A Handbook of

EMPLOYEE REWARD MANAGEMENT AND PRACTICE

A Handbook of

EMPLOYEE REWARD MANAGEMENT AND PRACTICE

Michael Armstrong • Tina Stephens

London and Sterling, VA

First published in Great Britain and the United States in 2005 by Kogan Page Limited.

Kogan Page Limited
120 Pentonville Road
London N1 9JN
United Kingdom
www.kogan-page.co.uk

Kogan Page US
22883 Quicksilver Drive
Sterling VA 20166–2012
USA

© Michael Armstrong and Tina Stephens, 2005

The right of Michael Armstrong and Tina Stephens to be identified as the authors of this work has been asserted by them in accordance with the Copyright, Designs and Patents Act 1988.

British Library Cataloguing in Publication Data

A CIP record for this book is available from the British Library.

ISBN 0 7494 4343 X

Typeset by Datamatics Technologies Ltd, Mumbai, India
Printed and bound in Great Britain by Bell & Bain, Glasgow

Contents

PART V REWARDING AND REVIEWING CONTRIBUTION AND PERFORMANCE

PART VI REWARD MANAGEMENT FOR SPECIAL GROUPS

30 Reward case studies **371**

Significant points 371; AEGON 373; Audit Commission 376; B&Q 377;
British Airways 380; Diageo 380; GlaxoSmithKline (GSK) 385; Lloyds
TSB 388; Nationwide 399; Norwich Union Insurance 401;
PricewaterhouseCoopers (PwC) 408; Tesco 411

Preface

This is a practical handbook designed to provide those concerned with rewarding employees guidance on the approaches they can adopt in developing and managing reward strategies, policies and processes. It is aligned to the professional standards of the Chartered Institute of Personnel and Development for employee reward. These standards are based on the application of good practice within a conceptual framework. They are intended to reflect what HR and reward specialists need to know and be able to do about rewarding people. The terms employee reward and reward management are synonymous and the latter is used throughout this book. The plan of the book is mapped below.

The contents and approach used in the handbook as a guide to students of the subject as well as practitioners are based on the experience of both authors, one (Michael Armstrong) a former Chief Examiner, Employee Reward for the CIPD and the other (Tina Stephens) the present Chief Examiner, Employee Reward.

PLAN OF THE BOOK

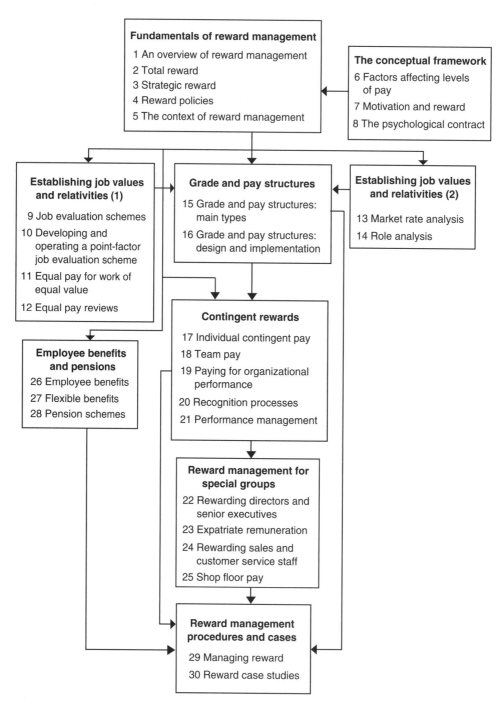

Figure 0.1 Plan of the book

Part I

The fundamentals of reward management

1

An overview of reward management

This chapter provides an overview of reward management. The concept of reward management, its strategic and detailed aims and its philosophy are discussed initially; this is followed by a description of the components of a reward management system. The chapter ends with a summary of the views of the writers who have made a major contribution to the development of the subject.

REWARD MANAGEMENT DEFINED

Reward management is concerned with the formulation and implementation of strategies and policies the purposes of which are to reward people fairly, equitably and consistently in accordance with their value to the organization and to help the organization to achieve its strategic goals. It deals with the design, implementation and maintenance of reward systems (reward processes, practices and procedures) which aim to meet the needs of both the organization and its stakeholders.

THE AIMS OF REWARD MANAGEMENT

The aims of reward management are to:

● reward people according to what the organization values and wants to pay for;

- reward people for the value they create;
- reward the right things to convey the right message about what is important in terms of outcomes and behaviours;
- develop a performance culture;
- motivate people and obtain their commitment and engagement;
- help to attract and retain the high quality people the organization needs;
- create total reward processes which recognize the importance of both financial and non-financial rewards;
- develop a positive employment relationship and psychological contract;
- align reward practices with both business goals and employee values; as Duncan Brown (1) emphasizes, the 'alignment of your reward practices with employee values and needs is every bit as important as alignment with business goals, and critical to the realisation of the latter', and Neil Buswell, International Reward Manager, British Airways, commented in response to an e-research survey in 2002 that: 'Reward can be a powerful communicator of business values and direction. People can, therefore benefit personally and deliver value to the company from a business-aligned reward strategy. The win–win is about the company getting value from the reward approach and the people need to feel that the company's expectations are reasonable for the rewards offered';
- operate in ways which are fair, equitable, consistent and transparent, as described below.

Fair

A fair reward system is one in which people are treated justly in accordance with what is due to them – their value to the organization. Fairness means that reward management processes operate in accordance with the principles of distributive and procedural justice.

Distributive justice

As defined by Leventhal (2), distributive justice refers to how rewards are provided to people. They will feel that they have been treated justly (fairly) if they believe that rewards have been distributed in accordance with the value of their contribution, that they receive what was promised to them and that they get what they need.

Procedural justice

Procedural justice refers to the ways in which managerial decisions are made and HR procedures are put into practice. The five factors that affect perceptions of procedural justice as identified by Tyler and Bies (3) are:

1. The viewpoint of employees is given proper consideration.
2. Personal bias towards employees is suppressed.
3. The criteria for decisions are applied consistently to all employees.
4. Employees are provided with early feedback about the outcome of decisions.
5. Employees are provided with adequate explanations of why decisions have been made.

The felt-fair principle

The influential 'felt-fair' principle was formulated by Eliot Jaques (4). This states that pay systems will be fair if they are felt to be fair. The assumptions underpinning the theory are that:

- there is an unrecognized standard of fair payment for any level of work;
- unconscious knowledge of the standard is shared among the population at work;
- to be equitable, pay must be felt to match the level of work and the capacity of the individual to do it;
- people should not receive less pay than they deserve by comparison with their fellow workers.

This felt-fair principle has passed into the common language of those concerned with reward management. It is often used as the final arbiter of how a job should be graded, sometimes overriding the conclusions reached by an analytical job evaluation exercise (the so-called 'felt-fair' test). Such tests are in danger of simply reproducing existing prejudices about relative job values.

Equity

Equity is achieved when people are rewarded appropriately in relation to others within the organization. Equitable reward processes ensure that relativities between jobs are measured as objectively as possible and that equal pay is provided for work of equal value.

Consistent

A consistent approach to the provision of rewards means that decisions on pay should not vary arbitrarily and without due cause between different people or at different times. They should not deviate irrationally from what would be generally regarded as fair and equitable.

Transparent

Transparency means that people understand how reward processes operate and how they are affected by them. The reasons for pay decisions are explained to them at the time they are made. Employees have a voice in the development of reward policies and practices and have the right to be given explanations of decisions and to comment on how they are made.

THE PHILOSOPHY OF REWARD MANAGEMENT

Reward management is based on a well-articulated philosophy – a set of beliefs and guiding principles that are consistent with the values of the organization and help to enact them. These include beliefs in the need to achieve fairness, equity, consistency and transparency in operating the reward system. The philosophy recognizes that if HRM is about investing in human capital from which a reasonable return is required, then it is proper to reward people differentially according to their contribution (that is, the return on investment they generate).

The philosophy of reward management recognizes that it must be strategic in the sense that it addresses longer-term issues relating to how people should be valued for what they do and what they achieve. Reward strategies and the processes that are required to implement them have to flow from the business strategy.

Reward management adopts a 'total reward' approach which emphasizes the importance of considering all aspects of reward as a coherent whole which is integrated with other HR initiatives designed to achieve the motivation, commitment, engagement and development of employees. This requires the integration of reward strategies with other human resource management (HRM) strategies, especially those concerning human resource development. Reward management is an integral part of an HRM approach to managing people.

REWARD MANAGEMENT COMPONENTS

The components of reward management are defined below.

Reward systems

Reward systems contain all the elements of reward, namely:

- *policies*, which provide guidelines on approaches to managing rewards;
- *practices*, which provide rewards including contingent pay;

- *processes*, which are concerned with evaluating the relative size of jobs (job evaluation) and assessing individual performance (performance management);
- *procedures*, which maintain the system;
- *structures,* which provide the framework for pay (grades or pay spines).

Reward strategy

Reward strategy sets out what the organization intends to do in the longer term to develop and implement reward policies, practices and processes which will further the achievement of its business goals.

Total reward

Total reward is the combination of financial and non-financial rewards available to employees.

Total remuneration

Total remuneration is the value of all cash payments (total earnings) and benefits received by employees.

Base or basic pay

The base rate is the amount of pay (the fixed salary or wage) that constitutes the rate for the job. It may be varied according to the grade of the job or, for shop floor workers, the level of skill required.

Base pay will be influenced by internal and external relativities. The internal relativities may be measured by some form of job evaluation. External relativities are assessed by tracking market rates. Alternatively, levels of pay may be agreed through collective bargaining with trade unions or by reaching individual agreements.

Base pay may be expressed as an annual, weekly or hourly rate. This is sometimes referred to as a time rate system of payment. Allowances as described later may be added to base pay. The rate may be adjusted to reflect increases in the cost of living or market rates by the organization unilaterally or by agreement with a trade union.

Job evaluation

Job evaluation is a systematic process for defining the relative worth or size of jobs within an organization in order to establish internal relativities and provide the basis for designing an equitable grade structure, grading jobs in the structure and managing relativities. It does not determine the level of pay directly. Job evaluation can be analytical or non-analytical. It is based on the analysis of jobs or roles which leads to the production of job descriptions or role profiles. Job evaluation is described in Chapters 9 and 10.

Market rate analysis

Market rate analysis is the process of identifying the rates of pay in the labour market for comparable jobs to inform decisions on levels of pay within the organization. A policy decision may be made on how internal rates of pay should compare with external rates – an organization's market stance. Market rate analysis is described in Chapter 13.

Grade and pay structures

Jobs may be placed in a graded structure according to their relative size. In such a structure pay is influenced by market rates and the pay ranges attached to grades provide scope for pay progression based on performance, competence, contribution or service. Alternatively, a 'spot rate' structure may be used for all or some jobs in which no provision is made for pay progression in a job. The various types of grade and pay structures are described in Chapter 15.

Contingent pay

Additional financial rewards may be provided that are related to performance, competence, contribution, skill or experience. These are referred to as 'contingent pay'. Contingent payments may be added to base pay, that is, 'consolidated'. If such payments are not consolidated (that is, paid as cash bonuses) they are described as 'variable pay'. Contingent pay schemes are described in Chapters 17 to 19 and 25.

Employee benefits

Employee benefits include pensions, sick pay, insurance cover, company cars and a number of other 'perks' as described in Chapters 26 to 28. They comprise elements of remuneration additional to the various forms of cash pay and also include provisions for employees that are not strictly remuneration, such as annual holidays.

Allowances

Allowances are paid in addition to basic pay for special circumstances (living in London) or features of employment (working unsocial hours). They may be determined unilaterally by the organization but they are often the subject of negotiation. The main types of allowances are:

- *Location allowances* – London and large town allowances to compensate for higher costs of living.
- *Overtime payments* – most manual workers are eligible for paid overtime as well as many staff employees up to management level. Higher-paid staff may receive time off in lieu if they work longer hours. Typically, organizations that make overtime payments give time and a half as an overtime premium from Monday to Saturday, with double time paid on Sundays and statutory holidays. Some firms also pay double time from around noon on Saturday. Work on major statutory holidays such as Christmas Day and Good Friday often attracts higher overtime premia.
- *Shift payments* are made at rates which usually vary according to the shift arrangement. A premium of, say, one-third of basic pay may be given to people working nights, while those on an early or late day shift may receive less – say, one-fifth of basic pay.
- *Working conditions allowances* may be paid where the work is unpleasant.
- *Subsistence allowances* may be paid for accommodation and meals when working away from home.
- *Stand-by and call-out allowances* may be made to those who have to be available to come in to work when required.

Performance management

Performance management processes (see Chapter 21) define individual performance and contribution expectations, assess performance against those expectations, provide for regular constructive feedback and result in agreed plans for performance improvement, learning and personal development. They are a means of providing non-financial motivation and may also inform contingent pay decisions.

Non-financial rewards

Rewards which do not involve any direct payments and often arise from the work itself, for example achievement, autonomy, recognition, scope to use and develop skills, training, career development opportunities and high quality leadership.

The interrelationships of these components are shown in Figure 1.1.

DEVELOPMENT OF THE CONCEPT OF REWARD MANAGEMENT

Much of the impetus for the development of the reward management concept has come from American writers, especially Lawler (5) with 'strategic pay' and, more recently, Schuster and Zingheim (6) with 'the new pay' and Flannery *et al* (7) with 'dynamic pay'.

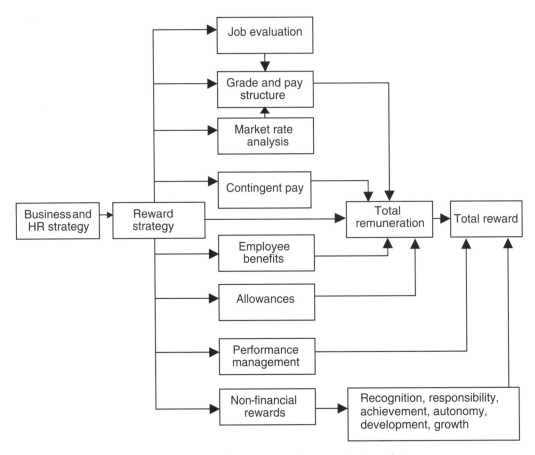

Figure 1.1 Reward management: elements and interrelationships

Strategic pay

Lawler emphasized that when developing reward policies it is necessary to think and act strategically about reward. Reward policies should take account of the organization's goals, values and culture and of the challenges of a more competitive global economy. New pay helps to develop the individual and organizational behaviour that a company needs if its business goals are to be met. Pay policies and practices must flow from the overall strategy and they can help to emphasize important objectives such as customer satisfaction and retention and product or service quality.

The new pay

Lawler's concept of the new pay was developed by Schuster and Zingheim who described its fundamental principles as follows:

- total compensation programmes should be designed to reward results and behaviour consistent with the key goals of the organization;
- pay can be a positive force for organizational change;
- the major thrust of new pay is in introducing variable (at risk) pay;
- the new pay emphasis is on team as well as individual rewards, with employees sharing financially in the organization's success;
- pay is an employee relations issue – employees have the right to determine whether the values, culture and reward systems of the organization match their own.

But Lawler (8) later emphasized that the 'new pay' ideology should be regarded as a conceptual approach to payment rather than a set of prescriptions:

> The new pay is not a set of compensation practices at all, but rather a way of thinking about reward systems in a complex organisation... The new pay does not necessarily mean implementing new reward practices or abandoning traditional ones; it means identifying pay practices that enhance the organization's strategic effectiveness.

Dynamic pay

Flannery *et al* expounded the concept of 'dynamic pay' and suggested that the nine principles which support a successful pay strategy are:

1. Align compensation with the organization's culture, values and strategic business goals.
2. Link compensation to the other changes.
3. Time the compensation programme to best support other change initiatives.
4. Integrate pay with other people processes.
5. Democratize the pay process.
6. Demystify compensation.
7. Measure results.
8. Refine. Refine again. Refine some more.
9. Be selective. Don't take to heart everything you hear or read about pay.

REFERENCES

1 Brown, D (2001) *Reward Strategies: From intent to impact*, CIPD, London
2 Leventhal, G S (1980) What should be done with equity theory? in *Social Exchange: Advances in Theory and Research*, ed G K Gergen, M S Greenberg and R H Willis, Plenum, New York

3   Tyler, T R and Bies, R J (1990) Beyond formal procedures: the interpersonal con-
     text of procedural justice, in *Applied Social Psychology and Organizational Settings* ed
     J S Carrol, Lawrence Erlbaum, Hillsdale, NJ
4   Jaques, E (1961) *Equitable Payment*, Heinemann, London
5   Lawler, E E (1990) *Strategic Pay*, Jossey-Bass, San Francisco
6   Schuster, J R and Zingheim, P K (1992) *The New Pay*, Lexington Books, New York
7   Flannery, T P, Hofrichter, D A and Platten, P E (1996) *People, Performance, and Pay*,
     The Free Press, New York
8   Lawler, E E (1995) The new pay: a strategic approach, *Compensation & Benefits
     Review*, November

2

Total reward

The concept of total reward has emerged quite recently and is exerting considerable influence on reward strategies. This chapter begins by defining what it means. The importance of the concept is then explained and the chapter continues with an analysis of the components of total reward. It concludes with a description of how a total reward approach to reward management can be developed.

TOTAL REWARD DEFINED

As defined by Manus and Graham (1), total reward 'includes all types of rewards – indirect as well as direct, and intrinsic as well as extrinsic'. Each aspect of reward, namely base pay, contingent pay, employee benefits and non-financial rewards, which include intrinsic rewards from the work itself, are linked together and treated as an integrated and coherent whole. Paul Bissell, Senior Manager – Rewards at Nationwide, defines their approach to total rewards as: 'A mixture of pay elements, with a defined cash value, benefits which have an intrinsic value, a positive and enjoyable work environment and opportunities for learning and development; all designed to make Nationwide an employer of choice.'

Total reward combines the impact of the two major categories of reward as defined below and illustrated in Figure 2.1:

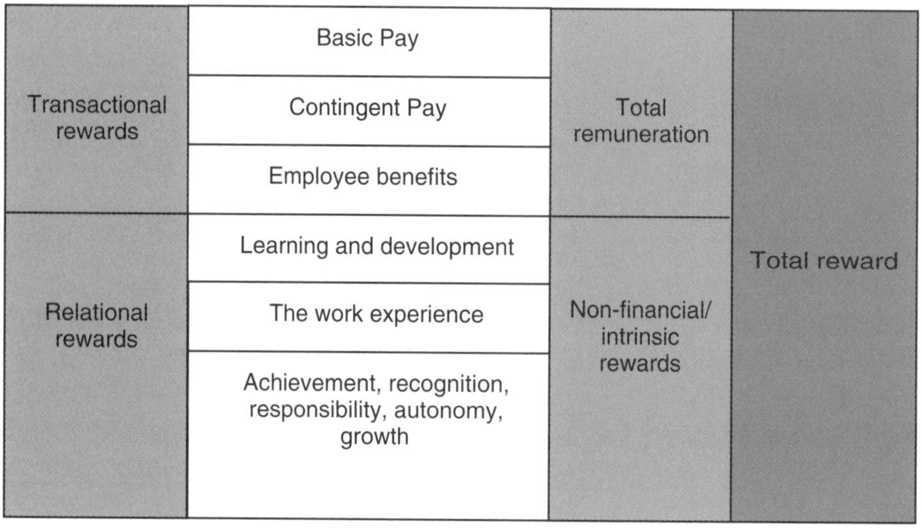

Transactional rewards	Basic Pay	Total remuneration	Total reward
	Contingent Pay		
	Employee benefits		
Relational rewards	Learning and development	Non-financial/ intrinsic rewards	
	The work experience		
	Achievement, recognition, responsibility, autonomy, growth		

Figure 2.1   The components of total reward

- *transactional rewards* – tangible rewards arising from transactions between the employer and employees concerning pay and benefits;
- *relational rewards* – intangible rewards concerned with learning and development and the work experience.

A total reward approach is holistic: reliance is not placed on one or two reward mechanisms operating in isolation, rather account is taken of every way in which people can be rewarded and obtain satisfaction through their work. The aim is to maximize the combined impact of a wide range of reward initiatives on motivation, commitment and job engagement. As Sandra O'Neal (2) has explained: 'Total reward embraces everything that employees value in the employment relationship.'

An equally wide definition of total reward is offered by WorldatWork (3), who state that total rewards are 'all of the employer's available tools that may be used to attract, retain, motivate and satisfy employees'. Paul Thompson (4) suggests that:

> Definitions of total reward typically encompass not only traditional, quantifiable elements like salary, variable pay and benefits, but also more intangible non-cash elements such as scope to achieve and exercise responsibility, career opportunities, learning and development, the intrinsic motivation provided by the work itself and the quality of working life provided by the organization.

The conceptual basis of total rewards is that of configuration or 'bundling', so that different reward processes are interrelated, complementary and mutually reinforcing. Total reward strategies are vertically integrated with business strategies, but they are also horizontally integrated with other HR strategies to achieve internal consistency.

THE SIGNIFICANCE OF TOTAL REWARD

Essentially, the notion of total reward says that there is more to rewarding people than throwing money at them.

For Sandra O'Neal (2), a total reward strategy is critical to addressing the issues created by recruitment and retention as well as providing a means of influencing behaviour: 'It can help create a work experience that meets the needs of employees and encourages them to contribute extra effort, by developing a deal that addresses a broad range of issues and by spending reward dollars where they will be most effective in addressing workers' shifting values.'

Perhaps the most powerful argument for a total rewards approach was produced by Pfeffer (5):

> Creating a fun, challenging, and empowered work environment in which individuals are able to use their abilities to do meaningful jobs for which they are shown appreciation is likely to be a more certain way to enhance motivation and performance – even though creating such an environment may be more difficult and take more time than simply turning the reward lever.

The benefits of a total reward approach are:

- *Greater impact* – the combined effect of the different types of rewards will make a deeper and longer-lasting impact on the motivation and commitment of people.
- *Enhancing the employment relationship* – the employment relationship created by a total rewards approach makes the maximum use of relational as well as transactional rewards and will therefore appeal more to individuals.
- *Flexibility to meet individual needs* – as pointed out by Bloom and Milkovich (6): 'Relational rewards may bind individuals more strongly to the organization because they can answer those special individual needs.'
- *Winning the war for talent* – relational rewards help to deliver a positive psychological contract and this can serve as a differentiator in the recruitment market which is much more difficult to replicate than individual pay practices. The organization can become an 'employer of choice' and 'a great place to work', thus attracting and retaining the talented people it needs.

MODEL OF TOTAL REWARD

A model of total reward developed by Duncan Brown (7) is shown in Figure 2.2.

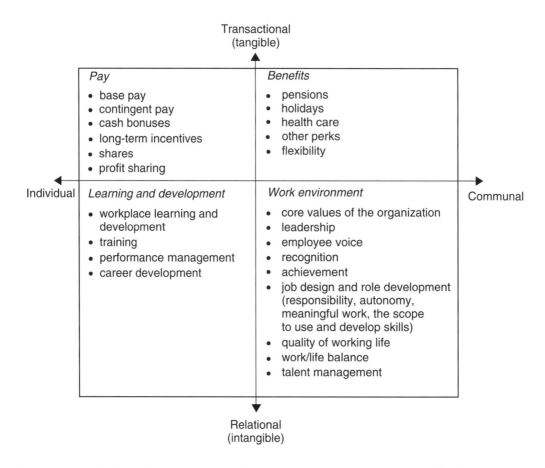

Figure 2.2 Model of total reward. (Source: Duncan Brown and Michael Armstrong (1999) *Paying for Contribution*, Kogan Page, London)

The upper two quadrants – pay and benefits – represent *transactional rewards.* These are financial in nature and are essential to recruit and retain staff but can be easily copied by competitors. By contrast, the *relational (non-financial) rewards* produced by the lower two quadrants are essential to enhancing the value of the upper two quadrants. The real power, as Thompson (4) states, comes when organizations combine relational and transactional rewards.

RELATIONAL REWARDS

Consideration is given below to the main areas of relational or non-financial rewards as set out in the lower quadrants of Figure 2.2.

Learning and development

Workplace learning

The workplace itself as an environment for learning can reward people by offering them opportunities to develop their skills and therefore their employability. Learning can be intentional and planned, aimed at training employees by supporting, structuring and monitoring their learning on the job. It should also be recognized that learning is an everyday part of the job. People develop skills, knowledge and understanding through dealing with the challenges posed by their work. This can be described as continuous learning and line managers can be encouraged and trained to enhance this process.

Training

The provision of systematic and planned instruction and development activities to promote learning can enable employees continually to upgrade their skills and progressively develop their careers. Many people now regard access to training as a key element in the overall reward package. The availability of learning opportunities, the selection of individuals for high-prestige training courses and programmes and the emphasis placed by the organization on the acquisition of new skills, as well as the enhancement of existing ones, can all act as powerful motivators. This is particularly important in de-layered organizations where upward growth through promotion is restricted but people can still develop laterally.

Performance management

Performance management processes are a powerful means of providing relational rewards. They can be the basis for developing a positive psychological contract by clarifying the mutual expectations of managers and their staff. Motivation can be provided by feedback. Performance reviews can inform personal development planning, thus encouraging self-managed learning but with the support as required of the manager and the organization.

Career development

Alderfer (8) emphasized the importance of the chance to grow as a means of rewarding people and therefore motivating them. He wrote: 'Satisfaction of growth needs depends on a person finding the opportunity to be what he is most fully and to become what he can.' The organization can offer this opportunity by providing people with a sequence of experience and training which will equip them for whatever level of responsibility they have the ability to reach. Talented individuals can be given the guidance and encouragement they need to fulfil their potential and achieve a successful career in tune with their abilities and aspirations. Paths can be defined which will map out how people can be rewarded by progressing their careers. Rewarding people through career development is associated with the process of talent management, which deals with the recruitment and retention of talented people and their career progression but is also associated with providing rewards through the working environment.

Work environment

Core values of the organization

The significance of the core values of an organization as a basis for creating a rewarding work environment was identified by the research conducted by John Purcell and his colleagues at Bath University (9). The most successful companies had what the researchers called 'the big idea'. The companies had a clear vision and a set of integrated values which were embedded, enduring, collective, measured and managed. They were concerned with sustaining performance and flexibility. Clear evidence existed between positive attitudes towards HR policies and practices, levels of satisfaction, motivation and commitment, and operational performance.

Leadership

Leaders play a vital role in reward management. They exist to get things done through people, ensuring that the task is achieved but also building and maintaining constructive and supportive relationships between themselves and members of their team and between the people within the group. They are there to motivate people and to obtain engaged performance. Leaders are the source of many relational rewards, such as recognition through feedback, scope to carry out meaningful work and exercise responsibility and the opportunity to grow through workplace learning and training. They are crucial to the success of performance management processes and may make or strongly influence contingent pay decisions.

Employee voice

As defined by Peter Boxall and John Purcell (10), 'Employee voice is the term increasingly used to cover a whole variety of processes and structures which enable, and sometimes empower employees, directly and indirectly, to contribute to decision-making in the firm.' Having a voice in the affairs of the firm is rewarding because it recognises the contribution people can make to the success of the organization or their team.

Employees can have a voice as an aspect of the normal working relationships between them and their managers, and this is linked closely to the other relational reward factors inherent in those relationships concerning recognition, achievement and responsibility. But the organization, through its policies for involvement, can provide motivation and increase commitment by putting people into situations where their views can be expressed, listened to and acted upon.

Recognition

Recognition is one of the most powerful methods of rewarding people. They need to know not only how well they have achieved their objectives or carried out their work but also that their achievements are appreciated. Recognition needs are linked to the esteem needs in Maslow's (11) hierarchy of needs. These are defined by Maslow as the need to have a stable, firmly based, high evaluation of oneself (self-esteem) and to have the respect of others (prestige). These needs are classified into two subsidiary sets: first, 'the desire for achievement, for adequacy, for confidence in the face of the world, and for independence and freedom', and second, 'the desire for reputation or status defined as respect or esteem from other people, and manifested by recognition, attention, importance or appreciation'.

Recognition can be provided by positive and immediate feedback from managers and colleagues which acknowledges individual and team contributions. It is also provided by managers who listen to and act upon the suggestions of their team members. Other actions that provide recognition include promotion, allocation to a high-profile project, and enlargement of the job to provide scope for more interesting and rewarding work.

There are other forms of recognition, such as public 'applause', status symbols of one kind or another, sabbaticals, treats, trips abroad and long-service awards, all of which can function as rewards. But they must be used with care. One person's recognition implies an element of non-recognition to others and the consequences of having winners and losers need to be carefully managed. Recognition schemes are examined more thoroughly in Chapter 20.

Financial rewards, especially achievement bonuses awarded immediately after the event, are clearly symbols of recognition to which are attached tangible benefits, and this is an important way in which a mutually reinforcing system of financial and non-financial rewards can operate.

Achievement

The need to achieve applies in varying degrees to all people in all jobs, although the level at which it operates will depend on the orientation of the individual and the scope provided by the work to fulfil a need for achievement. People feel rewarded and motivated if they have the scope to achieve as well as being recognized for the achievement. University researchers, for example, want to enhance their reputation as well as making a significant contribution to their institution's research rating.

If achievement motivation is high it will result in discretionary behaviour. As defined by Purcell *et al* (9), 'Discretionary behaviour refers to the choices that people make about how they carry out their work and the amount of effort, care, innovation and productive behaviour they display. It is the difference between people just doing a job and people doing a great job.' Self-discretionary or self-motivated behaviour occurs when people take control of situations or relationships, direct the course of events, create and seize opportunities, enjoy challenge, react swiftly and positively to new circumstances and relationships, and generally 'make things happen'. People who are driven by the need to achieve are likely to be proactive, to seek opportunities and to insist on recognition. Those whose orientations are not as strongly defined can be helped to satisfy possibly latent achievement needs by being given the scope and encouragement to develop and use their abilities productively.

Achievement motivation can be increased by organizations through processes and systems such as job design and performance management.

Job design and role development

Job design has two aims: first, to meet the needs of the organization for operational efficiency, quality of product or service and productivity, and second, to reward individuals by satisfying their needs for meaningful work which provides for interest, challenge and accomplishment. However, job design is not a static process. The roles people play at work develop as they respond to opportunities and changing demands, acquiring new skills and developing competencies. Managers and members of their teams have to work together to achieve mutual understanding of expectations as they change and to ensure that the role continues to provide intrinsic motivation from the work itself (the most powerful form of motivation). To be intrinsically motivating Ed Lawler (12) has suggested that roles should have the following characteristics:

- *Feedback* – individuals must receive meaningful feedback about their performance, preferably by evaluating their own performance and defining the feedback. This implies that they should ideally work on a complete process or product or a significant part of it that can be seen as a whole.
- *Use of abilities* – the role must be perceived by individuals as requiring them to use abilities they value to perform it effectively.
- *Self-control (autonomy)* – individuals must feel that they have a high degree of self-control over setting their own goals and defining the paths to these goals.

To develop rewarding jobs and roles, attention should be given to the following five principles set out by Robertson and Smith (13) which expand on the points made by Lawler:

1. *Influence skill variety*, providing opportunities for people to do several tasks and to combine tasks.
2. *Influence task identity*, combining tasks to form natural work units.

3. *Influence task significance*, forming natural work groups and informing people of the importance of their work.
4. *Influence autonomy*, giving people responsibility for determining their own working systems and making their own decisions.
5. *Influence feedback*, opening and using feedback channels.

Quality of working life

Rewards can be provided by the working environment if it improves the quality of working life. This is a matter of how the work is organized and the type of facilities provided as well as the design of the job or role. For example, research workers may feel well rewarded when they have excellent laboratory or other facilities which they can use to deliver exciting results.

Work/life balance

Work/life balance policies can reward people by recognizing their needs outside work by developing family-friendly policies. These include flexible hours, by offering flextime which gives employees some choice of when they start and finish around a core period when they have to be present, compressed hours (shorter working day), job sharing arrangements, part-time work or working at home (teleworking). The general approach is to provide more flexible working arrangements and make it clear that people will not be rewarded simply because they stay on after normal finishing time. It's what they deliver that counts, not how long they work.

Talent management

Talent management is about ensuring that the organization attracts, retains, motivates and develops the talented people it needs. It is associated with a number of other relational reward processes, such as designing jobs and developing roles that give people opportunities to apply and grow their skills and provide them with autonomy, interest and challenge. It is also concerned with creating a working environment in which work processes and facilities enable rewarding (in the broadest sense) jobs and roles to be designed and developed.

Talent management also means developing reward processes and a working environment that ensure that the organization is one for whom people want to work – an 'employer of choice'. There is a desire to join the organization and, once there, to want to stay. Employees are committed to the organization and engaged in the work they do. On the basis of their longitudinal research in 12 companies, Purcell *et al* (9) concluded that:

> What seems to be happening is that successful firms are able to meet people's needs both for a good job and to work 'in a great place'. They create good work and a conducive

working environment. In this way they become an 'employer of choice'. People will want to work there because their individual needs are met – for a good job with prospects linked to training, appraisal and working with a good boss who listens and gives some autonomy but helps with coaching and guidance.

Becoming an employer of choice starts with developing the image of the organization so that it is recognized as one that achieves results, delivers quality products and services, behaves ethically and provides good conditions of employment. Organizations with a clear vision and a set of integrated and enacted values are likely to project themselves as being rewarding to work for.

DEVELOPING A TOTAL REWARD APPROACH

The transactional and tangible elements of total reward (financial rewards) are quite clear cut. It may not be easy to make them work well but, as explained in later chapters of this book, it is not too difficult to decide on what needs to be done. There are plenty of guidelines available to help in selecting the approach and to indicate the means available for the design and implementation of tangible reward processes.

Relational or non-financial rewards are more difficult. By definition, they are intangible. Their provision may depend on top management providing the lead by developing what John Purcell and his colleagues call 'the big idea' – a clear vision and a set of integrated values which they ensure are embedded and enacted. It is not a matter of applying well-defined techniques. The organization can contribute by communicating the values, giving employees a voice, setting up performance management processes, instituting formal recognition schemes and taking steps to improve work/life balance. A conscious effort can be made to 'bundle' reward and HR practices together, for example developing career family structures where the emphasis is on mapping career paths rather than providing a pay structure.

Importantly, the organization can ensure that line managers appreciate the importance of using relational rewards – exercising effective leadership, giving feedback, recognizing achievement and providing meaningful work. Ultimately, relational rewards are in the hands of line managers, and what the organization must do is to ensure as far as possible that they understand the significance of this aspect of their work and are given the training and guidance needed to acquire the skills to do it well.

DEVELOPMENT STEPS

To summarize, the steps required to develop total rewards are:

1. Be clear about what the concept means and how it can benefit the organization as a foundation for its reward strategy.

2. Define what aspects of total reward, in terms of transactional and relational rewards, are relevant to the organization.
3. Prepare a statement of how each of the relevant components can be developed and applied in the organization, for example by adopting more systematic approaches to performance management, developing the capability of managers to become active participants in the reward system with special reference to relational rewards, improving career planning processes, dealing with work/life balance issues, or introducing a recognition scheme.
4. Convince top management that a total reward approach of this nature will benefit the organization in significant ways, eg recruitment and retention, motivation, commitment and job engagement, talent management.
5. Discuss with staff how a total reward approach will work and will benefit them.
6. Communicate to staff details of the proposed total reward strategy.
7. As part of the reward strategy, plan and implement each of the total reward initiatives that have been agreed with management and staff.
8. Conduct training as required to improve the capability of line managers to play a major part in providing relational rewards.
9. Ensure that HR is there to provide encouragement and guidance and to see that the total reward programme coheres.
10. Monitor the progress made in introducing total reward so that action can be taken to deal with any problems.

TOTAL REWARD AT BRITISH AIRWAYS

The total reward strategy at British Airways, as described in their response to the e-research 2002 survey, comprises four strands, with total pay and positive workplace viewed as the 'foundation' elements.

The four elements of the BA total reward model are:

- *Individual growth* – most individuals need to grow, learn and become more valuable/employable.
- *Compelling future* – people want a vision of the future for the company, since this links to their own future vision. There is an opportunity to create 'stakeholders' in the workforce.
- *Total pay* – the total pay solutions must be positive, attractive and performance related. Use reward principles to develop total pay.
- *Effective workplace* – positive people need effective leadership that gives direction and creates opportunities for delivering meaningful, challenging, interesting work, underpinned by an atmosphere of open communications, trust and commitment.

Neil Buswell, International Reward Manager, commented that: 'This total reward model makes a clear link between total pay and the other three key areas of employee reward. These are the reasons why people come to work and there is a balance to be achieved.' He continued: 'Whilst we may often focus on the "total pay" box it is important that the other areas are considered for their strengths and weaknesses to create an optimum mix – it's art as well as science!'

CONCLUSION

The rhetoric of the total reward concept is compelling. The reality of total reward – making it work – is much more difficult. It requires a lot of effort on the part of top management and line managers, with the determined encouragement and guidance of HR.

Examples of approaches to total reward in GlaxoSmithKline, LloydsTSB, Norwich Union Insurance and PricewaterhouseCoopers are given in Chapter 30.

REFERENCES

1 Manus, T M and Graham, M D (2002) *Creating a Total Rewards Strategy: A toolkit for designing business-based plans*, American Management Association, New York
2 O'Neal, S (1998) The phenomenon of total rewards, *ACA Journal*, **7** (3)
3 WorldatWork (2000) *Total Rewards: From strategy to implementation*, WorldatWork, Scottsdale, AZ
4 Thompson, P (2002) *Total Reward*, CIPD, London
5 Pfeffer, J (1998) *The Human Equation: Building profits by putting people first*, Harvard Business School Press, Boston
6 Bloom, M and Milkovich, G T (1998) Rethinking international compensation, *Compensation & Benefits Review*, April, pp 17–27
7 Brown, D (2003) Presentation to CIPD Conference, Bristol
8 Alderfer, C (1972) *Existence, Relatedness and Growth*, The Free Press, New York
9 Purcell, J, Kinnie, K, Hutchinson S, Rayton, B and Swart, J (2003) *Understanding the People and Performance Link: Unlocking the black box*, CIPD, London
10 Boxall, P and Purcell, J (2003) *Strategic Human Resource Management*, Palgrave Macmillan, Basingstoke
11 Maslow, A (1954) *Motivation and Personality*, Harper & Row, New York
12 Lawler, E E (1969) Job design and employee motivation, *Personnel Psychology*, 22
13 Robertson, I T and Smith, M (1985) *Motivation and Job Design*, IPM, London

3

Strategic reward

Strategic reward management is about the development and implementation of reward strategies and the philosophies and guiding principles that underpin them. It provides answers to two basic questions: (1) where do we want our reward practices to be in a few years' time and (2) how do we intend to get there? It therefore deals with both ends and means. As an end it describes a vision of what reward processes will look like in a few years' time. As a means, it shows how it is expected that the vision will be realized.

The chapter starts with a definition of reward strategy and an explanation of why it is necessary. Consideration is then given to the reality of strategic reward and the basis, structure and content of reward strategies. The guiding principles based upon a reward philosophy that may be incorporated in reward strategies are then discussed and this is followed by a description of the development process. The chapter ends with an examination of the important issue of line management capability.

REWARD STRATEGY DEFINED

Reward strategy is a declaration of intent which expresses what the organization wants to do in the longer term to develop and implement reward policies, practices and processes that will further the achievement of its business goals and meet the needs of its stakeholders.

Reward strategy provides a sense of purpose and direction and a framework for developing reward policies, practices and process. It is based on an understanding of the needs of the organization *and* its employees and how they can best be satisfied. It is also concerned with developing the values of the organization on how people should be rewarded and formulating guiding principles which will ensure that these values are enacted.

Reward strategy is underpinned by a reward philosophy which expresses what the organization believes should be the basis upon which people are valued and rewarded. Reward philosophies are often articulated as guiding principles.

INTEGRATED REWARD STRATEGY

One of the most important characteristics of an effective reward strategy is that it is integrated with other HR strategies. The approach adopted by Aon Ltd was described by them in response to an e-research survey in 2002 as follows:

> We are very keen to have 'joined up HR'. Hence we are trying to make the integrating links. So we want the performance culture and more effective performance management to be supported by reward.
>
> We are working on the identification of key talent and working on succession plans – the outputs are informing reward decisions. The new role level structure which was initiated as part of the harmonization of benefits has been clearly explained as a foundation for other HR initiatives – such as succession planning, management and leadership development and resourcing. These are, of course, where the role levels can have greatest impact and are made 'live'.

Neil Buswell, International Reward Manager, British Airways, commented in reply to the same e-research survey that: 'All people policies and priorities are linked and will influence and impact reward solutions.'

A model of the development of an integrated reward strategy is given in Figure 3.1.

WHY HAVE A REWARD STRATEGY?

Overall, in the words of Duncan Brown (1): 'Reward strategy is ultimately a way of thinking that you can apply to any reward issue arising in your organization, to see how you can create value from it.' More specifically, there are four arguments for developing reward strategies:

1. You must have some idea where you are going, or how do you know how to get there, and how do you know that you have arrived (if you ever do)?
2. Pay costs in most organizations are by far the largest item of expense – they can be 60 per cent and often much more in labour-intensive organizations – so doesn't it make sense to think about how they should be managed and invested in the longer term?

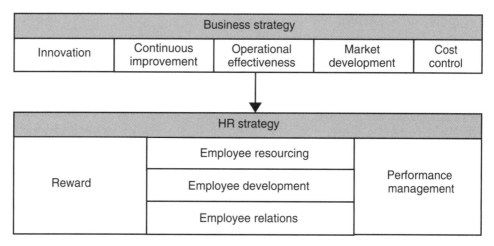

Figure 3.1 Developing integrated strategy

3. There can be a positive relationship between rewards, in the broadest sense, and performance, so shouldn't we think about how we can strengthen that link?
4. As Cox and Purcell (2) write, 'the real benefit in reward strategies lies in complex linkages with other human resource management policies and practices'. Isn't this a good reason for developing a reward strategic framework which indicates how reward processes will be linked to HR processes so that they are coherent and mutually supportive?

THE REALITY OF REWARD STRATEGY

Reward strategy in reality is not necessarily a formal, well-articulated and linear process which flows logically from the business strategy. Strategies may be formulated as they are used and Mintzberg (3) has emphasized that strategies emerge over time in response to evolving situations. Tyson (4) points out that:

- strategy is emergent and flexible – it is always 'about to be', it never exists at the present time;
- strategy is not only realized by formal statements but also comes about by actions and reactions;
- strategy is a description of a future-orientated action which is always directed towards change;
- the management process itself conditions the strategies that emerge.

Quinn (5) produced the concept of 'logical incrementalism' which states that strategy evolves in several steps rather than being perceived as whole. It has been suggested by Mintzberg *et al* (6) that strategy can have a number of meanings other than that of being 'a plan, or something equivalent – a direction, a guide, a course of action'. Strategy can also be a pattern, that is, consistency in behaviour over time, or a perspective, an organization's fundamental way of doing things.

All reward strategies are different, just as all organizations are different. Of course, similar aspects of reward will be covered in the strategies of different organizations but they will be treated differently in accordance with variations between organizations in their contexts, strategies and cultures. Examples of reward strategies are given in Chapter 30.

Reward strategists may have a clear idea of what needs to be done but they have to take account of the views of top management and be prepared to persuade them with convincing arguments that action needs to be taken. They have to take particular account of financial considerations – the concept of 'affordability' looms large in the minds of chief executives and financial directors who will need to be convinced that an investment in rewards will pay off. They also have to convince employees and their representatives that the reward strategy will meet their needs as well as business needs.

In short, the reality of strategic reward is that it is not such a clear-cut process as some believe. It evolves, it changes and it has sometimes to be reactive rather than proactive.

REWARD STRATEGY ISSUES

- 'Strategic decisions are event driven, not pre-planned.' *James Quinn* (5)
- 'Strategy is a pattern in a stream of activities.' *Henry Mintzberg* (6)
- 'Reward strategy will be characterized by diversity and conditioned both by the legacy of the past and the realities of the future.' *Helen Murlis* (7)
- 'Managing reward is a job of short-term damage limitation, not the strategic lever for change that appears so seductive in the writing of American commentators.' *Mark Thompson* (8)
- 'A general recognition that pay systems are not working well.' *HM Treasury Guidelines* (9)
- 'HR strategy is jumping onto the strategic bandwagon just when everyone else is jumping off.' *Rosabeth Moss Kanter* (10)
- 'The sceptre of best practice.' *Duncan Brown* (11)

THE STRUCTURE OF REWARD STRATEGY

Reward strategy should be based on a detailed analysis of the present arrangements for reward: the reward system. This, as suggested by the CIPD (12), could take the form of a 'gap analysis' which compares what is believed should be happening with what *is* happening and indicates which 'gaps' need to be filled. A format for the analysis is shown in Figure 3.2.

What should be happening	What is happening	What needs to be done
1. A total reward approach is adopted which emphasizes the significance of both financial and non-financial rewards.		
2. Reward policies and practices are developed within the framework of a well-articulated strategy which is designed to support the achievement of business objectives and meet the needs of stakeholders.		
3. An analytical job evaluation scheme is used which properly reflects the values of the organization, is up to date with regard to the jobs it covers and is non-discriminatory.		
4. Equal pay issues are given serious attention. This includes the conduct of equal pay reviews which lead to action.		
5. Market rates are tracked carefully so that a competitive pay structure exists which contributes to the attraction and retention of high-quality people.		
6. Grade and pay structures are based on job evaluation and market rate analysis, appropriate to the characteristics and needs of the organization and its employees, which facilitate the management of relativities, provide scope for rewarding contribution, clarify reward and career opportunities, are constructed logically, operate transparently and are easy to manage and maintain.		
7. Contingent pay schemes reward contribution fairly and consistently, support the motivation of staff and the development of a performance culture, deliver the right messages about the values of the organization, contain a clear 'line of sight' between contribution and reward and are cost-effective.		
8. Performance management processes contribute to performance improvement, people development and the management of expectations, operate effectively throughout the organization and are supported by line managers and staff.		
9. Employee benefits and pension schemes meet the needs of stakeholders and are cost-effective.		
10. A flexible benefits approach is adopted.		
11. Reward management procedures exist which ensure that reward processes are managed effectively and that costs are controlled.		
12. Appropriate use is made of computers (software and spreadsheets) to assist in the process of reward management.		
13. Reward management aims and arrangements are transparent and communicated well to staff.		
14. Surveys are used to assess the opinions of staff about reward and action is taken on the outcomes.		
15. An appropriate amount of responsibility for reward is devolved to line managers.		
16. Line managers are capable of carrying out their devolved responsibilities well.		
17. Steps are taken to train line managers and provide them with support and guidance as required.		
18. HR has the knowledge and skills to provide the required reward management advice and services and to guide and support line managers.		
19. Overall, reward management developments are conscious of the need to achieve affordability and to demonstrate that they are cost-effective.		
20. Steps are taken to evaluate the effectiveness of reward management processes and to ensure that they reflect changing needs.		

Figure 3.2   A reward gap analysis

A diagnosis should be made of the reasons for any gaps or problems so that decisions can be made on what needs to be done to overcome them. It can then be structured under the headings set out below.

1. *A statement of intentions* – the reward initiatives that it is proposed should be taken.
2. *A rationale* – the reasons why the proposals are being made. The rationale should make out the business case for the proposals, indicating how they will meet business needs and setting out the costs and the benefits. It should also refer to any people issues that need to be addressed and how the strategy will deal with them.
3. *A plan* – how, when and by whom the reward initiatives will be implemented. The plan should indicate what steps will need to be taken and should take account of resource constraints and the need for communications, involvement and training. The priorities attached to each element of the strategy should be indicated and a timetable for implementation should be drawn up. The plan should state who will be responsible for the development and implementation of the strategy.
4. *A definition of guiding principles* – the values that it is believed should be adopted in formulating and implementing the strategy (these are discussed in detail on pages 32–33).

THE CONTENT OF REWARD STRATEGY

Reward strategy may be a broad-brush affair simply indicating the general direction in which it is thought reward management should go. Additionally or alternatively, reward strategy may set out a list of specific intentions dealing with particular aspects of reward management.

Broad-brush reward strategy

A broad-brush reward strategy may commit the organization to the pursuit of a total rewards policy. The basic aim might be to achieve an appropriate balance between financial and non-financial rewards. A further aim could be to use other approaches to the development of the employment relationship and the work environment which will enhance commitment and engagement and provide more opportunities for the contribution of people to be valued and recognized.

Examples of other broad strategic aims include (1) introducing a more integrated approach to reward management – encouraging continuous personal development and spelling out career opportunities, (2) developing a more flexible approach to reward which includes the reduction of artificial barriers as a result of over-emphasis on grading and promotion, (3) generally rewarding people according to their contribution,

(4) supporting the development of a performance culture and building levels of competence, and (5) clarifying what behaviours will be rewarded and why.

Specific reward initiatives

The selection of reward initiatives and the priorities attached to them will be based on an analysis of the present circumstances of the organization and an assessment of the needs of the business and its employees. The following are examples of possible specific reward initiatives, one or more of which might feature in a reward strategy:

- the replacement of present methods of contingent pay with a pay for contribution scheme;
- the introduction of a new grade and pay structure, eg a broad-graded or career family structure;
- the replacement of an existing decayed job evaluation scheme with a computerized scheme which more clearly reflects organizational values;
- the improvement of performance management processes so that they provide better support for the development of a performance culture and more clearly identify development needs;
- the introduction of a formal recognition scheme;
- the development of a flexible benefits system;
- the conduct of equal pay reviews with the objective of ensuring that work of equal value is paid equally;
- communication programmes designed to inform everyone of the reward policies and practices of the organization;
- training, coaching and guidance programmes designed to increase line management capability (see also the last section of this chapter).

REWARD PHILOSOPHY

Reward philosophy consists of the set of beliefs which underpin the reward strategy of the organization and govern the reward policies that determine how reward processes operate. Reward philosophies may be implicit or stated explicitly as in the following example from COLT Telecom:

> COLT believes that talented and motivated people make a difference; talented people put us ahead of the competition and deliver the results on which the success of COLT is built. COLT seeks to offer a compensation and benefits package that rewards people for their contribution to the success of the company and ensures that external market competitiveness and internal relativities are taken into account. – *e-research report no 22, 2004*

Reward philosophy	Principles
• We will provide an innovative reward package that is valued by our staff and communicated brilliantly to reinforce the benefits of working for B&Q plc.	• Innovative and differentiated policies and benefits.
• Reward investment will be linked to company performance so that staff share in the success they create and, by going the extra mile, receive above-average reward compared to local competitors.	• Basic salaries will be competitive. • Total compensation will be upper quartile. • We share the success of B&Q with all employees. • Increase variable pay as a percentage of overall to drive company performance. • Pay for performance. • Performance objectives must have line of sight for individuals/team.
• All parts of the total reward investment will add value to the business and reinforce our core purpose, goals and values.	• Non-cash recognition is a powerful driver of business performance. • Pay can grow without promotion. • Rewards are flexible around individual aspirations. • We will not discriminate on anything other than performance.

Figure 3.3   Reward philosophy and guiding principles at B&Q

Alternatively, they may be defined alongside supporting guiding principles, as in the example from B&Q shown in Figure 3.3.

Many organizations simply draw up a set of guiding principles which in themselves define the philosophy.

GUIDING PRINCIPLES

Guiding principles define the approach an organization takes to dealing with reward. They are the basis for reward policies and provide guidelines for the actions contained in the reward strategy. They express the reward philosophy of the organization – its values and beliefs about how people should be rewarded.

Members of the organization should be involved in the definition of guiding principles which can then be communicated to everyone to increase understanding of what underpins reward policies and practices. However, employees will suspend their judgement of the principles until they experience how they are applied. What matters to them are not the philosophies themselves but the pay practices emanating from them and the messages about the employment 'deal' that they get as a consequence. It is the reality that is important, not the rhetoric.

Fundamental values

Guiding principles should incorporate, or be influenced by, general beliefs about fairness, equity, consistency and transparency as discussed in Chapter 1.

Specific guiding principles

Reward guiding principles may be concerned with such specific matters as:

- developing reward policies and practices that support the achievement of business goals;
- providing rewards that attract, retain and motivate staff and help to develop a high-performance culture;
- maintaining competitive rates of pay;
- rewarding people according to their contribution;
- recognizing the value of all staff who are making an effective contribution, not just the exceptional performers;
- allowing a reasonable degree of flexibility in the operation of reward processes and in the choice of benefits by employees;
- devolving more responsibility for reward decisions to line managers.

More examples of guiding principles are given in Appendix 2.

DEVELOPING REWARD STRATEGY

The formulation of reward strategy can be described as a process for developing and defining a sense of direction. The CIPD (13) suggests the following key development phases:

1. the *diagnosis* phase, when reward goals are agreed, current policies and practices assessed against them, options for improvement considered and any changes agreed;

2. the *detailed design* phase, when improvements and changes are detailed and any changes tested (pilot testing is important);
3. the final *testing and preparation* phase;
4. the *implementation* phase, followed by ongoing review and modification.

A logical step-by-step model for doing this is illustrated in Figure 3.4. This incorporates ample provision for consultation, involvement and communication with stakeholders, who include senior managers as the ultimate decision makers as well as employees and line managers.

In practice, however, the formulation of reward strategy is seldom as logical and linear a process as this. As explained earlier in this chapter, strategies evolve. Reward strategists have to respond to changes in organizational requirements which are happening all the time. They need to track emerging trends in reward management and may modify their views accordingly, as long as they do not leap too hastily on the latest bandwagon.

It may be helpful to set out reward strategies on paper for the record and as a basis for planning and communication. But this should be regarded as no more than a piece of paper that can be torn up when needs change – as they will – not a tablet of stone.

EFFECTIVE REWARD STRATEGIES

Components of an effective reward strategy

Duncan Brown (1) has suggested that effective reward strategies have three components:

1. They have to have clearly defined goals and a well-defined link to business objectives.
2. There have to be well-designed pay and reward programmes, tailored to the needs of the organization and its people, and consistent and integrated with one another.
3. Perhaps most important and most neglected, there needs to be effective and supportive HR and reward processes in place.

Criteria for effectiveness

The questions to be answered when assessing the effectiveness of a reward strategy are:

1. Does it support the achievement of the organization's business and HR strategies?
2. Will it reinforce organizational values?

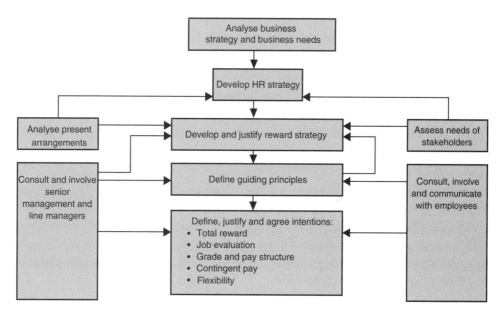

Figure 3.4 Developing reward strategy

3. Is there a convincing statement of how the business needs of the organization will be met and how the needs of stakeholders will be catered for?
4. Is it based on a thorough analysis and diagnosis of the reward situation in the organization?
5. Has a realistic assessment been made of the resources required to implement the strategy and the costs involved?
6. Is it affordable in the sense that the benefits will exceed any costs?
7. Have steps been taken to ensure that supporting processes such as performance management, communication and training are in place?
8. Is the programme for implementation realistic?
9. Have steps been taken to ensure that it is supported and understood by line managers and staff?
10. Will HR and line managers be capable of implementing and managing the strategy in practice?

REWARD STRATEGY AND LINE MANAGEMENT CAPABILITY

HR can initiate new policies and practices but it is the line that has the main responsibility for implementing them. In other words, 'HR proposes but the line disposes'. As pointed out by Purcell *et al* (13), high levels of organizational performance are not achieved simply by having a range of well-conceived HR policies and practices in place. What makes the difference is how these policies and practices are implemented. That is where the role of line managers in people management is crucial: 'The way line managers implement and enact policies, show leadership in dealing with employees and in exercising control comes through as a major issue.'

The trend is, rightly, to devolve more responsibility for managing reward to line managers. Some will have the ability to respond to the challenge and opportunity; others will be incapable of carrying out this responsibility without close guidance from HR; some may never be able to cope. Managers may not always do what HR expects them to do and if compelled to, they may be half-hearted about it. This puts a tremendous onus on HR and reward specialists to develop line management capability, to initiate processes which can readily be implemented by line managers, to promote understanding by communicating what is happening, why it is happening and how it will affect everyone, to provide guidance and help where required and to provide formal training as necessary.

EXAMPLES OF INTEGRATED REWARD STRATEGIES

The following are actual examples of integrated reward strategies summarized from research into how strategies are constructed carried out by e-research in 2003 (14). They are drawn from:

- a local authority with the emphasis on developing a performance culture;
- a financial services company which covers four typical aims of reward strategy;
- a retailer which sets out neatly for employees what reward strategy has to offer for them;
- a Scottish university where the strategy focuses on the development of a career family structure, as described in Chapter 15, designed not only to define the pay structure but also to clarify career paths between and within families and to achieve greater cohesion across career families (note that the top level extends across all three families);
- a service company where the description of the strategy emphasizes what's new.

Local authority

The fundamental business need that the reward strategy should meet is to develop and maintain a high-performance culture. The characteristics of such a culture are:

- A clear line of sight exists between the strategic aims of the authority and those of its departments and staff at all levels.

- Management defines what it requires in the shape of performance improvements, sets goals for success and monitors performance to ensure that goals are achieved.
- Leadership from the top which engenders a shared belief in continuous improvement.
- Performance management processes aligned to the authority's objectives to ensure that people are engaged in achieving the required goals and standards.
- Capabilities of people developed through learning at all levels to support performance improvement.
- People provided with opportunities to make full use of their skills and abilities.
- People valued and rewarded according to their contribution.

Integrated strategy in a financial services company

- Establish an integrated approach to performance management, development and reward of all staff and ensure that this is aligned with the needs of the business.
- Ensure that salaries and benefits remain competitive with regard to comparators in our industry so that we can attract and retain staff of the highest quality.
- Reduce the previous focus on grades in favour of broader bands so that personal development can be encouraged and rewarded.
- Motive staff so that they will ensure the Company remains successful, thereby allowing for continued competitive levels of reward for superior performance.

Integrated reward in a retailer

See Figure 3.5.

Integrated strategy in a Scottish university: career family structure

See Figure 3.6.

The development of reward strategy in British Airways

See Figure 3.7.

Reward strategy: The Children's Society

We intend to develop reward systems which will support our mission and corporate objectives. We will move towards processes which:

- recognize contribution;
- are transparent;

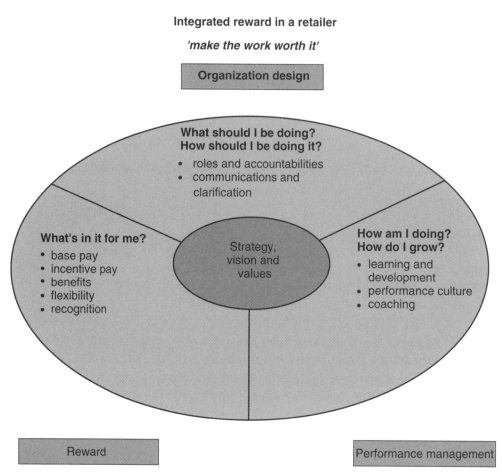

Figure 3.5 Strategic reward model

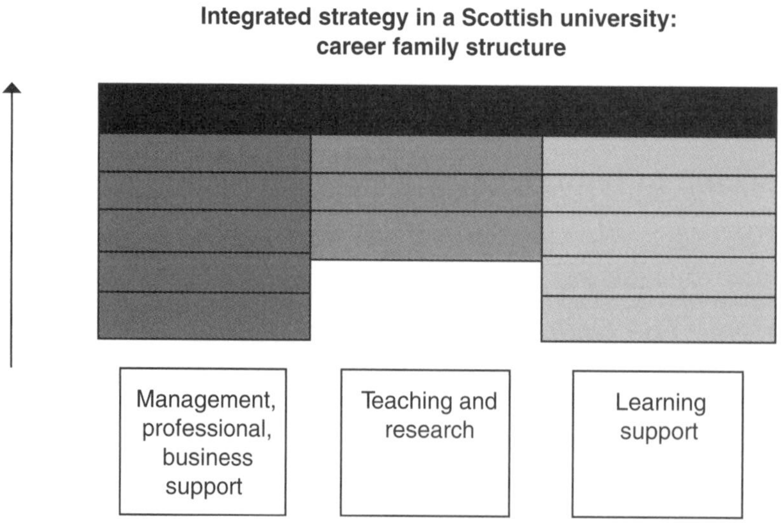

Figure 3.6 Career family structure

The development of reward strategy in British Airways

Reward inputs	→ Reward achievements
Uniform approach	→ Diverse approaches
Passive	→ Active
Internal equity focus	→ Market competitive
Reward job	→ Reward person
Self-perpetuating	→ Business driven
Base pay/fixed cost	→ Fixed and variable

Figure 3.7 Reward strategy development

- are owned by line managers and staff;
- reinforce leadership, accountability, team working and innovation;
- are market sensitive but not market led;
- are flexible and fair.

More examples of integrated reward strategies and guiding principles developed by The Audit Commission, B&Q, Diageo, GlaxoSmithKline, Lloyds TSB, Norwich Union Insurance and Tesco are given in Chapter 30.

REFERENCES

1 Brown, D (2001) *Reward Strategies; From intent to impact*, CIPD, London
2 Cox, A and Purcell, J (1998) Searching for leverage: pay systems, trust, motivation and commitment in SMEs, in *Trust, Motivation and Commitment*, ed S J Perkins and St John Sandringham, Strategic Remuneration Centre, Faringdon
3 Mintzberg, H (1987) Crafting strategy, *Harvard Business Review*, July–August, pp 66–74
4 Tyson, S (1997) Human resource strategy: a process for managing the contribution of HRM to organizational performance, *International Journal of Human Resource management*, **8** (3), pp 277–90
5 Quinn, J B (1980) Managing strategic change, *Sloane Management Review*, **11** (4/5), pp 3–30

6   Mintzberg, H, Quinn, J B and James, R M (1988) *The Strategy Process: Concepts, contexts and cases*, Prentice-Hall, Englewood Cliffs, NJ

7   Murlis, H (1996) *Pay at the Crossroads*, IPD, London

8   Thompson, M (1998) Trust and reward, in *Trust, Motivation and Commitment: A reader*, ed S Perkins, SRRC, Faringdon

9   HM Treasury Guidelines (2002), HM Stationery Office, Norwich

10 Kanter, R M (1989) *When Giants Learn to Dance*, Simon and Schuster, London

11 Brown, D (2003) *Presentation to CIPD Conference*, Bristol

12 Chartered Institute of Personnel and Development (2004) *How to Develop a Reward Strategy*, CIPD, London

13 Purcell, J, Kinnie, K, Hutchinson, S, Rayton, B and Swart, J (2003) *People and Performance: How people management impacts on organizational performance*, CIPD, London

14 e-research (2003) *Reward Strategies*, e-reward.co.uk Ltd, Stockport, Cheshire

4

Reward policies

In this chapter the purpose of reward policies is defined, the various headings under which policies may be formulated are discussed and the approach to their formulation is described.

THE PURPOSE OF REWARD POLICIES

Reward policies set guidelines for decision making and action. They indicate what the organization and its management are expected to do about managing reward and how they will behave in given circumstances when dealing with reward issues.

REWARD POLICY HEADINGS

Reward policies address the following broad issues:

- the level of rewards;
- achieving equal pay;
- the relative importance attached to external competitiveness and internal equity;
- the approach to total reward;
- the scope for the use of contingent rewards related to performance, competence, contribution or skill;

- the role of line managers;
- transparency – the publication of information on reward structures and processes to employees.

The more specific issues that may be covered by reward policies include assimilation, the use of job evaluation, the guidelines governing decisions on the rates of pay offered to staff on appointment or promotion and assimilation into new pay structures.

Level of rewards

The policy on the level of rewards indicates whether the company is a high payer, is content to pay median or average rates of pay or even, exceptionally, accepts that it has to pay below the average. Pay policy, which is sometimes referred to as the 'pay stance' or 'pay posture' of a company, will depend on a number of factors. These include the extent to which the company demands high levels of performance from its employees, the degree to which there is competition for good-quality people, the perceived need to demonstrate that people are valued highly, the traditional stance of the company, the organization culture, and whether or not it can or should afford to be a high payer. A firm may say that 'We will pay upper quartile salaries because we want our staff to be upper quartile performers and we want to show that we value them as such.'

Policies on pay levels will also refer to differentials and the number of steps or grades that should exist in the pay hierarchy. This will be influenced by the structure of the company. In today's flatter organizations an extended or complex pay hierarchy may not be required on the grounds that it does not reflect the way in which work is organized and will constrain flexibility.

Policies on the level of rewards also cover employee benefits – pensions, sick pay, health care, holidays and perks such as company cars.

Achieving equal pay

A policy is required on the degree to which equal pay considerations should drive the management of the reward system. Ideally, there should be no question that this should be the case, but some organizations may deliberately, if misguidedly, choose to ignore it or at least to minimize its importance. This raises the important policy issue of the degree to which pay levels should be market led, which, if it does take place, would involve reproducing inside the organization the pay inequities that exist outside it.

External competitiveness versus internal equity

A policy needs to be formulated on the extent to which rewards are market driven rather than equitable. This policy will be influenced by the culture and reward philosophies of the organization and the pressures on the business to obtain and keep high-quality staff. Any organizations that have to attract and retain staff who are much in demand and where market rates are therefore high may, to a degree, have to sacrifice their ideals (if they have them) of internal equity to the realism of the marketplace. They will provide 'market pay'; in other words, they will be 'market driven'.

The pay management process must cope as best it can when the irresistible force of market pressures meets the immovable object of internal equity. There will always be some degree of tension in these circumstances, and while no solution will ever be simple or entirely satisfactory, there is one basic principle which can enhance the likelihood of success. That principle is to make explicit and fully identifiable the compromises with internal equity that are made and have to be made in response to market pressures.

The policy may indicate that market considerations will drive levels of pay in the organization. It may, however, allow for the use of market supplements or premiums – additional payments to the rate for a job as determined by job evaluation (internal equity) which reflect market rates. The policy may lay down that these payments should be reviewed regularly and no longer offered if they are unnecessary. Market supplements for those who have them may not be withdrawn (they would not lose pay), but adjustments may be made to pay progression to bring their rates more into line with those for comparable jobs. Market pay and market supplements can lead to gender inequalities if, as is often the case, men in comparable jobs are paid more generally or more men get market supplements than women. Equal pay case law has ruled that market pay and market supplements should be 'objectively justified' and the requirement to do this should be included in the pay policy.

Total reward policy

A policy is required on the extent to which the organization wants to adopt a 'total reward' approach as described in Chapter 2. This will mean assessing the importance of the non-financial relational rewards and how they should complement the financial transactional rewards.

Contingent rewards

The policy will need to determine whether or not the organization wants to pay for performance, competence, contribution or skill and, if so, how much and under what circumstances. There may, for example, be a policy that bonuses should be paid for exceptional performance but that to be significant, they should not be less than, say, 10 per cent of basic pay, while their upper limit should be restricted to 30 per cent or so of basic pay. The policy may also indicate the approach to be used in relating pay to individual, team or organizational performance.

The role of line managers

Line managers play a crucial role in administering rewards and the policy should recognize this. The extent to which the responsibility for rewards should be devolved to line managers is a policy decision. The aim may be to devolve it as far as possible, bearing in mind the need to ensure that other reward policy guidelines are followed and that consistent decisions are made across the organization by line managers. The policy may cover the level of decisions managers can make, the guidance that should be made available to them and how consistency will be achieved. The training that line managers require to increase their capacity to exercise judgements on reward and to conduct performance management reviews could also be covered by the policy.

Transparency

Traditionally, organizations in the private sector have kept information about pay policies secret. This is no longer a tenable position. Employees will only feel that the reward management processes of an organization are fair if they know what they are and how they are used to determine their level of pay and methods of pay progression. Lack of understanding breeds suspicion and hostility. One of the aims of reward management should be to enhance commitment, but there is no possibility of this being achieved if the organization is secretive about pay.

Without transparency, people will believe that the organization has something to hide, often with reason. There is no chance of building a satisfactory psychological contract unless the organization spells out its reward policies and practices. Transparency is achieved through involvement and communication.

Policies on pay decisions

Policies may be required on the extent to which the level of pay offered on appointment can exceed the minimum pay for the grade into which the individual will be allocated. It is also necessary to consider the policy on what promotion increases should be awarded.

Assimilation policies

The introduction of a new or considerably revised pay structure means that policies have to be developed on how existing employees should be assimilated into it. These policies cover where they should be placed in their new grades and what happens to them if their new grade and pay range means that their existing rate is above or below the new scale for their job. The policy should therefore cover 'red-circling' (identifying and dealing with overpaid people) and 'green-circling' (identifying and dealing with underpaid people). In the case of red-circled staff, 'protection' policies may have to be formulated to safeguard their existing rates of pay. In the case of green-circled staff, the policy may have to determine when (not if) their pay should be increased to fit into the new scale. It is sometimes necessary to save costs by phasing the increase and this should be included as a possible policy. Assimilation policies are dealt with in greater detail in Chapter 16.

DEVELOPING REWARD POLICIES

Reward policies should be developed by:

- referring to the list of policy issues and adding or subtracting items which appear to be most relevant, taking into account the structure, culture, management style and values of the organization, its reward philosophy and its business, HR and reward strategies;
- deciding under each heading, in consultation with those concerned, what policy approach is likely to be most relevant to the business priorities of the organization and the needs of its employees;
- ensuring that the policies are practical (implementable) and will provide the requisite level of guidance for decision and action;
- deciding on the amount of training and guidance that will be required to enable line managers and others to implement policies with an appropriate degree of consistency;
- communicating the policies to all those affected by them – ideally, they should be expressed in writing and the communication process should include briefing-groups to ensure that employees have the opportunity to seek clarification and make suggestions.

Reviewing policies

It needs to be re-emphasized that all aspects of reward management are dynamic and evolutionary. They cannot stand still. They must be continually reviewed and modified in line with changes in organization structures, strategic priorities, core values, processes, technologies and the new demands such changes make on people.

It is necessary, therefore, to review current reward policies at regular intervals to answer such questions as:

- Are they still relevant?
- Are they providing the level of guidance required?
- What problems, if any, are being met in implementing them?
- Are there any new areas of reward policy that need to be covered?
- Does anyone (top managers, line managers, HR specialists, employees, union representatives) want them changed and, if so, how?

The review should be carried out by HR specialists or, possibly, outside consultants, working with a project team of staff and their representatives. The review should be based on an attitude survey supplemented by focus groups. The need to monitor reward policies regularly to identify the need for changes extends to all reward processes. It is a good idea to include a firm review date – one or two years ahead – following the introduction of any new reward system or structure. This should not preclude earlier reviews if the necessity arises.

5

The context of reward management

Reward management takes place within the contexts of the internal (corporate) and external environments. These can exert considerable influence on reward strategy and policies, as described in this chapter.

THE INTERNAL ENVIRONMENT

Reward policy and practice will be affected by the characteristics of the organization with regard to its purpose, products and services, processes, sector (private, public, voluntary or not for profit) and, importantly, its culture, which is influenced by all the other characteristics.

Corporate culture

The culture of the organization can make a significant impact on reward management policy and practice and must be taken into account when developing and implementing innovative reward strategies. Corporate or organizational culture consists of shared values, norms, beliefs, attitudes, and assumptions which influence the way people act and the way things get done. It is significant because it is rooted in deeply held beliefs and reflects what has worked in the past. A positive culture can work for an organization by creating an environment conducive to performance improvement and the management of change and a sense of identity and unity of purpose. It can help to shape behaviour by giving guidance on what is expected. The wrong culture can work against an organization by erecting barriers which prevent the attainment of reward strategic objectives. These barriers include resistance to change and lack of commitment.

- Reward management philosophies, strategies and policies should be developed by reference to the existing culture or, if it needs to be changed, the preferred culture. They can reinforce an existing culture or play an important part in changing it.
- In reward management, the most important aspect of culture which needs to be taken into account is the core values of the organization. Values are expressed in beliefs as to what is best for the organization and what sort of behaviour is desirable. The 'value set' of an organization may be recognized only at top level, or it may be shared throughout the firm, so that the enterprise can be described as 'value driven'. The stronger the values, the more they will affect behaviour.
- Values are concerned with such matters as care and consideration for people, the belief that employees should be treated as stakeholders, employee involvement, equity in the treatment of employees, equal opportunity, care for customers, innovation, quality, social responsibility and teamwork.
- These values may influence policies in such areas as performance management, paying for contribution, resolving the often competing pressures for internal equity and external competitiveness, the equity and 'transparency' of reward arrangements and the extent to which employees are involved in the development of reward processes and structures. They should be taken into account in determining the criteria to be used in reviewing performance and rewarding people for their contribution. The research into performance management conducted by the CIPD in 2003/4 (1) found that many organizations were aiming to become 'value driven' and were using their performance management processes to achieve that purpose, thus ensuring that their espoused values became 'values in use'.

The employees' point of view

Reward management policies should take account of the aspirations, expectations and needs of employees as stakeholders in the organization. Consideration has also to be given to the needs or views of other stakeholders, especially owners in the private sector and governments, local authorities and trustees elsewhere.

Employee involvement is crucial to the development of reward policies and programmes. The wishes of employees need to be ascertained. Their comments on existing practices should be listened to and acted upon. They should be involved in the development of new reward processes, for example job evaluation, performance management and contingent pay. They should continue to be involved in the implementation and evaluation of these processes.

THE EXTERNAL ENVIRONMENT

The external environment in the shape of global/EU and national competition, government interventions, the industrial relations scene and the characteristics of the organization's sector can all influence reward policies and practices.

Global/EU competition

Global and EU competition compels business to increase productivity, the quality of their goods or services and the level of service they provide to customers. They have to become world class. The existence of international and pan-European firms means that there is an international market for talent which has to be taken into account by any company with overseas operations when deciding on levels of pay. Approaches to reward management in international corporations will be particularly concerned with the payment of expatriates. And organizations with headquarters and their major operations overseas may impose their own pay systems on UK firms, not always successfully. The specific impact of global competition on reward systems in the UK has been to encourage the use of more flexible approaches to pay so that the business can react more swiftly to new demands and pressures, including recruitment and retention problems and market rate differentials.

The national context

The key features of the national context which affect reward practices and policies are:

- Structural changes in the demand for skills, with an emphasis on high levels of attainment and expertise.
- Structural changes in industry, consisting of a continuing shift from manufacturing to service industry.
- Fragmentation in the labour market, which has taken place as the old monolithic manufacturing organizations have broken up.
- Low inflation rates, which have contained the size of pay settlements and restricted the value of pay reviews.
- Skill shortages, which encourage the use of recruitment premia.
- The growth of part-time, temporary and self-employment so that most people are not working full-time. This challenges the reward policy emphasis on full-time employees with long-term employment prospects in large organizations.

● The end of the concept of a 'career for life', which has meant increased focus on short-term incentives and rewards and less interest in final salary (defined benefits) pension schemes.

UK legislation

The following pieces of UK legislation directly or indirectly affect pay policies and practices:

● *The Equal Pay Act 1970 and the Equal Pay (Amendment) Regulations 1983* provide that pay differences are allowable only if the reason for them is not related to the sex of the job holder. *The Employment Act 2002* provides for the use of equal pay questionnaires. Equal pay legislation is described in Chapter 11.

● *The National Minimum Wage Act 1998* provides workers in the UK with a level of pay below which their wages must not fall – regardless of where they live or work or the sector or size of company in which they work. It is *not* a going rate. The government prescribes by regulation the minimum wage.

● *The Working Time Regulations 1998* provide, *inter alia*, for a limit of 48 hours on average weekly working time, which an individual worker may voluntarily agree to exceed, and a minimum of four weeks' paid annual leave subject to a 13-week qualifying period.

● *The Data Protection Act 1998* provides, *inter alia*, that employees are entitled to make a formal request to access information on the personal data held on them and the uses to which this will be put. They have the right (1) to be provided as a matter of course with certain information about any data relating to them – the exceptions are those relating to confidential references, management forecasting and planning and negotiating positions, and (2) to access any purely automated decision-making process relating, for example, to work performance, which might affect them.

● *The Transfer of Undertakings (Protection of Employment) Regulations 1981 (TUPE)* provide that when a business or part of a business is transferred the workers in that business automatically transfer into the employment of the transferee together with their existing terms and conditions of employment (except for pensions) intact and with their accrued periods of continuous service.

● *The Financial Services Act 1986* places restrictions on the provision of financial advice to employees. Only those who are directly authorized by one of the regulatory organizations or professional bodies are permitted to give detailed financial advice on investments.

THE INDUSTRIAL RELATIONS SCENE

The trade unions influence reward practices at national level through national pay negotiations, pronouncements on such issues as top executives' pay, and exerting pressure to achieve equal pay. They produce policies and advice for their members on such matters as:

- the use of job evaluation (they are in favour of analytical schemes while emphasizing the need for involvement in their design);
- pay structures (they tend to be against broad-banded structures);
- contingent pay (they are universally hostile to it, preferring the traditional service-related incremental scales);
- protection policies (they accept limited periods but want these to be four or five years);
- the use of equal pay audits and questionnaires;
- employee benefits and pension schemes (they object to the move towards money purchase schemes).

In general, they also provide advice and support on conducting pay negotiations at local level and getting involved in developments and appeals.

Locally, at organizational or establishment levels, trade union representatives echo their national policies. They increasingly demand transparency in pay policies and practices and the right to be involved in developing new systems or revising existing ones. They will request membership of project steering groups and task forces and demand that no changes are made without their consent.

THE NATIONAL GOVERNMENT SCENE

The Cabinet Office and the Public Services Productivity Panel develop policy guidelines for implementation by government departments and agencies, although departments and, especially, agencies have some freedom to develop their own pay structures.

John Makinson, Group Finance Director, Pearson plc, recommended in his report (2) to the Public Services Productivity Panel the use of incentive schemes in government departments and agencies on the grounds that they 'clarify objectives, engage and motivate employees and reward achievement'. The report issued the following guidelines:

1. Managers must have the skills, experience, and delegated authority to implement the scheme.
2. The overall compensation structure should be flexible and motivational.
3. Management information systems should measure performance quickly and accurately.
4. Funding arrangements must permit the benefits of achievement to be shared with employees.

5. Targets must reinforce the psychological motivation of employees and be clearly communicated.
6. A high priority should be attached to consultation with employees, and their representatives, as well as to simple and regular communication.

As reported by Incomes Data Services (IDS) in 2004 (3), the pay modernization agenda of the government consists of the following elements:

- simplified grading structures based on job evaluation;
- harmonized scales for different groups of staff;
- new integrated bargaining structures;
- national pay spines;
- equality proofing in pay, progression and promotion;
- single status terms and conditions;
- harmonizing the length of the working week;
- shortening scales to aid retention;
- aiding skilled people to stay in the front line;
- introducing a target rate for the job.

In spite of the Makinson Report, IDS reported that there has been a move away from individual performance-related pay. Bands have been shortened and the link between progression and top performance markings has been removed so that all satisfactorily performing staff can get to the target rate for the job in four to five steps. Performance is now more likely to be rewarded by non-consolidated bonus payments.

THE LOCAL GOVERNMENT SCENE

In 2003 the Office of the Deputy Prime Minister and the Employers' Organization for Local Government (4) developed a pay and workforce strategy for local government. Their two main recommendations were:

1. Move from pay structures with a large number of narrow grades that do not reflect real differences in job size or levels of responsibility to broader, more flexible ranges that permit authorities to respond to local market pressures or to reward exceptional employee contribution.
2. Encourage the introduction of pay systems that align with service priorities and seek to motivate staff through a balanced assessment of an employee's competence and contribution to replace the traditional system based on time served.

THE VOLUNTARY AND NOT-FOR-PROFIT SECTORS

The voluntary and not-for-profit sectors are very diverse and it is difficult to detect any general trends in the development of pay systems. Most of the larger organizations have traditionally adopted public sector schemes with pay spines consisting of service-related incremental scales. In recent years, however, some of the larger charities and housing associations have introduced broad-banded structures and some form of contribution pay. In two examples the contribution pay scheme has involved an arrangement of four or five steps to a target rate or reference point, with progression based on competence. Above the target rate, bonuses are given for special achievements which can be consolidated if the high level of achievement is sustained.

REFERENCES

1   Armstrong, M and Baron, A (2004) *Performance Management: Action and impact*, CIPD, London
2   Makinson, J (2000) *Incentives for Change*, Public Services Productivity Panel, London
3   Incomes Data Services (2004) *Pay in the Public Services 2004*, IDS, London
4   Office of the Deputy Prime Minister and the Local Government Employers' Association (2003) *Pay and Workforce Strategy for Local Government*, London

Part II

The conceptual framework

6

Factors affecting levels of pay

Perhaps the most significant decisions that have to be made by those concerned with reward management are about levels of pay. In making these decisions it is necessary to be aware of the various factors that influence pay levels, including the key economic theories that explain those factors. The practical value of such awareness is that the parts to be played by job evaluation, labour market surveys and trade union negotiations in developing grade and pay structures, fixing pay levels and relativities and using recruitment premia will be understood and applied to produce equitable and competitive pay systems.

This chapter summarizes the main theoretical concepts drawn from the fields of labour economics and then deals with the factors influencing job values within organizations. Finally, conclusions are drawn on what these concepts and factors tell us about reward management.

ECONOMIC DETERMINANTS OF PAY

The following economic theories and concepts provide guidance on the factors that affect pay levels:

- the labour theory of value;
- the nature of the external and internal labour market;
- the economic 'laws' of supply and demand (classical economic theory);

- efficiency wage theory;
- human capital theory;
- agency theory (also known as principal agent theory);
- the effort bargain.

The labour theory of value

In 1865 Karl Marx wrote in *Das Kapital* that the value of goods and services is determined by the amount of labour that goes into them. It is not the marketplace that sets prices. Thus the *content* of labour determines the *price* of labour. Mainstream economists have never accepted this concept and assert the primacy of supply and demand in the marketplace in setting prices of goods and services. However, as pointed out by Niels Nielsen (1), conventional job evaluation schemes are based on the labour theory of value in that they are concerned only with job *content* and ignore market rate pressures. They make no attempt to price jobs directly.

The labour market

Markets consist of buyers and sellers of goods. Too many buyers for a limited number of goods forces prices up and a surplus of goods beyond what buyers want forces prices down. The labour market is a market like any other market; it has buyers (employers) and sellers (employees). The price of labour is the rate of pay required to attract and retain people in organizations.

The efforts of these buyers and sellers to transact and establish an employment relationship constitutes a labour market. An external market may be local, national or international. It may be related to specific occupations, sectors or industries in any of these areas. It is within these markets that the economic determinants of pay levels operate, which include not only supply and demand factors (see below) but also the impact of inflationary pressures.

In any sizeable organization there is also an internal labour market. This is the market that exists when firms fill their vacancies from the ranks of existing employees. Pay levels and relativities in the internal market may differ significantly between firms in spite of general external market pressures. These arise particularly when long-term relationships are usual, even though these are becoming less common. Pay in the internal market will be affected by views on the intrinsic value of jobs and what individuals are worth on the basis of their expertise and contribution, irrespective of the market rate for their job. Pay progression related to length of service and an 'annuity' approach to pay increments (that is, pay that goes up but does not come down, what economists call 'the sticky wage') may lead to higher internal rates. But the relationship between internal and external rates will also depend on policy decisions within the firm on its levels of pay generally, compared with the 'going rate' in the external market.

Classical economic theory (supply and demand)

Classical economic competitive theory states that pay levels in labour markets are determined by supply and demand considerations. Other things being equal, if there is a surplus of labour and supply exceeds the demand, pay levels go down; if there is a scarcity of labour and demand exceeds the supply, pay goes up. Pay stabilizes when demand equals supply at the 'market clearing' or 'market equilibrium' wage. This is sometimes known as the theory of equalizing differences and it was first stated by Adam Smith (2) over 200 years ago when he wrote that: 'The whole of the advantages and disadvantages of different employments and stock must, in the same neighbourhood, be either perfectly equal or continually tending to equality.'

As Elliott (3) has noted: 'Competitive theory predicts that the forces of supply in the market as a whole will determine the rates of pay within each firm. The relative pay of any two occupations in a single firm will be the mirror image of the relative pay of the same two occupations in the market as a whole.'

Classical theory, however, is based on the premises that 'other things are equal' and that a 'perfect market' for labour exists. In the real world, of course, other things are never equal and there is no such thing as a universally perfect market, that is, one in which everyone knows what the going rate is, there is free movement of labour within the market and there are no monopolistic or other forces interfering with the normal processes of supply and demand. The existence of internal markets means that individual firms exercise a good deal of discretion about how much they pay and how much attention they give to external market pressures. Human capital theory, as discussed in the next section, also explains why individual rates of pay may be influenced by other forces besides supply and demand. Imperfections in the market exist because of poor information, lack of opportunity and immobility. They also arise when employers or trade unions exert pressures on pay levels or when governments intervene in normal pay determination processes.

Efficiency wages theory

Efficiency wages theory proposes that firms will pay more than the market rate because they believe that high levels of pay will contribute to increases in productivity by motivating superior performance, attracting better candidates, reducing labour turnover and persuading workers that they are being treated fairly. This theory is also known as 'the economy of high wages'.

Organizations are using efficiency wages theory (although they will not call it that) when they formulate pay policies that place them as market leaders or at least above the average.

Human capital theory

Human capital theory, as stated by Ehrenberg and Smith (4): '... conceptualizes workers as embodying a set of skills which can be "rented out" to employers. The knowledge and skills a worker has – which comes from education and training, including the training that experience brings – generate a certain *stock* of productive capital.'

For the employee, the expected returns on human capital investments are a higher level of earnings, greater job satisfaction and, at one time, but less so now, a belief that security in employment is assured. For the employer, the return on investment in human capital is expected to be the improvements in performance, productivity, flexibility and the capacity to innovate which should result from enlarging the skill base and increasing levels of competence.

Agency theory

Agency theory, or principal agent theory, in its purest form recognizes that in most firms there is a separation between the owners (the principals) and the agents (the managers). However, the principals may not have complete control over their agents. The latter may therefore act in ways which are not fully revealed to their principals and which may not be in accordance with the wishes of those principals. This generates what economists call agency costs, which arise from the difference between what might have been earned if the principals had been the managers, and the earnings achieved under the stewardship of the actual managers. To reduce these agency costs, the principals have to develop ways of monitoring and controlling the actions of their agents.

Agency theory as described above can be extended to the employment contract within firms. The employment relationship may be regarded as a contract between a principal (the employer) and an agent (the employee). The payment aspect of the contract is the method used by the principal to motivate the agent to perform work to the satisfaction of the employer. But according to this theory, the problem of ensuring that agents do what they are told remains. It is necessary to clear up ambiguities by setting objectives and monitoring performance to ensure that those objectives are achieved.

Agency theory also indicates that it is desirable to operate a system of incentives to motivate and reward acceptable behaviour. This process of 'incentive alignment' consists of paying for measurable results which are deemed to be in the best interests of the owners. Such incentive systems track outcomes in the shape of quantifiable indices of the firm's performance such as earnings per share rather than being concerned with the behaviour that led up to them. The theory is that if the incentives schemes for top managers are designed properly, those managers will, out of self-interest, closely monitor performance throughout the organization.

Agency theory has been criticized by Gomez-Mejia and Balkin (5) as 'managerialist'. In other words, it looks at the employment relationship purely from the point of view of management and regards employees as objects to be motivated by carrot and stick methods. It is a dismal theory, which suggests that people cannot be trusted.

Agency theory is the basis of McGregor's (6) *Theory X* in which he described the traditional assumptions of managers about people and work as follows:

> The average human being has an inherent dislike of work and will avoid it if he (sic) can. Because of this human characteristic of dislike of work, most people must be coerced, controlled, threatened with punishment to get them to put forth adequate effort towards the achievement of organizational objectives.

McGregor, of course, advocated his much more optimistic *Theory Y* as an alternative approach. This states that:

> External control and the threat of punishment are not the only means for bringing about effort toward organizational objectives. Man will exercise self-direction and self-control in the service of objectives to which he is committed... Commitment to objectives is a function of the rewards associated with their achievement.

The effort bargain

The concept of the effort bargain is referred to less frequently nowadays and it is not strictly an economic theory. But it has its uses as a further means of describing the employment relationship on pay matters. The concept states that the task of management is to assess what level and type of inducements it has to offer in return for the contribution it requires from its workforce.

The aim of workers is to strike a bargain about the relationship between what they regard as a reasonable contribution and what their employer is prepared to offer to elicit that contribution. This is termed the 'effort bargain' and is, in effect, an agreement which lays down the amount of work to be done for a rate of pay or wage rate, not just the hours to be worked. Explicitly or implicitly, all employees are in a bargaining situation with regard to pay. A system will not be accepted as effective and workable until it is recognized as fair and equitable by both parties and unless it is applied consistently.

FACTORS AFFECTING PAY LEVELS
WITHIN ORGANIZATIONS

Within most organizations there are defined or generally understood pay levels for jobs. These are usually set out in the form of a pay structure which may cover the whole organization, or groups of related occupations (job families). There may be different structures at various levels, for example senior management, other staff, manual workers. In some organizations, however, the pay system is highly flexible and relatively unstructured. It may, for example, simply consist of individual rates for the various jobs (spot rates) which bear no apparent logical relationship to one another and are determined by management intuitively. Structures for manual workers may also consist of spot rates which are based on negotiations and custom and practice.

Where there are formal structures, pay levels and ranges may be influenced by the processes of job evaluation, which assesses the relative internal worth of jobs (internal relativities), and market pricing, which assesses external relativities. The type of processes used and the degree to which they are formal and analytical or informal and intuitive will vary widely.

Individual rates of pay may be governed by the structure in the form of a fixed rate for the job or by movement in the form of fixed increments up a scale (a fixed increment is a predetermined addition to an individual's rate of pay which is related to service in the job). These may take place within a pay bracket with fixed minima and maxima in a graded structure or by progression through defined pay ranges in a pay spine (a series of incremental pay points extending from the lowest to the highest jobs covered by the structure within which pay ranges for the jobs in the hierarchy are established). Alternatively, pay progression within brackets or bands or within job family structures may vary according to individual performance, competence or contribution.

The level of pay of employees within organizations is affected by the economic factors mentioned above which impact on the intrinsic value attached to the job, internal relativities, external relativities and the value of the person. It is also affected by the financial circumstances of the organization, the 'market stance' it adopts and trade union pressures.

Intrinsic value

The concept of intrinsic value states that jobs have value because of the impact they make on organizational results and by reference to the levels of responsibility and skill required to perform them. Increases in impact and these levels lead to higher rates of pay. This concept is in line with the labour theory of value and provides the theoretical base for job evaluation. However, as an explanation of the value attached to jobs it is limited because it ignores internal and external relativities.

Internal relativities

It can be argued that the value of anything, including jobs, is always relative to something else, that is, other jobs. Views on job values within organizations are based on perceptions of the worth of one job compared with others. This is the concept of internal equity which is achieved when people are rewarded appropriately in relation to others according to the value of their contribution. The case for equal pay for work of equal value is based on the imperative to achieve internal equity.

External relativities

The rates of pay for jobs and people will be influenced by market rates in accordance with the policy of the organization on how it wants its pay levels to relate to market levels and the degree to which market forces impact on the amounts required to attract and retain the quality of people the organization needs. It is often claimed that 'a job is worth what the market says it is worth' and this belief leads to reliance on 'market pricing' to value jobs rather than on job evaluation to establish internal relativities. But Rosabeth Moss Kanter (7) has argued that this process is circular: 'We know what people are worth because that's what they cost in the job market, but we also know that what people cost in the job market is just what they're worth.'

However, no organization can ignore external relativities if it wants to compete successfully in the labour market, just as no organization can ignore internal relativities if it believes in equitable pay. The problem is reconciling the two, that is, attempting to achieve external competitiveness while maintaining internal equity. This is always difficult and often impossible.

The value of the person

Individuals are valued by organizations for three main reasons: (1) the contribution they make to organizational success, (2) their skills and competences and (3) the experience they bring to their jobs. People also have their own value in the marketplace – their 'market worth', which has to be taken into account by employers in setting their rates of pay.

Financial circumstances of the organization

'Affordability' is an important concept in reward management. Pay systems cannot cost more than the organization can afford and this will influence the level of pay that can be offered to employees.

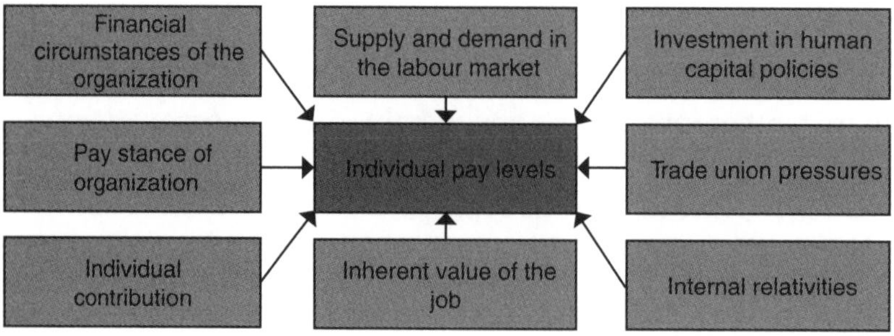

Figure 6.1 Factors affecting pay levels

Pay stance

Policy decisions on an organization's pay stance – whether it should be a high, medium or even low payer – will depend partly on what it can afford but it will also be affected by the extent to which it believes that it must be competitive in the labour market.

Trade union pressures

Pay levels may be determined through collective bargaining with trade unions. They will want their members' pay to keep ahead of inflation, to match market rates and to reflect any increases in the prosperity of the business. The amount of pressure they can exert on pay levels will depend on the relative bargaining strengths of the employer and the union, and this will reflect the amount of power either party can exert in pay negotiations.

The minimum wage

Minimum wage legislation in the UK sets minimum rates of pay. The amount is increased from time to time.

SUMMARY: FACTORS AFFECTING PAY LEVELS

The factors affecting individual pay levels are summarized in Figure 6.1.

THE SIGNIFICANCE OF THE FACTORS AFFECTING PAY LEVELS

The factors affecting pay levels described above are significant because they exert a major influence on how organizations manage their pay. That is why it is important to take them into account when making pay decisions, as described below.

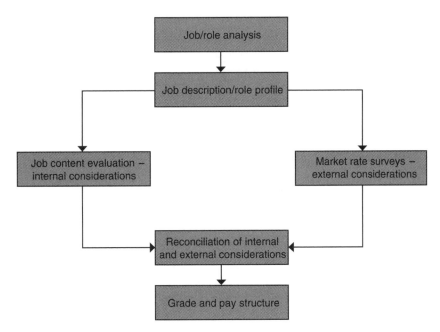

Figure 6.2   Developing a grade and pay structure

The labour theory of value

The labour theory of value in effect provides the rationale for job content job evaluation and the design of internally equitable grade structures but it is necessary to take into account market rates through 'market pricing' based on market rate analysis to ensure that pay is competitive as well as equitable. The process is illustrated in Figure 6.2.

Classical economic theory

The significance of classical economic theory is that it focuses attention on external pressures and the perceived need for 'competitive pay', that is, pay that matches or exceeds market rates. Classical theory is used as a justification for 'market' pricing rather than job evaluation, concentrating on external competitiveness at the expense of internal equity.

External competitiveness versus internal equity

Organizations must understand the other factors besides market pressures which may affect pay levels, such as perceived needs for equity and for rewarding individual contribution and competence, long service and loyalty. This means appreciating that there will be tension between pay determination policies based on external comparisons (market pricing) and those focusing on internal relativities (job evaluation). The problem is always how to reconcile the often conflicting requirements for internal equity and external competitiveness. Organizations cannot ignore the former because, if so, they will create unequal pay situations and dissatisfaction amongst employees. But they ignore the latter at their peril because if they do they may have problems in attracting and retaining quality employees. In any organizations relying on the external market, and this means most organizations, the need to be competitive may well prevail. The reconciliation process is often a balancing act involving the judicious use of recruitment premia to avoid permanently distorting internal relativities.

Labour markets

Organizations must be aware of the labour markets in which they are operating so that they can make appropriate decisions on pay levels in the light of market intelligence and policies on where they want to be in relation to the market.

Human capital theory

Organizations must appreciate the implication of human capital theory, which is that investment in people adds to their value to the firm. Individuals expect a return on their own investment and firms recognize that the increased value of their employees should be rewarded. Human capital theory encourages the use of competence-related or skill-based pay as a method of reward. It also underpins the concept of individual market worth. This indicates that individuals have their own value in the marketplace which they acquire and increase through investments by their employer and themselves in gaining extra expertise and competence through training, development and experience. The market worth of individuals may be considerably higher than the market rate of their jobs, and if they are not rewarded accordingly they may market their talents elsewhere.

Agency theory

Agency theory performs the useful function of directing attention to the ambiguities inherent in the employment relationship and to the importance of managing expectations. These aspects of reward are covered by the concepts of expectancy theory and the psychological contract as discussed in the next two chapters.

The effort bargain

The notion of an effort bargain highlights the fact that pay levels are subject to collective and individual negotiation. It also draws attention to the need for equity, fairness and consistency in reward systems.

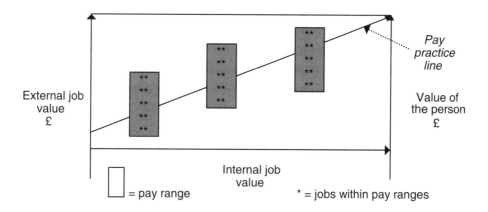

Figure 6.3   Interrelation of factors affecting individual pay

APPLICATION OF THE FACTORS

Within organizations the main factors affecting individual levels of pay interrelate as shown in Figure 6.3.

REFERENCES

1   Nielsen, N H (2002) Job content evaluation techniques based on Marxian economics, *WorldatWork Journal*, **11** (2), pp 52–62
2   Smith, Adam (1776) *The Wealth of Nations*
3   Elliott, R F (1991) *Labor Economics*, McGraw-Hill, Maidenhead
4   Ehrenberg, R G and Smith, R S (1994) *Modern Labor Economics*, HarperCollins, New York
5   Gomez-Mejia, L R and Balkin, D B (1992) *Compensation, Organizational Strategy, and Firm Performance*, South-Western Publishing Co., Cincinnati
6   McGregor, D (1960) *The Human Side of Enterprise*, McGraw-Hill, New York
7   Kanter, R M (1989) *When Giants Learn to Dance*, Simon and Schuster, London

7

Motivation and reward

One of the most fundamental concerns of reward management is how it can help to motivate people so that they achieve high levels of performance. The development of a performance culture is a typical aim of reward strategy.

It is therefore necessary to understand the factors that motivate people and how, in the light of these factors, reward processes and practices that will enhance motivation, commitment, job engagement and positive discretionary behaviour can be developed. Motivation theories provide essential guidance on the practical steps required to develop effective reward systems (there is nothing so practical as a good theory). This chapter examines the process of motivation and those theories that most influence reward. The relationship between money and motivation is then considered and the chapter ends with an analysis of how motivation theory can be put to good use.

THE PROCESS OF MOTIVATION

Motivation theory examines the process of motivation. It explains why people at work behave in the way they do in terms of their efforts, their discretionary behaviour and the directions they take.

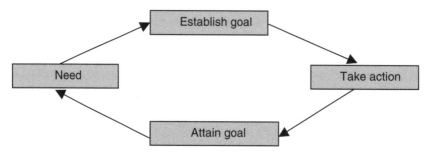

Figure 7.1 The process of motivation

Motivation defined

A motive is a reason for doing something. Motivation theory is concerned with the factors that influence people to behave in certain ways. People are motivated when they expect that a course of action is likely to lead to the attainment of a goal – a valued reward that satisfies their particular needs. Well-motivated people are those with clearly defined goals who take action that they expect will achieve those goals.

How motivation works

A model of motivation based on reinforcement, needs and goal theory as described later in this chapter is shown in Figure 7.1.

This model suggests that the process of motivation is initiated by the conscious or unconscious recognition of unsatisfied needs. These needs create wants, which are desires to achieve or attain something. Goals are then established which it is believed will satisfy these needs and a behaviour pathway is selected which it is believed will achieve the goal. If the goal is achieved, the need is satisfied and the behaviour is likely to be repeated the next time a similar need emerges. If the goal is not achieved, the same action is less likely to be repeated. However, as some needs are satisfied new needs emerge and the process continues. As Maslow (1) says, it is unsatisfied needs that motivate behaviour.

Individual differences

Some common needs headings have been established by theorists such as Maslow (1) and Herzberg (2) and these are described in the next section of this chapter. But it cannot be assumed that these are present at any moment to the same extent or even present at all in all the members of a population such as the employees of an organization. It is a cliché to say that all people are different but it is none the less true, and it is a truth that organizations sometimes fail to appreciate when they assume, for example, that all their employees will be motivated to the same degree by money.

Types of motivation

There are two types of motivation as originally described by Herzberg *et al* (2):

- *Intrinsic motivation* – this was described by Herzberg as 'motivation through the work itself'. It takes place when people feel that the work they do is intrinsically interesting, challenging and important and involves the exercise of responsibility (having control over one's own resources), autonomy or freedom to act, scope to use and develop skills and abilities and opportunities for advancement and growth.
- *Extrinsic motivation* – what is done to or for people to motivate them. This includes rewards such as increased pay, recognition, praise or promotion, and punishments such as disciplinary action, withholding pay, or criticism.

Extrinsic motivators can have an immediate and powerful effect, but it will not necessarily last long. The intrinsic motivators, which are concerned with the 'quality of working life' (a phrase and a movement promoted by proponents of the notion of intrinsic motivation), are likely to have a deeper and longer–term effect because they are inherent in individuals and not imposed from outside. But it should not be assumed that intrinsic motivation is good and extrinsic motivation is bad. They both have a part to play.

The role of job design in motivation

Intrinsic motivation is provided when jobs are well designed. This takes place when the job has the following characteristics:

- autonomy, discretion, self-control and responsibility;
- variety;
- use of abilities;
- availability of constructive feedback;
- belief that the work is significant.

The role of rewards and incentives in motivation

Rewards provide recognition to people for their achievements and contribution. If rewards are worth having and attainable and people know how they can attain them, they can act as motivators. Rewards can be either financial or non-financial.

Incentives are designed to encourage people to achieve objectives. They are intended to provide direct motivation: 'do this and we will make it worth your while'. Incentives are generally financial but they can promise non-financial rewards such as promotion or a particularly interesting assignment.

MOTIVATION THEORIES

The process of motivation as described above is broadly based on a number of motivation theories which attempt to explain in more detail what it is all about. The main theories as described below are:

- instrumentality, behaviourist and reinforcement theories;
- needs or content theories;
- Herzberg's two-factor theory;
- process or cognitive theories (expectancy, goal and equity).

Instrumentality theory

'Instrumentality' is the belief that if we do one thing it will lead to another. In its crudest form, instrumentality theory states that people work only for money. The theory emerged in the second half of the 19th century, when the emphasis was on the need to rationalize work and to concentrate on economic outcomes. It assumes that people will be motivated to work if rewards and penalties are tied directly to their performance. Instrumentality theory has its roots in the scientific management methods of Taylor (3), who wrote: 'It is impossible, through any long period of time, to get workmen to work much harder than the average men around them unless they are assured a large and permanent increase in their pay.'

This theory is based on the principle of reinforcement, which states that, with experience in taking action to satisfy needs, people perceive that certain actions help to achieve their goals while others are less successful. Success in achieving goals and rewards therefore acts as a positive incentive and reinforces the behaviour, which is repeated the next time a similar need emerges. Conversely, failure or punishment provides negative reinforcement, suggesting the need to seek alternative means of achieving goals. This process has been called the law of effect.

Motivation using this approach has been and still is widely adopted and can be successful in some circumstances. But it is based exclusively on a system of external controls and fails to recognize a number of other human needs. Nor does it take account of the fact that the formal control system can be seriously affected by the informal relations between workers.

Needs (content) theory

The basis of this theory is the belief that an unsatisfied need creates tension and disequilibrium. To restore the balance a goal is identified which will satisfy the need, and a behaviour pathway is selected which will lead to the achievement of the goal. All behaviour is therefore motivated by unsatisfied needs.

Not all needs are equally important to a person at any one time. Some may constitute a more powerful drive towards a goal than others, depending on the individual's background and situation. Complexity is increased because there is no simple relationship between needs and goals. The same need could be satisfied by a number of different goals. The stronger the need and the longer its duration, the broader the range of possible goals. At the same time, one goal may satisfy a number of needs. A new car provides transport as well as an opportunity to impress the neighbours.

The best-known contributor to needs theory is Maslow (1). He formulated the concept of a hierarchy of needs, which start from the fundamental physiological needs and lead through safety, social and esteem needs to the need for self-fulfilment, the highest need of all. He said that 'man is a wanting animal'; only an unsatisfied need can motivate behaviour, and the dominant need is the prime motivator of behaviour. This is the best-known theory of needs but it has never been verified by empirical research.

Herzberg's two-factor model

Herzberg's two-factor model theory states that the factors giving rise to job satisfaction (and motivation) are distinct from the factors that lead to job dissatisfaction. It is sometimes called the motivation–hygiene theory.

There are two groups of factors. The first consists of the satisfiers or motivators which are intrinsic to the job. These include achievement, recognition, the work itself, responsibility and growth. The second group comprises what Herzberg calls the 'dissatisfaction avoidance' or 'hygiene' factors, which are extrinsic to the job and include pay, company policy and administration, personal relations, status and security. These cannot create satisfaction but, unless preventive action is taken, they can cause dissatisfaction. He also noted that any feeling of satisfaction resulting from pay increases was likely to be short-lived compared with the long-lasting satisfaction from the work itself. One of the key conclusions derived from the research is therefore that pay is not a motivator, except in the short term, although unfair payment systems can lead to de-motivation.

Herzberg's two-factor model draws attention to the distinction between intrinsic and extrinsic motivators, and his contention that the satisfaction resulting from pay increases does not persist has some face validity. But his research and the conclusions he reached have been attacked – first because, it is asserted, the original research is flawed and fails to support the contention that pay is not a motivator, and secondly because no attempt was made to measure the relationship between satisfaction and performance. As David Guest (4) has written:

> Many managers' knowledge of motivation has not advanced beyond Herzberg and his generation. This is unfortunate. Their theories are now over thirty years old. Extensive research has shown that as general theories of motivation the theories of Herzberg and Maslow are wrong. They have been replaced by more relevant approaches.

Process or cognitive theory

The more relevant approaches to which Guest refers are the process or cognitive theories. They are known as process theories because they describe the psychological processes or forces which affect motivation, as well as basic needs. The term cognitive theories is used because they refer to people's perception of their working environment and the ways in which they interpret and understand it. Process theory can be more useful to managers than needs theory because it provides more realistic guidance on motivation techniques. The processes covered by the most relevant theories are:

- expectations (expectancy theory);
- goal achievement (goal theory);
- feelings about equity (equity theory).

Expectancy theory

The core process theory is expectancy theory. As Guest (4) notes, most other approaches adapt or build on it. The concept of expectancy was originally contained in the valency–instrumentality–expectancy (VIE) theory formulated by Vroom (5). Valency stands for value, instrumentality is the belief that if we do one thing it will lead to another, and expectancy is the probability that action or effort will lead to an outcome.

The strength of expectations may be based on past experience (reinforcement), but individuals are frequently presented with new situations – a change of job, payment system or working conditions imposed by management – where past experience is an inadequate guide to the implications of the change. In these circumstances, motivation may be reduced.

Motivation is likely only when a clearly perceived and usable relationship exists between performance and outcome, and the outcome is seen as a means of satisfying needs. This explains why extrinsic financial motivation – for example, an incentive or bonus scheme – works only if the link between effort and reward is understood (there is a clear 'line of sight') and the value of the reward is worth the effort. It also explains why intrinsic motivation arising from the work itself can be more powerful than

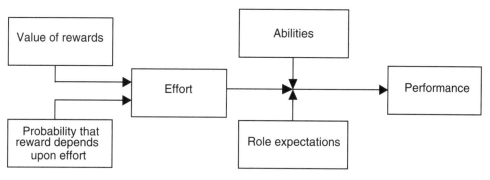

Figure 7.2 Motivation model (Porter and Lawler)

extrinsic motivation. Intrinsic motivation outcomes are more under the control of individuals, who can judge from past experience the extent to which advantageous results are likely to be obtained by their behaviour.

This theory was developed by Porter and Lawler (6) into a model which follows Vroom's ideas by suggesting that there are two factors determining the effort people put into their jobs: (1) the value of the reward to individuals in so far as they satisfy their need for security, social esteem, autonomy and self-actualization; (2) the probability that reward depends on effort, as perceived by individuals – in other words, their expectations of the relationship between effort and reward.

Thus, the greater the value of a set of rewards and the higher the probability that receiving each of these rewards depends on effort, the greater the effort that will be made in a given situation.

But, as Porter and Lawler emphasize, mere effort is not enough. It has to be effective effort if it is to produce the desired performance. The two variables additional to effort which affect task achievement are: (1) ability – individual characteristics such as intelligence, manual skills, know-how; (2) role perceptions – what individuals want to do or think they are required to do. They are good from the viewpoint of the organization if they correspond with what it thinks the individual ought to be doing. They are poor if the views of the individual and the organization do not coincide.

A model of expectancy theory as produced by Lawler and Porter is shown in Figure 7.2.

Goal theory

Goal theory, as developed by Latham and Locke (7), states that motivation and performance are higher when individuals are set specific goals, when the goals are difficult but accepted, and when there is feedback on performance. Participation in goal-setting is important as a means of securing agreement to the setting of higher goals. Difficult goals must be agreed and achieving them must be helped by guidance and advice. Finally, feedback is vital in maintaining motivation, particularly towards the achievement of even higher goals.

Goal theory provided the theoretical underpinning to processes such as management by objectives where the emphasis was on setting goals and measuring performance. Management by objectives, or MbO as it was known, is no longer a fashionable term, partly because MbO systems tended to be bureaucratic and over-emphasized quantitative targets. But they still provide the basis for traditional performance-related pay schemes where the focus is on objectives and the measurement of achievements as a means of providing financial rewards in the shape of performance pay.

Equity theory

Equity theory, as described by Adams (8), states that people will be better motivated if they are treated equitably and de-motivated if they are treated inequitably. It is concerned with people's perceptions of how they are being treated in relation to others. To be dealt with equitably is to be treated fairly in comparison with another group of people (a reference group) or a relevant other person. Equity involves feelings and perceptions, and it is always a comparative process. It is not synonymous with equality, which means treating everyone alike. That would be inequitable if they deserved to be treated differently.

Equity theory is linked with the 'felt fair' principle as defined by Jaques (9), which states in effect that pay systems will be fair if they are felt to be fair. A fuller description of his notion was set out in Chapter 1.

MOTIVATION AND FINANCIAL INCENTIVES AND REWARDS

Financial incentives and rewards can motivate. People need money and therefore want money. It can motivate but it is not the only motivator. It has been suggested by Wallace and Szilagyi (10) that money can serve the following reward functions:

- It can act as a goal that people generally strive for, although to different degrees.
- It can act as an instrument which provides valued outcomes.
- It can be a symbol which indicates the recipient's value to the organization.
- It can act as a general reinforcer because it is associated with valued rewards so often that it takes on reward value itself.

Money motivates because it is linked directly or indirectly with the satisfaction of many needs. It satisfies the basic need for survival and security, if income is regular.

It can also satisfy the need for self-esteem (it is a visible mark of appreciation) and status – money can set you in a grade apart from your fellows and can buy you things they cannot afford. Money satisfies the less desirable but nevertheless prevalent drives of acquisitiveness and cupidity. So money may in itself have no intrinsic meaning, but it acquires significant motivating power because it comes to symbolize so many intangible goals. It acts as a symbol in different ways for different people, and for the same person at different times. Pay is often a dominant factor in the choice of employer and pay is an important consideration when people are deciding whether or not to stay with an organization.

But doubts have been cast on the effectiveness of money as a motivator by Herzberg *et al* (2). As noted above, he claimed that while the lack of it may cause dissatisfaction, money does not result in lasting satisfaction. There is something in this, especially for people on fixed salaries or rates of pay who do not benefit directly from an incentive scheme. They may feel good when they get an increase, as, apart from the extra money, it is a highly effective way of making people feel they are valued. But the feeling of euphoria can rapidly die away. However, it must be re-emphasized that different people have different needs, and Herzberg's two-factor theory has not been validated. Some will be much more motivated by money than others. What cannot be assumed is that money motivates everyone in the same way and to the same extent.

But do financial incentives motivate people? The answer, according to Kohn (11), is absolutely not. He challenges what he calls the behaviourist dogma about money and motivation. And he claims that 'no controlled scientific study has ever found a long-term enhancement of the quality of work as a result of any reward system'. When you look at how people are motivated, claims Kohn: 'It becomes disturbingly clear that the more you use rewards to "motivate" people, the more they tend to lose interest in whatever they had to do to get the rewards.' He quotes research that has 'repeatedly shown that the more salient or reinforcing the reward is, the more it erodes intrinsic interest' and points out that 'various devices can be used to get people to do something, but that is a far cry from making people *want* to do something'.

Pfeffer (12) contends that: 'People do work for money – but they work even more for meaning in their lives. In fact, they work to have fun. Companies that ignore this fact are essentially bribing their employees and will pay the price in lack of loyalty and commitment.' He believes that pay cannot substitute for a working environment 'high on trust, fun and meaningful work'.

In contrast, Gupta and Shaw (13) emphasize the instrumental and symbolic meaning of money. The instrumental meaning of money concerns what we get for it – better houses, clothes, cars etc. The symbolic meaning of money concerns how it is viewed by ourselves and others – money signals our status in and worth to society. They take the basic behaviourist line on money: 'When certain behaviours are followed by money, then they are more likely to be repeated. This means that employees will do the things for which they are rewarded; it also means that they ignore the things for which they are not rewarded.'

The views expressed by Kohn are convincing except that he seems to think that the only types of rewards to be considered in this debate are financial. He does not seem to recognize that non-financial rewards *can* motivate if handled properly. Pfeffer, however, makes this point when he emphasizes the importance of trust and meaningful work. Gupta and Shaw weaken their argument by adopting a crude behaviourist viewpoint.

To assume that financial incentives will always motivate people to perform better is as simplistic as to assume, like Kohn, that they *never* motivate people to perform better. Some people will be more motivated by money than others and, if handled properly, an incentive scheme can encourage them to perform more effectively as long as they can link their effort to the reward and the reward is worth having. Sometimes cash sums (bonuses) can be more effective rewards because they can be immediately converted into things that people want. An increase of 3 per cent to someone's basic pay might not have such an effect. But others may be less interested in money and will respond more to intrinsic or non-financial rewards. The majority are likely to react positively to a judicious mix of both financial and non-financial rewards.

What is clear is that simplistic assumptions about the power of money to motivate can lead organizations into developing simplistic performance-related pay schemes or other forms of incentives. And we can be reasonably certain that a multiplicity of interdependent factors are involved in motivating people. Money is only one of those factors that may work for some people in some circumstances, but may not work for other people in other circumstances.

It should also be remembered that while an increase in pay arising from a contingent pay scheme may motivate people who get it, for a limited period perhaps, it will almost certainly de-motivate those who don't get it or feel that they are not getting enough compared with other people. The likelihood is that the number of people de-motivated in this way is likely to be larger than the number who have been motivated. Paradoxically, therefore, contingent pay schemes are in danger of increasing the amount of de-motivation existing in the organization rather than enhancing motivation.

FACTORS AFFECTING SATISFACTION WITH PAY

As Lawler (14) points out, people's feelings about the adequacy of their pay are based upon comparisons they make between their own and others'. External market comparisons are the most critical because they are the ones that strongly influence whether individuals want to stay with the organization. Many people, however, are unlikely to leave for pay reasons alone unless the increase they expect from a move is substantial, say 10 per cent.

Lawler also suggests, 'Sometimes it seems that individuals are never satisfied with the pay.' One of the reasons suggested by Lawler for low pay satisfaction seems to be that individuals seek out unfavourable comparisons. First they look externally: if comparisons there are favourable, they focus on internal comparisons. Only if these are favourable as well are they likely to be satisfied. He comments that: 'A finding that employees are dissatisfied with pay is, in effect, a non-finding. It is to be expected. The key thing that the organization needs to focus on is whether employees are more dissatisfied with their pay than are employees in other organizations.'

Reactions to reward policies and practices will depend largely on the values and needs of individuals and on their employment conditions. It is therefore dangerous to generalize about the causes of satisfaction or dissatisfaction. However, it seems reasonable to believe that, as mentioned above, feelings about external and internal equity (the 'felt fair' principle) will strongly influence most people. Research by Porter and Lawler (6) and others has also shown that higher-paid employees are likely to be more satisfied with their rewards but the satisfaction resulting from a large pay increase may be short-lived. People tend to want more of the same. In this respect, at least, the views of Maslow and Herzberg have been supported by research.

Other factors that may affect satisfaction or dissatisfaction with pay include the degree to which:

- individuals feel their rate of pay or increase has been determined fairly;
- rewards are commensurate with the perceptions of individuals about their ability, contribution and value to the organization (but this perception is likely to be founded on information or beliefs about what other people, inside and outside the organization, are paid);
- individuals are satisfied with other aspects of their employment – for example, their status, promotion prospects, opportunity to use and develop skills, and relations with their managers.

JOB SATISFACTION, MOTIVATION AND PERFORMANCE

There is no research evidence that there is always a strong and positive relationship between job satisfaction and performance. A satisfied worker is not necessarily a high performer and a high performer is not necessarily a satisfied worker. Satisfaction may lead to good performance but good performance may just as well be the cause of satisfaction. The relationship can be reciprocal.

The relationship between motivation and performance is even more complex. Vroom (5) formulated it as $P = M \times A$, where P is performance, M is motivation and A is ability. Note that the relationship is multiplicative – if the value of either M or A is zero, then there will be no performance. Performance depends on both motivation and ability.

A more recent formulation of the relationship has been produced by Boxall and Purcell (15). This is that $P = M + A + S$, where P is performance, M is motivation, A is ability and S is scope to use and develop abilities. Note that the relationship is not multiplicative as in Vroom, and scope is an additional factor.

By including ability and scope as factors, these formulations underline the importance of adopting an integrated approach to reward and other HR strategies. Motivation by pay or any other means is not enough. Reward strategies must be associated with human resource development and resourcing strategies to maximize their impact on performance.

THE KEY MESSAGES OF MOTIVATION THEORY

The key practical messages delivered by motivation theory are summarized below.

Extrinsic and intrinsic rewards

Extrinsic rewards provided by employers in the form of pay will help to attract and retain employees and, for limited periods, may increase effort and minimize dissatisfaction. Intrinsic non-financial rewards related to responsibility, achievement and the work itself may have a longer-term and deeper impact on motivation. Reward systems should therefore include a mix of extrinsic and intrinsic rewards.

The significance of needs

People will be better motivated if their work satisfies their social and psychological needs as well as their economic needs. Needs theory underpins the concept of total reward which recognizes the importance of the non-financial rewards as motivators. For example, recognition as a non-financial motivator is important because it addresses one of the most significant needs. A total reward policy makes use both of intrinsic and extrinsic rewards and of financial and non-financial rewards in a reward framework, as set out in Table 7.1.

Table 7.1 The reward framework

	Financial rewards	*Non-financial rewards*
Intrinsic rewards		Job design and role development (responsibility, autonomy, meaningful work, the scope to use and develop skills)
		Opportunities to achieve and develop
		Quality of working life
		Work/life balance
Extrinsic rewards	Pay and benefits	Recognition
		Praise
		Feedback

Performance management processes as described in Chapter 21 provide a basis for redesigning jobs or roles and for agreeing and implementing development programmes.

The importance of expectations

The degree to which people are motivated will depend not only upon the perceived value of the outcome of their actions – the goal or reward – but also on their perceptions of the likelihood of obtaining a worthwhile reward, that is, their expectations. They will be highly motivated if they can control the means of attaining their goals. This indicates that contingent pay schemes – that is, those where pay is related to performance, competence, contribution or skill – are effective as motivators only if (1) people know what they are going to get in return for certain efforts or achievements (this is sometimes called 'a line of sight'), (2) they feel that what they may get is worth having and (3) they expect to get it.

The influence of goals

Individuals are motivated by having specific goals to work for, and they perform better when they are aiming at difficult goals which they have accepted, and when they receive feedback on performance. This emphasizes the importance of performance management processes as motivators when they are based on *agreed* goals (note the emphasis) which are demanding but attainable and feedback on attainments in relation to those goals.

SUMMARY OF MOTIVATION THEORY AND ITS PRACTICAL APPLICATIONS

Table 7.2 Summary of motivation theories and their practical implications

Theory	Theorist	Summary of theory	Practical implications
Instrumentality	Taylor	People will be motivated to work if rewards and penalties are tied directly to their performance.	Conceptual basis of incentive and pay for performance schemes.
Needs	Maslow	Unsatisfied needs create tension and disequilibrium. To restore the balance a goal is identified which will satisfy the need, and a behaviour pathway is selected which will lead to the achievement of the goal. Only unsatisfied needs motivate.	Identifies a number of key needs for consideration in developing total reward policies.
Two-factor	Herzberg	The factors giving rise to job satisfaction (and motivation) are distinct from the factors that lead to job dissatisfaction. Any feeling of satisfaction resulting from pay increases is likely to be short-lived compared with the long-lasting satisfaction from the work itself. Makes a distinction between intrinsic motivation arising from the work itself and extrinsic motivation provided by the employer, eg pay.	A useful distinction is made between intrinsic and extrinsic motivation which influences total reward decisions. The limited motivational effects of pay increases are worth remembering when considering the part contingent pay can play in motivating people.
Expectancy	Vroom	Motivation is likely only when (1) a clearly perceived and usable relationship exists between performance and outcome and (2) the outcome is seen as a means of satisfying needs.	Provides the foundation for good practice in the design and management of contingent pay. The basis for the concept of the 'line of sight' which emphasizes the importance of establishing a clear link between the reward and what has to be done to achieve it.

(Continued)

Table 7.2 *Continued*

Theory	Theorist	Summary of theory	Practical implications
Goal	Latham and Locke	Motivation and performance are higher when individuals are set specific goals, when the goals are difficult but accepted, and when there is feedback on performance.	Provides a theoretical underpinning for performance management processes to ensure that they contribute to motivation through goal setting and feedback.
Equity	Adams	People will be better motivated if they are treated equitably and de-motivated if they are treated inequitably.	Emphasizes the need to develop an equitable reward system involving the use of job evaluation.

REFERENCES

1 Maslow, A (1954) *Motivation and Personality*, Harper & Row, New York
2 Herzberg, F, Mausner, B and Snyderman, B (1957) *The Motivation to Work*, Wiley, New York
3 Taylor, F W (1911) *Principles of Scientific Management*, Harper, New York
4 Guest, D (1992) Motivation after Herzberg, unpublished paper delivered at the Compensation Forum, London
5 Vroom, V (1964) *Work and Motivation*, Wiley, New York
6 Porter, L and Lawler, E E (1968) *Management Attitudes and Behaviour*, Irwin-Dorsey, Homewood, IL
7 Latham, G and Locke, E A (1979) Goal setting – a motivational technique that works, *Organizational Dynamics*, Autumn, pp 68–80
8 Adams, J (1965) Injustice in social exchange, in *Advances in Experimental Psychology*, ed L Berkowitz, Academic Press, New York
9 Jaques, E (1961) *Equitable Payment*, Heinemann, London.
10 Wallace, M J and Szilagyi, A D (1982) *Managing Behaviour in Organizations*, Scott, Glenview, IL
11 Kohn, A (1993) Why incentive plans cannot work, *Harvard Business Review*, September–October, pp 54–63
12 Pfeffer, J (1998) Six dangerous myths about pay, *Harvard Business Review*, May–June.
13 Gupta, N and Shaw, J D (1998) Financial incentives *are* effective!, *Compensation & Benefits Review*, March/April, pp 26, 28–32
14 Lawler E E (1990) *Strategic Pay*, Jossey-Bass, San Francisco
15 Boxall, P and Purcell, J (2003) *Strategy and Human Resource Management*, Palgrave Macmillan, Basingstoke

8

The psychological contract

The employment relationship contains a combination of beliefs held by individuals and their employers about what they expect of one another. This is the psychological contract, and it is necessary to understand what the psychological contract is and its significance when formulating and implementing reward policy as a key aspect of relationships with employees.

THE PSYCHOLOGICAL CONTRACT DEFINED

A psychological contract is a system of beliefs that encompasses the actions employees believe are expected of them and what response they expect in return from their employer. It has been defined by Stiles *et al* (1) as: 'The set of reciprocal expectations between an individual employee and the organization.' As described by Guest *et al* (2): 'It is concerned with assumptions, expectations, promises and mutual obligations.' It creates attitudes and emotions which form and govern behaviour. A psychological contract is implicit. It is also dynamic – it develops over time as experience accumulates, employment conditions change and employees re-evaluate their expectations.

The psychological contract may provide some indication of the answers to the two fundamental employment relationship questions that individuals pose: 'What can I reasonably expect from the organization?' and 'What should I reasonably be expected to contribute in return?' But it is difficult, often impossible, to ensure that the psychological contract and therefore the employment relationship will be fully understood by either party.

Employees may expect to be treated fairly as human beings, to be provided with work that uses their abilities, to be rewarded equitably in accordance with their contribution, to be able to display competence, to have opportunities for further growth, to know what is expected of them and to be given feedback (preferably positive) on how they are doing. Employers may expect employees to do their best on behalf of the organization – 'to put themselves out for the company', to be fully committed to its values, to be compliant and loyal, and to enhance the image of the organization with its customers and suppliers. Sometimes these assumptions are justified – often they are not. Mutual misunderstandings can cause friction and stress and lead to recriminations and poor performance, or to a termination of the employment relationship.

To summarize in the words of Guest and Conway (3), the psychological contract lacks many of the characteristics of the formal contract: 'It is not generally written down, it is somewhat blurred at the edges, and it cannot be enforced in a court or tribunal.' They believe that:

> The psychological contract is best seen as a metaphor; a word or phrase borrowed from another context which helps us make sense of our experience. The psychological contract is a way of interpreting the state of the employment relationship and helping to plot significant changes.

THE SIGNIFICANCE OF THE PSYCHOLOGICAL CONTRACT

As suggested by Spindler (4): 'A psychological contract creates emotions and attitudes which form and control behaviour.' The significance of the psychological contract was further explained by Sims (5) as follows:

> A balanced psychological contract is necessary for a continuing, harmonious relationship between the employee and the organization. However, the violation of the psychological contract can signal to the participants that the parties no longer shared (or never shared) a common set of values or goals.

The concept highlights the fact that employee/employer expectations take the form of unarticulated assumptions. Disappointments on the part of management as well as employees may therefore be inevitable. These disappointments can, however, be alleviated if managements appreciate that one of their key roles is to manage expectations, which means clarifying what they believe employees should achieve, the competencies they should possess and the values they should uphold. And this is a matter not just of articulating and stipulating these requirements but of discussing and agreeing them with people.

Guest *et al* (2) comment that:

> While employees may want what they have always wanted – security, a career, fair rewards, interesting work and so on – employers no longer feel able or obliged to provide these. Instead, they have been demanding more of their employees in terms of greater input and tolerance of uncertainty and change, while providing less in return, in particular less security and more limited career prospects.

DEVELOPING AND MAINTAINING A POSITIVE PSYCHOLOGICAL CONTRACT

As Guest *et al* (2) remark: 'A positive psychological contract is worth taking seriously because it is strongly linked to higher commitment to the organization, higher employee satisfaction and better employment relations. Again this reinforces the benefits of pursuing a set of progressive HRM practices.' They also emphasize the importance of a high-involvement climate and suggest in particular that HRM practices such as the provision of opportunities for learning, training and development, focus on job security, promotion and careers, minimizing status differentials, fair reward systems and comprehensive communication and involvement processes will all contribute to a positive psychological contract.

The part played by reward management in developing a positive psychological contract

Reward and, especially, performance management processes can help to clarify the psychological contract and make it more positive by:

- providing a basis for the joint agreement and definition of roles;
- communicating expectations in the form of targets, standards of performance, behavioural requirements (competencies) and upholding core values;
- obtaining agreement on the contribution both parties (the manager and the individual) have to make to getting the results expected;
- defining the level of support to be exercised by managers;
- providing financial rewards through schemes that deliver messages about what the organization believes to be important;
- providing non-financial rewards that reinforce the messages about expectations;
- giving employees opportunities at performance review discussions to clarify points about their work.

REFERENCES

1   Stiles, P, Gratton, L, Truss, C, Hope-Hailey, V and McGovern, P (1997) Performance management and the psychological contract, *Human Resource Management Journal*, **7** (1), pp 57–66

2   Guest, D E, Conway, N, Briner, R and Dickman, M (1996) *The State of the Psychological Contract in Employment*, IPD, London

3   Guest, D E and Conway, N (1998) *Fairness at Work and the Psychological Contract*, IPD, London

4   Spindler, G S (1994) Psychological contracts in the workplace: a lawyer's view, *Human Resource Management*, **33** (3), pp 325–33

5   Sims, R R (1994) Human resource management's role in clarifying the new psychological contract, *Human Resource Management*, **33** (3), Fall, pp 373–82

Part III

Establishing job values and relativities

9

Job evaluation schemes

Job evaluation is of fundamental importance in reward management. It provides the basis for achieving equitable pay and is essential as a means of dealing with equal pay for work of equal value issues. In the 1980s and 1990s job evaluation fell into disrepute because it was alleged to be bureaucratic, time consuming and irrelevant in a market economy where market rates dictate internal rates of pay and relativities. However, as the e-reward survey of job evaluation carried out in 2002 (1) showed, job evaluation is still practised widely and, indeed, its use is extending, not least because of the pressures to achieve equal pay.

In this chapter:

- job evaluation is defined;
- the different types of job evaluation schemes are described;
- information on the incidence of job evaluation is provided;
- the use of computers in job evaluation is discussed;
- the arguments for and against job evaluation are summarized and the limitations of job evaluation are discussed;
- consideration is given to criteria for choice;
- what is happening to job evaluation is examined;
- conclusions are reached about using job evaluation effectively.

JOB EVALUATION DEFINED

Job evaluation is a systematic process for defining the relative worth or size of jobs within an organization in order to establish internal relativities. It provides the basis for designing an equitable grade and pay structure, grading jobs in the structure and managing job and pay relativities.

Purpose

The purpose of job evaluation is to:

- establish the relative value or size of jobs, ie internal relativities based on fair, sound and consistent judgements;
- produce the information required to design and maintain equitable and defensible grade and pay structures;
- provide as objective as possible a basis for grading jobs within a grade structure, thus enabling consistent decisions to be made about job grading;
- enable sound market comparisons with jobs or roles of equivalent complexity and size;
- be transparent – the basis upon which grades are defined and jobs graded should be clear;
- ensure that the organization meets equal pay for work of equal value obligations.

The last aim is important. In its *Good Practice Guide – Job Evaluation Schemes Free of Sex Bias* the Equal Opportunities Commission (2) states that: 'Non-discriminatory job evaluation should lead to a payment system which is transparent and within which work of equal value receives equal pay regardless of sex.'

Methodology

Job evaluation can be analytical or non-analytical. Jobs can also be valued by reference to their market rates – 'market pricing'. These approaches are described below.

ANALYTICAL JOB EVALUATION

Defined

Analytical job evaluation is the process of making decisions about the value or size of jobs which are based on an analysis of the level at which various defined factors or elements are present in a job in order to establish relative job value. The set of factors used in a scheme is called the *factor plan* which defines each of the factors used (which should be present in all the jobs to be evaluated) and the levels within each factor. Analytical job evaluation is the most common approach to job evaluation (it was used by 89 per cent of the organizations with job evaluation responding to the e-research 2002 survey). The two main types of analytical job evaluation schemes are point-factor schemes and analytical factor comparison schemes, as described later.

Main features

The main features of analytical job evaluation, as explained below, are that it is systematic, judgemental, concerned with the job, not the person, and deals only with internal relativities.

Systematic

Analytical job evaluation is systematic and helps to reduce subjectivity by providing for the relative value or 'size' of jobs to be determined on the basis of factual evidence on the characteristics of the jobs which has been analysed within a structured framework of criteria or factors.

Judgemental

Human judgement has to be exercised at a number of points in the job evaluation process. Although job evaluations are based on factual evidence, this has to be interpreted. The information provided about jobs through job analysis can sometimes fail to provide a clear indication of the levels at which demands are present in a job. The definitions in the factor plan may not precisely indicate the level of demand that should be recorded. Judgement is required in making decisions on the level and therefore, in a point-factor or factor comparison scheme, the score. The aim is to maximize objectivity but it is difficult to eliminate a degree of subjectivity. A fundamental aim of any process of job evaluation is to provide frameworks or approaches that ensure, as far as possible, that consistent judgements are made based on objectively assessed information. To refer to an evaluation as 'judgemental' does not necessarily mean that it is inaccurate or unsound. Correct judgements are achieved when they are made within a defined framework and are based on clear evidence and sound reasoning. This is what a job evaluation scheme can do if the scheme is properly designed and properly applied.

Concerned with the job, not the person

This is the iron law of job evaluation. It means that when evaluating a job the only concern is the content of that job in terms of the demands made on the job holder. The performance of the individual in the job must not be taken into account. But it should be noted that while *performance* is excluded, in today's more flexible organizations the tendency is for some people, especially knowledge workers, to have flexible roles. Individuals may have the scope to enlarge or enrich their roles and this needs to be taken into account when evaluating what they do. Roles cannot necessarily be separated from the people who carry them out. It is people who create value, not jobs.

Concerned with internal relativities

When used within an organization, job evaluation in the true sense as defined above (that is, not market pricing as described later – an approach that values jobs on the basis of external relativities – market rates) can only assess the relative size of jobs in that organization. It is not concerned with external relativities, that is, the relationship between the rates of pay of jobs in the organization and the rates of pay of comparable jobs elsewhere (market rates).

Point-factor evaluation

Point-factor schemes are the most commonly used type of analytical method of job evaluation. The basic methodology is to break down jobs into factors or key elements representing the demands made by the job on job holders, the competences required and, in some cases, the impact the job makes. It is assumed that each of the factors will contribute to job size (that is, the value of the job) and is an aspect of all the jobs to be evaluated but to different degrees. Using numerical scales, points are allocated to a job under each factor heading according to the extent to which it is present in the job. The separate factor scores are then added together to give a total score which represents job size. Approaches to developing and operating a point-factor scheme are described in the next chapter.

Analytical factor comparison

Like point-factor job evaluation, analytical factor comparison (analytical job matching) is based on the analysis of a number of defined factors. Grade profiles are produced which define the characteristics of jobs in each grade in a grade structure in terms of factors. Role profiles are produced for the jobs to be evaluated, set out on the basis of analysis under the same factor headings as the grade profiles. Role profiles are 'matched' with the range of grade profiles to establish the best fit and thus grade the job. Examples of grade and role profiles are given in Appendix 3.

Alternatively, role profiles for jobs to be evaluated can be matched analytically with generic role profiles for jobs which have already been graded.

Analytical factor comparison by matching may be used to grade jobs following the initial evaluation of a sufficiently large and representative sample of 'benchmark' jobs, that is, jobs which can be used as a basis for comparison with other jobs. This can happen, especially in large organizations, when it is believed that it is not necessary to go through the whole process of point-factor evaluation for every job , especially where 'generic' roles are concerned, that is, roles which are performed by a number of job holders which are essentially similar, although there may be minor differences. When this follows a large job evaluation exercise as in the NHS Agenda for Change programme, the factors used in the grade and role profiles will be the same as those used in the point-factor job evaluation scheme. The example in Appendix 3 of a local authority level profile uses the factors in their job evaluation scheme as the headings for the profile. The same approach is used by the NHS in their Knowledge and Skills Frameworks.

Proprietary brands

There are a number of job evaluation schemes offered by management consultants. By far the most popular is the Hay Guide Chart Profile Method which is a factor comparison scheme. It uses three broad factors (know-how, problem solving and accountability), each of which is further divided into sub-factors, although these cannot be scored individually. Broad definitions of each level have been produced for each sub-factor to guide evaluators and ensure consistency of application.

NON-ANALYTICAL JOB EVALUATION

Non-analytical job evaluation compares whole jobs to place them in a grade or a rank order – they are not analysed by reference to their elements or factors. Non-analytical schemes do not meet the requirements of equal value law. The main non-analytical schemes are described below.

Job classification

This is the most common non-analytical approach. Roles as defined in job descriptions are slotted into grades in a hierarchy by comparing the whole job with a grade definition and selecting the grade that provides the best fit. It is based on an initial definition of the number and characteristics of the grades into which jobs will be placed. The grade definitions may therefore refer to such job characteristics as skill, decision making and responsibility. Job descriptions which include information on the presence of those characteristics may be used, but the characteristics are not assessed separately when comparing the description with the grade definition.

Job reference	a	b	c	d	e	f	Total score	Ranking
A	–	0	1	0	1	0	2	5=
B	2	–	2	2	2	0	8	2
C	1	0	–	1	1	0	3	4
D	2	0	1	–	2	0	5	3
E	1	0	1	0	–	0	2	5=
F	2	2	2	2	2	–	10	1

Figure 9.1 A paired comparison

Job ranking

Whole job ranking is the most primitive form of job evaluation. The process involves comparing whole jobs with one another and arranging them in order of their perceived size or value to the organization. In a sense, all evaluation schemes are ranking exercises because they place jobs in a hierarchy. The difference between simple ranking and analytical methods such as point-factor rating is that job ranking does not attempt to quantify judgements. Instead, whole jobs are compared – they are not broken down into factors or elements although, explicitly or implicitly, the comparison may be based on some generalized concept such as the level of responsibility.

Paired comparison ranking

Paired comparison ranking is a statistical technique which is used to provide a more sophisticated method of whole-job ranking. It is based on the assumption that it is always easier to compare one job with another than to consider a number of jobs and attempt to build up a rank order by multiple comparisons.

The technique requires the comparison of each job as a whole separately with every other job. If a job is considered to be of a higher value than the one with which it is being compared it receives two points; if it is thought to be equally important, it receives one point; if it is regarded as less important, no points are awarded. The scores are added for each job and a rank order is obtained.

A simplified version of a paired comparison ranking form is shown in Figure 9.1.

The advantage of paired comparison ranking over normal ranking is that it is easier to compare one job with another rather than having to make multi-comparisons. But it cannot overcome the fundamental objections to any form of whole-job ranking – that no defined standards for judging relative worth are provided and it is not an acceptable method of assessing equal value. There is also a limit to the number of jobs that can be compared using this method – to evaluate 50 jobs requires 1,225 comparisons.

Paired comparisons can also be used analytically to compare jobs on a factor-by-factor basis.

Internal benchmarking

Internal benchmarking is what people often do intuitively when they are deciding on the value of jobs, although it has never been dignified in the job evaluation texts as a formal method of job evaluation. It simply means comparing the job under review with any internal job which is believed to be properly graded and paid and placing the job under consideration into the same grade as that job. The comparison is often made on a whole-job basis without analysing the jobs factor by factor.

Market pricing

Market pricing is the process of assessing rates of pay by reference to the market rates for comparable jobs and is essentially external benchmarking. Strictly speaking, market pricing is not a process of job evaluation in the sense that those described above are – these only deal with internal relativities and are not directly concerned with market values, although in conjunction with a formal job evaluation scheme, establishing market rates is a necessary part of a programme for developing a pay structure.

However, the term market pricing in its extreme form is used to denote a process of directly pricing jobs on the basis of external relativities with no regard to internal relativities. This approach was widely publicized in the USA in the mid-1990s and sat alongside attempts at developing broad-banded pay structures (that is, structures as described in Chapter 15 with a limited number of grades or bands), and disillusionment with what was regarded as bureaucratic job evaluation. It is an approach that often has appeal at board level because of the focus on competitiveness in relation to the marketplace for talent.

The acceptability of market pricing is heavily dependent on the quality and detail of market matching as well as the availability of robust market data. It can therefore vary from analysis of data by job titles to detailed matched analysis collected through bespoke surveys focused on real market equivalence (see Chapter 13). Market pricing can produce an indication of internal relativities even if these are market driven. But it can lead to pay discrimination against women where the market has traditionally been discriminatory. It does not satisfy UK equal pay legislation.

Market pricing can be done formally by the analysis of published pay surveys, participating in 'pay clubs', conducting special surveys, obtaining the advice of recruitment consultants and agencies and, more doubtfully, by studying advertisements. In its crudest form, market pricing simply means fixing the rate for a job at the level necessary to recruit or retain someone. To avoid a successful equal pay claim, any difference in pay between men and women carrying out work of equal value based on market rate considerations has to be 'objectively justified'.

THE INCIDENCE OF JOB EVALUATION

Despite considerable criticism in the 1990s, job evaluation has not diminished in use in the UK or in many other countries. A survey of job evaluation practice in the UK conducted by e-research in late 2002 (1) found that 44 per cent of the 236 organizations contributing to the research had a formal job evaluation scheme, and 45 per cent of those who did not have such a scheme intended to introduce one. Analytical schemes were used by 89 per cent of the respondents. Of those, 70 per cent used point-factor rating. The most popular non-analytical approach was job classification. Schemes developed in-house ('home grown' schemes) were used by 37 per cent of the respondents.

A 'proprietary brand', that is, one provided by consultants, was used by 37 per cent of respondents and 26 per cent used a hybrid or tailored version of a proprietary brand. The Hay Guide Chart Profile Method dominated the market (83 per cent of the proprietary brand schemes). Organizations opting for a proprietary brand did so because of its credibility and, especially with Hay, its link to a market rate database. Organizations opting for a home-grown approach did so because they believed this would ensure that it could be shaped to meet the strategic needs of the organization and fit its technology, structure, work processes and business objectives. A minority of respondents mentioned the scope for aligning the scheme with their competency framework.

COMPUTER-ASSISTED JOB EVALUATION

Computers can be used to help directly with the job evaluation process.

Types of schemes

The two types of computer-assisted systems are:

1. *Job analysis-based schemes* such as that offered by Link Consultants in which the job analysis data is either entered direct into the computer or transferred to it from a paper questionnaire. The computer software applies predetermined rules based on an algorithm which reflects the organization's evaluation standards to convert the data into scores for each factor and produce a total score. The algorithm replicates panel judgements both on job factor levels and overall job score.

2. *Interactive schemes* using software such as that supplied by Pilat UK (Gauge) in which the job holder and his or her manager sit in front of a PC and are presented with a series of logically interrelated questions forming a question tree; the answers to these questions lead to a score for each of the built-in factors in turn and a total score.

Advantages of computer-assisted job evaluation

Computer-assisted job evaluation systems can:

- provide for greater consistency – the same input information will always give the same output result because the judgemental framework on which the scheme is based (the algorithm) can be applied consistently to the input data offering extensive database capabilities for sorting, analysing and reporting on the input information and system outputs;
- speed up the job evaluation process once the initial design is complete.

Disadvantages of computer-assisted job evaluation

Computer-assisted job evaluation systems can:

- lack transparency – the evaluation is made in a 'black box' and it can be difficult to trace the connection between the analysis and the evaluation and therefore to justify the score; this is not such a problem with interactive schemes in which job holders participate in evaluations and the link between the answer to a question and the score can be traced in the 'question trees';
- appear to bypass the evaluation process through joint management/employee panels which is typical in conventional schemes; however, this problem can be reduced if panels are used to validate the computer-generated scores.

CRITERIA FOR CHOICE

The main criteria for selecting a job evaluation scheme are that it should be:

- *Analytical* – it should be based on the analysis and evaluation of the degree to which various defined elements or factors are present in a job.
- *Thorough in analysis and capable of impartial application* – the scheme should have been carefully constructed to ensure that its analytical framework is sound and appropriate in terms of all the jobs it has to cater for. It should also have been tested and trialled to check that it can be applied impartially to those jobs.

- *Appropriate* – it should cater for the particular demands made on all the jobs to be covered by the scheme.
- *Comprehensive* – the scheme should be applicable to all the jobs in the organization covering all categories of staff, and the factors should be common to all those jobs. There should therefore be a single scheme which can be used to assess relativities across different occupations or job families and to enable benchmarking to take place as required.
- *Transparent* – the processes used in the scheme, from the initial role analysis through to the grading decision, should be clear to all concerned. If computers are used, information should not be perceived as being processed in a 'black box'.
- *Non-discriminatory* – the scheme must meet equal pay for work of equal value requirements.

A summary of the various approaches to job evaluation and their advantages and disadvantages is given in Table 9.1.

Making the choice

The choice has to be made by reference to the criteria referred to earlier and to the advantages and disadvantages of the alternative approaches listed above. But the overwhelming preference for analytical schemes shown by the e-research survey suggests that the choice is fairly obvious. The advantages of using a recognized analytical approach which satisfies equal value requirements appear to be overwhelming. Point-factor schemes were used by 70 per cent of those respondents and others used analytical matching, often in conjunction with the points scheme.

There is much to be said for adopting point-factor methodology as the main scheme but using analytical factor comparison in a supporting role to deal with large numbers of generic roles not covered in the original benchmarking exercise. Matching through analytical factor comparison can be used to allocate generic roles to grades as part of the normal job evaluation operating procedure to avoid having to resort to job evaluation in every case. The tendency in many organizations is to assign to job evaluation a supporting role of this nature rather than allowing it to dominate all grading decisions and thus involve the expenditure of much time and energy. Ways of using point-factor evaluation and analytical factor comparison in conjunction with one another and more details of matching procedures are described in the next chapter.

THE CASE FOR AND AGAINST JOB EVALUATION

The case for

The case for properly devised and applied job evaluation, especially analytical job evaluation, is that:

Table 9.1 Comparison of approaches to job evaluation

Scheme	Characteristics	Advantages	Disadvantages
Point-factor rating	An analytical approach in which separate factors are scored and added together to produce a total score for the job which can be used for comparison and grading purposes.	As long as they are based on proper job analysis, point-factor schemes provide evaluators with defined yardsticks which help to increase the objectivity and consistency of judgements and reduce the over-simplified judgement made in non-analytical job evaluation. They provide a defence against equal value claims as long as they are not in themselves discriminatory.	Can be complex and give a spurious impression of scientific accuracy – judgement is still needed in scoring jobs. Not easy to amend the scheme as circumstances, priorities or values change.
Analytical factor comparison	Grade profiles are produced which define the characteristics of jobs in each grade in a grade structure in terms of a selection of defined factors. Role profiles are produced for the jobs to be evaluated set out on the basis of analysis under the same factor headings as the grade profiles. Role profiles are 'matched' with the range of grade profiles to establish the best fit and thus grade the job.	If the matching process is truly analytical and carried out with great care, this approach saves time by enabling the evaluation of a large number of jobs, especially generic ones, to be conducted quickly and in a way that should satisfy equal value requirements.	The matching process could be more superficial and therefore suspect than evaluation through a point-factor scheme. In the latter approach there are factor-level definitions to guide judgements and the resulting scores provide a basis for ranking and grade design, which is not the case with analytical matching. Although matching on this basis may be claimed to be analytical, it might be difficult to prove this in an equal value case.
Job classification	Non-analytical – grades are defined in a structure in terms of	Simple to operate; standards of judgement when making	Can be difficult to fit complex jobs into a grade without using

(Continued)

Table 9.1 *Continued*

Scheme	Characteristics	Advantages	Disadvantages
	the level of responsibilities involved in a hierarchy. Jobs are allocated to grades by matching the job description with the grade description (jobslotting).	comparisons are provided in the shape of the grade definitions.	over-elaborate grade definitions; the definitions tend to be so generalized that they are not much help in evaluating border-line cases or making comparisons between individual jobs; does not provide a defence in an equal value case.
Ranking	Non-analytical – whole job comparisons are made to place them in rank order.	Easy to apply and understand.	No defined standards of judgement; differences between jobs not measured; does not provide a defence in an equal value case.
Internal bench-marking	Jobs or roles are compared with benchmark jobs that have been allocated to grades on the basis of ranking or job classification and placed in whatever grade provides the closest match of jobs. The job descriptions may be analytical in the sense that they cover a number of standard and defined elements.	Simple to operate; facilitates direct comparisons, especially when the jobs have been analysed in terms of a set of common criteria.	Relies on a considerable amount of judgement and may simply perpetuate existing relativities; dependent on accurate job/role analysis; may not provide a defence in an equal value case.
Market pricing	Rates of pay are aligned to market rates – internal relativities are therefore determined by relativities in the marketplace. Not strictly a job evaluation scheme.	In line with the belief that 'a job is worth what the market says it is worth'. Ensures that pay is competitive.	Relies on accurate market rate information which is not always available; relativities in the market may not properly reflect internal relativities; pay discrimination may be perpetuated.

- it can make the criteria against which jobs are valued explicit and provide a basis for structuring the judgement process;
- an equitable and defensible pay structure cannot be achieved unless a structured and systematic process is used to assess job values and relativities;
- a logical framework is required within which consistent decisions can be made on job grades and rates of pay;
- the factor plan and the process of job evaluation can be aligned to the organization's value system and competence framework and therefore reinforce them as part of an integrated approach to people management;
- analytical schemes provide the best basis for achieving equal pay for work of equal value and are the only acceptable defence in an equal pay case;
- a formal process of job evaluation is more likely to be accepted as fair and equitable than informal or ad hoc approaches – and the degree of acceptability will be considerably enhanced if the whole process is transparent.

The case against

The case against job evaluation has been presented vociferously. Critics emphasize that it can be bureaucratic, inflexible, time consuming and inappropriate in today's organizations. Opponents such as Niels Nielsen (3) take exception to the fact that job evaluation is not concerned with external relativities, which, they claim, are what really matter. Schemes can decay over time through use or misuse. People learn how to manipulate them to achieve a higher grade and this leads to the phenomenon known as grade drift – upgradings which are not justified by a sufficiently significant increase in responsibility. Job evaluators can fall into the trap of making *a priori* judgements. They may judge the validity of a job evaluation exercise according to the extent to which it corresponds with their preconceptions about relative worth. The so-called 'felt fair' test is used to assess the acceptability of job evaluations, but a rank order is felt to be fair if it reproduces their notion of what it ought to be.

These criticisms mainly focus on the way in which job evaluation is operated rather than the concept of job evaluation itself. Like any other management technique, job evaluation schemes can be misconceived and misused. And the grade and pay structures developed through job evaluation seldom last for more than a few years and need to be replaced or adjusted to remedy decay or reflect new ways of working.

Those who criticize job evaluation because it is only concerned with internal relativities fail to understand that job evaluation exists to grade jobs, not to price them. Of course, when developing the pay structures superimposed on grade structures it is necessary to take account of external relativities and this will mean reconciling the different messages provided by job evaluation and market rate surveys. If the latter indicate that attracting and retaining good-quality staff is only feasible if rates of pay higher than those indicated by the grading of the job are offered, then it may be necessary to pay market supplements, but to avoid claims that equal pay is not being provided, these must be objectively justified on the basis of evidence on competitive rates.

Limitations of job evaluation

Whatever arguments are used for and against job evaluation, its limitations must be recognized. These are:

- It can never be totally objective; it is probably more art than science.
- It can provide guidance when developing grade structures on where grades might be placed (see Chapter 16) but this is never definitive – there is always scope for judgement.
- It makes no allowance for the influence of external relativities.
- As the Equal Opportunities Commission (EOC) states in its *Good Practice Guide – Job Evaluation Schemes Free of Sex Bias* (2): '… it is recognized that to a certain extent any assessment of a job's total demands relative to another will always be subjective'.

WHAT IS HAPPENING TO JOB EVALUATION?

Traditional approaches to job evaluation have had to change for the following reasons:

- need for greater flexibility and speed;
- impatience with panels and committees;
- shift from 'job' to 'role' – different elements of work being valued, including competences;
- more emphasis on market forces;
- 'black box' reputation of some computerized schemes;
- less need for precision in broader grade structures;
- appreciation of the fact that in a very large job evaluation exercise it is not possible to evaluate every job in detail.

Organizations have responded by:

- using more tailor-made schemes to reflect key values rather than 'one size fits all';
- developing fully interactive and paperless employee-based PC schemes such as Gauge;
- giving job evaluation a supporting role rather than a primary focus;
- moving away from the wholesale use of point-factor schemes to a complementary and more flexible analytical matching approach.

CONCLUSIONS

It could be claimed that every time a decision is made on what a job should be paid it requires a form of job evaluation. Job evaluation is therefore unavoidable, but it should not be an intuitive, subjective and potentially biased process. The issue is how best to carry it out analytically, fairly, systematically, consistently, transparently and, so far as possible, objectively, without being bureaucratic, inflexible or resource intensive. There are four ways of dealing with this issue:

1. Use a tested and relevant analytical job evaluation scheme to inform and support the processes of designing grade structures, grading jobs, managing relativities and ensuring that work of equal value is paid equally. The approach to designing a point-factor scheme is described in Chapter 10.
2. Ensure that job evaluation is introduced and managed properly along the lines suggested in Chapter 10.
3. Consider using computers to speed up processing and decision making while at the same time generating more consistent evaluations and reducing bureaucracy.
4. Recognize that thorough training and continuing guidance for evaluators is essential, as is communication about the scheme, its operation and objectives to all concerned.
5. Review the operation of the scheme regularly to ensure that it is not decaying and continues to be appropriate and trusted.

Examples of approaches to the use of job evaluation in AEGON and Tesco are given in Chapter 30.

REFERENCES

1   e-research (2003) *Job Evaluation Survey*, e-reward.co.uk Ltd, Stockport, Cheshire
2   Equal Opportunities Commission (2003) *Good Practice Guide – Job Evaluation Schemes Free of Sex Bias*, EOC, Manchester
3   Nielsen, N H (2002) Job content evaluation techniques based on Marxian economics, *WorldatWork Journal*, **11** (2), pp 52–62

10

Developing and operating a point-factor job evaluation scheme

This chapter is solely concerned with describing methods of developing point-factor job evaluation schemes and explaining how they should be managed. The focus is on point-factor schemes simply because they are by far the most common approach and rightly so, because they are analytical and provide the best basis for developing an equitable grade and pay structure as long as steps are taken to ensure that the scheme is not discriminatory. However, reference will be made to the use of analytical factor comparison (matching) to supplement point-factor evaluation.

The chapter starts with a definition of the design and process criteria and then describes the basic point-factor job evaluation methodology. The steps required to design and implement job evaluation are then described and the chapter ends with a discussion of matching methodology.

DESIGN AND PROCESS CRITERIA

It is necessary to distinguish between the design of a scheme and the process of operating it. Equal pay considerations have to be taken into account in both design and process.

Design principles

The design principles are that:

- the scheme should be based on a thorough analysis of the jobs to be covered and the types of demands made on those jobs to determine what factors are appropriate;
- the scheme should facilitate impartial judgements of relative job size;
- the factors used in the scheme should cover the whole range of jobs to be evaluated at all levels without favouring any particular type of job or occupation and without discriminating on the grounds of gender, race disability or for any other reason – the scheme should fairly measure features of female-dominated jobs as well as male-dominated jobs;
- through the use of common factors and methods of analysis and evaluation, the scheme should enable benchmarking to take place of the relativities between jobs in different functions or job families;
- the factors should be clearly defined and differentiated – there should be no double-counting;
- the levels should be defined and graduated carefully;
- gender bias must be avoided in the choice of factors, the wording of factor and level definitions and the factor weightings – checks should be carried out to identify any bias (the guidelines set out in Chapter 12 should also be taken into account).

Process principles

The process principles are that:

- the scheme should be transparent, everyone concerned should know how it works – the basis upon which the evaluations are produced;
- appropriate proportions of women, those from ethnic minorities and people with disabilities should be involved in the process of developing and applying job evaluation;
- the quality of role analysis should be monitored to ensure that analyses produce accurate and relevant information which will inform the job evaluation process and will not be biased;
- consistency checks should be built into operating procedures;
- the outcomes of evaluations should be examined to ensure that gender or any other form of bias has not occurred;
- particular care is necessary to ensure that the outcomes of job evaluation do not simply replicate the existing hierarchy – it is to be expected that a job evaluation exercise will challenge present relativities;

- all those involved in role analysis and job evaluation should be thoroughly trained in the operation of the scheme and in how to avoid bias;
- special care should be taken in developing a grade structure following a job evaluation exercise to ensure that grade boundaries are placed appropriately and that the allocation of jobs to grades is not in itself discriminatory;
- there should be scope for the review of evaluations and for appeals against gradings;
- the scheme should be monitored to ensure that it is being operated properly and that it is still fit for its purpose.

POINT-FACTOR JOB EVALUATION SCHEME METHODOLOGY

Point-factor job evaluation is based on a factor plan which defines the factors or characteristics used to assess the demands made on jobs, divides each factor into defined levels and attaches a scoring scale which may be weighted, that is, some factors which are regarded as more important than others can be allocated a higher maximum number of points.

During the design phase a design team develops and tests the factor plan to produce an agreed version. A decision is made on whether or not to computerize the 'paper' plan produced in the earlier design stages. If a paper plan is used for the full evaluation, the design team becomes a job evaluation panel. The roles of the design team or panel members and the facilitator are defined below. If the scheme is computerized a panel is used to check and validate the job evaluation scores generated by the computer. The panel may also carry out role matching using the analytical scheme.

The role of the design team or panel

The role of the design team needs to be defined by reference to the following guidelines:

1. No untrained person should be allowed to take part in, or to influence, an evaluation.
2. All evaluators should have the input information at least a week prior to the evaluation meeting (to provide the opportunity to clarify anything that is unclear and thus save time at the meeting itself).
3. No aspect of the job holder as a person should influence any aspect of the evaluation (specifically not gender or ethnic origin).
4. The evaluation is concerned with the normal content of the job as defined in a job description or role analysis. It should not be affected by the activities of any individuals that vary the standard job requirements.

5. The aim of the design team is to achieve consensus on evaluations. Voting is undesirable because it can be divisive and lead to superficial discussions.
6. A full record of the scoring decisions should be kept and, where the decision was a marginal one, the reasons why that level was determined noted (a rationale). This is particularly important if the design team found it difficult to reach consensus, as it may be relevant if a review of that evaluation is called for.
7. All evaluation scores should be treated as provisional (and not disclosed) until they have been reviewed by a review or audit design team and confirmed.

Design team members will benefit from initial training in job analysis and the principles and practice of job evaluation. It may be helpful to start with one or two dummy runs – using the scheme to evaluate two or three made-up jobs. It is essential that they should be familiar with what they must do to avoid gender or any other form of bias.

The role of the facilitator

Good facilitation is crucial and the overall responsibility of the facilitator is to ensure that the team or panel discusses the evaluation thoroughly and reaches consensus on the evaluation. Consensus may be difficult to attain but experience has shown that it can always be achieved, although this may take time. The particular tasks of the facilitator are set out below:

1. Lay down the ground rules for evaluation and agree the procedure to be used by the team or panel.
2. Ensure that each job is fully understood (through examination of job information and round-table discussion) before any evaluation is attempted. The facilitator should have the authority to suspend an evaluation if the available information appears to be incomplete or misleading.
3. Initiate the discussion on each factor if a factor-by-factor approach is used.
4. Guide design team members through the evaluation, probing where necessary to test whether views have been properly justified on the basis of the evidence, but not giving any indication of the facilitator's own views – it is the design team members who carry out the evaluation, not the facilitator.
5. Continually reinforce the principles that it is the job and not the performance of the person that is being evaluated and the need to avoid gender or other bias.
6. Remind design team or panel members that it is the job content as it is intended to be carried out that is evaluated, not the job as carried out by a particular job holder.
7. Actively encourage the participation of every design team or panel member.
8. Stimulate reasoned debate.

9. Ensure that people respect alternative views and, where appropriate, are prepared to change their initial stance when presented with a valid reason to do so.

10. Bear in mind that a lone voice may have a significant contribution to make; dissenters should therefore be given a reasonable chance to express their view, subject to them not being allowed to dominate the discussion. Most seasoned job evaluation panel members will be able to recall at least one '12 Angry Men' situation where a presumed consensus for the 'obvious' conclusion was overturned by one person's persistence.

11. Be alert to, and suppress, any factions or cliques developing in the design team – one approach might be to change the seating plan each session.

12. Ensure that the consensus reached is not a 'false consensus' (one for which there is no dissenting voice only because one or more dissenters are too afraid to speak out against more dominant members). It will be up to the facilitator to be particularly sensitive to this and deliberately to encourage the more reticent members to state their views.

13. Be scrupulously neutral at all times. To achieve this, facilitators normally do not carry out any evaluations themselves, but they can when necessary challenge (gently) design team or panel members to justify their views, press for discussion based on the evidence rather than opinion and bring to the attention of members any evidence or relevant facts that will help them to reach an agreed conclusion.

14. Ensure that the decisions of the design team or panel and the rationale for those decisions are recorded.

15. Avoid trying to force the issue if the design team is unable to reach a true consensus within a reasonable time. But the facilitator should have the authority to put the job to one side for further reflection or so that more information about the points at issue can be obtained, for example a more specific job description.

16. Avoid putting design teams or panels to the vote because this will be divisive. The fundamental aim is to achieve consensus to give the evaluation the validity arising because a united view on the job size was achieved. This will help if a request is made to review the evaluation.

THE DESIGN AND IMPLEMENTATION PROGRAMME

The design and implementation of a point-factor job evaluation exercise can be a demanding and time-consuming affair. In a large organization it can take two years or more to complete a project. Even in a small organization it can take several months. Many organizations seek outside help from management consultants or ACAS in conducting the programme. An example of a programme is given in Figure 10.1.

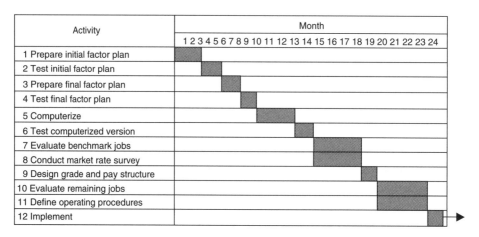

Figure 10.1 A typical job evaluation programme

Activities 1–6 form the initial design phase and activities 7–12 form the application of the design and implementation phases. Full descriptions of these phases follow.

THE SCHEME DESIGN PROGRAMME

Figure 10.2 shows the steps required to design a point-factor job evaluation scheme.

Step 1 Decide to develop scheme

The decision to develop a new point-factor job evaluation scheme follows an analysis of the existing arrangements, if any, for job evaluation, and a diagnosis of any problems.

Diagnostic review of existing scheme

The points that should be covered in the analysis and diagnosis if there is an existing scheme are:

1. Has the scheme decayed so that it is no longer appropriate for the new working arrangements and does not fit the values of the organization on rewarding staff?
2. Is the scheme taking up too much time and effort to administer?
3. Is the scheme being manipulated so that grade drift (ie staff wrongly upgraded) occurs?
4. Does the scheme provide a satisfactory basis for managing relativities?

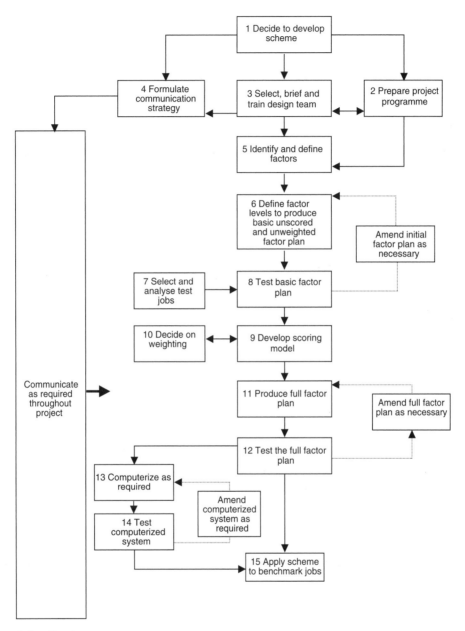

Figure 10.2 Design sequence

5. Would the scheme fail to provide a satisfactory response to an equal pay claim because it is discriminatory either in its design or in the way it is operated?
6. Do staff understand how the scheme works?
7. Do staff feel that the scheme is fair?
8. What is the business case for replacing the existing scheme?

9. What resources would be required (money and people) to develop and apply a tailor-made scheme or, alternatively, buy a proprietary brand?
10. What is the business case for developing a new tailor-made point-factor scheme rather than simply buying a proprietary brand?

Diagnostic review of arrangements for grading jobs if there is no scheme

The points that should be covered in the analysis and diagnosis if there is no existing scheme are:

1. How are jobs graded?
2. Is the process of grading fair and consistent?
3. Does it lead to equitable decisions on gradings?
4. Is the system understood and felt to be fair by staff?
5. Are we liable to expensive equal value claims in the absence of a scheme?
6. What is the business case for developing or purchasing an analytical point-factor scheme?

Programme planning

Assuming that a business case has been made and accepted for developing a new tailor-made scheme, the following programme planning activities are carried out:

1. Consider in broad terms what sort of scheme is required and, in particular, decide whether it should be computerized.
2. Develop an outline design and implementation programme for discussion with those involved in the project.
3. Assess the resource requirements (people, finance and time) for the programme and obtain agreement on a development budget.
4. Decide whether any outside help is needed and if the answer is yes, define what is required and brief and select the adviser.
5. Decide on arrangements for involving staff (it is important that members of staff and their trade union representatives, if any, participate fully in the project).
6. Decide how the project should be managed, eg overseen by a joint steering group with a design or project team carrying out the detailed development work.
7. Brief staff and trade unions and enlist their support.
8. Decide on the setting up of a steering group and design or project team.
9. Prepare an outline communications strategy so that staff are kept fully informed from the start to the finish of the programme of what is happening and how they will be affected.
10. Decide on the completion date of the project.

Step 2 Prepare detailed project programme

The detailed project programme could be set out in a bar chart as illustrated above in Figure 10.1. The programme should be discussed with, and agreed by, the steering group and the design team.

Step 3 Select, brief and train design team

The composition of the design team should have been determined broadly at step 1. Members are usually nominated by management and the staff or union(s) (if they exist). Some organizations have called for volunteers and in this case it is usually necessary to get the names approved by both sides. It is very desirable to have a representative number of women and men and the major ethnic groups employed in the organization. It is also necessary to appoint a facilitator.

The briefing to members of the design team should emphasize that it will be a demanding project in terms of both the time and the effort they will have to put into it. It should explain what they will be expected to do at each stage of the programme. Team members should be told how they should avoid being discriminatory.

Step 4 Formulate communication strategy

It is essential to have a communication strategy. The introduction of a new job evaluation will always create expectations. Some people think that they will inevitably benefit from pay increases, others believe that they are sure to lose money. It has to be explained carefully, and repeatedly, that no one should expect to get more and that no one will lose. The strategy should include a preliminary communication setting out what is proposed and why, and how people will be affected. Progress reports should be made at milestones throughout the programme, for example when the factor plan has been devised. A final communication should describe the new grade and pay structure and spell out exactly what is to happen to people when the structure is introduced.

Step 5 Identify and define factors

Job evaluation factors are the characteristics or key elements of jobs that are used to analyse and evaluate jobs in an analytical job evaluation scheme. The factors must be capable of identifying relevant and important differences between jobs that will support the creation of a rank order of jobs to be covered by the scheme. They should apply equally well to different types of work, including specialists and generalists, lower-level and higher-level jobs, and not be biased in favour of one gender or group. Although many of the job evaluation factors used across organizations capture similar job elements (this is an area where there are some enduring truths), the task of identifying and agreeing factors can be challenging.

Guidelines on the choice of factors

The following guidelines should be used when choosing factors:

1. The factors should between them measure all significant job features and should be of broadly comparable scope. As the EOC (1) emphasizes: 'The exclusion of a factor which is important to a job will result in it being undervalued.'
2. The whole range of jobs to be evaluated at all levels should be covered, without favouring men or women or any particular job or occupation.
3. Job features more commonly found in jobs carried out by women should not be omitted, for example manual dexterity, interpersonal skills and 'caring' responsibilities.
4. Double-counting should be avoided, ie each factor must be independent of every other factor – the more factors (or sub-factors) in the plan, the higher the probability that double-counting will take place.
5. Elision or compression of more than one significant job feature under a single factor heading should be avoided. If important factors are compressed with others it means that they would probably be undervalued. For example, trying to measure all forms of responsibility under a single factor heading can result in some people, often with people-related responsibilities, being disadvantaged by comparison with finance or other physical-resource-related responsibilities.
6. Acceptable criteria for identifying differences in the size of jobs should be provided.
7. The factor definitions should be clear, relevant and understandable and written in a way that is meaningful to those who will use the scheme.
8. The factors should be acceptable to those who will be covered by the scheme.
9. The choice should not lead to discrimination on the grounds of gender, race, disability or for any other reason. The scheme should fairly measure features of female-dominated jobs as well as male-dominated jobs. The EOC check list in their *Good Practice Guide* (1) on avoiding sex discrimination in the design of job evaluation schemes is summarized in Chapter 11.

The e-research survey (2) established that the most frequently used factors by the respondents with analytical schemes were:

1. knowledge and skill;
2. communications and contacts;
3. judgement and decision making;
4. impact;

5. people management;
6. freedom to act;
7. working environment;
8. responsibility for financial resources.

Step 6 Define factor levels to produce the basic factor plan

The factor plan is the key job evaluation document. It guides evaluators on making decisions about the levels of demand. The basic factor plan defines the levels within each of the selected factors. A decision has to be made on the number of levels (often five, six or seven) which has to reflect the range of responsibilities and demands in the jobs covered by the scheme. The starting points can be an analysis of what would characterize the highest or lowest level for each factor and how these should be described. For example, the highest level in a judgement and decision-making factor could be defined as: 'Deals with widely differing problems calling for extreme clarity of thought in assessing conflicting information and balancing the risks associated with possible solutions. Additionally, one of the main requirements of the role may be to develop fundamentally new strategies and approaches.' The lowest level could be defined as: 'The work is well defined and relatively few new situations are encountered. The causes of problems are readily identifiable and can be dealt with easily.' It might then be decided that there should be three levels between the highest and lowest level on the basis that this truly reflects the graduation in responsibilities or demands. The outcome would then be the definition of the factor and each of the five levels illustrated in Table 10.1. This process is repeated for each factor.

Guidelines for factor level definitions

The following guidelines should be used in defining levels:

1. Each level should be defined as clearly as possible as a guide to evaluators making 'best fit' decisions.
2. The levels should cover the whole range of demands in this factor which are likely to arise in the jobs with which the evaluation scheme is concerned.
3. The link between the content of level definitions should be related specifically to the definition of the factor concerned and should not overlap with other factors.
4. There should be uniform progression in the definitions level by level from the lowest to the highest level – there should be no gaps or undefined intermediate levels which might lead to evaluators finding it difficult to be confident about the allocation of a level of demand.
5. The level definitions should not rely upon a succession of undefined comparatives, eg small, medium, large – so far as possible, any dimensions should be defined.

Table 10.1 Example of factor level definitions

Judgement and decision making: The requirement to exercise judgement in making decisions and solving problems, including the degree to which the work involves choice of action or creativity.

1   The work is well defined and relatively few new situations are encountered. The causes of problems are readily identifiable and can be dealt with easily.
2   Evaluation of information is required to deal with occasional new problems and situations and to decide on a course of action from known alternatives. Occasionally required to participate in the modification of existing procedures and practices.
3   Exercises discriminating judgement in dealing with relatively new or unusual problems where a wide range of information has to be considered and the courses of action are not obvious. May fairly often be involved in devising new solutions.
4   Frequently exercises independent judgement when faced with unusual problems and situations where no policy guidelines or precedents are available. May also frequently be responsible for devising new strategies and approaches which require the use of imagination and ingenuity.
5   Deals with widely differing problems calling for extreme clarity of thought in assessing conflicting information and balancing the risks associated with possible solutions. Additionally, one of the main requirements of the role may be to develop fundamentally new strategies and approaches.

6. Each level definition should stand on its own. Level definitions should not be defined by reference to a lower or higher level, ie it is insufficient to define a level in words to the effect that it is a higher (or lower) version of an adjacent level.

Step 7 Select and analyse test jobs

A small representative sample of jobs should be identified to test the scheme. A typical proportion would be about 10 per cent of the jobs to be covered. These are then analysed in terms of the factors. This generally means using a questionnaire which will ask for information about the overall purpose of the job, the main activities carried out and the demands made by the job with regard to each factor. This is often a paper exercise but it can be carried out by direct input to a computer in response to questions that have been validated for use within the context for which they have been designed. Job and role analysis is covered in more detail in Chapter 14.

Step 8 Test basic factor plan

The factors forming the basic factor plan are tested by the design team on a representative sample of jobs. The aim of this initial test is to check on the extent to which the factors are appropriate, cover all aspects of the jobs to be evaluated, are non-discriminatory, avoid double-counting and are not compressed unduly. A check is also made on level definitions to ensure that they are worded clearly, graduated properly and cover the whole range of demands applicable to the jobs to be evaluated so that they enable consistent evaluations to be made. A more comprehensive test should be carried out later at step 12 when the full factor plan with scoring systems and weightings has been devised.

Step 9 Develop scoring model

The aim is to design a point-factor scheme which will operate fairly and consistently to produce a rank order of jobs, based on the total points score for each job. Each level in the factor plan has to be allocated a points value so that there is a scoring progression from the lowest to the highest level.

A decision needs to be made on how to set the scoring progression within each factor. There are two methods. The 'arithmetic' or linear approach assumes that there are consistent step differences between factor levels, for example a four-level factor might be scored 1,2,3,4. Alternatively, geometric scoring assumes that there are progressively larger score differences at each successive level in the hierarchy because the differences between levels of demand or responsibility progressively increase through successive levels. Geometric progression assumes that this distance needs to be reflected in the scoring system. Thus the levels may be scored 1,2,4,8 rather than 1,2,3,4. This appears to increase the scoring differentiation between higher-level jobs. The rank order produced by either of these methods is unlikely to differ much, but senior managers sometimes like to think that there should be larger gaps between levels at their end of the scale.

It is best to allocate a single finite score for each level as giving a choice from a range of scores can complicate evaluations. If it is decided that there should be some choice, this should be as simple as possible, for example low, standard and high. These graduations are then converted to scores within a range, for example a level range of from 200 to 280 points would provide for 220 points for a low assessment, 240 for a standard assessment and 260 for a high assessment. There should be no overlap in the scores between ranges.

Step 10 Decide on the factor weighting

Weighting is the process of attaching more importance to some factors than others through the scoring system (explicit weighting) or as a result of variations in the number of levels or the choice of factors (implicit weighting).

Explicit weighting

Explicit factor weighting is expressed as the maximum points available for a factor taken as a percentage of the total available points for all factors. In a scheme with six factors it may be decided that two factors such as expertise and problem solving should be weighted at 20 per cent and the remaining four factors weighted at 15 per cent. Thus, if the total score available were 800 points, the two weighted factors would have a maximum score of 160 points each and the remaining factors would each have a maximum of 120 points.

Explicit factor weighting can be determined by the design team who discuss the relative importance of the factors and agree on how they should be weighted. It is essentially a judgemental process; a matter of opinion which cannot be verified except in terms of the consensus achieved by the collective views (and prejudices) of the team. Attempts have been made to give this some validity by using the statistical technique of multiple regression analysis, but this does not produce a credible result.

Implicit weighting

In some schemes *implicit weighting* exists rather than the explicit weighting referred to above. Implicit weighting takes place whenever some factors are established which have more levels than others and for which the same scoring progression per level exists as in the other factors. Such factors would have more points available to them because of the extra levels and would have therefore been implicitly weighted. Thus a scheme with six factors, each with the same number of six levels and a score progression of 20 points per level, would have the same maximum score of 120 points for each factor and would therefore be unweighted. If, however, two factors had an additional level and the same scoring system were used, their maximum score would be 140 points and the scheme would be implicitly weighted at 18.42 per cent of the total score for the factors with additional levels, and 15.79 per cent of the total for the remaining factors.

The number and choice of factors may also implicitly weight a scheme. If two factors which would normally be treated as being of equal importance are compressed into one and the scoring has not been increased proportionately, then implicit weighting of that combined factor has taken place, that is, it is undervalued in terms of the significance of its characteristics.

Step 11 Prepare full factor plan

The outcome of steps 9 and 10 is the full scored and weighted factor plan which is tested in step 12.

Step 12 Test the full factor plan

The full factor plan incorporating a scoring scheme and either explicit or implicit weighting is tested on the same jobs used in the initial test of the draft factors. Further jobs may be added to extend the range of the test. Each test job is evaluated and scored by the design team and then ranked according to the total score. The design team then considers the extent to which it is believed the rank order is valid in the sense that the evaluations correctly indicate relative job size. There is no single, simple test which will establish the validity of a factor plan. The methods available are as follows:

1. *Reference ranking* – the team compares the ranking produced by the job evaluation with the ranking produced by a paired comparison ranking as described in Chapter 9. This should have been carried out by the team at an earlier stage in the project, say between steps 4 and 5. The facilitator needs to ensure so far as possible that team members set their prejudices aside when carrying out the paired comparisons. This may not happen in full but at least the facilitator can get team members to justify the ranking they have produced and ask searching questions if it is believed that prejudgements have been made. If this is done properly, reference ranking is probably the best way of testing a factor plan.

2. *Hierarchy comparisons* – the rank order produced by the test is compared with the existing organizational hierarchy and any obvious discrepancies are investigated. This method is a form of reference ranking and does not eliminate prejudice. But if the test produces rankings which are totally at variance with the hierarchy – if, for example, some managers are ranked lower than their subordinates – then there is clearly something wrong and it will need to be checked.

3. *The 'felt fair' test* – the rank order produced by the test is compared with what the panel 'feels' is the appropriate ranking and discrepancies are identified. If it is felt to be fair then it *is* fair. This test is in accordance with the felt-fair principle described in Chapter 1 and has been and probably still is the most commonly used testing method. But it is dangerous because it is liable simply to reproduce existing prejudices. Informed opinion such as that of Sue Hastings, a leading equal pay expert, rejects the felt fair test for this reason.

The EOC *Good Practice Guide* (1) states that job evaluation is in large part a social mechanism to establish agreed differentials within organizations. Therefore, the only final test available is whether the resulting rank order looks reasonable to all parties, and whether the appropriate tests have been made to ensure that the scheme applies fairly to the range of jobs it will cover. This is where caution must be exercised to ensure that the rank order review does not lead to weighting adjustments aimed at reverting to the previous hierarchy of roles, based on preconceptions about their relative worth, or *a priori* expectations about what results the job evaluation scheme should have produced. But the test may reveal a need to make further adjustments to the factor level definitions or the scoring and weighting plan. If these are revised, the validity of the rank order will need to be reconsidered. This can be an iterative process but no more than one or at most two iterations are usually required.

Step 13 Computerize

The steps set out above will produce a paper-based scheme and this is still the most popular approach. The e-research survey (2) found that only 28 per cent of respondents with job evaluation schemes used computers to aid evaluation. But full computerization as described in Chapter 9 can offer many advantages, including greater consistency, speed and the elimination of much of the paperwork. There is also the possibility of using computers to help manage and support the process without using computers as a substitute for grading design teams. Many HR software systems such as SAP and Peoplesoft provide for this.

Computer-assisted schemes use the software provided by suppliers but the system itself is derived from the paper-based scheme devised by the methods set out above. No job evaluation design team is required to conduct evaluations but it is necessary to set up a review panel which can validate and agree the outcomes of the computerized process. No one likes to feel that a decision about their grade has been made by a computer on its own and hard lessons have been learnt by organizations that have ended up with fully automated but discriminatory systems.

Step 14 Test the computerized scheme

It is essential to test the computerized scheme on the same jobs used to test the paper scheme to establish that similar results will be produced. If not, the computerized scheme will have to be amended.

Step 15 Apply and implement

When the final design of the paper or computerized scheme has been tested as satisfactory, the application and implementation programme can begin.

THE APPLICATION AND IMPLEMENTION PROGRAMME

The application and implementation of job evaluation is carried out by selecting benchmark jobs and then evaluating them to produce a rank order and a grade structure. This leads to the development and implementation of a pay structure taking into account the outcomes of a survey of market rates. The steps required are shown in Figure 10.3.

Step 1 Select and analyse benchmark jobs

When the design has been finalized, 'benchmark' jobs will need to be selected by the design team. Benchmark jobs provide the reference points for evaluation, bearing in

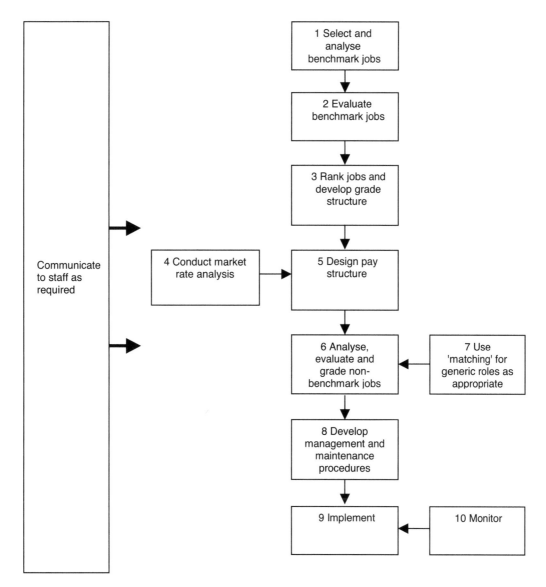

Figure 10.3 The application and implementation sequence

mind that job evaluation is essentially a comparative process. They are the representative jobs which enable standards to be developed and refined for making judgements about comparative worth and form the datum points which are the basis of the framework within which other jobs are evaluated.

Benchmarks will consist of the key jobs at different levels and in different functions of the organization and need to be selected whenever the total number of jobs is too large for them all to be compared with one another. As a rule of thumb, this may be the case when there are 40 jobs or more, although the number could be smaller if there are wide variations between the jobs. Normally between 15 and 30 per cent of the total number of jobs may be selected, depending on the complexity of the organization. Some jobs will be carried out by a number of people (generic jobs or roles) and the percentage of employees covered is therefore likely to be greater than the percentage of benchmarks. The jobs used for testing purposes can be used as benchmarks, although they will have to be re-evaluated if modifications to the design have taken place after the tests.

The criteria for selecting benchmarks are that they should:

- represent the entire range of jobs according to level and function and the extent to which job holders are predominantly male or female or members of different racial groups;
- be well-recognized jobs with which the members of the job evaluation design team between them are familiar;
- be reasonably stable, ie unlikely to change much in content (although this presents difficulties in a rapidly changing organization);
- be precisely defined with regard to skills, responsibilities and work requirements;
- stand out clearly from other jobs so that they can be easily identified;
- include at least some jobs which can form the basis of external comparisons.

Methods of job and role analysis and of preparing job descriptions or role profiles for evaluation purposes are described in Chapter 14.

Step 2 Evaluate benchmark jobs

The best approach is for the design team to evaluate one factor at a time in the benchmark jobs. Experience has shown that an in-depth factor-by-factor approach rather than a job-by-job approach makes it easier to achieve consensus. It means that design team members are less likely to make decisions on total scores based on *a priori* judgements about the relative value of the whole jobs, which they might find it hard to change. They are more likely to focus on 'read-across' analytical judgements about the level of particular factors and it will be easier for them to refer for guidance to previous evaluations of the same factor in other benchmark jobs. It also takes less time than other methods because it is possible to concentrate on factor evaluations that are questionable relative to the levels given to other jobs.

The design team exchanges views about the level appropriate for each factor by reference to the factor plan and the job description or role profile and, with guidance from the facilitator, reaches agreement. The scores are then computed for each of the jobs and the design team examines the comparative total scores to ensure that it is happy with the result. If not, decisions on the levels allocated to individual factors may have to be reconsidered. Note that the team is only deciding on levels. It is not directly scoring jobs.

When there are variations in factor evaluations, individual design team members are asked to give reasons for their conclusions. But the facilitator has to be careful not to allow them to be pressurized to change their views. If design team members have been properly trained and if there is a carefully designed, tested and understood factor plan and good information about the job, the extent to which evaluations vary is usually fairly limited, which enables consensus to be achieved more easily. Detailed notes on the roles of the facilitator and the design team were given earlier in this chapter (pages 109–11).

As the team gains experience in evaluating benchmark jobs it will gain better understanding of the meaning of level definitions by reference to the actual jobs being evaluated. This will enable them to interpret the level definitions in future more accurately and consistently. This understanding should be recorded as 'conventions' which can be referred to in future. Eventually a library of conventions will be created which can become part of the scheme, as took place in the NHS job evaluation programme as part of Agenda for Change.

The rank order produced by the benchmark evaluations provides the basis for the design of a grade structure, as described in Chapter 16. As noted above, organizations with a large number of jobs usually rely on matching the jobs not covered in the original evaluation with the grading of the benchmark jobs, especially in the case of generic roles. The procedure for matching is explained in the description of step 7 below.

Step 3 Rank benchmark jobs and develop grade structure

The benchmark jobs are ranked according to their scores and this provides the basis for developing a grade structure, as described in Chapter 16.

Step 4 Conduct market rate survey

A market rate survey, as described in Chapter 13, provides the information required to design a competitive pay structure.

Step 5 Design pay structure

Pay structure design, as described in Chapter 16, takes account of the results of the evaluation of benchmark jobs and the market rate survey.

Step 6 Analyse, evaluate and grade non-benchmark jobs

The next step is to analyse, evaluate and grade the jobs that have not been dealt with already as benchmarks. Generic roles will be identified and analysed so that multiple job evaluations do not have to be carried out. Generic roles are those with similar characteristics carried out by a number of role holders. Unique 'one-off' roles will have to be analysed and evaluated separately.

Step 7 Match roles

When a large number of similar jobs are included in the evaluation exercise it is the usual practice to adopt an analytical 'matching' approach as in the NHS rather than going through the time-consuming business of evaluating every job using the full scheme.

Analytical matching compares a generic role profile for the job to be matched with profiles for each of the levels in the grade structure and/or profiles for benchmark jobs that have already been evaluated and graded. An analytical framework of factors or role characteristics informs the matching process. A joint matching panel should be set up, which would probably include all or a high proportion of the job evaluation design team. This panel would need to be trained in matching methodology, possibly holding two or three dummy runs.

The analytical approach adopted by the panel involves matching role profiles with level or benchmark role profiles process on a factor-by-factor basis. The headings of the profile definitions should correspond with the factor headings in the job evaluation scheme, as illustrated in the example of a level profile in Appendix 3. The role profile descriptions for each heading should be compared (matched) with the level or benchmark profile definitions/descriptions for the corresponding headings. A decision is then made on the best fit for each heading. This is sometimes recorded as a good fit or as a comparison which places the role above or below the definition to which it is being matched in the level or benchmark profile. The judgements made for each of the headings are then assessed and a decision is made on whether or not there is a good match overall. It would normally be expected that a certain proportion, say 80 per cent, of the headings should provide a good fit to indicate that a match exists. In some procedures, it is required that certain key headings, such as expertise and decision making, should match as well to indicate that an overall match can be made. Where there is doubt about matching, jobs should be evaluated separately to ensure consistent and fair outcomes.

Step 8 Develop management and maintenance procedures

The management and maintenance procedures should cover setting up a job evaluation panel, conducting reviews of evaluations and maintenance procedures.

Job evaluation panel

A job evaluation panel should be set up to manage and maintain job evaluation, either by conducting 'paper' evaluations or by reviewing the outcomes of computerized job evaluations. The panel can also operate as a 'matching' panel as described above. It is usual for the design team to be converted into a panel but it will also be necessary to ensure that additional job evaluators are trained so that alternates are available. The training should include sitting in on design team meetings. It is important to include training in what needs to be done to avoid biased evaluations.

Evaluation reviews

Employees should be given the right to appeal against evaluations by requesting a review of the decisions made by the design team or job evaluation panel. There are essentially two situations where a review of the evaluation or grading of a job might properly be requested: (1) when the job is first allocated to a grade and that grade is made known to the parties concerned; (2) when the content of a job changes (or is about to change) sufficiently to place doubt on the existing grading of that job.

A formal evaluation review procedure should be prepared, agreed and issued before any evaluation results are made known. Reviews of the initial evaluations carried out by the design team should be conducted by a specially convened review group. This might be composed of two members of the original design team plus two additional trained evaluators who were not associated with the original decision and an independent chair. A request for the re-evaluation of a job should be dealt with by the job evaluation panel.

When reviewing the original evaluations of the design team the review stages are typically as follows:

1. The employee discusses their concern with their line manager who will decide whether or not to support the review.
2. The employee, supported if appropriate by their line manager, submits their case for a grading review.
3. The manager responsible for job evaluation should examine the request, add notes as necessary and submit it to the review group together with all available details of the original evaluation. If the request is based on a comparison with another job, details of that evaluation should also be provided.
4. The review group should examine the documents and decide whether a re-evaluation is justified. If the request is based on the way job information has been interpreted rather than on matters of fact, the review group should try to establish why this was not identified during the original evaluation or review.
5. The review group should re-evaluate the job.
6. If the review group believes that a request based on a comparison with another job is potentially valid but that it is the comparator job that was wrongly evaluated, it should re-evaluate both jobs.

Table 10.2 Tips on job evaluation scheme maintenance

'Need to ensure that regular reviews of scheme are built-in.'
'Provide adequate training for those operating the scheme.'
'Ensure trained evaluators don't get rusty.'
'Use IT in a smarter way.'
'Again, ensure better communications with employees.'
'More line accountability and involvement.'
'Find a less time-consuming way of managing it.'
'Have more robust process for challenging and slotting new roles.'
'Maintain better systems for record keeping and adopt smoother processes.'
'Ensure tighter policing and provide clearer rationale.'

7. The re-evaluation process should be the same as for the original evaluation but focusing only on the issues raised in stages 1 to 5 above.
8. The impact of any re-evaluation on the grading of the job under review should be assessed by the manager responsible for job evaluation and communicated to the employee and their manager as the outcome of the review design team's re-evaluation.

There should be no right of appeal to the review group but employees could be allowed to take up the case as a grievance through the normal grievance procedure.

If a re-evaluation is requested, this should be supported by evidence of changes in the role which indicate for consideration by the job evaluation panel why either the manager, the employee or both believe that re-grading is necessary.

Maintenance procedures

Job evaluation needs to be maintained with care, otherwise it will decay and become discredited. Ten suggestions on what needs to be done to maintain job evaluation, provided by respondents to the e-reward survey (2), are set out in Table 10.2.

Step 9 Implement

The implementation arrangements need to cover:

- how the new grade and pay structure will be introduced;
- how individuals will be affected;
- how individuals will be protected against any reductions in pay if the new structure means that they are overpaid in relation to their grade (this is called 'red-circling');

- what will be done about individuals whose pay range for the grade in the new structure to which they have been allocated is lower than their existing range (this is called 'green-circling').

Methods of dealing with the assimilation of jobs into new grade structures and dealing with red- and green-circled jobs, including 'protection' policies in the latter case, are examined in Chapter 16.

Step 10 Monitor

As suggested by Armstrong *et al* (3):

> All organizations are continually evolving, some more quickly than others. No matter how carefully the new job evaluation scheme has been developed, it can only be totally 'right' for the organization at the time of its development. Without regular review and re-tuning when necessary, it will gradually become viewed as 'yesterday's scheme', no longer valid for evaluating jobs in 'today's environment'. The review need not be time-consuming but it should be carried out on a regular basis which it is best to determine at the outset.

REFERENCES

1 Equal Opportunities Commission (2003) *Good Practice Guide – Job Evaluation Schemes Free of Sex Bias*, EOC, Manchester
2 e-research (2003) *Job Evaluation Survey*, e-reward.co.uk Ltd, Stockport, Cheshire
3 Armstrong, M, Cummins, A, Hastings, S and Wood W (2003) *Guide to Job Evaluation*, Kogan Page, London

11

Equal pay for work of equal value

This chapter deals with (1) why discrimination takes place, (2) the legislation concerning equal pay for work of equal value, (3) what organizations can do to avoid discrimination in their job evaluation practices to avoid gender bias, and (4) how pay structures can discriminate. Equal pay reviews or audits are dealt with in Chapter 12.

WHY DISCRIMINATION TAKES PLACE

As Robert Elliott (1) has stated: 'Discrimination arises when equals are treated unequally.' Historically, it has been generally accepted by men in a man's world that women's place was in the home, unless they were needed to carry out menial and therefore underpaid jobs. Women's work has been undervalued because of the low rates of pay. It has been a vicious circle. Prior to the Equal Pay Act in 1970, collective agreements tended to have only one rate of pay for women workers, with no differentiation between grades of work or levels of skill.

The entry of women into the professions in the 19th century and pressures for women's rights in the 20th heralded a very gradual change in this climate of discrimination. But it needed the Treaty of Rome (1957), Article 119 of which enshrined the principle of equal pay for equal work, to stimulate anti-discriminatory law in the

United Kingdom. The first British legislation was the Equal Pay Act of 1970, amended by the Equal Pay Amendment Regulations in 1983.

The incidence of discrimination

Discrimination in the determination of the relative rates of pay for men and women may not be so blatant now as it was before 1975, when the 1970 Equal Pay Act came into force, but there is still a significant gap nationally between the earnings of men and women. The government's New Earnings Survey of 2003 revealed that the gap between the hourly earnings for full-time men and women (the gender pay gap) was 18 per cent, while the gap between the hourly earnings of part-time women and full-time men was 40 per cent (NB: 44 per cent of women workers are part-timers while only 10 per cent of men are).

Causes of the gender pay gap

The 2001 Research conducted by The National Institution of Economics and Social Research (2) into the causes of the gender pay gap identified the following five key factors:

1. *Human capital differences* – ie differences in educational levels and work experience. Historical differences in the levels of qualifications held by men and women have contributed to the pay gap. Women are still more likely than men to have breaks from paid work to care for children and other dependants. These breaks impact on women's level of work experience, which in turn impacts on their pay rates.
2. *Part-time working* – the pay gap between women's part-time hourly earnings and men's full-time hourly earnings is particularly large and, because so many women work part-time, this is a major contributor to the gender pay gap. Some of this gap is due to part-time workers having lower levels of qualifications and less work experience. However, it is also due to part-time work being concentrated in less well-paid occupations.
3. *Travel patterns* – on average, women spend less time commuting than men. This may be because of time constraints due to balancing work and caring responsibilities. This can impact on women's work in two ways: smaller polls of jobs to choose from and/or lots of women wanting work in the same location (ie near to or where they live), which leads to lower wages for these jobs.
4. *Occupational segregation* – women's work is highly concentrated in certain occupations (60 per cent of working women work in just ten occupations). And these occupations which are female-dominated are often the lowest paid. In addition, women are still under-represented in the higher-paid jobs within occupations – the 'glass ceiling' effect.

5. *Workplace segregation* – at the level of individual workplaces, high concentrations of female employees are associated with relatively low rates of pay. And higher levels of part-time working are associated with lower rates of pay, even after other factors have been taken into account.

Other factors which affect the gender pay gap include: job grading practices, appraisal systems, reward systems, retention measures and wage-setting practices. In the latter case, wage levels set entirely on the basis of external comparisons (market rates) can lead to unequal pay for women within the organization simply because external rates may simply reflect the pay inequities already existing in the labour market.

The design and operation of pay structures can contribute to maintaining or even enlarging the pay gap. For example, experienced men with skills which, because of unequal opportunities, women do not have to the same extent may be started at higher rates of pay within a pay range for the job. Extended pay ranges, especially where progression is based on length of service, will favour men who are much less likely than women to have career breaks and may therefore progress further and faster. The assimilation of men on their present higher rates of pay in the upper reaches of new pay ranges may leave women behind and they may take a long time to catch up, if they ever do. Broad-banded pay structures as described in Chapter 15 can also lead to discrimination.

It is noteworthy that none of the key factors identified by the NIESR research refers specifically to pay inequities as a cause of the gender pay gap. Indeed, Diana Kingsmill, author of the 2001 Kingsmill *Review of Women's Employment and Pay* (3), commented that: 'Unlawful wage inequality – the occurrence of unequal pay... does not appear to be so commonplace as the 18 per cent headline gap would suggest.' This opinion seems to be backed up in part by the report of the 2001 Task Force on Equal Pay (4) to the Equal Opportunities Commission (EOC). The Task Force stated that in their view, pay discrimination contributed to 25 to 50 per cent of the pay gap – a wide range which seems to be matter of opinion rather than evidence.

However, the Kingsmill Review focused mainly on the other factors creating the pay gap and Diana Kingsmill commented that: 'Time and time again I have been confronted with data demonstrating that women are clustered towards the bottom of organizational hierarchies while men are clustered towards the top. This distribution clearly has a profound impact on the pay gap.'

The better use of human capital and the provision of equal opportunities for women are therefore important ways of reducing the pay gap. But this does not detract from the necessity of dealing with pay inequities. The rest of this chapter therefore concentrates on the equal pay legislation affecting pay policy and practice and how information on the incidence of unequal pay can be identified by equal pay audits as a basis for initiating corrective action.

THE LEGAL FRAMEWORK

The equal pay for work of equal value legal framework is based on the provisions of European legislation, the 1970 Equal Pay Act as amended by the Equal Pay (Amendment) Regulations 1983, plus the case law. The legislation essentially provides that pay differences are allowable only if the reason for them is not related to the sex of the job holder. The Act and its amendment are implemented through employment tribunals. The Employment Act 2002 provided for the use of equal pay questionnaires.

The same principles of fairness and equity of course apply to other potential areas of discrimination and although the rest of this chapter focuses on the equal pay legislation and its impact, the conduct of equal pay reviews which aim to identify any aspects of discrimination related to race, religion, disability or age which results in pay inequities is dealt with in the next chapter.

European legislation

Article 119 of the EC founding Treaty of Rome of 1957 (now subsumed and expanded as Article 142 of the Treaty of Maastricht) stated that men and women should receive equal pay for equal work – in order to achieve what is often described as a 'level playing field' in terms of wages. Article 119 was extended by the Equal Pay Directive of 1975, which stated that:

- men and women should receive equal pay for work of equal value;
- job classification systems (which is Euro-English for any formal grading system and thus encompasses job evaluation schemes) should be fair and non-discriminatory;
- EC member states should take steps to implement the equal pay principle.

The Equal Pay Act 1970

The 1970 Equal Pay Act effectively outlawed separate women's rates of pay by introducing an implied equality clause into all contracts of employment. Under the Act, which came into force in 1975, an employee in the United Kingdom is entitled to claim pay equal to that of an employee of the opposite sex in the same employing organization in only two situations:

1. where they are doing the same, or broadly similar work – 'like work';
2. where the work they do is rated equivalent under a job evaluation scheme.

The basis of the Act is that every contract of employment is deemed to contain an equality clause which is triggered in either situation. The equality clause modifies any terms in a woman's contract which are less favourable than those of the male comparator. Thus, if a woman is paid less than a man doing the same work, she is entitled to the same rate of pay. Although the Act refers to pay, it extends to all aspects of the employee benefits package

The three important points to note about the original Act are that:

1. Because it was confined to like work and work rated as equivalent, the scope of comparison was fairly narrow.
2. It did not make job evaluation compulsory, but did establish the important point (or made the important assumption) that where job evaluation did exist and valued two jobs equally, there was a prima facie entitlement to equal pay.
3. The Act recognized that a job evaluation scheme could be discriminatory if it set 'different values for men and women on the same demand under any heading'. It gave effort, skill, decision as examples of headings.

However, the European Commission's Equal Pay Directive of 1975 stated that the principle of equal pay should be applied to work of equal value. The Commission successfully argued before the European Court of Justice in 1982 that the United Kingdom had failed to implement the directive, because the Equal Pay Act enabled individuals to obtain equal pay for work of equal value only where their employer had implemented job evaluation. As a result, the United Kingdom government had to introduce the 1983 Equal Pay (Amendment) Regulations of the Act, which came into force in 1984. These are often referred to as the equal value regulations.

The Equal Pay (Amendment) Regulations, 1983

Under this equal value amendment women are entitled to the same pay as men (and vice versa) where the work is of equal value 'in terms of the demands made on a worker under various headings, for instance, effort, skill, decision'.

This removed the barrier built into the Act which had prevented women claiming equal pay where they were employed in women's jobs and no men were employed in the same work. Now any woman could claim equal pay with any man and vice versa, subject to the rules about being in the same employment. Equal value claims can now be brought even if there were no job evaluation arrangements, although the existence of a non-discriminatory job evaluation scheme, which has been applied properly to indicate that the jobs in question are not of equal value, can be a defence in an equal value case.

The amendment also provided for the assignment of 'independent experts' by employment tribunals to assess equality of value between claimant and comparator under such headings as effort, skill and decision without regard to the cost or the industrial relations consequences of a successful claim.

Employment Act 2002

One of the biggest barriers to bringing equal pay claims has been a lack of access to information regarding other people's pay. The Equal Pay (Questions and Replies) Order 2003 of the Employment Act 2002 provided for an Equal Pay questionnaire which can be used by an employee to request information from their employer about whether their remuneration is equal to that of named colleagues. Unions may also lodge these forms on behalf of their members.

The questionnaire includes:

- A statement of why the individual (the complainant) thinks they are not receiving equal pay, followed by a statement of who they believe the comparators are. A comparator is the person with whom the complainant is comparing themselves. A complainant can compare themselves with a predecessor or successor in the job. The comparator must be in the same employment as the complainant.
- Factual questions to ascertain whether the complainant is receiving less pay than their comparator and, if so, the reason why.
- A question asking whether the employer (the respondent) agrees or disagrees (with reasons) that the complainant is being paid less than the comparator.
- A question asking whether the employer agrees or disagrees (with reasons) that the complainant and the comparator are doing equal work.
- Space for the complainant's own questions.

The employer is asked to respond within eight weeks but is not required to reply to the complainant's questions. But if, without reasonable excuse, the employer fails to reply within eight weeks or replies in 'an evasive or ambiguous way', the employment tribunal may conclude that a respondent did not provide a proper explanation for a difference in pay because there was no genuine reason for the difference.

Case law

The following are some of the leading cases which provide guidance in a number of areas as indicated on how the equal pay legislation should be applied in a number of areas.

The basis of comparison

In the case of *Hayward v Cammell Laird* (1988) the House of Lords ruled that the Act required a comparison of each term of the contract considered in isolation. The applicant was therefore entitled to the same rates of basic and overtime pay as the comparator, even though the other terms of her contract were more favourable.

The definition of pay

In *Barber v Guardian Royal Exchange Assurance Group* (1990) the European Court of Justice held that occupational pensions under a contracted-out pensions scheme constitute 'pay' under Article 119 and so must be offered to men and women on equal terms.

Extended pay scales

In *Crossley v ACAS* (1999) the applicant claimed that she was doing work of equal value to the comparator but earned significantly less due to the fact that the ACAS pay scales required many years' experience to reach the top of the pay band which, it was argued, discriminated against women who are more likely to have shorter periods of service. Although the tribunal accepted that there was a period during which the job was being learnt, it agreed the period in this case was too long.

Market forces

In *Enderby v Frenchay Health Authority* (1993) the European Court of Justice ruled that 'the state of the employment market, which may lead an employer to increase the pay of a particular job in order to attract candidates, may constitute an objectively justified ground' for a difference in pay. But tribunals will want clear evidence that a market-forces material factor defence is based on 'objectively justified grounds', bearing in mind that the labour market generally discriminates against women. They may view with suspicion evidence gleaned only from published surveys which they may hold to be inherently discriminatory because they simply represent the status quo.

Red-circling

In *Snoxell v Vauxhall Motors Ltd* (1977) it was held that if an employee's pay is not reduced, ie is 'protected', following a re-grading exercise when their pay falls above the maximum for their new grade (red-circling), the protection should not last indefinitely.

Transparency

In what is usually referred to abbreviated form as the 'Danfoss' case, the European Court of Justice in 1989 ruled that:

> The Equal Pay Directive must be interpreted as meaning that when an undertaking applies a pay system which is characterized by a total lack of transparency, the burden of proof is on the employer to show that his [sic] pay practice is not discriminating

where a female worker has established, by comparison with a relatively large number of employees, that the average pay of female workers is lower than that of male workers.

Use of job evaluation as a defence in an equal pay claim

In *Bromley v Quick* (1988) the Court of Appeal ruled that a job evaluation system can provide a defence only if it is analytical in nature. The employer must demonstrate the absence of sex bias in the job evaluation scheme, and jobs will be held to be covered by a job evaluation scheme only if they have been fully evaluated using the scheme's factors.

THE EOC CODE OF PRACTICE ON EQUAL PAY

The Code of Practice on Equal Pay as reissued by the Equal Opportunities Commission in December 2003 (5) describes:

- the equal pay legislation;
- the scope of the Equal Pay Act;
- how individuals can raise equal pay matters with their employers, request information and bring an equal pay claim;
- how to conduct equal pay reviews.

It also provides an example of an equal pay policy as referred to in Chapter 12 of this book.

EQUAL PAY CLAIMS

Claims for equal pay, which may be supported by a completed equal pay questionnaire, can be made to an employment tribunal on any of the following three grounds:

1. where the work is *like work*, meaning the same or very similar work;
2. where the work is *work rated as equivalent* under a job evaluation 'study';
3. where the work is of *equal value* 'in terms of the demands made on a worker under various headings, for instance, effort, skill, decision'.

If a tribunal finds that the work is like, equivalent or of equal value it can invoke the equality clause in the legislation and rule that the man and the woman should be paid the same.

Defending an equal pay claim

The two most common grounds for defending a claim are (1) that the work is not equal and (2) that even if they are equal, there is a genuine material factor which justifies the difference in pay as long as the justification is objective. As the EOC Code of practice states, objective justification has to demonstrate that:

- the purpose of the provision or practice is to meet a real business need;
- the provision or practice is appropriate and necessary as a means of meeting that need.

Employers cannot defend equal value cases on the grounds of the cost of implementation or the effect a decision could have on industrial relations, and part-time working *per se* cannot provide a defence to a claim. A tribunal can ask an independent expert to analyse the jobs and report on whether or not they are of equal value.

Proving that the work is not equal

The onus is on the employer to prove that the complainant is not carrying out like work, work rated as equivalent or work of equal value when compared with the comparator. If the employer invokes job evaluation to provide support to a claim that the jobs are not equal, the scheme must be analytical, unbiased and applied in a non-discriminatory way.

Analytical means that the scheme must analyse and compare jobs by reference to factors such as, in the words of the Equal Pay Regulations, 'effort, skill, decision'. Slotting jobs on a whole-job comparison basis is not acceptable as a defence. The legislation and case law does not specify that a point-factor or a scored factor comparison scheme should be used, but even if an 'analytical matching' process is followed (see Chapter 9) a tribunal may need to be convinced that this is analytical within the meaning of the Act and has not led to biased decisions.

Genuine material factor

The legislation provides for a case to be made by the employer that there is a 'genuine material factor' creating and justifying the difference between the pay of the applicant and the comparator. A genuine material factor could be the level of performance or length of service of the comparator which means that he is paid at a higher level than the applicant in the pay range for a job. But this only applies if the basis for deciding on additions to pay and the process of doing so is not discriminatory. The Crossley case referred to above is an example of where a tribunal found that length of service criteria could be discriminatory if they meant that women are paid less than men and find it hard to catch up.

Pay differences because of market supplements can be treated as genuine material factors as long as they are 'objectively justified'. In the case of a claim that market pressures justify unequal pay, the tribunal will need to be convinced that this was not simply a matter of opinion and that adequate evidence from a number of sources was available. In such cases, the tribunal will also require proof that the recruitment and retention of the people required by the organization was difficult because pay levels were uncompetitive.

Independent experts

If there is any doubt as to whether or not work is of equal value, employment tribunals will require an independent expert to prepare a report. The expert must:

- evaluate the jobs concerned analytically;
- take account of all information supplied and representations which have a bearing on the question;
- before reporting, send the parties a written summary of the information and invite representations;
- include the representations in the report, together with the conclusion reached on the case and the reason for that conclusion;
- take no account of the difference in sex, and at all times act fairly.

The independent expert's task differs in a number of ways from that of someone carrying out a conventional job evaluation within an organization. This is because the aim in the latter case is to establish relative value by ranking a number of jobs, while an independent expert will be concerned with comparative value – comparing the value of a fairly narrow range of jobs.

Avoiding equal pay claims

To avoid successful equal pay claims, which can be very expensive, there are four things an organization must do:

1. Use a non-discriminatory analytical job evaluation scheme designed and operated to avoid discrimination as explained later in this chapter.
2. Conduct regular equal pay reviews or audits as described in the next chapter and take action if they reveal pay discrimination.
3. Ensure that there is objective and non-discriminatory justification for any differences in pay between men and women.
4. Ensure that everyone is aware that one of the most important core values of the organization is the provision of equal opportunities to enable women to have the

same chance as men to progress their careers and therefore their pay and to be given equal pay for work of equal value. Steps must be taken to ensure that this core value is acted upon.

AVOIDING DISCRIMINATION IN JOB EVALUATION

EOC guidelines

The main points on avoiding discrimination made by the Equal Opportunities Commission in its *Good Practice Guide – Job Evaluation Schemes Free of Sex Bias* (6) are:

- The scheme should be analytical.
- The scheme should be appropriate for the jobs it is intended to cover – it should incorporate all the important and relevant differentiating characteristics of those jobs.
- The scheme should be designed and operated to measure fairly all significant features of jobs typically carried out by women as well as of those generally carried out by men.
- The factors should operate fairly.
- The factor and level definitions should be exact and detailed descriptions should be provided for each factor.
- The factors should cover all important job demands – a scheme will be discriminatory if it fails to include or properly take into account a demand such as caring that is an important element in the jobs carried out by women – the exclusion of an important factor will result in its being undervalued compared with other jobs.
- There should be no double-counting of factors.
- Factors which are characteristic of jobs largely held by one sex should not unjustifiably have a greater number of levels than the number of levels in factors mainly held by the other sex.
- Factors which are characteristic of male-dominated jobs should not have a wider dispersion of scores than factors which are characteristic of female-dominated jobs.
- The method of scoring for each factor should be reasonably similar.
- Variation between points should reflect real differences in demand.
- The weighting system should not favour men or women.
- The selection of benchmark jobs should not favour men or women.
- Job evaluation on the basis of a traditional organizational job description is likely to be unsatisfactory because it leaves evaluators to use their own experience or make assumptions when assessing jobs against factors for which no information is provided.
- Job analysts, facilitators and evaluators should be trained on how to avoid bias.

- The selection of grade boundaries should be objectively based on the evidence provided by job evaluation, irrespective of the sex of the job holders.
- The outcome of a new job evaluation scheme should be monitored to check for sex bias; other things being equal, it is to be expected that a new job evaluation scheme will result in some upward movement of female-dominated jobs as historical pay discrimination is eliminated, particularly those which show typical features of work carried out by women, relative to other jobs.
- Existing schemes should be reviewed to ensure that sex discrimination has not crept in.

The application of these guidelines was considered in Chapter 10.

Use of slotting

The use of traditional 'slotting' techniques is a further potential cause of discrimination. In even a medium-size organization, it is time consuming to evaluate the job of every individual employee separately. In a large organization, it is impossible. Historically, therefore, it was common practice in larger organizations to evaluate only a benchmark sample of jobs and to 'slot' other jobs against the benchmark through some form of whole job comparison.

However, in its decision in the case of *Bromley v Quick*, the Court of Appeal said that the applicant and comparator jobs which had been 'slotted' in this way had not been analysed and evaluated under the scheme in question, so were not covered by the 'job evaluation study' defence. There was not such a study 'where the jobs of the women and their comparators were slotted into the structure on a "whole job" basis and no comparison was made by reference to the selected factors between the demands made on the individual workers under the selected headings'. This decision has significant implications for job evaluation in large organizations, as it implies that all employees should be attached to a job description, which has either been analysed and evaluated, or, at minimum, has been matched to an evaluated benchmark job, using an analytical process.

The process of analytical matching as described in Chapters 9 and 10 aims to avoid the problems of slotting by ensuring that the comparisons are made by reference to an analytical framework.

DISCRIMINATORY PAY STRUCTURES

Pay structures can be discriminatory in the following ways:

- The grade boundary lines in a multi-graded structure are based purely on judgements which may simply reinforce existing inequalities.

- Generic job descriptions take insufficient account of significant differences between male and female roles.
- Whole jobs are slotted into a graded, broad-banded or job family structure by a process of internal benchmarking which is not analytical in itself and is not underpinned by an analytical job evaluation scheme, with the result that the outcome could simply be the perpetuation of existing discrimination.
- Benchmark jobs do not fairly represent the distribution of male and female jobs.
- Market-related pay levels and differentials reproduce marketplace gender discrimination and do not take account of internal relativities.

Approaches to designing non-discriminatory pay structures are described in Chapter 16.

REFERENCES

1   Elliott, R F (1991) *Labor Economics*, McGraw-Hill, Maidenhead
2   National Institute for Economic and Social Research (2001) *The Gender Pay Gap*, Women and Equality Unit, Department of Trade and Industry, London
3   Kingsmill, D (2001) *Review of Women's Employment and Pay*, Department of Trade and Industry, London
4   Equal Opportunities Commission (2001) *Just Pay*, Report of the Equal Pay Task Force to the Equal Opportunities Commission, EOC, Manchester
5   Equal Opportunities Commission (2003) *Code of Practice on Equal Pay*, EOC, Manchester
6   Equal Opportunities Commission (2003) *Good Practice Guide – Job Evaluation Schemes Free of Sex Bias*, EOC, Manchester

12

Equal pay reviews

As described in Chapter 11, UK organizations have a legal obligation to provide equal pay for equal work that is free from sex bias. They therefore need to understand whether their practices and policies are achieving this outcome. The Equal Opportunity Commission's (EOC's) Code of Practice on Equal Pay (1) says that an internal review is 'the most appropriate method of ensuring that a pay system delivers equal pay free from sex bias'.

This section of the chapter describes the equal pay review process (sometimes termed equal pay audits). However, it does not intend to replicate the comprehensive guidance that is available through other sources such as the EOC Equal Pay Review Kit (2) or the CIPD Equal Pay Guide (3). It focuses instead on how organizations can respond to the analysis challenges presented by equal pay reviews in the context of their existing approach(es) to valuing jobs.

PURPOSE OF EQUAL PAY REVIEWS

The purpose of equal pay reviews is to:

- establish whether any gender-related pay inequities have arisen;
- analyse the nature of any inequities and diagnose the cause or causes;
- determine what action is required to deal with any inequities that are revealed.

In doing so they should give organizations confidence about whether they are meeting their legal obligations with respect to equal pay for equal work. There is also the broader benefit from being seen to apply a fair and equitable reward system, and the positive impact this has on employee perceptions and satisfaction.

Equal pay reviews will also support an organization's ability to respond to employee requests for information about their pay practices in accordance with the 2002 Employment Act. This provides for a statutory equal pay questionnaire to help individuals who believe that they may not have received equal pay to obtain information from their employer on whether this is the case, and why, before deciding whether to submit an equal pay claim.

PLANNING A REVIEW

Before embarking on the data collection and analysis that are essential parts of an equal pay review, it is necessary to decide on the scope of the review: whether it should focus on gender only, or include other possible areas of pay inequity such as racial groups and those with disabilities. It is certainly advisable to consider the conduct and outcomes of an equal pay review in the context of all the other equality policies, procedures and processes in the organization.

The review should cover employees on different employment terms, specifically part-time and hourly paid staff if there are any, and those on short-term or contracts of unspecified duration as well as full-time staff.

Part of the planning process will inevitably involve consideration of how to source and access the data that will be needed to feed the analysis. The initial data required may well sit across payroll and the HR database. The data for follow-up analyses may rest in individual files, or reside in the memory of longer-serving staff – if it exists at all. Issues that have come up in equal pay reviews include data that is not retrievable without HR support, data not collected in standardized form and the need to convert data from multiple sources onto a common database in order to generate reports.

Some software tools are available to support analyses. These range from database tools that enable data to be imported from a range of sources to generate pay gap analyses such as the e-review Equal Pay toolkit, to more sophisticated tools that allow for a broader range of analysis possibilities using different data cuts, including the tool developed by Link Consultants. What is clear is that analysis needs will vary from one organization to the next and it is not always possible to specify in advance what analyses will be needed. Therefore advice to organizations planning to replace their HR database is that one criterion should be the flexibility of customized reporting to support future equal pay review analyses.

There are other process decisions to be made – for example, about how intensive the review should be and at what point staff or unions should be involved. These process decisions are all well covered in the EOC Equal Pay Review toolkit and other sources.

THE EQUAL PAY REVIEW PROCESS

Although the EOC Equal Pay Review toolkit describes a five-stage process, there are essentially three main stages to an equal pay review:

1. *analysis*: the collection and analysis of relevant data to identify any gender gaps;
2. *diagnosis*: the process of reviewing gender gaps, understanding why they have occurred and what remedial action might be required if the differences cannot be objectively justified;
3. *action*: agreeing and enacting an action plan that eliminates any inequalities.

These stages are described below and the chapter continues with a review of analysis options, based around an organization's existing approach to valuing jobs.

Stage one: analysis

This stage involves collecting and analysing pay and benefits practices and policies in order to test the extent of any differences in policy or application that might lead to unequal pay between men and women. There are three elements to this analysis stage:

1. Review the organization's equal pay policy

This is the most straightforward part of the initial analysis. It involves establishing whether or not an equal pay policy exists. If there is one, the organization should:

- compare the policy with the model policy set out in the EOC Code of Practice on Equal Pay (see below);
- examine the extent to which it has been communicated internally;
- identify who is responsible for implementing the policy and what steps have been taken to ensure that it has been implemented.

Where there is no existing equal pay policy, the EOC model as set out below can be used as a basis for establishing one.

MODEL EQUAL PAY POLICY: THE EQUAL OPPORTUNITIES COMMISSION

We are committed to the principle of equal pay for all our employees. We aim to eliminate any bias in our pay systems.

We understand that equal pay between men and women is a legal right under both domestic and European law.

It is in the interest of the organization to ensure that we have a fair and just pay system. It is important that employees have confidence in the process of eliminating sex bias and we are therefore committed to working in partnership with the recognized trade unions. As good business practice we are committed to working with trade union/employee representatives to take action to ensure that we provide equal pay.

We believe that in eliminating sex bias in our pay system we are sending a positive message to our staff and customers. It makes good business sense to have a fair, transparent reward system and it helps us to control costs. We recognize that avoiding discrimination will improve morale and enhance efficiency.

Our objectives are to:
• Eliminate any unfair, unjust or unlawful practices that impact on pay
• Take appropriate remedial action.

We will:

• Implement an equal pay review in line with EOC guidance for all current staff and starting pay for new staff (including those on maternity leave, career breaks, or non-standard contracts)
• Plan and implement actions in partnership with trade union/employee representatives
• Provide training and guidance for those involved in determining pay
• Inform employees of how these practices work and how their own pay is determined
• Respond to grievances on equal pay as a priority
• In conjunction with trade union/employee representatives, monitor pay statistics annually.

---

2. Pay analysis

This is about generating the first set of statistics that will help to indicate whether or not an organization may have an equal pay issue, and the extent to which further analysis will be needed. The analysis requirements are discussed later in this chapter.

3. Benefits comparison

This involves establishing the extent to which men and women have access to, and on average receive, equal benefits for equal work, such as pensions, sick pay, medical insurance, company cars and holidays. Benefits design, eligibility criteria and actual practice will need to be examined.

Benefits comparison is an essential part of the analysis phase because, although the publicity surrounding equal pay reviews focuses mainly on cash reward, equal pay legislation allows comparison to be made in respect of any remuneration item. There is no 'total remuneration' concept in equal pay law. This means that an equal pay claim can be submitted in respect of any remuneration item where an individual feels that they are not being fairly treated in comparison with a colleague of the opposite sex doing equal work – even if their total remuneration package is worth the same.

Stage two: diagnosis

The aim of stage two is to establish the nature of any inequities and their causes with the intent of establishing whether the difference in pay is genuinely due to a material difference between the man's and the woman's jobs rather than due to their gender. The review should first seek explanations of why the gap exists and then establish the extent to which the gap can be objectively justified. This stage involves delving into the data, using intuition and judgement about where to focus effort, in order not to be overwhelmed by the mass of options for further analysis.

If this diagnostic phase suggests that any pay differences are gender based, the remedial action needed to rectify the situation should feed into stage three. Tables 12.1(a) and 12.1(b) give examples of the types of analyses and issues that could arise from this diagnostic phase, together with the remedial actions that may be required.

Stage three: action

Any issues that have been identified in phase two must be remedied. The course of action that will remove pay gaps must be defined, planned and implemented. The action plan should incorporate proposals on:

- introducing or amending an equal pay policy if necessary;
- the steps required to remove pay gaps;
- how future bias can be eliminated by changing the processes, rules or practices that gave rise to unequal pay;
- a programme for implementing change;
- accountabilities for drawing up and implementing the plan;
- how employee representatives or recognized trade unions should be involved in preparing and implementing the plan;
- the arrangements for monitoring the implementation of the plan and for evaluating outcomes.

With regard to how long an organization should take to address any inequities, the answer depends on the scale of change that is needed; the causes and costs

Table 12.1(a) Factors creating pay gaps and remedial actions

Possible factors	Data required to identify factors	Possible remedial actions
Men and women on like work, work rated equivalent or work of equal value are paid differently.	(1) An analysis of the average and individual rates of pay of all those on like work, work rated equivalent or work of equal value. (2) An assessment of possible reasons for differences, eg traditional differentials, higher entry pay levels for certain categories of staff, market rate supplements, red- or green-circling and any of the other reasons set out below.	Investigate each case to establish whether or not there is a material factor such as differences in the performance of those concerned, market forces, or red-circling which might justify the inequality. But a claim by an employer that a difference arose from different levels of performance or market forces would have to be objectively justified and red-circling which favours any category could be regarded as discriminatory. If there is no material factor that demonstrably justifies the difference, the jobs in question should be compared by means of an analytical job evaluation scheme. If this indicates that the jobs are of equal value, steps would have to be taken to equalize pay.
Other measures of equal value, eg qualification levels, show pay inequalities between jobs in different occupational groups.	The use of a job evaluation scheme to establish whether the inequalities are caused by the systematic under-evaluation of one occupational group as against another.	As set out above.
Disproportionate distribution of men or women at the upper or lower part of a pay range or an incremental scale. This might result from the unequal impact of women's family responsibilities such as the effect of career interruptions because of maternity.	Distribution of men or women in the range or scale.	Review: (1) the length of the range or scale. If this is longer than is necessary to reflect the additional value that experience can bring to a role, this will discriminate against women and others who have less opportunity to obtain continuous experience; (2) the policy on fixing recruitment salaries (see below).

(Continued)

Table 12.1(a) *Continued*

Possible factors	Data required to identify factors	Possible remedial actions
Men or women placed at higher points in the scale on appointment or promotion.	The most common point on the pay scale for the grade at which men or women are placed on appointment or promotion.	Ensure that policies and procedures are implemented which will prevent such discrimination. For example, produce guidelines which specify when staff can be recruited or promoted to higher points in the range or scale and emphasize the importance of adopting a non-discriminatory approach. Monitor such decisions to ensure that they are objectively justified and do not discriminate.

involved in rectifying inequities are wide and varied. However, the timetable should be realistic in the light of change required, while demonstrating an immediate intention to implement change. In the interim the organization remains at risk of an equal pay claim – the intent to redress the difference is not sufficient to avoid a claim.

It is, of course, important to address both the cause and the effect of the inequity. For example, if the cause of pay differences within grades rests in an organization's recruitment processes, the short-term remedy may be to rectify existing pay differentials – but to avoid the situation arising again, more fundamental issues will need to be addressed relating to recruitment, perhaps including actions such as manager training and generating new guidelines on how to set recruitment salaries.

ANALYSING PAY

The rest of this chapter focuses on the types of pay analyses that may be involved in an equal pay review. In particular, it focuses on the initial analyses that are needed to check whether there appears to be a gender-related pay gap. The nature of analyses that are possible will be affected by the existing pay and grading structure. Some preparatory analysis of the employee population is needed before the statistical analyses can start.

Table 12.1(b)   Factors creating pay gaps and remedial actions

Possible factors	Data required to identify factors	Possible remedial actions
Men or women receive higher merit or performance pay awards or benefit more from accelerated increments.	The comparative level of merit or performance pay awards or the comparative incidence of the award of accelerated increments. The comparative distribution of performance ratings. The extent to which differences can be objectively justified.	Ensure that: ● Men and women are equally entitled to participate in merit or performance pay schemes or to obtain accelerated increments. ● The criteria and processes used to determine merit or performance pay increases are not biased. ● Managers are aware of the possibility of gender or race bias and are trained in how to avoid it. ● Proposals for merit or performance pay or for accelerated increments are monitored to ensure that they are objectively justified and to detect and correct any bias.
Discriminatory use of a threshold merit bar resulting in more men or women achieving a level of pay above the merit bar.	The proportion of men and women whose pay is above the threshold merit bar.	● Review criteria for crossing the threshold or merit bar to ensure that they are not discriminatory. ● Monitor threshold or merit bar decisions to ensure that they have been objectively justified and are free of bias.
Market supplements applied differentially to men or women.	The comparative number of men and women receiving market supplements and their relative value.	Ensure that no supplements are awarded unless they have been objectively justified. Such justification to include evidence that the recruitment and retention of the staff concerned would be seriously prejudiced unless market rates were paid. It should use a number of information sources and should not rely solely on published survey material which could simply reproduce existing marketplace inequalities.
'Red- or green-circling' applied in a way that results in pay discrimination between men and women doing work of equal value or like work.	The incidence and duration and impact in terms of pay differentials of red- or green-circling for the different categories being compared.	Ensure that red- or green-circling does not unjustifiably favour either women or men.

(Continued)

Table 12.1(b) *Continued*

Possible factors	Data required to identify factors	Possible remedial actions
Men or women in work of equal value or like work receive higher allowances.	The distribution and amount of allowances for the different categories being compared.	Equalize the distribution and amount of allowances.
A discriminating job evaluation scheme in terms of factors or weightings or the job evaluation scheme is applied in a discriminatory way.	Details of the factor plan and an analysis of the process of job evaluation followed by an assessment.	Revise the plan or the process to take account of any bias revealed by its assessment.

Determining initial analysis options

In the experience of organizations that have undertaken equal pay reviews, this step can be the most difficult part of the process. This is determining what kind of analyses an organization is able to do in relation to the three definitions of equal work. These are:

- *Like work* – this means identifying jobs anywhere in the organization where the work is the same or broadly similar. Where there is no job evaluation this is the only type of equal work comparison that can readily be made. Although this should be a straightforward comparison, there are potential pitfalls, such as over-reliance on unrepresentative job titles. If existing job titles are not a good guide, it might be necessary to re-categorize jobs in order to arrive at who is doing 'like work'.
- *Work rated as equivalent* – this means work that has been rated as equivalent using the organization's own analytical job evaluation scheme. Clearly, analyses can only be readily applied where the organization has a job evaluation scheme that covers the whole organization.
- *Work of equal value* – this is the 'catch all' in equal pay legislation. It means that an equal pay claim can be brought by any employee where they believe that their job is of equal worth to any other role in the organization that is occupied by someone of the opposite sex. As with the 'work rated as equivalent' test, the only organizations that can readily conduct analyses under this heading are those with an

organization-wide job evaluation scheme that enables different types of jobs to be compared using criteria that apply equally across the organization.

These last two definitions of equal pay rely on job evaluation, and fully to satisfy an equal pay test in law the scheme should be analytical. But it is unrealistic to expect that every organization will introduce an analytical job evaluation scheme in order to provide a legal defence to equal pay claims, even those organizations that aim to be fair and equitable employers. Decisions about how to value and reward jobs are based on a wide range of organizational and business factors, and organizations must balance the relative benefits and risks of alternative approaches, of which the ability to meet all the tests laid down in equal pay legislation is just one – albeit an important one.

However, it is reasonable to expect organizations to apply a range of tests in good faith that will enable them to be satisfied that their pay practices and outcomes are non-discriminatory.

Undertaking the initial pay analyses

As a minimum, organizations need to be able to undertake straightforward statistical checks to investigate the percentage pay difference between men and women doing the same or similar ('like') work and thus define any 'pay gap' that exists.

To do this women's base pay and total pay should be calculated as a percentage of men's pay for all incumbents doing like work. It is helpful to separate the calculation into the different elements of total earnings in order to see where any pay differences lie. As mentioned earlier, in order to compare like with like this analysis needs to be based on a standard norm, for example annual or hourly pay.

The aim is to establish the degree to which inequality exists in the form of a significant pay gap. The EOC recommends that a pay gap in favour of one gender of more than 5 per cent for one job is significant enough to warrant further investigation, as is a pattern of differences in favour of one group of 3 per cent or more (for example, a pay gap in favour of men at all or most levels of the organization).

However, the guideline percentages are, at best, a rule of thumb. It is more important to get an understanding of the pattern of differences and to investigate suspected problem areas, even if the results do not lie within these guideline percentages. It is also important to remember that an individual can make a claim whatever the aggregate statistics say.

The discovery of a gender pay gap does not automatically mean that there is a problem. However, differences must be objectively justifiable – so further investigation will be needed to check whether this is so. If the reason for the pay difference is gender related, the law requires that the inequity is remedied.

If job evaluation is used on an organization-wide basis it is possible to conduct pay gap analyses that meet all three equal work categories. This can be done by conducting both a like work and an organization-wide comparison between the pay for men and women in the same grade irrespective of their occupational groups. This is because where organizations use analytical job evaluation, different types of jobs on the same grade, defined in terms of a range of job evaluation scores, will generally be regarded as being of 'equal worth', thus enabling a pay gap analysis that covers all employees in the same grade.

However, this is unlikely to be a satisfactory assessment of equal worth where bands or grades are so broad that they include jobs with a wide range of responsibilities and skills. Where this is the case, it may be necessary to split the grades/bands into narrower groups. This can be done fairly easily using a points-factor scheme's total job scores, but will not be so straightforward where other job evaluation techniques have been used (for example, classification), without some adaptation to the scheme or alternative approach to deriving additional levels. Of course, the type of job evaluation approach used also impacts on the perceived robustness of the equal worth comparison in the first place.

Where there is no organization-wide job evaluation scheme, further steps need to be taken by an organization if it wants to satisfy itself that there is no potential pay gender gap. The extent to which an organization may need to extend analysis beyond the initial 'like' work check will depend on a number of factors:

● the outcome of the 'like work' analysis;
● the extent to which it wants to explore the potential risk of an equal pay claim;
● the extent to which it wants to be seen as adhering to 'best practice' in conducting an equal pay review.

The options for extending the analysis depend both on the level of rigour that the organization wants to apply and the nature of existing remuneration arrangements. In particular, the options for further analysis will depend on whether:

● analytical job evaluation is used in one or more parts of the organization – and can be extended across the organization;
● analytical job evaluation is not normally used, but where the organization may be prepared to apply it purely for equal pay review purposes;
● the organization is not prepared to formally apply analytical job evaluation.

CONCLUSION

As those organizations that have conducted equal pay reviews have found out, the causes of pay inequity are many and varied – there is the risk of getting overwhelmed by the data requirements needed to carry out a comprehensive review. It is therefore important to prioritize effort, and to undertake those analyses that are most likely to throw light on whether any potential inequities exist.

It should be noted that where an organization satisfies itself through an equal pay review and continuing monitoring that there is no systematic pay discrimination, it is still possible to be subject to an equal pay claim. However, the likelihood of claims occurring should be reduced, and any claims that do occur are more likely to be one-offs rather than reflecting a wider problem.

Ultimately, the test of an equal pay review is whether the organization has reached evidence-based conclusions that it is systematically applying non-discriminatory criteria for determining pay and for achieving outcomes that are defensible and justifiable; or, if not, it knows what is needed to address any inequities. Looking for such evidence should be an ongoing responsibility of any organization to enable organizations to demonstrate that employees are being treated fairly. For this reason, the demand for robust, analytical approaches to valuing jobs will remain a constant organizational requirement.

REFERENCES

1   Equal Opportunities Commission (2003) *Code of Practice on Equal Pay*, EOC, Manchester
2   Equal Opportunities Commission (2002) *Equal Pay Review Kit*, EOC, Manchester
3   Chartered Institute of Personnel and Development (2002) *Equal Pay Guide*, CIPD, London

13

Market rate analysis

Competitive pay structures can only be developed and maintained if data on the levels of pay in the external market are systematically monitored by a process of market rate analysis. This chapter deals with:

- the purpose and aims of market rate analysis;
- the concept of a market rate;
- the process of market rate analysis;
- the sources of market rate data;
- how market data should be used.

THE PURPOSE OF MARKET RATE ANALYSIS

Market rate analysis aims to collect two types of data to provide for competitive pay: (1) the levels of pay – the 'going rates' and benefits for similar jobs provided by comparable organizations (external relativities) and (2) trends in pay settlements.

Data on pay and benefit levels

The data on levels of pay and benefits is collected for similar jobs in comparable organizations. The data may be used in three ways:

1. To provide guidance on the pay ranges to be attached to grades or bands when designing a pay structure.
2. To support a market pricing approach to valuing jobs as described in Chapter 9. This will be particularly important when the organization decides that its pay levels should be 'market driven'. In spite of equal pay considerations, some organizations decide that internal equity should be a secondary consideration, especially if the market for their key staff is highly competitive. Others may state that their policy is to be sensitive to market rates without being driven by them, which means that they have to resolve the competing claims of competitiveness and equity.
3. To inform decisions on market supplements added to base rates to ensure that pay will attract and retain the people the organization needs.

Decisions on levels of pay following market rate analysis will be guided by the pay policy of the organization – its 'market stance' – that is, how it wants its pay levels to relate to market levels.

Data on pay settlement trends

Information on the levels at which organizations are settling pay negotiations or giving 'across the board' pay increases to all employees will be used to guide pay negotiations or to provide the basis for decisions on the level of a general, probably annual, pay review. Information on settlements and trends is published by Incomes Data Services and the IRS Pay and Benefits Bulletin.

Aims of market analysis

When making market comparisons, the aims are to:

- obtain relevant, accurate and representative data on market rates;
- compare like with like, in terms of data, regional and organizational variations and, importantly, type and size of job or role;
- obtain information which is as up to date as possible;
- interpret data in a way that clearly indicates the action required.

THE CONCEPT OF A MARKET RATE

People often refer to the 'market rate' but it is a much more elusive concept than it seems. There is no such thing as a definitive market rate for any job, even when comparing identically sized organizations in the same industry and location. There are local markets and there are national markets, and none of them is perfect in the economist's sense. Different market information sources for the same types of jobs produce different results because of variations in the sample, the difficulty of obtaining precise matches between jobs in the organization and jobs elsewhere (job matching), and timing (the dates on which the data is collected may differ).

This means that market rate analysis is most unlikely to produce information on *the* rate for the job. The possibly incomplete data from a number of sources, some more reliable than others, has to be interpreted to indicate what the organization should do about it. Data may be available for some jobs but not for others which are unique to the organization.

THE PROCESS OF MARKET ANALYSIS

The process of market analysis consists of the following steps as described below:

1. Assess requirements.
2. Consider method of analysis.
3. Identify sources of pay and benefit data and, if required, data on settlement trends.
4. Obtain and analyse data from sources.

Assess requirements

The assessment of requirements will define the purpose of the market rate analysis and when and how often data is required. The jobs and job markets to be covered will need to be identified.

The data to be collected will have to be defined. Pay and benefits data will include as a minimum the actual base rates paid for jobs, together with additional information on earnings from contingent pay, bonus or payment by results schemes to indicate total earnings. Additional information may be collected on pay structures, financial benefits, pension schemes, location or other allowances, holidays, working hours and overtime and shift or unsocial hours premium payments. Data on settlement trends may also be required.

Consider methods of analysis

Before identifying sources and analysing pay and benefits data it is necessary to appreciate how the data can and will be presented and how job matching will be achieved.

Data analysis – statistical terms

Market analysis requires the understanding of a number of statistical terms as described below:

1. *Measures of central tendency*, ie the point about which the several values cluster. These consist of:
   - The arithmetic mean or *average* (A), which is the total of the values of the items in the set divided by the number of individual items in the set. The average, can, however, be distorted by extreme values on either side of the centre.
   - The *median* (M), which is the middle item in the distribution of individual items – 50 per cent of the sample falls above the median, 50 per cent below. This is unaffected by extremes and is generally preferred to the arithmetical mean, as long as there are a sufficient number of individual items (the median of a sample much less than 10 is suspect). Medians are often lower than arithmetic means because of the tendency in the latter case for there to be a number of high values at the top of the range.
2. *Measures of dispersion*, ie the range of values in the set, which provides guidance on the variations in the distribution of values of items around the median. These consist of:
   - The upper quartile (UQ): the value above which one-quarter of the individual values fall (this term is generally used loosely to indicate the range of values above the upper quartile). An organization that says that its policy is to pay upper quartile rates means that its rates are at above the upper quartile of the rates paid by other organizations.
   - The lower quartile (LQ); the bottom 25 per cent of a distribution, the value below which one-quarter of the individual values fall (also sometimes used loosely as in the case of the upper quartile).
   - The inter-quartile range: the difference between the upper and lower quartile values; this is a good measure of dispersion.
   - Upper and lower deciles: the values above and below which 10 per cent of the individual values fall. This is less frequently used but does provide for greater refinement in the analysis of distribution.
   - Total range: the difference between the highest and lowest values. This can be misleading if there are extreme values at either end, and is less often used than the inter-quartile range, except where the sample is very small.

Job matching

Inadequate job matching is a major cause of inaccuracies in the data collected by market analysis. So far as possible, the aim is to match the jobs within the organization and those outside (the comparators) so that like is being compared with like. It is essential to avoid crude and misleading comparisons based on job titles alone or vague descriptions of job content. It is first necessary to ensure that a broad match is achieved between the organization and the types of organizations used as comparators in terms of sector, industry classification, size and location.

The next step is to match jobs within the organizations concerned. The various methods in ascending order of accuracy are:

- *Job title:* this can be misleading. Job titles by themselves give no indication of the range of duties or the level of responsibility and are sometimes even used to convey additional status to employees or their customers unrelated to the real level of work done.
- *Brief description of duties and level or zone of responsibility:* national surveys frequently restrict their job-matching definitions to a two- or three-line description of duties and an indication of levels of responsibility in rank order. The latter is often limited to a one-line definition for each level or zone in a hierarchy. This approach provides some guidance on job matching, which reduces major discrepancies, but it still leaves considerable scope for discretion and can therefore provide only generalized comparisons.
- *Capsule job descriptions:* club or specialist 'bespoke' surveys frequently use capsule job descriptions that define main responsibilities and duties in about 100 to 200 words. To increase the refinement of comparisons, modifying statements may be made indicating where responsibilities are higher or lower than the norm. Capsule job descriptions considerably increase the accuracy of comparisons as long as they are based on a careful analysis of actual jobs and include modifying statements. But they are not always capable of dealing with specialist jobs and the accuracy of comparisons in relation to levels of responsibility may be limited, even when modifiers are used. An example of a capsule job description is given in Figure 13.1.
- *Full job descriptions:* full job descriptions of individual jobs, sometimes including a factor analysis of the levels of responsibility involved, may be used in special surveys when direct comparisons are made between jobs in different organizations. They can be more accurate on a one-for-one basis but their use is limited because of the time and labour involved in preparing job descriptions. A further limitation is that comparator organizations may not have available, or be prepared to make available, their own full job descriptions for comparison.
- *Job evaluation:* job evaluation can be used in support of capsule or full job descriptions and provides a more accurate measure of relative job size or weight. A common method of evaluation is necessary. In the UK market information sources are created on this basis by both Hay and Watson Wyatt. This approach will further increase the accuracy of comparisons but the degree of accuracy will depend on

---

CAPSULE JOB DESCRIPTION

Retail marketing analyst

1   Provide annual and monthly forecasts of retail sales on the basis of given
    assumptions to assist in generating retail one- and three-year plans.
2   Maintain database of information on sales, retail prices and customer discounts.
3   Provide information on products to the trade and other interested parties.
4   Deal with queries on products and prices from customers.
5   Provide general support to marketing and sales managers in analysing retail sales
    data.
6   Undertake special investigations and ad hoc exercises as required to support
    marketing and sales planning activities.

Figure 13.1   Example of a capsule job description

the quality of the job evaluation process. Consistency depends on quality assurance of the evaluation process, both within organizations and across participants.

Sources of data

A check on the going rate for a job in local labour markets can be carried out simply by ringing round or writing to a few local organizations, studying advertisements in the local paper and checking with an agency or two. A more comprehensive study involves referring to published surveys, conducting a wider-ranging special survey or, possibly, joining or forming a pay club (a group of organizations which regularly exchange information on levels of pay and benefits). It is advisable to obtain data from more than one published source and to supplement it by information from other sources – journals, market intelligence and even advertisements, as long as the latter are treated with caution.

Information on what published surveys are available is published regularly by Incomes Data Services in its Directory of Salary Surveys. This summarizes what the surveys provide in the shape of jobs covered, sample data, cost and availability, as well as comments on the quality and reliability of the data.

Criteria for data

- Does it cover relevant jobs in similar organizations?
- Does it provide the information on pay and benefits required?
- Are there enough participants to provide acceptable comparisons?
- Is the sample adequate?
- Is the quality of job matching reasonably precise?

- Is the data reasonably up to date?
- Are the results well presented?
- Does it provide value for money?

The main sources of pay and benefits data are described below.

General national and regional published surveys

General published surveys can be purchased from providers such as Monks, Remuneration Economics and Reward. They contain data on a variety of occupations (often restricted to managerial and professional jobs), usually for the whole of the United Kingdom, and often analysed by regions. They may be produced as paper-based books but paper publication is increasingly being replaced by electronic formats such as standard computer spreadsheet presentations or PDF documents that can be delivered directly via e-mail or published on and downloaded from websites.

The data in published surveys comprises details of base salary and total earnings levels at a given date, with some information on the provision of employee benefits. Pay movements may also be included. The data is presented by job title and function. There is usually some indication of the level of the job and sometimes a brief description of typical responsibilities. The data will probably be analysed in terms of organization size (sales turnover or number of employees), location and industry sector.

General surveys give an overall picture of pay levels in the national and regional labour markets but their value is diminished by the problems of job matching. It is difficult to be certain that either the surveys or the analyst is comparing like with like. This difficulty, and differences in sampling, explains why data on seemingly similar jobs may vary widely between the surveys. Variations are also caused because the surveys may have been conducted on different dates and some time ago.

General local published surveys

Some organizations such as locally based management consultants and recruitment agencies conduct and publish surveys of the local labour market, covering office and manual occupations as well as managerial and professional jobs.

Such surveys can usefully provide relevant information for the market in which an organization is doing most of its recruiting. It is necessary, however, to ensure that the survey includes data from a reasonable number of organizations (no fewer than twenty or so), and that it has been conducted professionally, with some care to ensure an acceptable level of job matching.

Sector surveys

Sector surveys produced by consultants can produce useful information on a sector where pay levels and occupations may be distinct from those in other sectors, for example the electronics industry, the insurance industry and the voluntary sector.

Occupational surveys

Occupational surveys conducted by consultants or professional firms obtain information on the pay of members of professional institutions such as chartered accountants and specific categories of people such as computer specialists, sales or office staff. The data from professional institutions is often confined to pay in relation to age, qualifications and membership status rather than to jobs. But it gives useful information on general levels of salary for professional people.

Special surveys conducted by the organization

An organization can conduct its own special survey or arrange for a firm of management consultants to conduct one on its behalf. This may be a national, regional or sector survey, or it may be confined to the local labour market. It could cover a range of occupations or focus on particular jobs.

Such surveys can be as sophisticated as those conducted by the organizations that publish general surveys, or they can be relatively simple. They have the advantage of being able to concentrate on the jobs in which the organization is particularly interested. They can also seek information from competitor organizations in the national or local labour market who may be quite willing to cooperate as long as they think the benefit of the extra information with which they are provided on a reciprocal basis justifies the time and effort in replying to a survey questionnaire. The steps required are described below.

1. Draw up a list of participating organizations

The first step in conducting a special pay survey is to draw up a list of participating organizations. Those invited to take part should be chosen on the basis of their compatibility with regard to sector, size and the sort of jobs they have. Selection will also be governed by estimates of the likelihood of the organizations agreeing to participate. It is obviously best to start with organizations and individuals known to the originator of the survey, who can be contacted informally by telephone. Preferably the organizations selected should be ones where there are HR or pay specialists who will be able to obtain and present the information required. It is generally easier to conduct a local market survey because good networks are more likely to exist.

Job title	No. in job	Base rates £			Total earnings £		
		Lower quartile	Median	Upper quartile	Lower quartile	Median	Upper quartile

Figure 13.2   Example of a pay and benefits survey form

The number of organizations invited will depend on the time available and on whether the survey is to be by post or by personal visit. Personal visits are ideal, but they are time consuming and the participating organizations may prefer to deal quickly with a return rather than having to entertain a visitor. Clearly, the more sources of information the better. The aim should be to attract at least twenty participants, although in a specialized area it may be necessary to be content with a smaller number. Experience has shown that, unless the originating company is fortunate, at least a third of the companies invited to take part will decline on the grounds that they do not reveal pay data, or that they will get nothing out of it, or that they have contributed to enough surveys already. The proportion of refusals can be minimized by adopting an impressively professional approach, but some refusals are inevitable and should be allowed for when drawing up the list of organizations.

2. Decide on data required, the format in which it should be made available and the information that should accompany the invitation to participate

The data requested will include levels of pay for specified jobs (base rates and earnings) and details of benefits provision as required. The format usually includes a request for information on the median rate for particular jobs and an indication of dispersion, for example the upper and lower quartile rate. The format for the survey should be as simple as possible to encourage comparators to participate. An example of a survey form restricted to pay data is given in Figure 13.2. Further columns could be added as required to obtain information on such benefits, allowances and terms and conditions as pension schemes, life insurance, company cars, location allowances, holidays and hours of work. The terms used, for example base rates, total earnings and median and quartiles, would need to be defined. Capsule job descriptions would have to be supplied.

3. Approach comparators

When approaching potential comparator organizations it is best to deal with known contacts but a direct approach often has to be made out of the blue. There is much to be said for making the approach by e-mail, possibly followed up by a telephone call. The e-mail can lead to the use of electronic means to collect and analyse data, which is infinitely preferable to the traditional paper exercise from the points of view of both the participant and the originator of the survey. When inviting someone you do not know to participate, the three messages to be got across are that: (1) a responsible individual is conducting the survey, which will be carried out competently, (2) the respondent organization will obtain relevant and useful information in return in the form of a summary of the survey results and (3) they will not be put to too much trouble. The date by which it is hoped responses will be made available should also be stated. People tend to complete such forms at the last minute and it is best to restrict the time to three or four weeks.

4. Collect, analyse and distribute data

Respondents may have to be reminded to supply the data. If the worst comes to the worst, an attempt can be made to collect the data over the telephone. When sufficient data is received, a summary should be provided to participants on an anonymous basis.

Pay clubs

Pay clubs consist of members who regularly exchange information among themselves on the pay and benefits provided for a selected range of jobs. The methods used to produce and analyse the data and the format of the capsule descriptions are similar to those used for special surveys as described above. A considerable number of such clubs have been set up by employers in a particular sector or part of a sector and in industries or localities.

Their advantage is that more accurate job matching can be achieved and the information is obtained in a standardized form on a regular basis.

Pay clubs should consist of a sufficient number of members, ten or more, to ensure that a good spread of information is obtained. They can be set up by an existing network, the members of which already exchange information informally and who want to obtain comparative data more systematically. If such a network does not exist, a company may decide to form a club. In that case, other companies with which the originating organization has no contacts may have to be invited to join.

It is useful to invite interested parties to a meeting at which agreement can be reached on the jobs to be covered, the data to be collected for those jobs, the preparation of capsule job descriptions, the method of analysis and presentation, and how the club may be run. The originating company may undertake to administer the drawing up of capsule job descriptions and the initial survey. However, the aim would be to get club members interested enough to take turns in administering the survey. They may agree to contribute to retaining a management consultant to conduct the survey.

Published data in journals

Up-to-date company and national pay data can be obtained from:

- Incomes Data Services and IRS Employment Review (Pay and Benefits Section) which monitor pay settlements and publish details of agreements. Details of pay structures and trends in individual companies are also supplied.
- The government's Labour Force Survey and New Earnings Survey for information on trends.
- The business news sections of the *Financial Times* and other quality newspapers.

Job advertisements

A lot of people, especially line managers, rely on job advertisements in the national and local press or in specialist journals. Advertisements provide some indication of levels of pay but they should be treated with caution, especially in the case of managerial and professional jobs advertised nationally. Differences in the levels of responsibility and scope of jobs with the same job title can be considerable and levels of pay vary accordingly. The brief descriptions of the jobs are often full of hyperbole and may be misleading. The quoted pay levels may be misleading. This problem is not so acute for the clerical, sales and manual workers who are advertised for in local papers.

Nevertheless, even for managerial and professional jobs, advertisements provide an additional source of information which cannot be ignored. Employees will also be looking at them and will be drawing their own conclusions about what they are worth in the market place.

Recruitment consultants and agencies

Recruitment consultants and agencies should have a good 'feel' for levels of pay in the posts which they are helping to fill. They obtain data from employers and from applications. Executive search consultants are particularly knowledgeable about rates of pay in the senior management job market. They will sometimes conduct their own surveys which can provide useful information.

Management consultants' databases

Management consultancy firms such as the Hay Group, Towers Perrin and Watson Wyatt, especially those specializing in pay, maintain their own database of pay levels which can be accessed by clients or, at a cost, by non-clients. The Hay Group, for example, provides clients who use the Hay job evaluation system with market rate data where job matching is achieved through the use of a common evaluation process by survey contributors.

Interactive data sources are available from consultancies such as the Hay Group and Watson Wyatt. They provide users with the choice of different types of analysis which they can relate to their own database and information requirements.

Analysis of recruitment data

It is sometimes possible to get ancillary data about levels of pay by analysing information obtained from recruitment campaigns. Data provided in CVs, if any, may be suspect, but some indication of what is the going rate can be obtained by establishing how much money is required to attract a particular type and level of applicant.

Other market intelligence

Data on market rates can be obtained from informal contacts or networks. Information can usefully be exchanged on rates of pay for specific jobs, increases in pay levels, performance or merit pay increases, and data obtained from separate market rate surveys. Building up and maintaining an informal or semi-formal network can be very helpful, especially if it consists of employers or personnel managers who are interested in the local labour market.

Selecting data sources

More than one source should be used to provide a reasonably convincing basis for analysis and to obtain objective justification for any market premia which might create unequal pay.

General market data can be supplemented by specialist surveys covering particular jobs. A company-administered survey or a salary club can provide information on local market rates. If the quality of job matching is important, an individual survey can be conducted or a salary club can be joined if there is room (some clubs are oversubscribed) or formed. Published surveys, which are readily accessible and are based on a large sample, can be used to back up individual or club surveys. But the information has to be relevant to the needs of the organization and particular attention should always be paid to the range of data and the quality of job matching.

Market intelligence and published data from journals and associated sources should always be used as back-up material and for information on going rates and trends. They can provide invaluable help with updating.

Although the analysis of job advertisements has its dangers, it can be used as further back up, or to give an instant snapshot of current rates, but it is risky to rely on this source alone.

Table 13.1 Summary of sources of market data

Source	Brief description	Advantages	Disadvantages
General national published surveys	Available for purchase – provide an overall picture of pay levels for different occupations in national and regional labour markets.	Wide coverage, readily available, continuity allows trend analyses over time, expert providers.	Risk of imprecise job matching, insufficiently specific, quickly out of date.
Local published surveys	Available for purchase – provide an overall picture of pay levels for different occupations in the local labour market.	Focus on local labour market, especially for administrative staff and manual workers.	Risk of imprecise job matching, insufficiently specific, quickly out of date, providers may not have expertise in pay surveys.
Sector/industrial	Available for purchase – provide data on a sector such as charities or provided by an employer's association.	Focus on a sector or industry where pay levels may differ from national rates, deal with particular categories in depth.	Risk of imprecise job matching, insufficiently specific, quickly out of date.
Special surveys	Surveys specially conducted by an organization.	Focused, reasonably good job matching, control of participants, control of analysis methodology.	Takes time and trouble, may be difficult to get participation, sample size may therefore be inadequate.
Pay clubs	Groups of employers who regularly exchange data on pay levels.	Focused, precise job matching, control of participants, control of analysis methodology, regular data, trends data, more information may be available on benefits and pay policies.	Sample size may be too small, involve a considerable amount of administration, may be difficult to maintain enthusiasm of participants.
Published data in journals	Data on settlements and pay levels available from IDS or IRS, and on national trends in earnings from the New Earnings Survey.	Readily accessible.	Mainly about settlements and trends, little specific well-matched information on pay levels for individual jobs.

(Continued)

Table 13.1 *Continued*

Source	Brief description	Advantages	Disadvantages
Job advertisements	Pay data obtained from job advertisements.	Readily accessible, highly visible (to employees as well as employers), up to date.	Job matching very imprecise, pay information may be misleading.
Recruitment agencies	Data obtained from local recruitment agencies on going rates.	Localized and specific, especially for more junior jobs.	Sample may be small and job matching poor.
Management consultants' databases	Pay data obtained from the databases maintained by management consultants.	Based on well-researched and well-matched data.	Only obtainable from specific consultants.
Analysis of recruitment data	Pay data derived from analysis of pay levels required to recruit staff.	Immediate data.	Data random and can be misleading because of small sample.
Other market intelligence	Pay data obtained from informal contacts or networks.	Provide good background.	Imprecise, not regularly available.

Presentation of market information

Analysed pay data can be presented in tabular or graphical form.

Presentation in tabular form

Data from information sources are usually presented in tabular form. *Tabular formats should identify the job, the size of the sample and, where appropriate, include analyses criteria such as the size and type of organization and its location.* An example is given in Table 13.2.

Table 13.2 Presentation of market data

Job title: Marketing Executive					
Turnover	Sample number		Lower quartile £	Median £	Upper quartile £
£5m – 10m	25	Base salary	34,135	39,434	46,756
		Total earnings	36,544	42,908	49,778
£11m – 20m	33	Base salary	34,668	41,409	48,873
		Total earnings	37,821	44,002	51,546

Marketing Director	Survey data	
		LQ M UQ
	Actual pay	X
UK Sales Director	Survey data	
		LQ M UQ
	Actual pay	X
Marketing Executive	Survey data	
		LQ M UQ
	Actual pay	X X X
Annual pay		35K 40K 50K 55K 60K 65K

Figure 13.3 Comparison of survey data and actual salaries

Presentation in graphical form

The significance of the information can sometimes be revealed more clearly if the tables are supplemented by graphs, which can highlight significant data, and comparisons as in the example in Figure 13.3.

Figure 13.4 shows how a graphical presentation can be made of the outcome of a pay survey based on job evaluation scores compared with the organization's practice

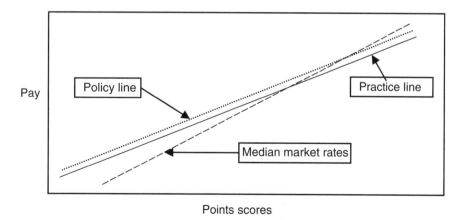

Figure 13.4 A graphical presentation of comparative survey data

line of actual salaries and the policy line defining where the organization would like its pay levels to be. This example shows that pay practice is falling behind pay policy and is ahead of median market rates in the lower part of the scale but market rates are higher in the upper part of the scale.

USING MARKET DATA

The translation of salary market data into competitive pay levels for individuals, or into an acceptable company pay structure, is a process based on judgement and compromise. The aim is to extract a derived market rate based on informed and effective estimates of the reliability of data. It means striking a reasonable balance between the competing merits of the different sources used. To a large extent, this is an intuitive process.

Once all the data available have been collected and presented in the most accessible manner possible (that is, job by job for all the areas the structure is to cover), a proposed scale mid-point or 'spot' salary/rate (often called the 'reference point') has to be established for each level based on the place in the market the company wishes to occupy, that is, its 'market stance'. The establishment of this reference point will be based not only on assessment of current and updated pay data, but also on indications of movements in earnings and the cost of living which are likely to affect the life of the whole structure. For organizations needing to stay ahead of the market, this point will often be between the median and the upper quartile (of a significant population). For others, closer alignment with the median is adequate. Once the series of reference points in relation to the market has been established and assessed, the principles of grade and pay structure design construction set out in Chapter 16 can be applied.

14

Role analysis

Role analysis provides the essential framework for job evaluation, as described in Chapters 9 and 10, for market rate analysis (Chapter 13) and grade structure design (Chapter 16). It also produces information for performance management (Chapter 21) and many other key HR processes such as human resource development, talent management and career planning. In this chapter consideration is given initially to the distinction between jobs and roles and why role profiles are being used nowadays rather than job descriptions for reward management purposes. This is followed by an assessment of the contribution made by role analysis to reward management and a description of the techniques of role analysis and the preparation of role profiles.

JOB DESCRIPTIONS AND ROLE PROFILES

It is necessary to make a distinction between jobs and roles:

- A *job* consists of a group of finite tasks to be performed, responsibilities to be exercised and duties to be carried out as set out in a job description.
- A *role* is the part played by people in meeting their objectives. It refers to the behaviours expected of them as well as the outcomes of that behaviour and is set out in a role profile.

Traditionally, job descriptions consisting of a list of duties have been used for job evaluation and other reward management purposes. But a job description is essentially a prescriptive and static document which tells people in detail what they do on a continuing basis. For reward management purposes they have been largely replaced by role profiles.

Role profiles describe the part played by role holders in fulfilling their work requirements, focusing on outputs and outcomes and frequently referring to knowledge and skill requirements and expected behaviours. They may be for individual roles or they may be generic, that is, describing a role which is carried out by a number of role holders. The same approach to role analysis and role profiling is used for both individual and generic roles.

Role profiles do not follow the typical job description approach of simply listing a number of tasks or duties. They are therefore more dynamic and, potentially, less restrictive than job descriptions. In effect they indicate to people what they are expected to achieve without spelling out what tasks they have to carry out to meet expectations.

ROLE ANALYSIS AND REWARD MANAGEMENT

The contribution made by job and role analysis to job evaluation, market rate analysis, the design of graded pay structures and performance management is described below.

Job evaluation

For job evaluation purposes, job and role analysis generates the information required to enable evaluators to form a judgement on the levels of demand and responsibility in a role. This judgement determines what levels in the various factors in the factor plan are appropriate for that role or enables evaluators to match the role with a grade profile/description or a benchmark role.

It is therefore necessary to structure the analysis around the factor plan to ensure that information about the demands made by the role or the levels of responsibility for each factor is available to the evaluator. The analysis will establish what the key result areas of the role are and then produce the information required to summarize the demands under each of the factor plan headings.

Market rate analysis

Role analysis provides the essential data needed to produce the capsule job descriptions used to provide for good job matching.

Graded pay structure design

The design of grade structures may involve the production of grade definitions or profiles which will enable matching to take place. Guidance on producing these will be provided by role analysis.

Performance management

As described in Chapter 21, an essential start to the performance management process is an agreement on role expectations. This agreement may start by referring to an existing role profile but it is necessary to update and revise that as necessary, and this means further role analysis.

ROLE ANALYSIS TECHNIQUES

Role analysis is not easy. The 'facts' about roles may have to be interpreted because responsibilities are ill defined or because there is a difference of opinion between role holders and their managers about exactly what the role entails. Some people find it difficult to explain what they are doing succinctly, and role analysts can be overwhelmed with detail.

Role analysis can be conducted by means of interviews or questionnaires. The latter may be paper based or the data can be input to a computer if computer-assisted job evaluation is used.

Interviews

Interviews can be structured around questions designed to elicit information about the characteristics of the job and the role played by the job holder. Where appropriate, these questions should be linked explicitly with the factors included in the evaluation scheme. The questions could cover:

- *Overall purpose*. What is the role for?
- *Outputs and outcomes*. What is the role holder expected to achieve? The number of headings under which outcomes are described should be restricted to no more than seven or eight.
- *Knowledge and skill requirements*. What is the role holder expected to know and be able to do?
- *Behavioural expectations (competencies)*. How is the role holder expected to behave under each of the main headings in the organization's competency framework? If no such framework exists then it is highly desirable that one should be created.

Competency analysis is often based on interviews and/or questionnaires, although a 'workshop' approach can be adopted in which a number of people who are in the jobs being analysed, or have extensive knowledge of them, get together as a group to analyse the job. During the interview or workshop, the questions concentrate on what people do, the results they have to achieve, the situations they face and what distinguishes performers at different levels of competence in terms of behaviours.

● *Factor analysis.* What demands are made on the role holder under each of the headings in the factor plan? This assumes that an analytical form of job evaluation is used, as it should be.

The interview should be based on a logical sequence of questions which help interviewees to order their thoughts. It may be necessary to probe to establish what people really do. Answers to questions are often vague. Information may be given by means of untypical instances and people can inflate descriptions of their work. The answers to questions may produce a lot of irrelevant data which must be sifted before preparing the role definition.

It is always advisable to check the information provided by individuals with their managers or team leaders. Different views can be held about the role, and if so, they should be reconciled. Role analysis often reveals such differences as well as various organizational problems. This information can provide a useful spin-off from the analysis process.

Questionnaires

Questionnaires covering points such as those mentioned above can be completed by individuals and approved by their manager or team leader. They are helpful when a large number of roles are to be covered. They can also save interviewing time by recording purely factual information and by enabling the analyst to structure questions in advance to cover areas which need to be explored in greater depth. Questionnaires can produce information quickly and cheaply on a large number of roles and can be phrased in non-discriminatory ways. But a substantial sample is needed and the construction of a questionnaire is a skilled job which should be done only on the basis of preliminary fieldwork. It is highly advisable to pilot-test questionnaires before launching into a full-scale exercise. The accuracy of the results also depends on the willingness and ability of individuals to complete questionnaires. Many people find it difficult to express themselves in writing about their work, however well they know and do it.

Questionnaires can be structured to cover every aspect of the role as specifically as possible and to facilitate the subsequent evaluation of the role. Structured questionnaires are often used in computer-assisted job evaluation systems – the answers are loaded into the computer and the software generates a score. Such questionnaires can eliminate the need for job descriptions as the basis of job evaluation and therefore reduce the often tedious time it usually takes to prepare such descriptions.

ROLE PROFILES

The following is a typical role profile format (examples are given in Appendix 3).

Purpose

This is a short statement of why the job exists. It should be expressed in a single sentence. When defining the purpose of a job it is helpful to consider questions like:

- What part of the organization's or team's total purpose is accomplished by people in this job?
- What is the unique contribution of this job that distinguishes it from other jobs?
- How would you summarize the overall responsibility of individuals in this job?

Organization

This section explains where the job fits into the organization. It sets out the job title of the person to whom the individual is responsible and the job titles of the people who are directly responsible to the job holder.

Key result areas

Key result areas (also known as key tasks, main responsibilities or principal accountabilities) are statements of the end results or outputs required of the job. They answer the question 'What are the main areas in which people in this job must get results to achieve its purpose?'

For most roles, up to seven or eight headings are sufficient to cover the major result areas. Fewer than four or five headings probably means something is missing; more than eight may mean that the job description is going into too much detail.

The complete key result area schedule should be expressed on the proverbial one side of one sheet of paper. The emphasis should be on contribution and outcomes.

Key result area statements should have the following characteristics:

- Taken together, they represent all the major outputs expected of the job.
- They focus on what is required (results and outputs), not on how the job is done (detailed tasks and duties).

- Each key result area is distinct from the others and describes an important aspect of the job in which results are to be achieved.
- They suggest (but need not state explicitly) measures or tests which could determine the extent to which results are being achieved.

A key result area statement is written in the form: 'Do something in order to achieve a stated result or standard.' Where possible, it should point to performance measures. Each statement is made in one sentence beginning with an active verb such as 'prepare', 'produce', 'plan', 'schedule', 'test', 'maintain', 'develop', 'monitor', 'ensure'.

Factor analysis

If an analytical job evaluation scheme is used, an additional section may be added to the role profile which describes the demands made by the job under such headings as skills, responsibilities, complexity, interpersonal relations and mental and physical demands.

Part IV

Grade and pay structures

15

Grade and pay structures: main types

The purpose of grade and pay structures is to provide a logically designed framework within which an organization's pay policies can be implemented. They enable the organization to determine where jobs should be placed in a hierarchy, define pay levels and the scope for pay progression and provide the basis upon which relativities can be managed, equal pay achieved and the processes of monitoring and controlling the implementation of pay practices can take place. A grade structure can also serve as a medium through which the organization communicates the career and pay opportunities available to employees.

This chapter starts with definitions of grade and pay structures and then describes the following types of grade and pay structures: narrow-graded, broad-graded, broad-banded, job level, career family and job family. Spot rate and individual job grades are also described as methods of establishing and defining pay levels and pay ranges, although, strictly speaking, neither of these is an overall grade and pay structure in the way the others are.

GRADE STRUCTURES

A grade structure consists of a sequence or hierarchy of grades, bands or levels into which groups of jobs which are broadly comparable in size are placed. There may be a single structure which contains grades or bands and which is defined by their number and width (width is the scope the grade or band provides for pay progression). Alternatively, the structure may be divided into a number of career or job families consisting of groups of jobs where the essential nature and purpose of the work are similar but the work is carried out at different levels.

The main types of graded structures as described in this chapter are:

- *Narrow-graded structures* – which consist of a sequence of narrow grades (ten or more).
- *Broad-graded structures* – which have fewer grades (six to nine).
- *Broad-banded structures* – which consist of a limited number of grades or bands (often four to five).
- *Career family structures* – which consist of a number of families (groups of jobs with similar characteristics) each divided typically into six to eight levels. The levels are described in terms of key responsibilities and knowledge, skill and competence requirements and therefore define career progression routes within and between career families. There is a common grade and pay structure across all the career families.
- *Job family structures* – which are similar to career families except that pay levels in each family may differ to reflect market rate considerations (this is sometimes referred to as market grouping). The structure is therefore more concerned with market rate relativities than mapping careers. The number of levels in families may also vary.

The e-research 2004 Survey of Grade and Pay Structures (1) found that narrow-graded structures with ten or more grades were used by 18 per cent of respondents, 24 per cent of respondents had a broad-graded structure with six to nine grades, 8 per cent had a broad-banded structure with five bands or less and 17 per cent had a career or job family structure. The remaining respondents used pay spines, spot rates or individual ranges as described later in this chapter.

PAY STRUCTURES

A grade structure becomes a pay structure when pay ranges, brackets or scales are attached to each grade, band or level. In some broad-banded structures, as described later in this chapter, reference points and pay zones may be placed within the bands and these define the range of pay for jobs allocated to each band.

Pay structures define the different levels of pay for jobs or groups of jobs by reference to their relative internal value as determined by job evaluation, to external relativities as established by market rate surveys and, sometimes, to negotiated rates for jobs. They provide scope for pay progression in accordance with performance, competence, contribution or service.

There may be a single pay structure covering the whole organization or there may be one structure for staff and another for manual workers, but this is becoming less common. There has in recent years been a trend towards 'harmonizing' terms and conditions between different groups of staff as part of a move towards single status. This has been particularly evident in many public sector organizations in the UK, supported by national agreements on 'single status'. Executive directors are sometimes treated separately where reward policy for them is decided by a remuneration committee of non-executive directors (see Chapter 22).

NARROW-GRADED STRUCTURES

Until fairly recently the typical type of structure was the narrow multi-graded pay structure illustrated in Figure 15.1. However, this type of structure is being replaced by structures which have fewer grades (broad-grade structures) or with broadbanded, career family or job family structures.

Defined

A narrow-graded structure consists of a sequence of job grades into which jobs of broadly equivalent value are placed. There may be ten or more grades and long-established structures, especially in the public sector, may have as many as 18 grades. Grades may be defined by a bracket of job evaluation points so that any job for which the job evaluation score falls within the points bracket for a grade would be allocated to that grade. Alternatively, grades may be defined by grade definitions or profiles which, if analytical factor comparison is used as described in Chapter 9, provide the information required to match jobs set out under job demand factor headings. This information can be supplemented by reference to benchmark jobs which have been already graded as part of the structure design exercise. An example of grade definitions is given in Appendix 3.

Pay ranges

A pay range is attached to each grade. The maximum of each range is typically between 20 and 50 per cent above the minimum. For example, a '40 per cent' range

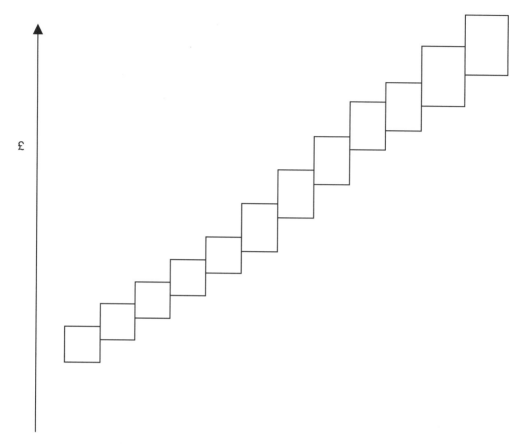

Figure 15.1 A narrow, multi-graded structure

could span from £20,000 to £28,000. Pay ranges are also described as a percentage of the mid-point; for example, the range could be expressed as 80 to 120 per cent, where the mid-point is £25,000 and the minimum and maximum are £20,000 and £30,000 respectively. A reference point or target rate is defined in each grade which is the rate for a fully competent individual who is completely qualified to carry out the job. It is usually aligned to market rates in accordance with company policies on the relationship between its pay levels and market rates for similar jobs (its 'market stance'). The reference point is commonly the mid-point of the pay range for a grade. It may be called a target rate when it is regarded as the consolidated rate for a fully competent and experienced job holder above which awards for special achievement in the role are paid in the form of non-consolidated cash bonuses (this approach is becoming increasingly common in public sector organizations).

The pay ranges provide scope for pay progression which is usually related to performance, competence or contribution (in a narrow-graded pay spine, progression is through fixed increments based on length of service in the job). Differentials between pay ranges are typically around 20 per cent and there is usually an overlap between ranges, which can be as high as 50 per cent. This overlap provides more flexibility to recognize that a highly experienced individual at the top of a range may be contributing more than someone who is still in the learning curve portion of the next higher grade.

What are sometimes called 'mid-point management' techniques analyse and control pay policies by comparing actual pay with the reference point which is regarded as the policy pay level. 'Compa-ratios' can be used to measure the relationship between actual and policy rates of pay as a percentage. If the two coincide, the compa-ratio is 100 per cent. Compa-ratio analysis can be used to establish how pay practice (actual pay) compares with pay policy (the rate for a person who is fully qualified and competent in their job). This can be an analysis of the pay of all job holders which, for example, might indicate that if the compa-ratio is less than 100 per cent pay practice is falling behind pay policy and something might have be done to ensure that pay levels remain competitive. Compa-ratio analysis is also carried out for individuals, so that a compa-ratio of, say, 95 per cent shows that if the individual is fully competent an increase of 5 per cent is required to bring pay into line. Individual compa-ratio analysis is also used as a means of guiding contingent pay increases through a pay matrix as described in Chapter 17.

Advantages and disadvantages

Narrow-graded structures provide a framework for managing relativities and for ensuring that jobs of equal value are paid equally. In theory they are easy to manage because the large number of grades enables fine distinctions to be made between different levels of responsibility. They define career ladders and staff may favour them because they appear to offer plenty of opportunities for increasing pay by upgrading.

The main problem with narrow, multi-graded structures is that if there are too many grades, there will be constant pressure for upgrading, leading to grade drift (unjustified upgradings). They can represent an extended hierarchy which may no longer exist in a de-layered organization, and can function rigidly which is at odds with the requirement of flexibility in new team and process-based organizations. They also reinforce the importance of promotion as a means of progression which may run counter to the need for organizations to be more flexible and grow capability by moving people within grades to broaden their experience and capability.

BROAD-GRADED STRUCTURES

Broad-graded structures have six to nine grades rather than the ten or more grades contained in narrow-graded structures. The grades and pay ranges are defined and managed in the same way as narrow-graded structures except that the increased width of the grades means that organizations sometimes introduce mechanisms to control progression in the grade so that staff do not inevitably reach its upper pay limit. The mechanisms available consist of:

- *Reference point control* – scope is provided for progression according to competence by increments to the reference point. Thereafter, individuals may earn cash bonuses for high achievement which may be consolidated up to the maximum pay for the grade if high achievement levels are sustained.
- *Threshold control* – a point is defined in the pay range beyond which pay cannot increase unless individuals achieve a defined level of competence and achievement.
- *Segment or zone control* – an extension of threshold control which involves dividing the grade into, usually, three segments or zones.

All these mechanisms require the use of some form of contingent pay as described in Chapter 17.

Broad-graded structures are used to overcome or at least alleviate the grade drift problem endemic in multi-graded structures. If the grades are defined, it is easier to differentiate them, and matching (comparing role profiles with grade definitions or profiles to find the best fit) becomes more accurate. But it may be difficult to control progression and this would increase the costs of operating them, although these costs could be offset by better control of grade drift.

BROAD-BANDED STRUCTURES

Broad-banded structures compress multi-graded structures into four or five 'bands' as illustrated in Figure 15.2. The process of developing broad-banded structures is called 'broad-banding'.

Origin of the concept

The notion of broad-banding first crossed the Atlantic in the early 1990s, although it was referred to, briefly, by Michael Armstrong and Helen Murlis (2) in 1988. An article by Leblanc (3) in 1992 produced one of the earliest definitions of broad-banding – 'Fewer pay grades for all types of jobs and more horizontal (lateral) movement'. Broad-banding really came to the fore in the mid-1990s when Gilbert and Abosch (4) wrote about how it had been developed in General Electric in support of the Jack Welch philosophy of boundary-less (and de-layered) organizations. Since then it has burgeoned.

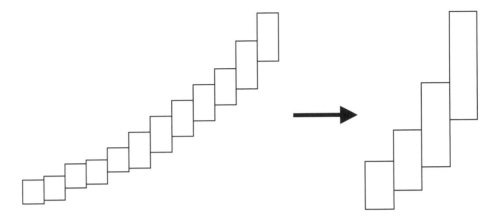

Figure 15.2 Narrow and broad-banded structures

The difference between a broad-graded structure and a broad-banded structure is important. It was originally made by Gilbert and Abosch in 1996. They referred to broad-grade structures with seven or eight grades in which a fairly conventional approach to pay management is often adopted using mid-point management, compa-ratio analysis and pay matrix techniques. They contrasted these with what they called 'career band' structures with four to five bands where the emphasis is on individual career development, flexible roles and competence growth.

The original concept of broad-banding

In its original version, a broad-banded structure contained no more than five bands, each with, typically, a span of 70 to 100 per cent. Bands were unstructured and pay was managed much more flexibly than in a conventional graded structure (no limits may be defined for progression) and much more attention was paid to market rates, which governed what were in effect the spot rates for jobs within bands. Progression in bands depended on competence and the assumption of wider role responsibilities. Bands were described verbally, not by reference to the results of analytical job evaluation. More authority was devolved to line managers to make pay decisions within a looser framework.

Armstrong and Brown (5) established that in organizations with broad bands, 62 per cent had bands with widths between 50 and 75 per cent, while the rest had bands with widths between 75 and 100 per cent. Typically, there were between four and six bands in such structures. The band boundaries were often, but not always, defined by job evaluation. Jobs were placed in the bands purely by reference to market rates or by a combination of job evaluation and market rate analysis. Bands were described by an overall description of the jobs allocated to them (senior management etc) or by reference to the generic roles they contained, for example technical support.

This concept was, and still is, beguiling. It satisfied the desire for more flexibility, and the research conducted by Armstrong and Brown (5) in 2001 established that this was by far the most important reason for introducing broad bands. It is achieved by catering for broader roles rather than tightly defined jobs, by adopting less rigid approaches to the allocation of roles to bands and how people progress within them, and by responding more quickly to market rate pressures. An aspect of flexibility which is seldom discussed in public is that when introducing broad bands the wider span of pay means that fewer anomalies are created and the cost of implementation is reduced.

Moreover, broad-banding was in accord with the drive for de-layering. The reduction in the number of grades meant that the pressure for upgrading was reduced, there was less likelihood of grade drift and it was thought that they would be easier to manage.

Further developments in the concept

The original notion of unstructured broad bands is now no longer general practice. It created expectations of the scope for progression which could not be met. Progression had to stop somewhere if costs were going to be controlled, and no rationale was available for deciding when and why to stop. Line managers felt adrift without adequate guidance and staff missed the structure they were used to. Questions were asked on the point of having broad bands at all when in effect all they consisted of was spot rates determined mainly by market relativities. Why, people asked, should organizations not be honest with themselves and their staff and revert to the complete freedom and therefore flexibility that spot rates provide?

Inevitably, therefore, structure crept in. It started with reference points aligned to market rates around which similar roles could be clustered. These were then extended into zones for individual jobs or groups of jobs as illustrated in Figure 15.3 which define the scope for pay progression around reference points. Reference points are frequently placed in zones so that they increasingly resemble conventional structure grades. The research conducted by Armstrong and Brown (5) established that 80 per cent of organizations had introduced some controls in the form of zones (43 per cent) and zones with reference points (37 per cent). Job evaluation was used not only to define the boundaries of the band but to size jobs as a basis for deciding where reference points should be placed in conjunction with market pricing. Progressively, therefore, the original concept of broad-banding was eroded as more structure was introduced and job evaluation became more prominent to define the structure and meet equal pay requirements. Zones within broad bands began to look very like conventional grades. An example of a broad-banded structure linked to job evaluation in a housing association is given in Figure 15.4.

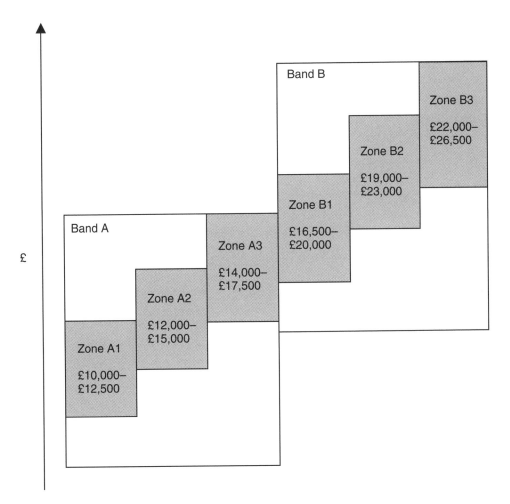

Figure 15.3 Zones in a broad-banded structure

Reservations about broad-banding

The two reservations that emerged from the experience of developing broad bands in the 1990s and early 2000s were: (1) What's the point of unstructured broad bands if they simply consist of spot rates? and (2) What's the difference between, say, a four-banded structure with three zones in each band and a twelve-graded structure? The answer given by broad-band devotees to the first question was that at least there was some overall structure within which spot rates could be managed. In reply to the second question, the usual answer was that as roles develop, movements between zones within bands could be dealt with more flexibly. Neither of these responses is particularly convincing.

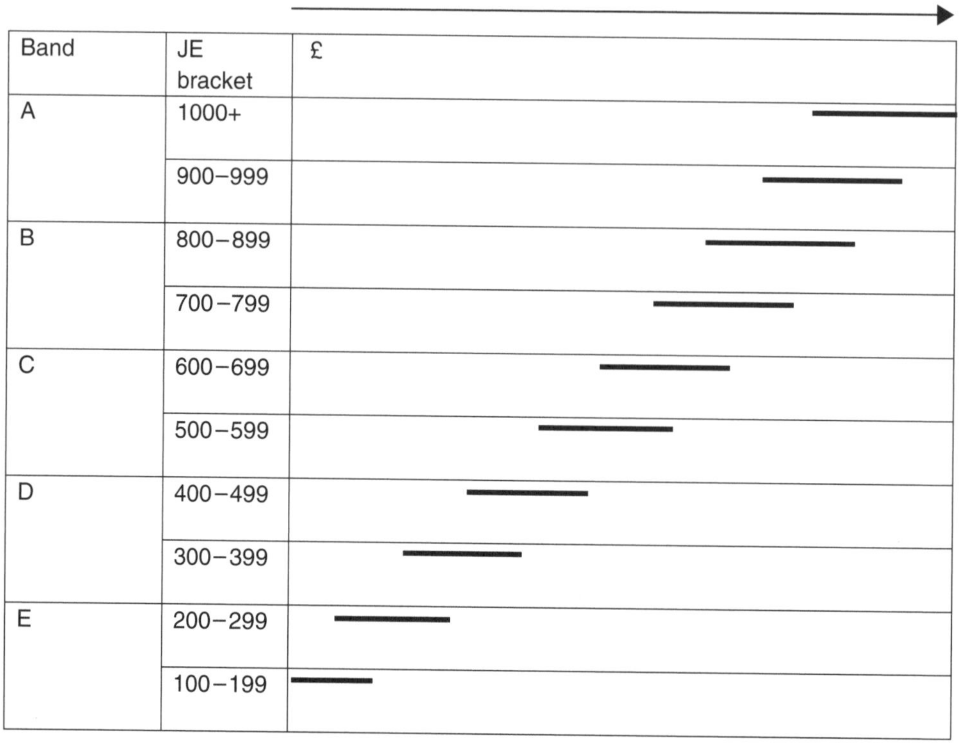

Figure 15.4 A broad-banded structure with zones defined by job evaluation score brackets

Objections to broad-banding

Apart from these fundamental reservations, there are a number of other objections to broad-banding. In general, it has been found that broad-banded structures are harder to manage than narrower-graded structures in spite of the original claim that they would be easier – they make considerable demands on line managers as well as HR. Broad-banding can build employee expectations of significant pay opportunities which are doomed in many cases if proper control of the system is maintained. It can be difficult to explain to people how broad-banding works and how they will be affected and they may be concerned by the apparent lack of structure and precision. Decisions on movements within bands can be harder to justify objectively than in other types of grade and pay structures.

Broad-banded structures may be more costly than more conventional structures because there is less control over pay progression. Research conducted by Charles Fay and others in the United States in 2000–1 (6) found that both wages and total cash compensation was significantly higher in the companies with broad-banded structures than in those with more conventional structures. They estimated that broad-banding increased pay roll costs by 7 per cent plus.

Another major objection to broad-banding is that it can create the following equal pay problems:

- Reliance on external relativities (market rates) to place jobs in bands can reproduce existing inequalities in the labour market.
- The broader pay ranges within bands mean that they include jobs of widely different values or sizes which may result in gender discrimination.
- Women may be assimilated at their present rates in the lower regions of bands and find it impossible, or at least very difficult, to catch up with their male colleagues who, because of their existing higher rates of pay, are assimilated in the upper reaches of bands.

Broad-banding in its original sense is therefore not the panacea it was once thought to be. More organizations are settling for a broad-graded structure with six to eight grades with the possibility of restricting the number to five but recognizing that they have to contain control mechanisms which might take the form of a series of zones.

Examples of broad-banded structures at GlaxoSmithKline, Norwich Union Insurance and Tesco are given in Chapter 30. The structure at Tesco has no zones.

The AEGON approach to broad-banding

Distinct roles within each career family at AEGON UK are analysed and placed into four broader pay bands. Each of the bands spans the pay opportunities covered by several separate grade and pay ranges in the old structure. The bands are described in general terms by reference to the type of roles allocated to them, as follows:

- Band A – operations delivery
- Band B – team leader and technical
- Band C – junior management, professional and senior technical
- Band D – management and senior professional.

The emphasis is on external relativities – market pricing is used to define target rates for roles in the band and to place jobs in the bands. But positioning people into bands and decisions on pay increases are still governed in part by internal equity considerations through comparisons between the pay of people with similar roles in job clusters or job families.

JOB-LEVEL STRUCTURES: THE COLT EXPERIENCE

Job-level structures have been introduced by firms such as Unilever and COLT Telecom as an alternative to broad-banded structures. The COLT Telecom structure was described by Vivian Leinster, Director of Compensation and Benefits (e-research report, no. 21, 2004), as follows.

Prior to early 2003 all employees were on spot salaries. In July 2003 senior managers were moved onto new pay levels, and everyone moved in 2004. Generally, an organization drawing up a new function-based structure and determining job levels would then seek to attach salaries to each level. But COLT did not want to set up the job families structure it saw as the conventional option in this case. Instead, it decided to map its nine job levels as set out in Appendix 4 of this book directly to the 15 Towers Perrin *Insite* survey points. This enables it to benchmark jobs by discipline and country directly to the survey. One of the advantages of going straight to the survey is that pay outcomes are perceived as fair. The fact that there are two *Insite* points for each job level provides managers with a broad pay range for each individual, within which they can be rewarded as appropriate for their knowledge, skills and performance.

Job levels were introduced as a way of:

- providing transparency in the organizational structure;
- providing an equitable reward framework for base pay, variable pay and long-term incentives;
- ensuring consistency and fairness across functions and countries;
- allowing cross-function and cross-country comparison;
- beginning to clarify career development and progression;
- supporting the *One COLT* culture and values of open and honest communication;
- aid internal and external benchmarking of remuneration.

Vivian Leinster says: 'COLT levels seek to aid succession planning and promotion; an advantage of having a formal job-level structure is that managers will be able to communicate how and when their teams can progress within COLT. As the levels are fairly broad, not all promotions or role changes will result in a level change. However, if your role changes or you move within the organization to a different department, the job level will be reviewed and adjusted as appropriate.'

CAREER FAMILY STRUCTURES

Career families consist of jobs in a function or occupation such as marketing, operations, finance, IT, HR, administration or support services which are related through the activities carried out and the basic knowledge and skills required, but in which the

Career families			
Operations	Administration	Finance	IT
Level 1	Level 1	Level 1	Level 1
Level 2	Level 2	Level 2	Level 2
Level 3	Level 3	Level 3	Level 3
Level 4	Level 4	Level 4	Level 4
Level 5	Level 5	Level 5	Level 5
Level 6	Level 6	Level 6	Level 6

Figure 15.5   A career family structure

levels of responsibility, knowledge, skill or competence needed differ. In a career family structure the different career families are identified and the successive levels in each family are defined by reference to the key activities carried out and the knowledge and skills or competences required to perform them effectively. They therefore define career paths – what people have to know and be able to do to advance their career within a family and to develop career opportunities in other families. Typically, career families have between six and eight levels as in broad-graded structures. Some families may have more levels than others.

In a career family structure as distinct from a job family structure there is a common grade and pay structure. Jobs in the same level in each career family are deemed to be the same size as assessed by job evaluation and the pay ranges in corresponding levels across the career families are the same. In effect, a career structure is a single graded structure in which each grade has been divided into families. The difference is that the level definitions in any one career family in a career family structure are specific to jobs in that family and therefore differ between families, while the grade definitions in a single graded structure are all the same. This is the essential characteristic of career family structures, which are as much about defining career progression routes as they are about defining a pay structure. A career family structure is illustrated in Figure 15.5.

Advantages and disadvantages

Career family structures provide the foundation for personal development planning by defining the knowledge, skills and competencies required at higher levels or in different functions and what needs to be learnt through experience, education or training. Level definitions in a family can be more accurate than in a conventional structure because they concentrate on roles within the family with common characteristics and do not attempt to cover wide and in some ways unconnected sets of skills across the whole organization. Furthermore, the existence of a common grading system, when it is supported by job evaluation, facilitates the achievement of equal pay for work of equal value. Finally, by linking pay and grade management with career development it is in accordance with good practice human resource management in the shape of 'bundling' – the belief, supported by extensive research, that HR practices will be more effective if they are interrelated and therefore complement and reinforce one another.

But career structures can be more difficult to develop, explain and manage than single grade structures. A considerable amount of work is required to produce clear analytical level definitions which are properly graded and provide good career guidelines. A broad-graded structure, for example, is a simple and straightforward concept and splitting it into families may increase the complexity without providing commensurate benefits. Maintaining the accuracy of the level definitions also demands much care and attention. It is these problems that are perhaps the main reason why career structures have not yet caught on.

Furthermore, whatever emphasis is placed on career development between as well as within families, they could be perceived as being divisive and in conflict with the principle of identical treatment for all enshrined in a single grade structure. It may be inferred that progression can only take place in an occupational 'silo'. This has meant that career family approaches have been abandoned where the silos have been narrowly drawn and managed rigidly – the simpler they are the better.

The Xansa approach to career families (e-research report 2003)

Xansa is an international business process and IT services company with 3,500 employees in the UK and 5,000 worldwide. There are about 150 generic job titles covering everyone from receptionists to the board directors, which are positioned on a 'job map' in 7 broad bands and 14 career families. The bands reflect the accountability, complexity and influence in the nature of the work undertaken, while career families are groups of jobs with similar skills. For each job there is a generic job description which outlines the main purpose of the job, its key responsibilities and a skills profile which identifies the generic requirements of the job. There is also a competency framework which defines the attributes which contribute to high performance.

The career job families fall into four groups:

- *delivery* – design; build/integrate; run and support; management; business services; and training;
- *consultancy*;
- *business development* – general management; sales and strategic development; and client development;
- *professional support* – business support; finance; human resources; and marketing/communications.

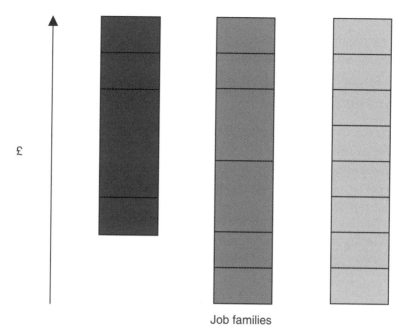

£

Job families

Figure 15.6 A job family structure

JOB FAMILY STRUCTURES

Job family structures, as illustrated in Figure 15.6, resemble career structures in that separate families are identified and levels of knowledge, skills and competency requirements defined for each level, thus indicating career paths and providing the basis for grading jobs by matching role profiles to level definitions. Like career families, job families may have different numbers of levels depending on the range of responsibility they cover.

The main difference between job family and career family structures is that each job family has in effect its own pay structure which takes account of different levels of market rates between families (this is sometimes called 'market grouping'). The level or grade structures may also differ to reflect the special characteristics of roles in the various families. In contrast, career family structures have common ranges of pay or job evaluation points for similar levels in different families. Because the size of jobs and rates of pay can vary between the same levels in different job families, there may be no read-across between them unless they are underpinned by job evaluation.

Another difference between career and job families is that the former usually cover distinct occupations or functions such as finance, IT and HR while the latter are typically based on common processes. Thus, while finance, IT and HR roles might be identified as separate in a career family structure, a job family structure might combine all these roles into a 'business support' family.

Advantages and disadvantages

Job family structures can help organizations to flex rates of pay for different occupations to reflect variations in market rates and therefore provide for competitive pay to attract and retain people with essential skills. They can also indicate career paths within and, to a certain extent, between families. Nationwide decided to opt for a system of job families as described in Chapter 30 because they:

- offer the flexibility to respond to occupational and labour market pressures, in contrast to more rigid systems where market rates may fall outside the grading structure;
- encourage flexible working practices and multiskilling;
- encourage people to move jobs and build up a broad base of skills in different areas while still remaining in the same job family, although there must be flexibility in the pay ranges to reward people for this;
- clarify routes to career progression;
- flatten the organizational structure, driving accountability down to the lowest possible level so that the person dealing with the customer is empowered to solve their problems.

But job family structures can result in unequal pay for work of equal value between job families. This can arise if jobs of the same size are paid differently when pay levels vary between families to cater for market rate pressures. Such variations may be difficult to justify objectively because the market pay differentials in job family structures are common to a whole family. In other structures, including career family structures, the alternative and preferable approach can be adopted of using market supplements, which are easier to justify on an individual basis. Pay inequities in job family structures can also arise because of read-across difficulties when trying to assess the relative size of jobs is different families. In theory this problem can be solved by the use of job evaluation but in practice this is difficult when there are considerable differences in the structure and definition of family levels.

In addition, like career family structures, job families can be more difficult to develop, explain and manage than single grade structures.

Broad-graded job family structure at Friends Provident

The following are the seven elements of a job family structure developed at Friends Provident (e-research report no. 21, 2004):

- five broad career bands for non-management staff, to replace the nine previous grades, with generic skills and competency levels established to describe the broad requirements for each band; three additional bands cover everyone below executive director;
- 18 job families, with a small number of generic role profiles, based on key skills and competency levels, in each of the five career bands;
- job family salary ranges for each career band;
- an annual salary review, with individual reviews analysed by a range of criteria, such as gender, to help ensure fairness and equity across the company;
- regional salary ranges, to reflect the influence of regional pay where appropriate;
- performance management;
- a discretionary non-consolidated performance bonus.

PAY SPINES

Pay spines are found in the public sector or in agencies and charities which have adopted a public sector approach to reward management. They consist of a series of incremental 'pay points' extending from the lowest- to the highest-paid jobs covered by the structure. Typically, pay spine increments are between 2.5 and 3 per cent. They may be standardized from the top to the bottom of the spine, or the increments may vary at different levels, sometimes widening towards the top. Job grades are aligned to the pay spine and the pay ranges for the grades are defined by the relevant scale of pay points. The width of grades can vary and job families may have different pay spines. Progression through a grade is based on service, although an increasing number of organizations provide scope for accelerating increments or providing additional increments above the top of the scale for the grade to reward merit.

Advantages and disadvantages

The advantages of pay spines are first that they just about manage themselves. Either no decisions on pay progression have to be made by management and line managers, or decisions on additional increments, if they are provided for, are made within an explicit framework. Secondly, because the need for managers to make possibly biased or inconsistent judgements on pay increases does not exist or is severely limited, they give the impression of being fairer than structures where progression is governed by managerial decisions on performance or contribution. For this reason they are favoured by trade unions and many managements in the public sector.

The disadvantages are that: (1) relating pay almost entirely to service means that people are rewarded for 'being there' and not for the value of their contribution, (2) pay spines can be costly in organizations with low staff turnover where everyone drifts to the top of the scale, and (3) where there are a large number of incremental points in the scale, equal value complications can arise as men progress to the top while the progress of women is delayed because of career breaks. For this reason the Local Government Pay Commission in 2003 recommended a move away from service-related increments to pay for contribution, restricting increments to the first few years in a job.

SPOT RATES

Some organizations do not have a graded structure at all for any jobs or for certain jobs such as directors. Instead they use 'spot rates'. They may also be called the 'rate for the job', more typically for manual jobs where there is a defined skilled or semi-skilled market rate which may be negotiated with a trade union. Spot rates are quite often used in retail firms such as B&Q for customer service staff (see Chapter 30).

Spot rates are sometimes attached to a person rather than a job. Unless they are negotiated, rates of pay and therefore relativities are governed by market rates and managerial judgement. Spot rates are not located within grades and there is no defined scope for progression while on the spot rate. There may, however, be scope for moving on to higher spot rates as skill, competence or contribution increases, as at B&Q (see Chapter 30). Job holders may be eligible for incentive bonuses on top of the spot rate.

Spot rates may be used where there is a very simple hierarchy of jobs as in some manufacturing and retailing companies. They may be adopted by organizations that want the maximum amount of scope to pay what they like. They often exist in small or start-up organizations which do not want to be constrained by a formal grade structure and prefer to retain the maximum amount of flexibility. But they can result in serious inequities which may be difficult to justify.

INDIVIDUAL JOB GRADES

Individual job grades are, in effect, spot rates to which a defined pay range of, say, 20 per cent on either side of the rate has been attached to provide scope for pay progression based on performance, competence or contribution. Again, the mid-point of the range is fixed by reference to job evaluation and market rate comparisons.

Individual grades are attached to jobs, not persons, but there may be more flexibility for movement between grades than in a conventional grade structure. This can arise when people have expanded their role and it is considered that this growth in the level of responsibility needs to be recognized without having to upgrade the job. Individual job grades may be restricted to certain jobs, for example more senior managers where flexibility in fixing and increasing rates of pay is felt to be desirable. They provide for greater flexibility than more conventional structures but can be difficult to manage and justify and can result in pay inequities. As described earlier in this chapter, the 'zones' that are often established in broad-banded structures have some of the characteristics of individual job grades.

REFERENCES

1   e-research (2004) *Survey of Grade and Pay Structures*, e-reward.co.uk Ltd, Stockport, Cheshire

2   Armstrong, M and Murlis, H (1988) *Reward Management*, 1st edn, Kogan Page, London

3   Leblanc, P V (1992) Banding – the new pay structure for the transformed organization, *Journal of Compensation and Benefits*, January–February, pp 34–8

4   Gilbert, D and Abosch, K S (1996) *Improving Organizational Effectiveness Through Broad-banding*, American Compensation Association, Scottsdale, AZ

5   Armstrong, M and Brown, D (2001) *New Dimensions in Pay Management*, CIPD, London

6   Fay, C H, Schulz, E, Gross, S E and Van De Voort, D (2004) Broadbanding, pay ranges and labour costs: an empirical test, *WorldatWork Journal*, **13** (2), second quarter

16

Grade and pay structures: design and implementation

This chapter is concerned with the overall principles, approaches, options and guidelines for the design of grade and pay structures and, in more detail, how these principles and guidelines can be applied to the design of the different types of grade and pay structures. The focus is on the design of graded, broad-banded and career or job family structures. Because the approach to developing narrow- and broad-graded structures is the same, even if the result in terms of the number of grades is different, these two types of structure are considered together. The chapter also examines the process of implementing new or radically changed structures with particular reference to assimilation and protection issues.

GUIDING PRINCIPLES FOR GRADE AND PAY STRUCTURES

Grade and pay structures should:

- be appropriate to the culture, characteristics and needs of the organization and its employees;
- facilitate the management of relativities and the achievement of equity, fairness, consistency and transparency in managing gradings and pay;

- be capable of adapting to pressures arising from market rate changes and skill shortages;
- facilitate operational flexibility and continuous development;
- provide scope as required for rewarding performance, contribution and increases in skill and competence;
- clarify reward, lateral development and career opportunities;
- be constructed logically and clearly so that the basis upon which they operate can readily be communicated to employees;
- enable the organization to exercise control over the implementation of pay policies and budgets.

APPROACH TO DESIGN

The design process should be governed by the guiding principles. Initially, the present existing arrangements should be reviewed. This is to establish the extent to which these fit the changing requirements of the organization, to check on how far the guiding principles are satisfied, and to identify any specific problems that need to be dealt with. The ten most common problems are:

1. Too many grades causing grade drift.
2. Lack of precision in grade definitions.
3. Inconsistent and poorly justified decisions on grading.
4. Too many anomalies (over-graded or under-graded jobs).
5. Equal pay for work of equal value is not provided for adequately.
6. The structure no longer fits the way in which work is organized.
7. A satisfactory basis is not provided for rewarding contribution.
8. The structure does not help with the management of relativities.
9. Pay levels are not sufficiently aligned to market rates.
10. Career paths are not clarified by the structure.

If it is decided that the changing requirements of the organization or the problems of the existing arrangements mean that a new or substantially changed structure is required then decisions should be made on communications and involvement policies. These decisions will be concerned with how employees will participate in the design process and the communications strategy required to inform them of what is happening and why. The importance of involvement and communications cannot be overestimated and these aspects of the development of reward processes are considered specifically in Chapter 29.

The next step is to consider the options concerning the type of structure and its design. The different types of structures and their advantages and disadvantages are

Table 16.1 Summary description of different grade and pay structures

Type of structure	Features	Advantages	Disadvantages
Narrow-graded	• A sequence of job grades – 10 or more	• Clearly indicate pay relativities	• Create hierarchical rigidity
	• Narrow pay ranges, eg 20–40%	• Facilitate control	• Prone to grade drift
	• Progression usually linked to performance	• Easy to understand	• Inappropriate in a de-layered organization
Broad-graded	• A sequence of between 6 and 9 grades	As for narrow-graded structures but in addition:	• Too much scope for pay progression
	• Fairly broad pay ranges, eg 40–50%	• the broader grades can be defined more clearly	• Control mechanisms can be provided but they can be difficult to manage
	• Progression linked to contribution and may be controlled by thresholds or zones	• better control can be exercised over grade drift	• May be costly
Broad-banded	• A series of, often, 5 or 6 'broad' bands	• More flexible	• Create unrealistic expectations of scope for pay rises
	• Wide pay bands – typically between 50 and 80%	• Reward lateral development and growth in competence	• Seem to restrict scope for promotion
			• Difficult to understand
	• Progression linked to contribution and competence	• Fit new-style organizations	• Equal pay problems
Career family	• Career families identified and defined	• Clarify career paths within and between families	• Could be difficult to manage
	• Career paths defined for each family in terms of key activities and competence requirements	• Facilitate the achievement of equity between families and therefore equal pay	• May appear to be divisive if 'silos' emerge
	• Same grade and pay structure for each family	• Facilitate level definitions	
Job family	• Separate grade and pay structures for job families containing similar jobs	• Can appear to be divisive	• Facilitate pay differentiation between market groups
		• May inhibit lateral career development	

(Continued)

Table 16.1 *Continued*

Type of structure	Features	Advantages	Disadvantages
	● Progression linked to competence and/or contribution	● May be difficult to maintain internal equity between job families unless underpinned by job evaluation	● Define career paths against clear criteria
Pay spine	● A series of incremental pay points covering all jobs	● Easy to manage ● Pay progression not based on managerial judgement	● No scope for differentiating rewards according to performance
	● Grades may be superimposed	● Progression linked to service	● May be costly as staff drift up the spine

summarized in Table 16.1 and this is followed by an assessment of the criteria for choice of structure and a description of the design options.

Criteria for choice

The chosen structure should be the one that most closely fits the requirement of the organization. The considerations affecting this choice are described below.

Narrow-graded structure

A narrow-graded structure may be considered more appropriate when:

- the organization is large and bureaucratic with well defined and extended hierarchies;
- pay progression is expected to occur in small but relatively frequent steps;
- the culture is one in which much significance is attached to status as indicated by gradings;
- when some but not too much scope for pay progression is wanted.

Broad-graded structure

A broad-graded structure may be considered more appropriate when:

- it is believed that if there is a relatively limited number of grades it will be possible to define and therefore differentiate them more accurately as an aid to better precision when grading jobs;

- an existing narrow-graded structure is the main cause of grade drift;
- it is considered that pay progression through grades can be related to contribution and that it is possible to introduce effective control mechanisms.

Broad-banded structure

A broad-banded structure may be considered more appropriate when:

- greater flexibility in pay determination and management is required;
- it is believed that job evaluation should no longer drive grading decisions;
- the focus is on rewarding people for lateral development;
- the organization has been de-layered.

Career family structure

A career family structure may be considered more appropriate when:

- there are distinct families and different career paths within and between families can be identified and defined;
- there is a strong emphasis on career development in the organization;
- robust methods of defining competencies exist.

Job family structure

A job family structure may be considered more appropriate when:

- there are distinct market groups that need to be rewarded differently;
- the range of responsibility and the basis upon which levels exist vary between families;
- it is believed that career paths need to be defined in terms of competence requirements.

Pay spine

A pay spine may be considered more appropriate when:

- this is the traditional approach in a public or voluntary sector organization and it fits the culture;
- it is believed to be impossible to measure different levels of contribution fairly and consistently;
- ease of administration is an important consideration.

Design options

Whichever structure is selected, there will be a number of design options. These comprise the number of grades, bands or levels, the width of the grades and pay ranges, the differentials between grades, the degree to which there should be overlap between grades, if any, and the method of pay progression within grades. In broad-banded structures there is also choice on the infrastructure (the use of reference points or zones), and in career or job family structures there are options concerning the number of families, the composition of families and the basis upon which levels should be defined.

Number of grades, levels or bands

The considerations to be taken into account when deciding on the number of grades levels or bands are:

- the range and types of roles to be covered by the structure;
- the range of pay and job evaluation points scores to be accommodated;
- the number of levels in the organizational hierarchy (this will be an important factor in a broad-banded structure);
- decisions on where grade boundaries should be placed following a job evaluation exercise which has produced a ranked order of jobs – this might identify the existence of clearly defined clusters of jobs at the various levels in the hierarchy between which there are significant differences in job size;
- the fact that within a given range of pay and responsibility, the greater the number of grades, the smaller their width and vice versa – this is associated with views on what is regarded as the desirable width of a range, taking into account the scope for progression, the size of increments in a pay spine and equal pay issues;
- the problem of 'grade drift' (unjustified upgradings in response to pressure, lack of promotion opportunities or because job evaluation has been applied laxly) which can be increased if there are too many narrow grades.

Width of grades

The factors affecting decisions on the width of grades or bands are:

- views on the scope that should be allowed for performance, contribution or career progression within grade;
- equal pay considerations – wide grades, especially extended incremental scales, are a major cause of pay gaps between men and women, simply because women, who are more likely to have career breaks than men, may not have the same

opportunity as men to progress to the upper regions of the range; male jobs may therefore cluster towards the top of the range while women's may cluster towards the bottom;

- decisions on the number of grades – the greater the number, the smaller the width;
- decisions on the value of increments in a pay spine – if it is believed, as in local government and as a result of the ACAS equal pay case, that the number of increments should be restricted, for equal pay or other reasons, but that the number of grades should also be limited, then it is necessary to increase the value of the increments;
- in a broad-banded structure, the range of market rates and job evaluation scores covering the jobs allocated to the band.

Differentials between pay ranges

Differentials between pay ranges should provide scope to recognize increases in job size between successive grades. If differentials are too close – less than 10 per cent – many jobs become borderline cases which can result in a proliferation of appeals and arguments about grading. Large differentials below senior management level of more than 25 per cent can create problems for marginal or borderline cases because of the amount at stake. Experience has shown that in most organizations with conventional grade structures a differential of between 16 and 20 per cent is appropriate except, perhaps, at the highest levels.

Pay range overlap

There is a choice on whether or not pay ranges should overlap and, if so, by how much. The amount of overlap, if any, is a function of range width and differentials. Large overlaps of more than 10 per cent can create equal pay problems where, as is quite common, men are clustered at the top of their grades and women are more likely to be found at the lower end.

Pay progression

There is a choice of methods of pay progression between the fixed service-related increments common in the public sector, and the other forms of contingent pay, namely performance, competence or contribution-related as described in Chapter 17.

The grade and pay structure design process

The design process will vary according to the type of structure and on the approach adopted to the use of job evaluation. The main variations are between the design of narrow- and broad-graded structures (dealt with together as the design process is similar), broad-banded structures or career or job family structures as described later.

An analytical job evaluation scheme is usually the basis for designing a graded structure and it can be used in the initial stages of designing a broad-banded or career/job family structure. In the case of graded structures, decisions on the number and width of grades are generally based on an analysis of the rank order of scores produced by job evaluation.

This approach is used less often in the design of broad-banded or career/job family structures where the most common method is to make a provisional advance decision on the number of bands or career family levels, and then position roles in bands (often by reference to market rates) or allocate roles into levels by a 'matching' process as described in Chapter 9. Job evaluation may only be used at a later stage to validate the positioning of roles in bands or the allocation of jobs to family levels, check on relativities and, sometimes, define the bands or levels in job evaluation score terms. The initial decision on the number of bands or levels and their definition may, however, be changed in the light of the outcome of the allocation, matching and evaluation processes.

More rarely, the grade and pay structure design is conducted by means of a non-analytical job classification exercise (see Chapter 9) which defines a number of single grades. Jobs are then slotted into the grades by reference to the grade definitions. The basic sequence of steps for designing a grade and pay structure is illustrated in the flow chart in Figure 16.1. Note the emphasis on communication and involvement at all stages.

GRADED PAY STRUCTURE DESIGN

The steps required to design a graded pay structure are defined in Figure 16.1. The particular considerations described below concern decisions on grading and pay ranges.

Grading decisions following a job evaluation exercise

Grading decisions can follow an analytical job evaluation exercise. This will produce a rank order of jobs according to their job evaluation scores either for all jobs or by job families. A decision then has to be made on where the boundaries which will define grades should be placed in the rank order. So far as possible, boundaries should divide groups or clusters of jobs which are significantly different in size so that all the jobs placed in a grade are clearly smaller than the jobs in the next higher grade and larger than the jobs placed in the next lower grade.

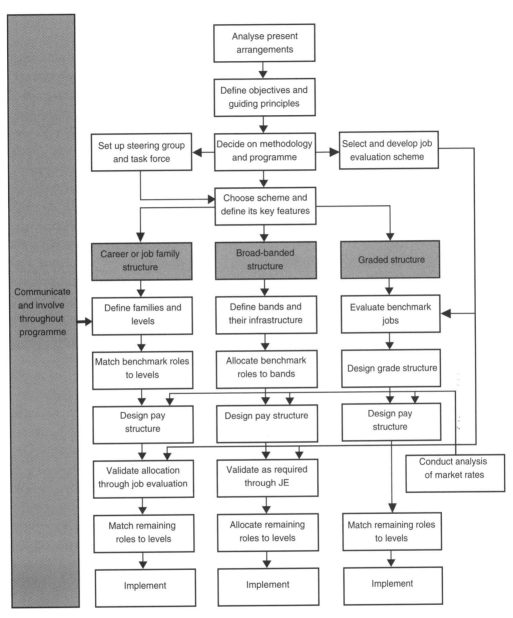

Figure 16.1 Flow chart: design of a new grade and pay structure

Fixing grade boundaries is one of the most critical aspects of grade structure design following an analytical job evaluation exercise. It requires judgement – the process is not scientific and it is rare to find a situation when there is one right and obvious answer. In theory, grade boundaries could be determined by deciding on the number of grades in advance and then dividing the rank order into equal parts. But this would mean drawing grade boundary lines arbitrarily and the result could be the separation of groups of jobs which should properly be placed in the same grade.

The best approach is to analyse the rank order to identify any significant gaps in the points scores between adjacent jobs. These natural breaks in points scores will then constitute the boundaries between clusters of jobs which can be allocated to adjacent grades. A distinct gap between the highest-rated job in one grade and the lowest-rated job in the grade above will help to justify the allocation of jobs between grades. It will therefore reduce boundary problems leading to dissatisfaction with gradings when the distinction is less well defined. Clear grade breaks appear more naturally when job evaluation scores are based on geometric progression than when progression is arithmetic. This is because a 'step difference' principle is implicit in the former.

Provisionally, it may be decided in advance when designing a conventional graded structure that a certain number of grades is required but the gap analysis will confirm the number of grades that is appropriate, taking into account the natural divisions between jobs in the rank order. However, the existence of a number of natural breaks cannot be guaranteed, which means that judgement has to be exercised as to where boundaries should be drawn when the scores between adjacent jobs are close.

In cases where there are no obvious natural breaks the guidelines that should be considered when deciding on boundaries are as follows:

● Jobs with common features as indicated by the job evaluation factors are grouped together so that a distinction can be made between the characteristics of the jobs in different grades – it should be possible to demonstrate that the jobs grouped into one grade resemble each other more than they resemble jobs placed in adjacent grades.
● The grade hierarchy should take account of the organizational hierarchy, ie jobs in which the job holder reports to a higher-level job holder should be placed in a lower grade, although this principle should not be followed slavishly when an organization is over-hierarchical with, perhaps, a series of one-over-one reporting relationships.
● The boundaries should not be placed between jobs mainly carried out by men and jobs mainly carried out by women.
● The boundaries should ideally not be placed immediately above jobs in which large numbers of people are employed.
● The grade width in terms of job evaluation points should represent a significant step in demands on job holders as indicated by the job evaluation scheme.

Organizations often form *a priori* views on the number of grades required to reflect how work is organized in hierarchies. A rigid application of the empirical approach described above may produce a grade structure that is unacceptable and the final decision may be a fudged one. To avoid this, grade structure design programmes may start with a provisional decision on the number of grades required and then determine grade boundaries that will produce the desired number of grades. But it is still necessary to follow the guidelines on fixing grade boundaries outlined above, paying particular attention to the need to avoid discrimination through the structure (the points to be considered on designing non-discriminatory grade structures are set out later in this chapter).

Pay range design

1. List the jobs placed within each grade on the basis of job evaluation (these might be limited to benchmark jobs that have been evaluated but there must be an adequate number of them if a proper basis for the design is to be provided).
2. Establish the actual rates of pay of the job holders.
3. For each grade set out the range of pay for job holders and calculate their average or median rate of pay (the pay practice point). It is helpful to plot this pay practice data as illustrated in Figure 16.2, which shows pay in each grade against job evaluation scores and includes a pay practice trend line.
4. Obtain information on the market rates for benchmark jobs where available. If possible, this should indicate the median rate and the upper and lower quartiles.
5. Agree policy on how the organization's pay levels should relate to market rates – its 'market stance'. This could be at the median, or above the median if it is believed that pay levels should be more competitive.
6. Calculate the average market rates for the benchmark jobs in each grade according to pay stance policy, eg the median rates. This produces the range market reference point.
7. Compare the practice and market reference points in each range and decide on the range reference point. This usually becomes the mid-point of the pay range for the grade and is regarded as the competitive rate for a fully competent job holder in that grade. This is a judgemental process which takes into account the difference between the practice and policy points, the perceived need to be more competitive if policy rates are higher, and the likely costs of increasing rates.
8. Examine the pay differentials between reference points in adjacent grades. These should provide scope to recognize increases in job size and, so far as possible, variations between differentials should be kept to a minimum. If differentials are too close – less than 10 per cent – many jobs become borderline cases which can result in a proliferation of appeals and arguments about grading. Large differentials below senior management level of more than 25 per cent can create problems for marginal or borderline cases because of the amount at stake. Experience has shown that in most organizations with conventional grade structures, a differential of between 15 and 20 per cent is appropriate except, perhaps, at the highest levels.

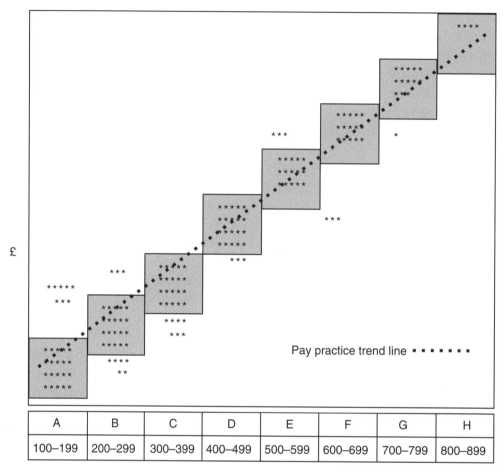

Figure 16.2 Scattergram of evaluations and pay

9. Decide on the range of pay around the reference point. This might be 20 per cent on either side of the reference point, thus if that point is 100 per cent, the range is from 80 per cent to 120 per cent. The range can, however, vary in accordance with policy on the scope for progression and if a given range of pay has to be covered by the structure, the fewer the grades the wider the ranges.

10. Decide on the extent, if any, to which pay ranges should overlap. Overlap recognizes that an experienced job holder at the top of a range may be making a greater contribution than an inexperienced job holder at the lower end of the range above. Large overlaps of more than 10 per cent can create equal pay problems where men are at the top of their grades and women are likely to be found at the lower end.

11. Review the impact of the above pay range decisions on the pay of existing staff in order to calculate implementation costs. Establish the number of staff whose present rate of pay is above or below the pay range for the grade into which their jobs have been placed and the extent of the difference between the rate of pay of those

below the minimum and the lowest point of that pay range. Calculate the costs of bringing them up to the minimum. Software such as the pay modellers produced by Link and Pilat or locally tailored Excel spreadsheets can be used for this purpose. Modelling alternative pay structures is considered in more detail later in this chapter.

12. When the above steps have been completed it may be necessary to review the decisions made on the grade structure and pay reference points and ranges. Iteration is almost always necessary to obtain a satisfactory result which conforms to the criteria for grade and pay structures mentioned earlier and minimizes the cost of pay.

BROAD-BANDED STRUCTURE DESIGN

The steps required to design a broad-banded structure are set out below.

1. Decide on objectives

The objectives of the structure should be set out in terms of what it is expected to achieve, for example increase flexibility in the provision of rewards, reflect organization structure, provide a better base for rewarding lateral development and growth in competence, replace an over-complex and inappropriate grade and pay structure.

2. Decide on number of bands

The decision on the number of bands will be based on an analysis of the existing organization structure and hierarchy of jobs. The aim is to identify the value-adding tiers that exist in the business. An initial assessment can be made, for example that there are six tiers comprising: (1) senior managers, (2) middle managers, (3) first-line managers and senior specialists, (4) team leaders and specialists, (5) senior administrators and support staff, (6) administrators and support staff. This structure should be regarded as provisional at this stage – it could be changed after the more detailed work in the next two stages.

3. Decide on band infrastructure

A decision has to be made at this stage on the use of reference points and zones. If reference points are to be used, which is most often the case, the method of determining where they should be placed in bands (by market pricing, job evaluation or both) should be decided. If zones are to be used, decisions need to be made on the width of the zones and the basis upon which people should progress within and between zones. The scope for flexibility in creating special reference points and zones for individuals should also be considered.

4. Define the bands

Broad initial definitions are now made of each of the bands. For example, a band for senior administrators and support staff could be defined as:

Key activities

- Provide a range of fairly complex administrative or higher-level support services.
- May have responsibility for a small section or sub-section of work.
- May prepare non-standard documentation.
- May deal with non-routine queries.
- Take action to deliver improved performance.

Performance requirements

- Plan and prioritize own day-to-day activities in order to achieve performance objectives.
- Work under general supervision.

Relationships

- Maintain helpful and supportive relationships with colleagues in own and other areas and with internal and external customers.
- Take a leadership role within team when appropriate.

Communications

- Communicate orally or in writing internally and externally on non-routine matters.

People management

- May act as instructor or mentor to more junior staff.
- May allocate work to members of section or sub-section.

---

5. Prepare role profiles for benchmark jobs

Identify benchmark jobs which are representative of different functions at the levels covered by the structure and for which market price data can probably be obtained.

They should include as many of the key generic roles as possible. Role profiles for each of them are then prepared. The profiles should provide sufficient information to enable them to be matched with the band definitions and, ideally, for market comparisons.

6. Match the benchmark roles to the bands

The matching process should provisionally allocate each benchmark role to a band. It is best carried out by a team consisting of line managers and employee representatives facilitated by HR or an outside consultant. This initial matching may indicate that the bands need to be redefined.

7. Obtain market prices

Conduct surveys and/or access pay information databases to establish the market rates of the benchmark roles.

8. Evaluate benchmark roles

Use an analytical job evaluation method to evaluate the benchmark roles.

9. Decide on reference points

Assuming a decision has been made to have reference points and zones, decide on the reference points for the benchmark roles, taking into account market rates and internal relativities as determined by job evaluation. This is a judgemental process because it means striking a balance between the two criteria. The weight given to either criterion will be a policy matter depending on the extent to which pay is market driven and the extent to which it is believed that internal equity is important.

10. Decide on zones

Assuming a decision has been made to use zones, these should now be attached to the reference points for the benchmark roles in accordance with the policy determined at stage 3.

11. Define pay ranges of bands

This is usually done empirically by reference to the earlier decisions on reference points and zones – the range of pay for a band will be the range of pay from the bottom of the lowest zone in the band to the top of the highest zone.

12. Define bands in terms of job evaluation scores

If the benchmark roles have been evaluated, this will indicate the bracket of job evaluation scores that can be used to define each band, which might provide a guide to allocating non-benchmark or new roles to bands.

13. Allocate non-benchmark roles to bands

In theory the remaining non-benchmark jobs could be allocated to bands on the basis of job evaluation, but in practice, most organizations match role profiles for such jobs (which are often generic) with the profiles of the benchmark jobs. This is more likely to work well if a reasonably representative range of benchmark jobs have been used and if there is well-developed management capability to work on this process and deal with its implications.

14. Communicate outcomes

Staff should have been involved and kept informed of the progress of the design process throughout the exercise but in this final stage the way in which broad-banding works and how it will affect them must be explained in detail.

CAREER FAMILY STRUCTURE DESIGN

The steps required to design a career family structure are described below.

1. Make strategic decisions

- Reason for developing career family structure.
- How the structure would meet business needs.
- How the structure would fit with other aspects of HR and reward strategy.
- Initial views on number of families, number of levels, use of job evaluation, scope for contribution pay and market rate relativities.
- Communications strategy – it is important to keep people informed of the purpose of the programme, the proposed arrangements and how they will be affected throughout the programme.
- Involvement strategy – line managers, staff and trade union representatives. This may include setting up a steering group and a joint task force.
- Project direction and management – steering committee, project team, project management arrangements, resources and help required, programme, likely costs of implementation.

2. Identify all distinct roles

The roles that will be covered by the structure should be listed. This is the preliminary step to the division of roles into career families, the selection of benchmark roles and the identification of generic roles.

3. Select and define career families

Decide on what career families are required. Typically, not more than four or five families are identified. The choice of families is between functions, for example marketing, finance, or activities, for example administration, support staff, or a combination of functions and activities.

4. Select/design analytical job evaluation scheme

- This could be an existing scheme if it is satisfactory, a proprietary brand or a specially designed (custom built) scheme.
- Remember that a custom-built scheme will take some time to develop and test, especially if it is computerized. The development programme could last 12 months or more and this will affect the timing of the rest of the structure design programme.
- The factor plan provides a framework for the level role profiles in the structure.

5. Decide on number of levels in career families and define them with level profiles

- Career family structures tend to have no more than seven or eight levels, which is appropriate in most organizations. Using more than eight levels can create difficulties in differentiating level definitions.
- Level definitions or profiles generally summarize the key activities or main tasks carried out at each level and the competence or knowledge and skill requirements. They should facilitate analytical role matching (step 14).
- It is best to relate level profiles to the factor definitions used in the job evaluation scheme as long as the latter cover competence and skill requirements. If not, competences will need to be covered specifically in the family level profiles.
- Level profiles can be derived from the analysis of benchmark roles as described for step 6.

6. Select and analyse generic or typical benchmark roles to produce role profiles

- If there is an existing job evaluation scheme, the selection of benchmark roles involves identifying already profiled and evaluated generic or typical roles representing each of the levels in all the career families. A generic role is one that is carried out by a number of role holders. A typical role is one that is significant enough to be included in the list. Additional roles may have to be identified if a fully representative sample is not available.

- If a new scheme is being introduced or developed, a representative number of generic or typical roles which can serve as benchmarks would similarly have to be identified.
- The number of benchmarks will depend on the number of families, the total number of levels and the range of roles in each family. Around three benchmarks are typically required for each level so that in a structure of four families with a total of 24 levels, 70 to 80 benchmarks will be needed.
- When developing a new scheme it is usually necessary to identify between 20 per cent and 30 per cent of the distinct generic or typical roles as benchmarks. At this stage of developing a career family structure, however, it might not be necessary to have so many. As long as each level is represented adequately, the initial analysis of benchmark roles may involve fewer roles than will be eventually required for the full development and testing programme.
- The generic benchmark role profiles will contribute to the definitions of the family level profiles.

7. Match benchmark role profiles to level profiles

- Matching benchmark role profiles with level profiles to establish the level at which a benchmark should be placed is best carried out analytically. This means making comparisons element by element in order to establish the best fit between a benchmark profile and a level profile.

8. Evaluate benchmark roles

- Assuming that there is an established scheme or a new scheme has been developed and tested, an evaluation of the benchmark roles used in defining the level profiles which have been matched to levels at stage 7 can now take place.

9. Validate allocation of benchmark roles to family levels

- The outcome of the evaluation provides the basis for validating the allocation of benchmark roles to levels.
- If inequities are revealed, some iteration may be required to resolve them.
- When validation has been completed it will be possible to define each career family level in terms of a range of job evaluation scores as indicated by the scores attached to the benchmark roles.

10. Check relativities between career families

- A check is carried out by reference to job evaluation scores of the allocation through matching across the career families to ensure that the relativities between them look reasonable.
- Some adjustment may need to be made as a result of this cross-check if it exposes inequities between families.

11. Analyse and match remaining generic and typical roles to levels

- The generic and typical roles are matched to career family levels. This may include additional generic roles not covered in the original sample.

12. Analyse and evaluate atypical roles

- It may be possible to match some non-generic but typical roles from existing role analysis data. There may, however, be some atypical roles for which special role profiles will have to be developed. If necessary, these roles can be evaluated and allocated to family levels according to their score.

13. Conduct analysis of market rates

- An analysis of market rates for benchmark roles should also be conducted. This could be started at an earlier stage, eg when the benchmark roles have been identified to ensure that it is available as required. This analysis will contribute to the design of the pay structure (step 15).

14. Analyse current salaries by role and gender

- This analysis will inform the design of the pay structure.

15. Develop draft pay structure and pay progression arrangements

- The pay ranges for each level should be established by reference to the data assembled at steps 13 and 14.
- Initial decisions can be made on how pay will be progressed within the structure.

16. Model alternative pay structure and calculate cost of implementation

- The cost implications of the draft pay structure should be calculated by modelling the impact of the structure in terms of the amount it would cost to bring the pay of individuals whose existing rate is below the minimum for their new grade up to the minimum for that grade.

● Alternative structures can be modelled and by a process of iteration the cost of the structure can be optimized.

17. Define final grade and pay structure

● After optimization has taken place the final structure can be defined and preparations made for implementation.
● Final decisions can be made on how pay will be progressed within the structure.

18. Develop assimilation rules and assimilate to structure

● The assimilation rules will indicate where individuals should be placed within the new structure. Normal practice is that they are assimilated at their existing rate but in some cases this could mean that they are overpaid in relation to their new pay range and would therefore have to be 'red-circled' and dealt with under the protection policy. In other cases they may be underpaid and they are therefore green-circled with the understanding that their pay will be brought to their new minimum.

19. Formulate implementation policies

● Prior to implementation, agreement will have to be reached on policies for the protection of the pay of those who have been red-circled and on how the pay of those who have been green-circled should be increased to the minimum for their new range.

20. Implementation

● Implementation will take place in accordance with the assimilation and protection policies.
● The impact on individuals will need to be explained carefully. However, the communications that should have been made earlier on the new structure and the organization's pay policies should have prepared individuals for what is going to happen.

JOB FAMILY STRUCTURE DESIGN

The process of designing job family structures is essentially the same as that used for career family structures. The differences are that, because individual families may have their own pay and level structure, the analysis of market rates and the organization of work in families will have a stronger influence on the design.

GRADE STRUCTURE DESIGN BASED UPON JOB CLASSIFICATION

The non-analytical job classification method of job evaluation as described in Chapter 9 starts with a definition of the number and characteristics of the grades into which jobs will be placed. These *a priori* decisions are made without reference to job evaluation scores, as is sometimes the case when designing other types of structures. There are therefore no problems in defining grade boundaries, as can occur when the structure is derived from the rank order produced by an analytical evaluation exercise.

When the grade definitions have been produced, jobs are slotted into the grades. This should ideally be carried out by means of a matching process which is analytical to the degree that it specifically compares the characteristics of whole jobs with the characteristics set out in the grade definitions.

Job classification is the simplest method of grade design but when there is no analytical base, grading decisions may be arbitrary and inequitable. They may also change over time as different people become involved in the process who may not share the understanding or the values of the original team that worked on the project. Most importantly, no reliable defence will be available in the event of an equal pay claim. The solution to these problems adopted by some organizations is to use an analytical point-factor scheme to validate the gradings and check on internal equity.

DESIGNING NON-DISCRIMINATORY PAY STRUCTURES

To design a non-discriminatory pay structure it is necessary to ensure that:

- great care is taken over grade boundary decisions – the aim should be to avoid placing them between jobs which have been evaluated as virtually indistinguishable, bearing in mind that the problem will be most acute if grade boundaries are placed between traditionally male and female jobs (in any situation where such boundary problems exist it is good practice to re-evaluate the jobs, possibly using a direct 'comparable worth' or equal value approach which concentrates on the particular jobs);
- 'read-across' mechanisms exist between different job families and occupational groups if they are not all covered by the same plan;
- market rate comparisons are treated with caution to ensure that differentials arising from market forces can be objectively justified;

- care is taken over the implementation of the pay structure to ensure that female employees (indeed, any employees) are not disadvantaged by the methods used to adjust their pay following re-grading;
- a non-discriminatory analytical job evaluation system is used to define grade boundaries and grade jobs;
- discriminatory job descriptions are not used as a basis for designing and managing the structure;
- men's jobs or women's jobs do not cluster respectively at the higher and lower levels in the grade of the hierarchy;
- any variation between pay levels for men and women in similarly evaluated jobs (for example, for market rate reasons) can be objectively justified;
- red-circling is free of sex bias;
- there are objectively justifiable reasons for any inconsistency in the relation of the grading of jobs in the structure to job evaluation results.

IMPLEMENTING NEW GRADE AND PAY STRUCTURES

The implementation of new or revised grade and pay structures provides a change management challenge of considerable proportions. The scale of this challenge will be reduced if employees have a voice in its design. But it is essential to communicate the purpose and features of the new structure and how everyone will be affected. If, as is usual, the new structure follows a job evaluation programme, it is necessary to manage the expectations of staff. They should be informed that while no one will necessarily get extra pay, no one will lose. This means that assimilation and protection policies should be discussed and agreed prior to implementation. It is also necessary to ensure that training is provided for everyone concerned in administering reward.

Above all, it is important to think about how implementation is to take place and plan each aspect carefully. As Armstrong and Brown (1) comment:

> Perhaps the worst thing you can do if you are in a situation where you think your pay structures need to be redesigned is to start with the solution and to rapidly implement it. Yes, in these fast moving times, the HR function needs to be agile, responsive and results-oriented, as Ulrich (2) tells us. But in respect of such a sensitive and politically and emotionally charged issue as base pay management, this is not an area where you want to be acting first and then thinking, or perhaps regretting later.

A planned approach to managing implementation

It is essential to plan implementation. Approaches to change management and enlisting the understanding and support of stakeholders should be given close consideration at the project planning stage. It is essential to provide for both involvement and participation in the design and development programme. As suggested by Armstrong and Brown (1), the implementation steps are:

1. Decide at the planning stage the overall change/transition strategy and timing.
2. Model the transition into the new structure and develop policies to manage this transition. This means formulating assimilation and protection policies as explained later in this chapter.
3. Develop detailed operating responsibilities and guidelines for the new structure, including the procedures for grading or re-grading jobs and managing pay progression. The authority to make pay and grading decisions and methods of budgetary control should also be covered.
4. Negotiate the introduction of the new arrangements with staff representatives and trade unions. They should have been involved throughout the process, but here, the detailed 'nitty-gritty' of actual pay levels and assimilation policies and procedures need to be thrashed out.
5. Produce and distribute communications about the new structure – how it works, who will be involved in managing it and how people will be affected. It is now that the benefits of regularly involving and communicating with staff throughout the design and development programme will become apparent. Broad details of the proposed changes and the reasons for them should thereby be known already. The focus at the implementation stage can then be on the detailed designs and their individual impact. It is best to use line managers as the main communicators, helping them with relevant support (booklets, question and answer sheets, PowerPoint presentations etc) to get the key messages over to their staff. Information technology (the intranet) can be used to identify and address specific staff concerns.
6. Design and run training workshops for managers, and possibly all staff. In the case of broad-banded structures and some career/job family structures, managers are likely to have more freedom and discretion in positioning staff in bands or family levels and adjusting their pay. But they may well need more than an operating manual and entries on the intranet to help them manage this in an appropriate and fair manner. HR should be prepared to provide coaching to managers as well as more formal courses. They must make themselves available to give guidance, especially to the less committed or experienced managers. A cadre of line managers can be trained to coach their colleagues on managing pay in the new structure.
7. Run a pilot or simulation exercise, operating the new approach in parts of the organization, to test its workability and robustness. In one organization recently, for example, the new system was initially introduced in the IT Department, where the market pressures were greatest; this assisted in estimating the HR

support required for full rollout, and also indicated the emphasis required in the staff communication and 'branding' of the changes when full implementation occurred.

8. Full implementation and rollout. This will include giving every individual information on how the new structure affects them and on their right to ask for a review of their grading if they are dissatisfied.

Assimilation policy

The hard part of implementing arrives when the assimilation of staff to the new structure has to take place. It is necessary to have a policy on where staff will be assimilated to the new structure. This is usually at their existing salary or, in the case of a revised pay spine, on the nearest point in a new incremental scale above their existing salary. The following categories of staff should be covered by the assimilation policy.

Employees with current pay and pay potential both within the new pay range

In some ways this group is the easiest to deal with and the majority of staff will normally be included in it. The wider the grades the more likely that is to be the case. One point at issue is whether or not any increase should be awarded on transition and the answer should be 'no' except when, as mentioned above, the policy is to move each person's pay to the nearest higher pay point.

Good advance communications should have conveyed the fact that job evaluation and a new pay structure do not necessarily mean any increase in pay. But some people in this group may still feel disadvantaged at seeing others getting increases. This negative reaction can be decreased by introducing the new structure at the same time as any annual pay increase, so that everyone gets at least something.

It is necessary to be aware of the possibility of creating equal pay problems when assimilating staff to their new scale. For example, if two people with broadly equivalent experience and skills are on different current salaries and are assimilated into the same new grade but at those rates, it would appear that there is no equal pay problem – they are both on the same grade with the same grade and salary potential. But an equal value issue is only avoided if a lower-paid woman or man has the opportunity to catch up with the higher-paid man or woman within a reasonable period (say three or four years).

Employees whose current pay is within the new pay range but pay potential higher than new maximum

No immediate increase is necessary in this circumstance but employees should be told what will happen. If progression to the old maximum was based on service only, that is, automatic annual increases to the maximum, this guarantee will have to be retained and, contractually, it may be necessary to go on awarding increments to the maximum of the previous scale. However, once a person's pay passes the maximum for the grade as a result of service-related increases, this will then become a 'red-circle' situation and should be treated as such (see below).

If progression to the old maximum were not guaranteed, but was based on performance, competencies etc, then the new range maximum should normally be applied. Care will be needed to ensure that this does not adversely affect any specific category of employees, particularly female staff.

Employees whose current pay is below the minimum for the new grade

Both justice and equity demand that, if someone has now been identified as being underpaid, the situation should be rectified as quickly as possible. Correcting this situation, by raising the pay to the minimum of the new pay range, should normally be the first call on any money allocated to the assimilation process. Each case should, however, be taken on its merits. If someone has recently been appointed to a post and given a pay increase at that time, it may be appropriate to wait until that person has completed a probationary period before awarding another pay increase.

If the total cost of rectifying underpayments is more than the organization can afford, it may be necessary, however unpalatable, to phase the necessary increases, say one portion in the current year and the rest next year – it is undesirable to phase increases over a longer period unless the circumstances are exceptional. The simplest approach is to place a maximum on the increase that any one person may receive. This can be in absolute terms (for example, maximum of £2,000) or in percentage increase terms (for example, maximum of 20 per cent of current pay). Another alternative is to use an annual 'gap reduction' approach (for example, pay increase of 50 per cent of the difference between current pay and range minimum or £500, whichever is the greater).

Again, if any delay in rectifying underpayment situations is necessary and some staff have therefore to be 'green-circled', it must not disadvantage one staff group more than another. Most organizations introducing job evaluation for the first time (or replacing an outdated scheme) and using the outcome to devise a new pay structure will find that more women than men have to be green-circled. Failure to correct these would be a perpetuation of gender bias.

Employees whose current pay is above the maximum for the new grade

These situations, which lead to red-circling, are usually the most difficult to deal with. They normally include a high proportion of people (often male) who have been in their current job a long time and who have been able to benefit from a lax approach to pay management in the past. People can take very different attitudes about what should be done about these situations and, as a result, the most protracted of the implementation negotiations are often centred on 'how to handle the red circles' (protection policy).

At one end of the scale is the argument that these people are now known to be receiving more pay than the job is worth and that this should be stopped as soon as possible, especially if the organization needs that money to pay more to those people who have been (or are still) receiving less than they should. The opposite stance is that these people have become accustomed to a standard of living based on the pay that the organization has been willing to provide up to now and they should not suffer just because new standards are being applied. This is the principle that is usually adopted but there are different ways of applying it.

Any assimilation policy must set out how the 'red-circle' situations will be handled. The starting point is normally that no one should suffer a reduction in pay – it should be 'protected' or 'safeguarded'. Thereafter, it is a matter of how quickly pay can and should be brought in line. Approaches to protection are discussed below.

Protection policies

'Indefinite protection', that is, maintaining the difference between current pay and range maximum for as long as the employee remains in the job, is highly undesirable, first because it will create permanent anomalies, and second because, where there are a lot of men in this situation (which is often the case), it will perpetuate unacceptable gender gaps. The Equal Opportunities Commission in its *Good Practice Guide – Job Evaluation Schemes Free of Sex Bias* states that red-circling 'should not be used on such a scale that it amounts to sex discrimination'. And, as stated by the Equal Pay Task Force: 'The use of red or green circling which maintains a difference in pay between men and women over more than a phase-in period of time will be difficult to justify.'

Because of these considerations, the most common approach is now to provide for red-circled employees to receive any across-the-board (cost of living) increase awarded to staff generally for a protection period which is usually limited to three or four years. They will no longer be entitled to general increases after the time limit has been reached (that is, they will 'mark time') until their rate of pay falls within the new scale for their job. They will then be entitled to the same increases as any other staff in their grade up to the grade maximum. If a red-circled individual leaves the job, the scale of pay for the job reverts to the standard range as set up following job evaluation. Where there is an incremental pay structure it is usual to allow staff to continue to earn any increments to which they are entitled under existing arrangements up to the maximum of their present scale.

If there is no limit to the protection period, red-circled staff continue to be eligible for general increases for as long as they remain in their present job. They are then on what is sometimes called a 'personal to job holder' scale.

Throughout the protection period, and particularly at the start of it, every attempt should be made to resolve the 'red-circle' cases by other means. If job holders are thought to be worth the current salary, then they may well be underused in their existing job. Attempts should be made to resolve this by either increasing the job responsibilities so that the job will justify re-grading to a higher grade, or moving the person concerned to a higher-graded job as soon as an appropriate vacancy arises.

REFERENCES

1   Armstrong, M and Brown, D (2001) *New Dimensions in Pay Management*, CIPD, London
2   Ulrich, D (1998) A new mandate for human resources, *Harvard Business Review*, January–February, pp 124–34

Part V

Rewarding and reviewing contribution and performance

17

Individual contingent pay

Contingent pay is the standard term used to describe schemes for providing financial rewards which are related to individual performance, competence, contribution or skill, and this chapter focuses on such schemes. However, pay related to service is also in a sense contingent pay and is therefore considered separately towards the end of the chapter.

Contingent pay may be provided for teams, which is dealt with in Chapter 18. It also covers schemes rewarding people according to organizational performance (Chapter 19). Shop floor and sales force incentive schemes can be classified as contingent pay but, because of their special nature, they are examined specifically in Chapters 21 and 22 respectively.

This chapter deals with individual contingent pay under the following headings:

- contingent pay defined;
- the incidence of contingent pay;
- contingent pay as a motivator;
- arguments for and against contingent pay;
- alternatives to contingent pay;
- criteria for success;
- performance-related pay;
- competence-related pay;
- contribution-related pay;
- skill-based pay;

- service-related pay;
- choice of scheme;
- readiness for contribution pay;
- developing and implementing contingent pay.

INDIVIDUAL CONTINGENT PAY DEFINED

Individual contingent pay relates financial rewards to the performance, competence, contribution or skill of individual employees. It provides an answer to the two fundamental reward management questions: (1) What do we value? and (2) What are we prepared to pay for?

Contingent pay may be consolidated in base pay or provided in the form of cash lump-sum bonuses. The latter arrangement is called 'variable pay'. This is sometimes referred to as 'pay at risk' which has to be re-earned, as distinct from consolidated pay which is usually regarded as continuing as long as the person remains in the job and performs it satisfactorily.

Contingent pay schemes are based on processes for measuring or assessing performance, competence, contribution or skill. These may be expressed as ratings which are converted by means of a formula to a payment. Alternatively, there may be no formal ratings and pay decisions are based on broad assessments rather than a formula.

A distinction can be made between performance (what a person achieves) and contribution (the impact made by that person on the performance of the team and the organization). The level of contribution will depend on the competence, knowledge, skill and motivation of individuals, the opportunities they have to apply their knowledge and skills, and the use they make of the leadership, support and guidance they receive.

THE INCIDENCE OF CONTINGENT PAY

The CIPD 2004 survey of performance management (1) found that 42 per cent of the 566 respondents had some form of contingent pay.

The e-research 2004 survey of contingent pay (2) established that 189 schemes were used by the 100 respondents in the following proportions:

- performance-related pay – 65%;
- contribution-related pay – 33%;
- service-related pay – 15%;
- competence-related pay – 8%.

CONTINGENT PAY AS A MOTIVATOR

Many people see contingent pay as the best way to motivate people. But it is simplistic to assume that it is only the extrinsic motivators in the form of pay that create long-term motivation about financial rewards. The total reward concept, as explained in Chapter 2, emphasizes the importance of non-financial rewards as an integral part of a complete package. The intrinsic motivators which can arise from the work itself and the working environment may have a deeper and longer-lasting effect.

Incentives and rewards

When considering contingent pay as a motivator a distinction should be made between financial incentives and rewards.

Financial incentives are designed to provide direct motivation. They tell people how much money they will get in the future if they perform well – 'Do this and you will get that.' A shop floor payment-by-result scheme and a sales representative's commission system are examples of financial incentives.

Financial rewards act as indirect motivators because they provide a tangible means of recognizing achievements, as long as people expect that what they do in the future will produce something worth while. Rewards can be retrospective: 'You have achieved this, therefore we will pay you that.' But rewards can also be prospective: 'We will pay you more now because we believe you have reached a level of competence which will produce high levels of performance in the future.'

ARGUMENTS FOR AND AGAINST CONTINGENT PAY

Arguments for

The most powerful argument for contingent pay is that those who contribute more should be paid more. It is right and proper to recognize achievement with a financial and therefore tangible reward. This is preferable to paying people just for 'being there' as happens in a service-related system.

The e-research 2004 survey of contingent pay (2) found that, in order of importance, the following were the main reasons produced by the respondents for using contingent pay:

1. To recognize and reward better performance.
2. To attract and retain high quality people.
3. To improve organizational performance.
4. To focus attention on key results and values.

5. To deliver a message about the importance of performance.
6. To motivate people.
7. To influence behaviour.
8. To support cultural change.

Arguments against

The main arguments against contingent pay are that:

- the extent to which contingent pay schemes motivate is questionable – the amounts available for distribution are usually so small that they cannot act as an incentive;
- the requirements for success as set out below are exacting and difficult to achieve;
- money by itself it will not result in sustained motivation – as Kohn (3) points out, money rarely acts in a crude, behaviourist, Pavlov's dog manner;
- people react in widely different ways to any form of motivation – it cannot be assumed that money will motivate all people equally, yet that is the premise on which contribution pay schemes are based;
- financial rewards may possibly motivate those who receive them but they can de-motivate those that don't and the numbers who are de-motivated could be much higher than those who are motivated;
- contingent pay schemes can create more dissatisfaction than satisfaction if they are perceived to be unfair, inadequate or badly managed, and, as explained below, they can be difficult to manage well;
- contingent pay schemes depend on the existence of accurate and reliable methods of measuring performance, competence, contribution or skill, which might not exist:
- contingent pay decisions depend on the judgement of managers which, in the absence of reliable criteria, could be partial, prejudiced, inconsistent or ill-informed;
- the concept of contingent is based on the assumption that performance is completely under the control of individuals when, in fact, it is affected by the system in which they work;
- contingent pay, especially performance-related pay schemes, can militate against quality and teamwork.

Another powerful argument against contingent pay is that it has proved difficult to manage. Organizations, including the civil service, rushed into performance-related pay in the 1980s without really understanding how to make it work. Inevitably problems of implementation arose. Studies such as those conducted by Bowey (4), Kessler and Purcell (5), Marsden and Richardson (6) and Thompson (7) have all revealed these difficulties. Failures are usually rooted in implementation and operating processes, especially those concerned with performance management, the need for effective communication and involvement, and line management capability.

The last factor is crucial. The success of contingent pay rests largely in the hands of line managers. They have to believe in it as something that will help them as well as the organization. They must also be good at practising the crucial skills of agreeing targets, measuring performance fairly and consistently, and providing feedback to their staff on the outcome of performance management and its impact on pay. Line managers can make or break contingent pay schemes.

Vicky Wright (8) has summed it all up: 'Even the most ardent supporters of performance-related pay recognize that it is difficult to manage well' and Oliver (9) made the point that 'performance pay is beautiful in theory but difficult in practice'.

Conclusions

A comprehensive study by Brown and Armstrong (10) into the effectiveness of contingent pay, as revealed by a number of research projects, produced two overall conclusions: (1) contingent pay cannot be endorsed or rejected universally as a principle and (2) no type of contingent pay is universally successful or unsuccessful. They concluded their analysis of the research findings by stating that 'the research does show that the effectiveness of pay-for-performance schemes is highly context and situation-specific; and it has highlighted the practical problems which many companies have experienced with these schemes'.

ALTERNATIVES TO CONTINGENT PAY

The arguments against contribution pay set out above convince many people that it is unsatisfactory, but what is the alternative? One answer is to rely more on non-financial motivators. But it is still necessary to consider what should be done about pay. The reaction in the 1990s to the adverse criticisms of performance-related pay (PRP) was to develop the concept of competence-related pay, which fitted in well with the emphasis on competences (the competence industry). This approach, as described later, in theory overcame some of the cruder features of PRP but still created a number of practical difficulties and has never really taken off. In the late 1990s the idea of contribution-related pay emerged, as advocated by Brown and Armstrong (10). This combines the output-driven approach of PRP with the input (competence)-orientated approach of competence-related pay and has proved to be much more appealing than either performance- or competence-related pay.

However, many people still have reservations about this approach from the viewpoint of achieving the fair and consistent measurement of contribution. So what are the alternatives for them? Team pay is often advocated because it removes the individualistic aspect of PRP and accords with the belief in the importance of teamwork but, as explained in Chapter 18, although team pay is attractive, it is often difficult to apply and it still relies on performance measurement.

The traditional alternative is service-related pay, as described at the end of this chapter. This certainly treats everyone equally (and therefore appeals to trade unions) but pays people simply for being there and this could be regarded as inequitable in that rewards take no account of relative levels of contribution.

The other common alternative is a spot rate system where there is a single rate for the job and no defined scope for pay progression. Spot rates are often used for senior management and, at the other end of the hierarchy, for manual workers and sales representatives. They are sometimes adopted by start-up organizations and in smaller companies where pay is market driven and a matter for individual contracts rather than being determined by a company-wide system. Provision is usually made for payment by results in the form of cash bonuses (variable pay) or, for management, shares. Most people, however, want and expect a range of base pay progression, however that is determined, and spot rates are not much used in larger organizations apart from the exceptions noted above.

CRITERIA FOR SUCCESS

The following are the criteria for effective contingent pay:

1. Individuals should have a clear line of sight between what they do and what they will get for doing it. A line-of-sight model adapted from Lawler (11) is shown in Figure 17.1. The concept expresses the essence of expectancy theory: that motivation only takes place when people *expect* that their effort and contribution will be rewarded. The reward should be clearly and closely linked to accomplishment or effort – people know what they will get if they achieve defined and agreed targets or standards and can track their performance against them.
2. Rewards are worth having.
3. Fair and consistent means are available for measuring or assessing performance, competence, contribution or skill.
4. People must be able to influence their performance by changing their behaviour and developing their competences and skills.
5. The reward should follow as closely as possible the accomplishment that generated it.

These are ideal requirements and few schemes meet them in full. That is why contingent pay arrangements can often promise more than they deliver.

Figure 17.1   Line-of-sight model

PERFORMANCE-RELATED PAY

Methods of operating PRP vary considerably but its typical main features are summarized in Figure 17.2 and described below.

Basis of scheme

Pay increases are related to the achievement of agreed results defined as targets or outcomes.

Consolidated pay increases

Scope is provided for consolidated pay progression within pay brackets attached to grades or levels in a graded or career family structure or zones in a broad-banded structure. Such increases are permanent – they are seldom if ever withdrawn.

Cash bonuses (variable pay)

Alternatively or additionally, high levels of performance or special achievements may be rewarded by cash bonuses which are not consolidated and have to be re-earned. Individuals may be eligible for such bonuses when they have reached the top of the pay bracket for their grade, or when they are assessed as being fully competent, having completely progressed along their learning curve. The rate of pay for someone who reaches the required level of competence can be aligned to market rates according to the organization's pay policy.

Pay progression

The rate and limits of progression through the pay brackets are typically but not inevitably determined by performance ratings, which are often made at the time of

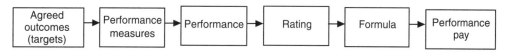

Figure 17.2   Performance-related pay

	Percentage pay increase according to performance rating and position in pay range (compa-ratio)			
	Position in pay range			
Rating	80–90%	91–100%	101–110%	111–120%
Excellent	12%	10%	8%	6%
Very effective	10%	8%	6%	4%
Effective	6%	4%	3%	0
Developing	4%	3%	0	0
Ineligible	0	0	0	0

Figure 17.3   PRP pay matrix

the performance management review but may be made separately in a special pay review. Some organizations do not base PRP increases on formal ratings and instead rely on a general assessment of how much the pay of individuals should increase by reference to performance, potential, the pay levels of their peers and their 'market worth' (the rate of pay it is believed they could earn elsewhere).

A formula in the shape of a pay matrix, as illustrated in Figure 17.3, is often used to decide on the size of increases. This indicates the percentage increase payable for different performance ratings according to the position of the individual's pay in the pay range. This is sometimes referred to as an individual 'compa-ratio' (short for comparison ratio) and expresses pay as a percentage of the mid-point in a range. A compa-ratio of 100 per cent means that the salary would be at the mid-point.

Pay progression in a graded structure is typically planned to decelerate through the grade, for two reasons. First, it is argued, in line with learning curve theory, that pay increases should be higher during the earlier period in a job when learning is at its highest rate. Second, it may be assumed that the central or reference point in a grade represents the market value of fully competent people. According to the pay policy of the organization this may be at or higher than the median. Especially in the latter case, it may be believed that employees should progress quite quickly to that level but, beyond it, they are already being paid well and their pay need not progress so rapidly. This notion may be reasonable but it can be difficult to explain to someone why they get smaller percentage increases when they are performing well at the upper end of their scale.

Amount of increases

The e-research 2004 survey (2) found that the average increase was 3.3 per cent.

Conclusions on PRP

PRP has all the advantages and disadvantages listed for contingent pay. Many people feel the latter outweigh the former. It has attracted a lot of adverse comment, primarily

Figure 17.4   Competence-related pay

because of the difficulties organizations have met in managing it. Contribution-related pay schemes are becoming much more popular.

COMPETENCE-RELATED PAY

The main features of competence-related pay schemes are illustrated in Figure 17.4 and described below.

Basis of scheme

People receive financial rewards in the shape of increases to their base pay by reference to the level of competence they demonstrate in carrying out their roles. It is a method of paying people for the ability to perform now and in the future.

Consolidated pay increases

As in the case of PRP, scope is provided for consolidated pay progression within pay brackets attached to grades or levels in a narrow-graded or career family structure or zones in a broad-banded structure (competence pay is often regarded as a feature of such structures).

Pay progression

The rate and limits of progression through the pay brackets can be based on ratings of competence using a PRP-type matrix, but they may be governed by more general assessments of competence development.

Conclusions on competence-related pay

Competence-related pay is attractive in theory because it can be part of an integrated competency-based approach to HRM. As Brown and Armstrong (10) comment: 'Increasingly, organizations are finding that success depends on a competent workforce. Paying for competence means that an organization is looking forward, not back.' Pay based on competence avoids the over-emphasis in PRP schemes on quantitative, and often unrealistic targets. It is attractive because it rewards people for what they are capable of doing, not for results over which they might have little control.

However, the idea of competence-related pay raises two questions. The fundamental question is 'What are we paying for?'. Are we are paying for competencies, that is, how people behave, or competences, that is, what people have to know and be able to do to perform well? If we are rewarding good behaviour (competencies) then a number of difficulties arise. It has been suggested by Sparrow (12) that these include the performance criteria on which competencies are based, the complex nature of what is being measured, the relevance of the results to the organization, and the problem of measurement. He concluded that 'we should avoid over-egging our ability to test, measure and reward competencies'.

Other fundamental objections to the behavioural approach have been raised by Ed Lawler (13). He expresses concern about schemes that pay for an individual's personality traits and emphasizes that such plans work best 'when they are tied to the ability of an individual to perform a particular task and when there are valid measures available of how well an individual can perform a task'. He also points out that 'generic competencies are not only hard to measure, they are not necessarily related to successful task performance in a particular work assignment or work role'.

This raises the second question: 'Are we paying for the possession of competence or the use of competence?' Clearly it must be the latter. But we can only assess the effective use of competence by reference to performance. The focus is therefore on results and if that is the case, competence-related pay begins to look suspiciously like performance-related pay. It can be said that the difference between the two in these circumstances is all 'smoke and mirrors'. Competence-related pay could be regarded as no more than a more acceptable name for PRP.

Competence-related pay sounds like a good idea but it has never been taken up to a great extent because of the problems mentioned above.

There may be a case for rewarding the possession of competence but an even stronger one for linking the reward to outcomes (performance) as well as inputs (competence). This is the basis of the notion of contribution-related pay, as described below, and provides the explanation for the growing popularity of that approach compared with the more rarefied notion of competence-related pay.

CONTRIBUTION-RELATED PAY

Contribution-related pay, as modelled in Figures 17.5 and 17.6, is a process for making pay decisions which are based on assessments of both the outcomes of the work carried out by individuals and the inputs in terms of levels of competence and

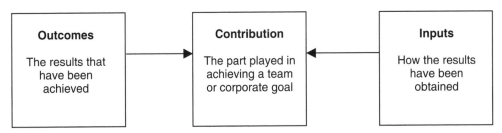

Figure 17.5 Contribution pay model (1)

competency which have influenced these outcomes. It focuses on what people in organizations are there to do, that is, to contribute by their skill and efforts to the achievement of the purpose of their organization or team.

Contribution-related pay is a holistic process, taking into account all aspects of a person's performance in accordance with the definition produced by Brumbach (14):

> Performance means both behaviours and results. Behaviours emanate from the performer and transform performance from abstraction to action. Not just the instruments for results, behaviours are also outcomes in their own right – the product of mental and physical effort applied to tasks – and can be judged apart from results.

The case for contribution-related pay was made by Brown and Armstrong (10) as follows:

> Contribution captures the full scope of what people do, the level of skill and competence they apply and the results they achieve, which all contribute to the organization achieving its long-term goals. Contribution pay works by applying the mixed model of performance management: assessing inputs and outputs and coming to a conclusion on the level of pay for people in their roles and their work; both to the organization and in the market; considering both past performance and their future potential.

Main features

The main features of contribution-related pay are illustrated in Figure 17.7.

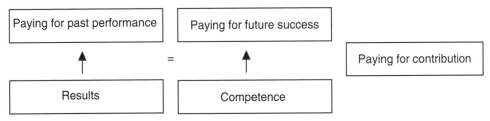

Figure 17.6 Contribution pay model (2)

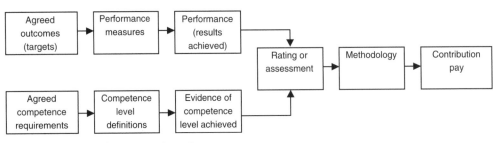

Figure 17.7 Contribution-related pay

An example of a pay for contribution scheme in a UK bank is shown in Figure 17.8. (The balanced scorecard is a set of performance measures which have to be taken equally into account when assessing overall performance.)

Basis of contribution pay

Contribution-related pay rewards people for both their performance (outcomes) and their competence (inputs).

Pay awards

Pay awards can be made as consolidated pay increases but in some schemes there is also scope for cash bonuses.

Methods of deciding contribution awards

There are six basic approaches as described below.

1. Matrix formula

Pay awards are governed by assessments of performance and competence and the amount is determined by a pay matrix such as the one illustrated in Figure 17.9.

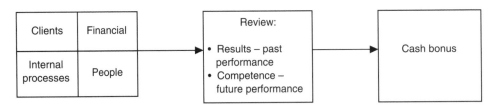

Figure 17.8 Paying for contribution in a UK bank

	Percentage pay increase according to performance rating and competence assessment		
	Competence assessment		
Performance rating	Developing – does not yet meet all competence standards	Fully competent – meets all competence standards	Highly competent – exceeds most competence standards
Exceptional	–	8%	10%
Very effective	–	6%	7%
Effective	–	4%	5%
Developing	3%	–	–
Ineligible	0	–	–

Figure 17.9   Contribution pay matrix

This approach is somewhat mechanistic.

2. Separate consolidated increases and bonuses

Output is the only factor that governs cash bonuses but it is treated as a subsidiary factor when considering base salary. In contrast, competence is used as the major component in determining salary.

3. Relate consolidated increases to competence up to a reference point

The main features of the scheme are:

● A 'reference point' rate of pay is determined within each grade, band or level which includes jobs of broadly equal size.
● The reference point is defined as the rate of pay for a person in a job who is highly competent, ie fully competent in all aspects of the job and therefore achieving high levels of performance.
● The reference point takes account of both internal relativities and market rates.
● The level of comparison for market rates is in accordance with the pay policy of the organization – this might be to set at above the median, eg at the upper quartile, to ensure that the high quality of staff required can be attracted and retained.
● The reference point is the maximum level of consolidated pay a high performer can expect to attain.
● A minimum level of pay for each grade is determined and progression to the reference point depends on achieving defined levels of competence – there may be three or four levels.

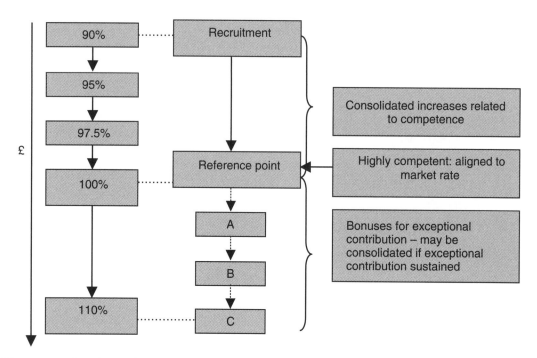

Figure 17.10 Contribution-related pay model

- There is scope to reward those who perform exceptionally well with a re-earnable cash bonus which could be consolidated if the level of exceptional performance is sustained over two to three years up to a maximum level defined for the grade.

This pay for contribution scheme is modelled in Figure 17.10.

4. Rewards as either consolidated increases or bonuses

In this approach, as illustrated in Figure 17.11, performers can earn a mix of base pay increase and bonus which varies according to their position in the pay range. However, all outstanding performers receive a payment of 10 per cent of their base pay. Line managers would therefore not have to pass on the difficult message to outstanding individuals who are high in their pay range that they would be getting a smaller increase in spite of their contribution (this would be the case in a scheme using a typical PRP matrix as illustrated in Figure 17.1). Here, the higher up the range individuals are, the greater the proportion of their increase which is payable as a bonus. So those high in the range who are assessed as outstanding get 8 per cent as bonus and 2 per cent addition to their base pay, while outstanding individuals low in their range and below their market rates would get an 8 per cent addition to their base pay and a 2 per cent bonus.

Position In range	High –expert	Bonus	0%	2%	3%	6%	8%
		Base pay	0%	1%	2%	2%	2%
	Mid-competent market rate	Bonus	0%	1%	2%	4%	6%
		Base pay	0%	2%	3%	4%	4%
	Low – learning	Bonus	0%	0%	0%	1%	2%
		Base pay	0%	3%	6%	7%	8%
			U	S	G	E	O

Competency assessment*

* O = outstanding, E = excellent, G = good, S = satisfactory, U = unsatisfactory

Figure 17.11 Contribution matrix for base pay increases and bonuses. (Source: adapted from Duncan Brown and Michael Armstrong (1999) *Paying for Contribution,* Kogan Page, London

5. Threshold payments

A threshold is built into the pay range, as illustrated in Figure 17.12 for an incremental payment scheme. To cross the threshold into a higher part of the range, individuals must meet contribution criteria which will define the level of competence required and indicate any performance (outcome) criteria that may be relevant.

Threshold systems are often associated with incremental scales, as in the NHS where they are called gateways. They may be particularly relevant where there are extended incremental scales and it is felt that progression needs to be controlled. They could be regarded as a halfway house to a full contribution pay scheme and, because they do not rely on a suspect formula and contain defined and transparent criteria, they may be more acceptable to staff and their trade unions. However, their effectiveness depends on the definition of clear and assessable criteria and the willingness of

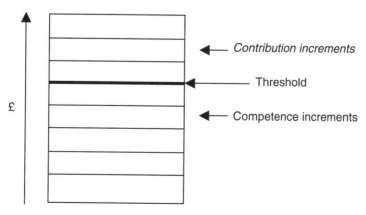

Figure 17.12 Contribution thresholds in a pay range

all those concerned to assess contribution on the basis of evidence about the extent to which individuals meet the criteria. Judgements are still involved and this depends on the ability of managers to exercise them fairly and consistently and to be prepared to make hard decisions on the basis of objective evidence which may mean that staff do not progress through the threshold. There is a real danger that if managers do not have the courage of their convictions, staff will more or less automatically progress through the thresholds, as happened in the time of 'merit bars', although the criteria for crossing those bars were seldom defined explicitly.

6. Holistic assessment

A holistic approach can be adopted to assessing the level of contribution and therefore possible awards in the shape of base pay increases or bonuses. This approach leads to a decision on the level of pay appropriate for an individual in relation to the comparative levels of contribution of their peers and their own market worth, which will include consideration of their potential and the need to retain them.

Consideration is given both to what individuals have contributed to the success of their team and to the level of competence they have achieved and deployed. Team members who are contributing at the expected level will be paid at or around the reference point for the grade or zone and this reference point will be aligned to market rates in accordance with the organization's market pay policies. If, in the judgement of the line manager, individuals are achieving this level of contribution but are paid below their peers at the reference point, the pay of the individuals would be brought up to the level of their peers or towards that level if it is felt that the increase should be phased. Individuals may be paid above the reference point if they are making a particularly strong contribution or if their market worth is higher.

The policy guideline would be that the average pay of those in the grade should broadly be in line with the reference point (a compa-ratio of 100) unless there are special market rate considerations which justify a higher rate. Those at or above the reference point who are contributing well could be eligible for a cash bonus. A 'pay pot' would be made available for distribution, with guidelines on how it should be used.

This approach depends largely on the judgement of line managers, although they would be guided and helped in the exercise of that judgement by HR. Its acceptability to staff as a fair process depends on precise communications generally on how it operates and equally precise communications individually on why decisions have been made. The assessment of contribution should be a joint one as part of performance management and the link between that assessment and the pay decision should be clear.

Other characteristics

The other characteristics of contribution pay are that:

- it is concerned with people as team members contributing to team performance, not acting as individuals;
- it can operate flexibly – approaches may be varied between different groups of people;
- it is tailored to suit the business and HR strategy of the organization;
- there is a clear business-related rationale which serves stated HR and reward purposes – individual and team contribution expectations are defined on the basis of the corporate and team business goals to be achieved and measured accordingly;
- it operates transparently – everyone understands how the scheme operates and how it affects them and staff, and their representatives will have contributed to the design of the system and will take part in regular reviews of its effectiveness leading to modifications when required.

Conclusions

Contribution pay and performance pay are significantly different concepts, as is shown in Table 17.1.

However, contribution-related pay decisions still ultimately depend on the judgement of line managers and contribution pay will only work if line managers are capable of making sound judgements and are willing to spend time in doing so. Training and guidance are required and HR has an important role in providing them. The requirements for success are demanding and, as explained in the last two sections of this chapter, it is essential to ensure that the organization is ready for contribution pay and to plan its introduction with great care, including ample consultation and involvement. Organizations should never rush into contribution pay – more time than is usually thought necessary is needed to plan and implement it.

SKILL-BASED PAY

Defined

Skill-based pay provides employees with a direct link between their pay progression and the skills they have acquired and can use effectively. It focuses on what skills the business wants to pay for and what employees must do to demonstrate them. It is therefore a people-based rather than a job-based approach to pay. Rewards are related to the employee's ability to apply a wider range or a higher level of skills to different jobs or tasks. It is not linked simply with the scope of a defined job or a prescribed set of tasks.

Table 17.1 Pay for performance compared with pay for contribution

	Pay for performance	*Pay for contribution*
Organizing philosophy	Formulae, systems	Processes
HR approach	Instrumentalist, people as costs	Commitment, people as assets
Measurement	Pay for results (the whats) – achieving individual objectives	Multidimensional, pay for results and how they are achieved
Measures	Financial goals	Broad variety of strategic goals: financial service operating etc (balanced scorecard)
Focus of measurement	Individual	Multi-level: business, team
Design	Uniform merit pay and/or individual bonus approach throughout the organization	Diverse approaches using wide variety of reward methods to suit the needs of individual groups
Time-scales	Immediate past performance	Past performance and contribution to future goals
Performance assessment	Performance appraisal – past review and ratings focus; top down and quantitative	Performance management mixed model – past review and future development; partnership approach, quantitative and qualitative (possibly 360º)
Pay linkage	Fixed formula, matrix	Looser, more flexible linkages
Administration	Controlled by HR	Owned/operated by users
Communication and involvement	Top down, non-transparent, imposed	Face-to-face, transparent, high involvement
Evaluation of effectiveness	Act of faith	Regular review and monitoring against clearly defined success criteria
Change over time	All or nothing	Regular incremental modification

(Source: adapted from Duncan Brown and Michael Armstrong (1999) *Paying for Contribution*, Kogan Page, London)

A skill may be defined broadly as a learnt ability which improves with practice in time. For skill-based pay purposes the skills must be relevant to the work. Skill-based pay is also known as knowledge-based pay, but the terms are used interchangeably, knowledge being regarded loosely as the understanding of how to do a job or certain tasks.

Application

Skill-based pay was originally applied mainly to operatives in manufacturing firms. But it has been extended to technicians and workers in retailing, distribution, catering and other service industries. The broad equivalent of skill-based pay for managerial, professional and administrative staff and knowledge workers is competence-related pay, which refers to expected behaviour as well as, often, to knowledge and skill requirements. There is clearly a strong family resemblance between skill-based and competence-related pay – each is concerned with rewarding the person as well as the job. But they can be distinguished both by the way in which they are applied, as described below, and by the criteria used.

Main features

Skill-based pay works as follows:

- Skill blocks or modules are defined. These incorporate individual skills or clusters of skills which workers need to use and which will be rewarded by extra pay when they have been acquired and the employee has demonstrated the ability to use them effectively.
- The skill blocks are arranged in a hierarchy with natural break points between clearly definable different levels of skills.
- The successful completion of a skill module or skill block will result in an increment in pay. This will define how the pay of individuals can progress as they gain extra skills.
- Methods of verifying that employees have acquired and can use the skills at defined levels are established.
- Arrangements for 'cross-training' are made. These will include learning modules and training programmes for each skill block.

Conclusions

Skill-based pay systems are expensive to introduce and maintain. They require a considerable investment in skill analysis, training and testing. Although in theory a skill-based scheme will pay only for necessary skills, in practice individuals will not be using them all at the same time and some may be used infrequently, if at all. Inevitably, therefore, payroll costs will rise. If this increase is added to the cost of training and certification, the total of additional costs may be considerable. The advocates of skill-based pay claim that their schemes are self-financing because of the resulting increases in productivity and operational efficiency. But there is little evidence that such is the case. For this reason, skill-based schemes have never been very popular in the UK and some companies have discontinued them.

SERVICE-RELATED PAY

Defined

Service-related pay provides fixed increments which are usually paid annually to people on the basis of continued service either in a job or a grade in a pay spine structure. Increments may be withheld for unacceptable performance (although this is rare) and some structures have a 'merit bar' which limits increments unless a defined level of 'merit' has been achieved. This is the traditional form of contingent pay and is still common in the public and voluntary sectors and in education and the health service, although it has largely been abandoned in the private sector.

Arguments for

Service-related pay is supported by many unions because they perceive it as being fair – everyone is treated equally. It is felt that linking pay to time in the job rather than performance or competence avoids the partial and ill-informed judgements about people which managers are prone to make. Some people believe that the principle of rewarding people for loyalty through continued service is a good one.

Arguments against

The arguments against service-related pay are that:

- it is inequitable in the sense that an equal allocation of pay increases according to service does not recognize the fact that some people will be contributing more than others and should be rewarded accordingly;
- it does not encourage good performance; indeed, it rewards poor performance equally;
- it is based on the assumption that performance improves with experience but this is not automatically the case – it has been said that a person with five years' experience may in practice only have had one year's experience repeated five times;
- it can be expensive – everyone may drift to the top of the scale, especially in times of low staff turnover, but the cost of their pay is not justified by the added value they provide.

The arguments against service-related pay have convinced most managements, although some are concerned about managing any other form of contingent-pay schemes (incremental pay scales do not need to be managed at all). They may also have to face strong resistance from their unions and can be unsure of what exit strategy they should adopt if they want to change. They may therefore stick with the status quo.

CHOICE OF APPROACH

The first choice is whether or not to have contingent pay related to performance, competence, contribution or skill. Public or voluntary sector organizations with fixed incremental systems (pay spines) where progression is solely based on service may want to retain them because they do not depend on possibly biased judgements by managers and they are perceived as being fair – everyone gets the same – and easily managed. However, the fairness of such systems can be questioned. Is it fair for a poor performer to be paid more than a good performer simply for being there?

The alternatives to fixed increments are either spot rates or some form of contingent pay. Spot rate systems in their purest form are generally only used for senior managers, shop floor or retail workers and in smaller organizations and new businesses where the need for formal practices has not yet been recognized.

If it is decided that a more formal type of contingent pay for individuals should be adopted, the choice is between the various types of performance pay, competence-related or contribution-related pay and skill-based pay as summarized in Table 17.2.

Although contribution-related pay shares the disadvantages of other forms of contingent pay in that it relies on managerial judgement and is difficult to manage well, it is probably the best choice in most circumstances. As the CIPD survey showed, it is certainly the most popular. The last two sections of this chapter therefore concentrate on discussions of readiness for contribution pay and methods of developing and implementing it.

READINESS FOR CONTRIBUTION PAY

The ten questions to be answered when assessing readiness for contribution pay are:

1. Is it believed that contribution pay will benefit the organization in the sense of enhancing its ability to achieve its strategic goals?
2. Are there valid and reliable means of measuring performance?
3. Is there a competence framework and are there methods of assessing levels of competence objectively (or could such a framework be readily developed)?
4. Are there effective performance management processes which line managers believe in and carry out conscientiously?
5. Are line managers willing to assess contribution and capable of doing so?
6. Are line managers capable of making and communicating contribution pay decisions?
7. Is the HR function capable of providing advice and guidance to line managers on managing contribution pay?
8. Can procedures be developed to ensure fairness and consistency in assessments and pay decisions?

Table 17.2 Comparison of contingent pay schemes

Type of scheme	Main features	Advantages	Disadvantages	When appropriate
Performance-related pay	Increases to basic pay or bonuses are related to assessment of performance.	May motivate (but this is uncertain). Links rewards to objectives. Meets the need to be rewarded for achievement. Delivers message that good performance is important and will be rewarded.	May not motivate. Relies on judgements of performance which may be subjective. Prejudicial to teamwork. Focuses on outputs, not quality. Relies on good performance management processes. Difficult to manage well.	For people who are likely to be motivated by money. In organizations with a perform-ance-orientated culture. When performance can be measured objectively.
Competence-related pay	Pay increases are related to the level of competence.	Focuses attention on need to achieve higher levels of competence. Encourages competence development. Can be integrated with other applications of competency-based HR management.	Assessment of competence levels may be difficult. Ignores outputs – danger of paying for competences that will not be used. Relies on well-trained and committed line managers.	As part of an integrated approach to HRM where competencies are used across a number of activities. Where competence is a key factor. Where it may be inappropriate or hard to measure outputs. Where well-established competency frameworks exist.
Contribution-related pay	Increases in pay or bonuses are related both to inputs (competence) and outputs (performance).	Rewards people not only for what they do but how they do it.	As for both PRP and competence-related pay – it may be hard to measure contribution and it is difficult to manage well.	When it is believed that a well-rounded approach covering both inputs and outputs is appropriate.

(Continued)

Table 17.2 *Continued*

Type of scheme	Main features	Advantages	Disadvantages	When appropriate
Skill-based pay	Increments related to the acquisition of skills.	Encourages and rewards the acquisition of skills.	Can be expensive when people are paid for skills they don't use.	On the shop floor or in retail organizations.
Service-related pay	Increments related to service in grade.	No scope for bias, easy to manage.	Fails to reward those who contribute more.	Where this is the traditional approach and trade unions oppose alternatives.

9. Are employees and trade unions willing to accept the scheme?
10. Do employees trust management to deliver the deal?

DEVELOPING AND IMPLEMENTING CONTRIBUTION PAY

The ten steps required to develop and implement contribution pay are:

1. Analyse culture, strategy and existing processes, including the grade and pay structure, performance management and methods of progressing pay or awarding cash bonuses.
2. Set out aims which demonstrate how contribution pay will help to achieve the organization's strategic goals.
3. Communicate aims to line manager's staff and involve them in the development of the scheme.
4. Determine how the scheme will operate covering:
   ● the use of performance and competence measures;
   ● the performance management processes required;
   ● the scope for awarding cash bonuses as well as base pay increases;
   ● the approach to making decisions on awards – one of the six approaches listed on pages 242–47 or any other suitable method of deciding on pay progression and cash payments;
   ● the amount of money that will be available for contribution pay, and how that money should be distributed;

- the guidelines and procedures needed to govern contribution pay reviews and ensure that they are carried out fairly and consistently and within available budgets;
- the basis upon which the effectiveness of contribution pay will be evaluated.

5. Develop competence framework and role profiles.
6. Develop or improve performance management processes covering the selection of performance measures, decisions on competence requirements, methods of agreeing objectives and the procedure for conducting joint reviews.
7. Communicate intentions to line managers and staff.
8. Pilot test the scheme and amend as necessary.
9. Provide training to all concerned.
10. Launch the scheme and evaluate its effectiveness after the first review.

REFERENCES

1 Armstrong, M and Baron, A (2004) *Performance Management: Action and Impact*, CIPD, London
2 e-research (2004) *Survey of Contingent Pay*, e-reward.co.uk Ltd, Stockport, Cheshire
3 Kohn, A (1993) Why incentive plans cannot work, *Harvard Business Review*, September–October
4 Bowey, A (1982) *The Effects of Incentive Pay Systems*, Department of Employment, Research Paper N 36, DOE, London
5 Kessler, J and Purcell, J (1992) Performance-related pay: objectives and application, *Human Resource Management Journal*, **2** (3), Spring
6 Marsden, D and Richardson, R (1994) Performing for pay? *British Journal of Industrial Relations*, June
7 Thompson, M (1992) *Pay and Performance: The Employer Experience*, Institute of Manpower Studies Report No 218, Brighton
8 Wright, V (1991) Performance related pay, in *The Performance Management Handbook*, ed E Neale, IPM, London
9 Oliver, J (1996) Cash on delivery, *Management Today*, August
10 Brown, D and Armstrong, M (1999), *Paying for Contribution*, Kogan Page, London
11 Lawler, E E (1988) Pay for performance: making it work, *Personnel*, October
12 Sparrow, P A (1996) Too good to be true, *People Management*, December
13 Lawler, E E (1993) Who uses skill-based pay, and why, *Compensation & Benefits Review*, March–April
14 Brumbach, G B (1988) Some ideas, issues and predictions about performance management, *Public Personnel Management*, Winter

18

Team pay

Two factors have combined to create interest in rewarding teams rather than individuals. The first is the significance attached to good teamwork and the belief that team pay would enhance it, and the second is dissatisfaction with the individual nature of performance-related pay which is believed to be prejudicial to teamwork. The notion of team pay appeals to many people but the number of organizations that use it is small. The e-research 2004 survey (1) of contingent pay found that only 11 per cent of respondents had team pay and in the organizations covered by the CIPD 2003 reward survey (2) the proportion was even smaller (6 per cent).

Team pay is an attractive idea but one difficult to put into practice. The limited number of schemes may arise because organizations find it difficult to meet the quite exacting conditions for team pay set out later in this chapter. Others may believe that they have to focus their incentive schemes on individual rather than group effort.

This chapter starts with a definition of team pay and its aims and continues with a description of how team pay works, an analysis of the arguments for and against team pay and suggestions on how team pay can be introduced.

TEAM PAY DEFINED

Team pay links payments to members of a formally established team to the performance of that team. The rewards are shared among the members of the team in accordance with a published formula or on an ad hoc basis in the case of exceptional achievements. Rewards for individuals may also be influenced by assessments of their contribution to team results. To appreciate how team pay works it is necessary to understand the nature of a team and the various types of teams to which it can apply.

The nature of a team

A team has been defined by Katzenbach and Smith (3) as: 'A small number of people with complementary skills who are committed to a common purpose, performance goals and approach for which they hold themselves mutually accountable.'

Types of teams

There are four types of teams as described below.

Organizational teams

These consist of individuals who are linked together organizationally as members of, for example, the 'top management team', departmental heads in an operational or research division, section heads or team leaders in a department, or even people carrying out distinct and often separate functions, as long as they are all contributing to the achievement of the objectives of their department or section.

Members of organizational teams can be related to one another by the requirement to achieve an overall objective, but this may be loosely defined and the degree to which they act in consort will vary considerably. In a sense, organizations are entirely constructed of such 'teams', but team reward processes may be inappropriate unless their members are strongly united by a common purpose and are clearly interdependent. If such is not the case, some form of bonus related to organizational performance might be preferable.

Work teams

These are self-contained and permanent teams whose members work closely together to achieve results in terms of output, the development of products or processes, or the delivery of services to customers. This type of team will be focused on a common purpose and its members will be interdependent – results are a function of the degree to which they can work well together. It is for this type of team that continuing team pay schemes rewards may be appropriate, as long as team targets can be established and team performance can be measured accurately and fairly.

Project teams

These consist of people brought together from different functions to complete a task lasting several months to several years. When the project is completed the team disbands. Examples include product development teams or a team formed to open a new plant. Project teams may be rewarded with cash bonuses payable on satisfactory completion of the project to specification, on time and within the cost budget. Interim 'milestone' payments may be made as predetermined stages of the project are completed satisfactorily.

Ad hoc teams

These are functional or cross-functional teams set up to deal with an immediate problem. They are usually short-lived and operate as a task force. It is unusual to pay bonuses to such teams unless they deliver exceptional results.

AIM OF TEAM PAY

The aim of team pay is to encourage and reinforce the sort of behaviour that leads to and sustains effective team performance by:

- providing incentives and other means of recognizing team achievements;
- clarifying what teams are expected to achieve by relating rewards to the attainment of predetermined and agreed targets and standards of performance or to the satisfactory completion of a project or a stage of a project;
- conveying the message that one of the organization's core values is effective teamwork.

Research conducted by the Institute of Personnel and Development (4) established that the main reason organizations gave for developing team reward processes was the perceived need to encourage group endeavour and cooperation rather than to concentrate only on individual performance. It was argued that 'pay for individual performance' systems prejudice team performance in two ways. First, they encourage individuals to focus on their own interests rather than on those of the team. Second, they result in managers and team leaders treating their team members only as individuals rather than relating to them in terms of what the team is there to do and what they can do for the team.

HOW TEAM PAY WORKS

The most common method of providing team pay is to distribute a cash sum related to team performance among team members. There are a number of formulas and ways of distributing team pay as described below.

The team pay formula

This establishes the relationship between team performance, as measured or assessed in quantitative or qualitative terms, and the reward. It also fixes the size of the bonus pool or fund earned by the team to be distributed among its members, or the scale of payments made to team members in relation to team performance with regard to certain criteria. Bonuses may be related to performance in such specific areas as sales, throughput, achievement of targets in the form of the delivery of results for a project, levels of service or an index of customer satisfaction. Targets are agreed and performance is measured against the targets.

Alternatively, bonuses may be related to an overall criterion which can be a more subjective assessment of the contribution of the team to organizational performance.

Method of distributing bonuses

Bonuses can be distributed to team members in the form of either a percentage of base salary or the same sum for each member, usually based on a scale of payments. Payment of bonus as a percentage of base salary is the most popular method. The assumption behind it is that base salary reflects the value of the individual's contribution to the team. The correctness of this assumption clearly depends on the extent to which base salary truly indicates the level of performance of individuals as team members.

Team pay and individual pay

Some organizations pay team bonuses only. A minority pay individual bonuses as well, which are often related to an assessment of the competence of the person, thus, it is thought, providing encouragement to develop skills and rewarding them for their particular contribution.

Dealing with high and low individual performance in a team

It is sometimes assumed by advocates of team pay that all members of a team contribute equally and should therefore be rewarded equally. In practice the contribution of individual team members will vary and if this is the case, for example, in shop floor groups, team pressure may be forcing everyone to work at the same rate so as to avoid 'rate busting'. (This is an example of how a highly cohesive team can work against the interests of the organization.)

When designing a team pay scheme, decisions have to be made on the likelihood that some people will perform better or worse than others. It may be decided that, even if this happens, it would be invidious and detrimental to single anyone out for different treatment. It could, however, be considered that 'special achievement' or 'sustained high performance' bonuses should be payable to individuals who make an exceptional contribution, while poor performers should receive a lower bonus or no bonus at all.

Project team bonuses

The design considerations described above apply to permanent work teams. Different arrangements are required for project teams specially set up to achieve a task and, usually, disbanded after the task has been completed. Project team bonuses should, wherever possible, be self-financing – they should be related to increases in income or productivity or cost savings arising from the project. Project teams can be set targets and their bonus can be linked to achieving or surpassing targeted results. Alternatively, a fixed bonus can be promised if the project is on time, meets the specification and does not exceed the cost budget. The bonus could be increased for early completion or to reflect cost savings. For lengthy projects, interim payments may be made at defined 'milestones'.

Ad hoc bonuses

Where there are no predetermined arrangements for paying bonuses to teams, a retrospective bonus can be paid to a project or ad hoc team in recognition of exceptional achievement.

REQUIREMENTS FOR TEAM PAY

Team pay works best if teams:

- stand alone as performing units for which clear targets and standards can be agreed;
- have a considerable degree of autonomy – team pay is likely to be most effective in self-managed teams;
- are composed of people whose work is interdependent – it is acknowledged by members that the team will deliver the results expected of it only if they work well together and share the responsibility for success;
- are stable – members are used to working with one another, know what is expected of them by fellow team members and know where they stand in the regard of those members;
- are mature – teams are well established, used to working flexibly to meet targets and deadlines, and capable of making good use of the complementary skills of their members.

These are exacting requirements, which helps to explain why the take-up of team pay is low. If the requirements above can be met there may be a good case for team pay.

ADVANTAGES AND DISADVANTAGES OF TEAM PAY

Team pay can:

- encourage team working and cooperative behaviour;
- enhance flexible working within teams and encourage multiskilling, clarify team goals and priorities and provide for the integration of organizational and team objectives;
- encourage less effective performers to improve in order to meet team standards;
- serve as a means of developing self-managed or self-directed teams.

But:

- the effectiveness of team pay depends on the existence of well-defined and mature teams and they may be difficult to identify and, even if they can be, do they need to be motivated by a purely financial reward?
- team pay may seem unfair to individuals who could feel that their own efforts are unrewarded;
- pressure to conform, which is accentuated by team pay, could result in the team maintaining its output at lowest common denominator levels – sufficient to gain what is thought collectively to be a reasonable reward but no more;
- it can be difficult to develop performance measures and methods of rating team performance that are seen to be fair – team pay formulae may well be based on arbitrary assumptions about the correct relationship between effort and reward;
- there may be pressure from employees to migrate from poorly performing teams to high-performing teams which, if allowed, could cause disruption and stigmatize the teams from which individuals transfer, or if refused, could leave dissatisfied employees in the inadequate teams, making them even worse (this was a serious problem experienced by Pearl Assurance, one of the pioneers of team pay).

To many organizations, the disadvantages outweigh the advantages.

DEVELOPING TEAM PAY

If, in spite of the problems that may beset team pay, it is decided to introduce it, the development steps are as follows.

1. Initial analysis

This should identify whether there are teams which satisfy the requirements set out above.

2. Scheme design

Decisions need to be made on which teams will be eligible for team pay and why, the team bonus formula (the criteria to be used in judging performance, the amount available for team pay and the method of distributing team pay).

3. Scheme introduction

Team pay is likely to be unfamiliar and it should therefore be introduced with care, especially if it is replacing an existing system of individual PRP. The process will be easier if employees have been involved in developing the scheme, but it is still essential to communicate in detail to all employees the reasons for introducing team pay, how it will work and how it will affect them.

It is easier to introduce team pay into mature teams whose members are used to working together, trust one another and can recognize that team pay will work to their mutual advantage. Although it may seem an attractive proposition to use team pay as a means of welding new work teams together, there are dangers in forcing people who are already having to adapt to a different situation to accept a radical change in their method of remuneration. It should be remembered that it may not be easy to get people in work teams to think of their performance in terms of how it impacts on others. It can take time for employees to adapt to a system in which a proportion of their pay is based on team achievement.

When it comes to launching team pay it may be advisable to pilot it initially in one or two well-established teams. Experience gained from the pilot scheme can then be used to modify the scheme before it is extended elsewhere. If the pilot scheme teams think it has been a success, other teams may be more willing to convert to team pay.

REFERENCES

1   e-research (2004) *Survey of Contingent Pay*, e-reward.co.uk Ltd, Stockport, Cheshire
2   Chartered Institute of Personnel and Development (2003) *Reward Management 2003: A survey of policy and practice*, CIPD, London
3   Katzenbach, J and Smith, D (1993) *The Magic of Teams*, Harvard Business School Press, Boston, MA
4   Armstrong, M and Ryden, O (1996) *The IPD Guide to Team Reward*, IPD, London

19

Paying for organizational performance

Many organizations believe that their financial reward systems should extend beyond individual contingent pay, which does not recognize collective effort, or team pay, which is difficult. They believe that their system should help to create a sense of stake-holding in the organization among their employees as well as providing them with additional financial rewards. The response to this belief is to offer financial rewards which are related to organizational performance (sometimes known as company-wide or factory-wide schemes) and both the CIPD (1) and e-research (2) surveys in 2003 found that 40 per cent of respondents had one or more of the types of schemes described below.

TYPES OF SCHEMES

The three types of formal organizational schemes are:

1. *Profit-sharing* – the payment of sums in cash or shares related to the profits of the business; 13 per cent of the respondents to the e-research survey had such schemes.

2. *Share ownership schemes* – employees are given the opportunity to purchase shares in the company; 23 per cent of the respondents to the e-research survey had such schemes.
3. *Gain-sharing* – the payment of cash sums to employees related to the financial gains made by the company because of its improved performance; only 4 per cent of the e-research respondents had such schemes.

Less formally, managements can make decisions on the amount to be paid out in the form of individual performance or contribution-related increments or individual/team cash bonuses. These decisions are made on the basis of what they believe the organization can afford. This creates what is sometimes called a 'pot' from which payments are funded. The assessment of affordability (a potent word for many managements) can determine pay review budgets on the proportion of the pay roll, for example 3 per cent, that can be allocated for increments or bonuses.

Research carried out by IRS in 2003 (3) established that there was a high degree of 'mix and match' among the profit-sharing and share ownership schemes offered by companies to their employees. Half of the respondents to the survey with schemes in place ran more than one. Organizations may also provide for payments related to organizational performance in addition to individual contingent pay.

AIMS

The aims of relating rewards to organizational performance are to:

- increase the commitment of employees to the organization;
- enable employees to share in the success of the organization;
- stimulate more interest in the affairs of the organization;
- focus employees' attention on what employees can contribute to organizational success and bring areas for improvement to their attention;
- obtain tax advantages for employees through approved share schemes – such 'tax-efficient' schemes enable the business to get better value for money from its expenditure on employee remuneration.

Perhaps the two most important reasons for organizational schemes are the beliefs that they increase the identification of employees with the company and that the company is morally bound to share its success with their employee stakeholders – those who collectively make a major contribution to it. However, it is generally recognized that they do not provide a direct incentive because the links between individual effort and the collective reward are too obscure.

PROFIT-SHARING

Profit-sharing is a plan under which an employer pays to eligible employees, as an addition to their normal remuneration, special sums related to the profits of the business. The amount shared is determined either by an established formula or entirely at the discretion of management. As a percentage of pay, the value of profit shares varies considerably between companies and within companies from year to year. Between 2 and 5 per cent is a fairly typical range of payments but it can be 20 per cent or more. It is unlikely that profit distributions of less than 5 per cent will make much impact on commitment, never mind motivation. Employees tend to take the smallish sums they receive for granted.

There used to be two types of profit-sharing schemes: Inland Revenue Approved Schemes which provided tax advantages, and the more traditional 'non-approved schemes'. Approved schemes were phased out from 2001 and only the non-approved schemes remain.

Profits can be distributed in the form of cash or shares, usually share options. The arrangements for profit-sharing are concerned with eligibility, the basis for calculating profit shares and the method of distribution. They vary considerably between companies.

Eligibility

In most schemes all employees except directors are eligible. A period of time, often one year's service, is usually required before profit shares can be received.

Basis of calculation

There are three approaches to calculating profit shares:

1. *A predetermined formula* – a fixed percentage of profits is distributed. This clarifies the relationship of payout to profits and demonstrates the good faith of management but it lacks flexibility and the amount available may fluctuate widely.
2. *No predetermined formula* – the board determines profit shares entirely at its own discretion in accordance with their assessment of what the company can afford. This gives them complete control over the amount distributed but, because of the secrecy involved, is at odds with the principle of getting employees more involved with the organization. This is the most typical approach.
3. *A threshold formula* – a profit threshold is set below which no profits will be distributed and a maximum limit is defined. Between these, the board exercise discretion on the amount to be distributed.

Methods of distributing profit shares

There are four methods of distribution:

1. *Percentage of pay with no allowance for service* – this is a fairly common method which recognizes that profit shares should be related to the employee's basic contribution as measured by their level of pay which takes into account service.
2. *Percentage of pay with an allowance for service* – this approach is also frequently used on the grounds that it rewards loyalty.
3. *Percentage of pay with an allowance for individual performance* – this method is fairly rare below board level because of the difficulty of measuring the relationship between individual performance and profit.
4. *As a fixed sum irrespective of earnings, service or performance* – this is an egalitarian approach but is fairly rare.

SHARE OWNERSHIP SCHEMES

There are two main forms of share ownership plans: Share Incentive Plans (SIPS) and Save-as-you-earn (SAYE) schemes. These can be Inland Revenue approved and, if so, produce tax advantages as well as linking financial rewards in the longer term to the prosperity of the company.

Share incentive plans

Share incentive plans must be Inland Revenue approved. They provide employees with a tax-efficient way of purchasing shares in their organization to which the employer can add 'free', 'partnership' or 'matching' shares. There is a limit to the amount of free shares that can be provided to employees (£3,000 a year in 2004). Employees can use up to £1,500 a year (in 2004) out of pre-tax and pre-National Insurance Contributions pay to buy partnership shares and employers can give matching shares at a ratio of up to two matching shares for each partnership share.

Save-as-you-earn schemes

Save-as-you-earn (SAYE) schemes must be Inland Revenue approved. They provide employees with the option to buy shares in the company in three, five or seven years' time at today's price or a discount of up to 20 per cent of that price. Purchases are made from a savings account from which the employee pays an agreed sum each month. The monthly savings must be between £5 and £250. Income tax is not chargeable when the option is granted.

GAIN-SHARING

Gain-sharing is a formula-based company or factory-wide bonus plan which provides for employees to share in the financial gains made by a company as a result of its improved performance. The formula determines the share by reference to a performance indicator such as added value or another measure of productivity. In some schemes the formula also incorporates performance measures relating to quality, customer service, delivery or cost reduction.

The most popular performance indicator is value added, which is calculated by deducting expenditure on materials and other purchased services from the income derived from sales of the product. It is, in effect, the wealth created by the people in the business. A manufacturing business 'adds value' by the process of production as carried out by the combined contribution of management and employees.

Gain-sharing differs from profit-sharing in that the latter is based on more than improved productivity. A number of factors outside the individual employee's control contribute to profit, such as depreciation procedures, bad debt expenses, taxation and economic changes. Gain-sharing aims to relate its payouts more specifically to productivity and performance improvements within the control of employees.

Although the financial element is obviously a key feature of gain-sharing, its strength as a means of improving performance lies equally in its other important features – ownership, involvement and communication. The success of a gain-sharing plan depends on creating a feeling of ownership that first applies to the plan and then extends to the operation. When implementing gain-sharing, companies enlist the support of employees in order to increase their commitment to the plan. The involvement aspect of gain-sharing means that information generated on the company's results is used as a basis for giving employees the opportunity to make suggestions on ways of improving performance, and for giving them scope to make decisions concerning their implementation.

However, gain-sharing has never been popular in the UK, perhaps because its use is mainly limited to the manufacturing sector and it takes time to plan and operate if it is to work well. Conventional profit-sharing and share ownership schemes are much easier to manage.

REFERENCES

1   Chartered Institute of Personnel and Development (CIPD) (2003) *Reward Management 2003: A survey of policy and practice*, CIPD, London.
2   e-research (2004) *Survey of Contingent Pay*, e-reward.co.uk Ltd, Stockport, Cheshire
3   Industrial Relations Services (IRS) (2003) Sharing the spoils: profit-share and bonus scheme, *IRS Employment Review*, **784**, Pay and Benefit Bulletin, 19 September, pp 28–33.

20

Recognition processes

Formal recognition processes acknowledge success. They are based on the belief that taking steps to ensure that people's achievements and contribution are recognized is an effective way of motivating them. This belief is supported by motivation theory (see Chapter 7).

Recognition processes can form an important part of a total reward approach, as described in Chapter 2. They complement direct financial rewards and therefore enhance the reward system.

RECOGNITION PROCESSES DEFINED

Recognition processes enable appreciation to be shown to individuals for their achievements either informally on a day-to-day basis or through formal recognition schemes. They can take place quietly between managers and individuals in their teams or be visible celebrations of success.

A recognition scheme as defined by Michael Rose (1) typically provides for 'non-cash awards given in recognition of a high level of accomplishment or performance, which is not dependent on achievement against a given target'. A recognition scheme can be formal and organization wide, providing scope to recognize achievements by gifts or treats or by public applause. Importantly, recognition is also given less formally when managers simply say 'well done', 'thank you' or 'congratulations' face-to-face or in a brief note of appreciation.

PRINCIPLES OF RECOGNITION

The principles that need to be borne in mind when developing recognition processes are that recognition:

- should be given for specially valued behaviours and exceptional effort as well as for special achievements;
- is about valuing people; it should be personalized so that people appreciate that it applies to them;
- needs to be applied equitably, fairly and consistently throughout the organization;
- must be genuine, not used as a mechanistic motivating device;
- should not be given formally as part of a scheme if the achievement has been rewarded under another arrangement, for example a bonus scheme;
- needs to be given as soon as possible after the achievement;
- should be available to all – there should be no limits on the numbers who can be recognized;
- should not be predicated on the belief that they are just about rewarding winners – Kohn (2) argues against any such system because 'for each person who wins, there are many others who have lost';
- should be available for teams as well as individuals to reward collective effort and avoid creating isolated winners;
- should not be based on an over-elaborate scheme.

It is also necessary to bear in mind that awards above £100 are subject to income tax. The award can be grossed up for tax and NIC and it is then possible for the organization to meet the tax and NIC liabilities annually.

TYPES OF RECOGNITION

Day-to-day recognition

The most effective form of recognition is that provided by managers to their staff on a day-to-day basis. This is an aspect of good management practice, such as getting to know people, monitoring performance (without being oppressive) and providing positive feedback. It is provided orally on the spot or in a short note (preferably hand-written) of appreciation, and should take place soon after the event (not delayed until an annual performance review). It must be genuine – people can easily spot insincerity, or someone simply going through the motions.

This type of recognition should be a natural part of the daily routine. The organization should aim to develop a recognition culture which is nurtured by the management style of senior managers and permeates the organization through each level of management so that it becomes 'the way we do things around here'. Managers can be encouraged to adopt this style but this should be more by example than by precept, not the subject of a scheme, process or system. Such recognition should be a part of the organizational culture. If it is not, it needs to be before any more structured scheme will pay dividends.

Public recognition

Recognition for particular achievements or continuing effective contributions can be provided by public 'applause' through an 'employee of the month scheme' or some other announcement using an intranet, the house journal or notice boards.

Formal recognition

Formal recognition schemes provide individuals (and importantly, through them, their partners) with tangible means of recognition in the forms of gifts, vouchers, holidays or trips in the UK or abroad, days or weekends at health spas, or meals out. Team awards may be through outings, parties and meals. Such schemes may be centrally driven, with formal award ceremonies. Managers and employees can nominate individuals for awards. If the awards are substantial, organizations can set up a recognition committee with employee representatives to agree on who should be eligible, thus ensuring that decisions are transparent.

Formal schemes can provide for different levels of recognition and rewards as illustrated in the schedule in Table 20.1, developed for a large local authority. This provides for a graduated series of awards which can be made by managers within a budget. At the lowest level, managers may be given quite a lot of autonomy to make immediate small recognition awards. The next higher-level rewards would have to be approved by a senior manager and the highest level would be reviewed by a recognition committee for final approval by top management.

EXAMPLES OF NON-CASH AWARDS

Some ideas for non-cash awards include:

● Basket of fruit
● Books
● Bottle of champagne (with a personalized label)
● Cinema or theatre vouchers
● Dinner out for two (include a taxi and organize a babysitter)

Table 20.1 Levels of recognition

Level	Examples
1 Below £25	• Volunteering to help others when the workload is heavy • Providing extra help to a customer • Working late or at weekends without extra pay to meet an important deadline • Taking on a temporary extra task which is not part of normal duties • Demonstrating valued behaviours
2 £25 to £150	• Identifying improved work practices • Providing a sustained level of customer service • Making or recommending cost savings when not part of role • Demonstrating valued behaviours which make a significant short-term impact
3 £500 to £1,000	• Generating significant extra revenue when not part of role • Reducing costs significantly when not part of role • Successfully completing a major project which is not part of normal role • Demonstrating valued behaviours which make a significant long-term impact

- Experience days (eg hot air balloon ride, or a day at a health and beauty spa)
- Flowers (delivered to the workplace or at home)
- Food hamper
- Fridays off for a month
- Gift certificates
- Jewellery
- Personal letter from the chairman or chief executive
- Plaques or certificates
- Points-based catalogue gifts
- Retail shopping vouchers
- Tickets to a concert, theatre or sports event
- Trip for two to Amsterdam, Barcelona or Paris
- Trophy (passed from one person to another)
- Weekend in an hotel for two.

CONCIERGE SERVICES

Concierge services as provided by PwC (see Chapter 30) originated in the USA in response to the long-hours culture which limited personal time away from the workplace. Businesses benefit from providing these services because they enable staff to concentrate on their jobs by freeing them from mundane personal tasks such as waiting at home for deliveries or getting their car serviced. Services can include dealing with home and car repair and maintenance, financial services, buying presents, restaurant reservations, theatre tickets and travel arrangements.

At PwC, staff may pay £10 a month for a limited number of requests, and £15 a month for unlimited requests. Requests can be for anything from shopping or arranging a plumber, to event planning – 'so long as it's legal'.

Concierge services can be run by outside providers.

DESIGNING A RECOGNITION SCHEME

The principles set out earlier in this chapter should be borne in mind when designing and implementing a recognition scheme. Line managers and employees should be consulted, guidelines should be prepared and explained to managers and the details of the scheme publicized.

The implementation of the scheme should be monitored and steps taken to maintain the impetus – managers can lose interest. Progress reports should be made to employees so that they know that the scheme is working well.

EXAMPLE OF A RECOGNITION SCHEME AT XANSA

Objectives

- To recognize and celebrate exceptional achievement that demonstrates the company's values.
- To reward performance that is above and beyond the 'norm'.
- To promote recipients as role models.

Eligibility and scheme features

The policy applies to all employees working in the UK at the time of the award. The objectives include:

- Awards will be made as soon as possible after the event.
- It will not be bureaucratic, for example there will not be a formal sign-off process.
- Groups can be rewarded as well as individuals.

The only prerequisites are that:

- Recognition is fair and consistent.
- Budgets are not exceeded.
- No cash payments are made.

Type of reward

At the very least, extra effort deserves a personal thank you in the form of a conversation or letter. Written communication will often be more appreciated than verbal because the recipient can keep it.

Where more than a verbal or written thank you is warranted, the choice of a more formal award is really only limited by imagination.

The following are some ideas:

- Food and drink, for example a bottle of champagne or a food hamper. But remember that a bottle of champagne may not be appreciated by a teetotaller.
- Outings, for example cinema tickets, family outing to Legoland, a stay at a health farm.
- Charity donation.
- Vouchers, for example either for a particular shop or for experiences such as rally driving or a spa day.

Tax and accounting requirement

The company will meet the tax liabilities annually. The value of the award must be grossed up for tax and NIC.

REFERENCES

1   Rose, M (2001) *Recognising Performance*, CIPD, London
2   Kohn, A (1993) Why incentive plans cannot work, *Harvard Business Review*, September–October, pp 54–63

21

Performance management and reward

Performance management plays an important part in reward management. This chapter starts with a definition of performance management and its purpose. A summary of the processes involved follows. The chapter continues with a description of how performance management functions as part of total reward with particular reference to motivation and the generation of information to inform contingent pay decisions. In conclusion, the criteria for evaluating performance management are listed.

PERFORMANCE MANAGEMENT DEFINED

Performance management is a strategic and integrated process which delivers sustained success to organizations by improving the performance of the people who work in them and by developing the capabilities of individual contributors and teams.

It is strategic in the sense that it is concerned with the broader issues facing the business if it is to function effectively in its environment, and with the general direction in which it intends to go to achieve longer-term goals. It is integrated in two senses: (1) *vertical integration* – linking or aligning business, team and individual objectives and core competences, and (2) *horizontal integration* – linking different aspects of human resource management, especially organizational development, human resource development and reward, to achieve a coherent approach to the management, development and motivation of people.

AIMS OF PERFORMANCE MANAGEMENT

The fundamental aim of performance management is to get better results from the organization, teams and individuals by understanding and managing performance within an agreed framework of planned goals, standards and competence requirements. It is a process for establishing shared understanding about what *is* to be achieved, and an approach to managing and developing people in a way that increases the probability that it *will* be achieved in the short and longer term. It is owned and driven by line management.

Performance management can also make a major contribution to the motivation of people by providing the foundation upon which many non-financial motivation approaches can be built.

Essentially, performance management is concerned with the encouragement of productive discretionary behaviour. As defined by John Purcell and his team at Bath University (1), 'Discretionary behaviour refers to the choices that people make about how they carry out their work and the amount of effort, care, innovation and productive behaviour they display. It is the difference between people just doing a job and people doing a great job.' On the basis of their research into the relationship between HR practice and business performance, Purcell and his colleagues noted that 'the experience of success seen in performance outcomes helps to reinforce positive attitudes'. Performance management can help to define what success is and how it can be attained.

PRINCIPLES OF PERFORMANCE MANAGEMENT

Egan (2) proposes the following guiding principles for performance management:

> Most employees want direction, freedom to get their work done, and encouragement not control. The performance management system should be a control system only by exception. The solution is to make it a collaborative development system, in two ways. First, the entire performance management process – coaching, counselling, feedback, tracking, recognition, and so forth – should encourage development. Ideally, team members grow and develop through these interactions. Second, when managers and team members ask what they need to be able to do to do bigger and better things, they move to strategic development.

The principles of performance management have also been well summarized by IDS (3) as follows:

- It translates corporate goals into individual, team, department and divisional goals.
- It helps to clarify corporate goals.
- It is a continuous and evolutionary process, in which performance improves over time.
- It relies on consensus and cooperation rather than control or coercion.
- It creates a shared understanding of what is required to improve performance and how this will be achieved.
- It encourages self-management of individual performance.
- It requires a management style that is open and honest and encourages two-way communication between superiors and subordinates.
- It requires continuous feedback.
- Feedback loops enable the experiences and knowledge gained on the job by individuals to modify corporate objectives.
- It measures and assesses all performance against jointly agreed goals.
- It should apply to all staff.
- It is not primarily concerned with linking performance to financial reward.

To which could be added that performance management is about providing support as well as direction.

The extensive research conducted by the CIPD in 1997 and 2003/4 (Armstrong and Baron, (4) and (5)) identified ten maxims from practitioners on how these principles should be applied:

1. 'A management tool which helps managers to manage.'
2. 'Driven by corporate purpose and values.'
3. 'To obtain solutions that work.'
4. 'Only interested in things you can do something about and get a visible improvement.'
5. 'Focus on changing behaviour rather than paperwork.'
6. 'It's about how we manage people – it's not a system.'
7. 'Performance management is what managers do: a natural process of management.'
8. 'Based on accepted principle but operates flexibly.'
9. 'Focus on development not pay.'
10. 'Success depends on what the organization is and needs to be in its performance culture.'

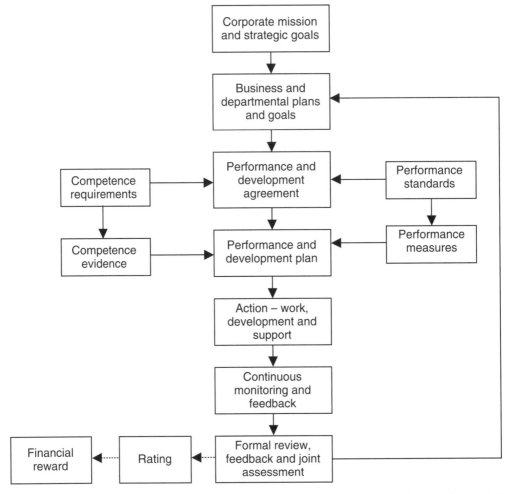

Figure 21.1 The performance management sequence. (Source: adapted from A Cave and C Thomas (1998) *The Reward Portfolio*, IPD, London)

THE PERFORMANCE MANAGEMENT SEQUENCE

Performance management involves a sequence of interconnected activities as shown in Figure 21.1.

THE PERFORMANCE MANAGEMENT CYCLE

Performance management is a natural process of management. It is not an HRM technique or tool. As a natural process of management the performance management cycle

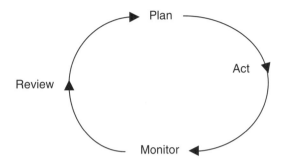

Figure 21.2 The performance management cycle

as shown in Figure 21.2 corresponds with William Deming's (6) Plan–Do–Check–Act model.

The performance management processes taking place in this cycle are:

- *Plan:* agreeing objectives, standards and competence requirements; identifying the required behaviours; producing plans expressed in performance agreements for meeting objectives and improving performance; preparing personal development plans to enhance knowledge and skills and reinforce the desired behaviours.
- *Act:* carrying out the work required to achieve objectives by reference to the plans and in response to new demands.
- *Monitor:* checking on progress in achieving objectives and responding to new demands; treating performance management as a continuous process – 'managing performance all the year round' – rather than an annual appraisal event.
- *Review:* a 'stocktaking' discussion of progress and achievements held in a review meeting and identifying where action is required to develop performance as a basis for completing the cycle by moving into the planning stage.

The basis upon which performance management works is further illustrated in Figure 21.3.

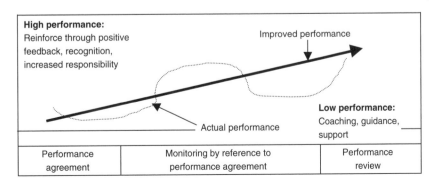

Figure 21.3 Stages of performance management

KEY FEATURES OF PERFORMANCE MANAGEMENT

The key features of performance management are that:

- at every stage the aim is to obtain agreement between managers and individuals on how well the latter are doing and what can be done *jointly* to develop strengths and deal with any weaknesses;
- discussions between managers and individuals should take the form of a dialogue; managers should not attempt to dominate the process and it should not be perceived as an alternative method of control;
- performance management is largely about managing expectations – both managers and individuals understand and agree what they expect of one another, thus developing a more positive psychological contract;
- positive feedback is used to motivate people by recognizing their achievements and potential;
- the process is forward looking – it does not dwell on the past and the dialogue is about what can be done in the future to give individuals the opportunity to develop and grow (this is an important means of motivation);
- performance management is a continuous process, it is not an annual event; managers and individuals are there to manage performance throughout the year.

PERFORMANCE MANAGEMENT AS A MOTIVATING PROCESS

Performance management, if carried out properly, can motivate people by functioning as a key component of the total reward process. It provides rewards in the form of recognition through feedback, opportunities to achieve, the scope to develop skills, and guidance on career paths. It can encourage job engagement and promote commitment. All these are non-financial rewards which can make a longer-lasting and more powerful impact than financial rewards such as performance-related pay.

Performance management is, of course, also associated with pay by generating the information required to decide on pay increases or bonuses related to performance, competence or contribution. In some organizations this is its main purpose, but performance management is, or should be, much more about developing people and rewarding them in the broadest sense. Approaches to using performance management to motivate by non-financial means are discussed below. The rest of this chapter then deals with performance management and pay.

PERFORMANCE MANAGEMENT AND NON-FINANCIAL MOTIVATION

Non-financial motivation is provided by performance management through recognition, the provision of opportunities to succeed, skills development and career planning, and by enhancing job engagement and commitment.

Performance management and recognition

Performance management involves recognizing people's achievements and strengths. They can be thanked, formally and informally, for what they have done.

Performance management and the provision of opportunities to achieve

Performance management processes are founded on joint agreements between managers and their people on what the roles of the latter are and how their role can be developed (enriched). It is therefore an essential part of job or role design and development activities.

Performance management and skills development

Performance management can provide a basis for motivating people by enabling them to develop their skills. It provides an agreed framework for coaching and support to enhance and focus learning.

Performance management and career planning

Performance management reviews provide opportunities to discuss the direction in which the careers of individuals are going and what they can do – with the help of the organization – to ensure that they follow the best career path for themselves and the organization.

Performance management and job engagement

People are engaged with their jobs when they have interest in what they do and a sense of excitement in their work. This can be created by performance management when it concentrates on intrinsic motivating factors such as taking responsibility for job outcomes, job satisfaction and achievement and fulfilment of personal goals and objectives.

Performance management and commitment

One of the prime aims of performance management is to promote commitment to the organization and its goals by integrating individual and organizational objectives.

PERFORMANCE MANAGEMENT AND PAY

Performance management is not inevitably associated with pay, although this is often assumed to be the case. Only 42 per cent of respondents to the CIPD 2003/4 survey (5) with performance management had contingent pay. The proportion in public sector organizations was even less – 29 per cent.

However, those with contingent pay must have a means of deciding on increases, which has to be based on some form of assessment. The most typical approach is performance appraisal, which generates ratings to inform contingent pay decisions, often through a formula (a pay matrix as described in Chapter 17). This may conflict with the developmental purposes of performance management – the performance review meeting will focus on the ratings that emerge from it and how much money will be forthcoming. Issues concerning development and the non-financial reward approaches discussed earlier will be subordinated to this preoccupation with pay. Many organizations attempt to get over this problem by holding development and pay review meetings on separate dates, often several months apart (decoupling). Some try to do without formulaic approaches (ratings and pay matrices) altogether, although it is impossible to dissociate contingent pay completely from some form of assessment.

Reconciling performance management and pay

The problem of reconciling the developmental aspects of performance management or appraisal and pay has been with us for decades. Armstrong commented as long ago as 1976 (7) that:

> It is undesirable to have a direct link between the performance review and the reward review. The former must aim primarily at improving performance and, possibly, assessing potential. If this is confused with a salary review, everyone becomes over-concerned about the impact of the assessment on the increment.... It is better to separate the two.

Many people since then have accepted this view in principle but have found it difficult to apply in practice. As Kessler and Purcell (8) argue:

> How distinct these processes (performance review and performance-related pay) can ever be or, in managerial terms, should ever be, is perhaps debatable. It is unrealistic to

assume that a manager can separate these two processes easily and it could be argued that the evaluations in a broad sense should be congruent.

And Armstrong and Murlis (9) comment that:

> Some organizations separate entirely performance pay ratings from the performance management review. But there will, of course, inevitably be a read-across from the performance management review to the pay-for-performance review.

The issue is that if you want to pay for performance or competence you have to measure performance or competence. And if you want, as you should do, the process of measurement to be fair, equitable, consistent and transparent, then you cannot make pay decisions, on whatever evidence, behind closed doors. You must convey to individuals or teams how the assessment has been made and how it has been converted into a pay increase. This is a matter of procedural justice, the rules of which, as expressed by Leventhal (10), were set out in Chapter 1.

Procedural justice demands that there is a system for assessing performance and competence, that the assessment should be based on 'good information and informed opinion', that the person affected should be able to contribute to the process of obtaining evidence to support the assessment, that the person should know how and why the assessment has been made, and that the person should be able to appeal against the assessment.

Rating performance

Traditional performance appraisal schemes almost always included some form of overall rating of performance. There are arguments for the use of rating as a summary of the assessment and to inform performance-related or contribution-related pay decisions. But there are also powerful arguments against. The arguments for rating are that:

- it is useful to sum up judgements about people;
- you cannot have contingent pay without ratings, although this is not actually the case – 52 per cent of the organizations with contingent pay that responded to the CIPD 2003/4 survey did not include ratings as part of the performance management process;
- they give people something to strive for along the lines of 'You have given me a "C" rating – what have I to do to get a "B" rating?'

The arguments against ratings are that:

- they are largely subjective and it is difficult to achieve consistency between the ratings given by different managers;
- to sum up the total performance of a person with a single rating is a gross over-simplification of what may be a complex set of factors influencing that performance – to do this after a detailed discussion of strengths and weaknesses suggests that the rating will be a superficial and arbitrary judgement;
- the whole performance review meeting may be dominated by the fact that it will end with a rating, especially if that governs contingent pay increases; this will severely limit the forward-looking and developmental focus of the meeting which is all-important;
- it *may* be feasible to rate performance against clearly defined quantitative objectives but it becomes much more difficult to rate fairly and consistently when dealing with more qualitative aspects of performance. It is particularly invidious to attempt to rate competency levels because they tend to be generalized statements of behavioural expectations which cannot support precise ratings, even if evidence of actual behaviour is available (which for assessment purposes it must be).

The arguments against ratings are more powerful than the arguments in favour and more and more organizations have turned against them. This is shown by a comparison on the basis of the CIPD surveys of the proportion of organizations which used ratings for any purpose (not just to inform performance pay decisions) in 1992, which was 78 per cent, with the proportion in 2003 which was 59 per cent.

If, in spite of the problems, it is decided that ratings are necessary the following things need to be considered:

1. the basis upon which levels of performance will be defined;
2. the number of rating levels to be used;
3. methods of achieving a reasonable degree of accuracy and consistency in ratings.

Performance level definitions

The rating scale format can either be behavioural, with examples of good, average and inadequate performance, or graphic, which simply presents a number of scale points along a continuum. The scale points or anchors in the latter may be defined alphabetically (a,b,c etc), numerically (1,2,3 etc) or by means of initials (ex for excellent etc) which purport to disguise the hierarchical nature of the scale. The scale points may be further described adjectivally (for example, exceptional, acceptable, unsatisfactory).

The following is a typical example of a five-point rating scale which progresses downwards from highly positive to negative:

A   Outstanding performance in all respects.
B   Superior performance, significantly above normal job requirements.
C   Good all-round performance which meets the normal requirements of the job.
D   Performance not fully up to requirements. Clear weaknesses requiring improvement have been identified.
E   Unacceptable; constant guidance is required and performance of many aspects of the job is well below a reasonable standard.

An alternative and increasingly popular approach is to have a rating scale such as the following four-point one which provides positive reinforcement or at least emphasizes development needs at every level.

Very effective   Consistently performs in a thoroughly proficient manner beyond normal expectations.
Effective   Achieves required objectives and standards of performance and meets the normal expectations of the job.
Developing   A contribution which is stronger in some aspects of the job than others, where most objectives are met but where performance improvements should still take place.
Basic   A contribution which indicates that there is considerable room for improvement in several definable areas.

Note also that in order to dispel any unfortunate associations with other systems such as school reports, this 'positive' scale does not include alphabetic or numerical ratings.

Number of rating levels

The most common number of rating levels in those respondents to the 2003/4 CIPD survey who used them was four (28 per cent of respondents) and five (47 per cent of respondents). Three levels were used by 5 per cent of respondents.

Traditionally, five-level scales have been used on the grounds that raters prefer this degree of fineness in performance definition and can easily recognize the middle grade and distinguish those who fall into higher or lower categories. Four-level scales are used when it is believed that they avoid the problem inherent in five-level scales of taking the easy route of rating in the middle of the scale. Three-level scales are advocated by some organizations because they believe that people are not capable of making any finer distinctions between performance levels. Managers know the really good and poor performers when they see them and have no difficulty in placing the majority where they belong, that is, in the middle category.

The number of levels to use is a matter of choice and judgement but there is no evidence that any single approach is superior to the others. It is, however, preferable for level definitions to be positive rather than negative and for them to provide a degree of reliable guidance on the choice of ratings.

Achieving consistency

The problem with rating scales is that it is difficult to ensure that a consistent approach to rating is adopted by managers throughout an organization. There is plenty of room for subjective and biased judgements and this creates difficulties when rating decisions are converted into contingent pay decisions. Performance-related pay schemes have often failed because the people affected do not trust their managers to be fair. The approaches that can be adopted to achieving consistency are as follows.

1. Forced distribution

This requires managers to conform to a pattern which quite often corresponds broadly with the normal curve of distribution. A typical distribution would be:

Rating	%
A	5
B	15
C	60
D	15
E	5

But the distribution of ability between different departments may vary and managers rightly dislike being forced to conform to some arbitrary pattern. Only 8 per cent of the respondents to the CIPD survey used forced distribution.

2. Ranking systems

An alternative approach is to rank staff in order of merit and then to divide the rank order into segments which define ratings. A forced distribution in a ranking system might involve giving the top 10 per cent an A rating, the next 15 per cent a B rating, the next 60 per cent a C rating and the remaining 15 per cent a D rating. Such distribution systems do ensure a consistent distribution of ratings but still depend on the relative objectivity and accuracy of the rankings.

3. Training

Training can take place in the form of 'consistency' workshops for managers who discuss how ratings can be objectively justified and test rating decisions on case study performance review data. This can build a level of common understanding about rating levels.

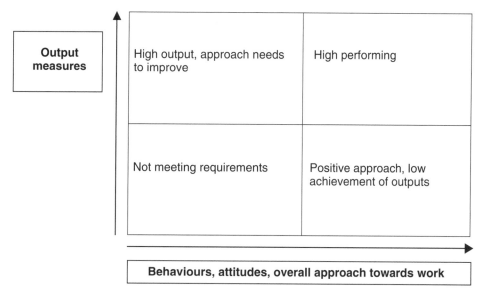

Figure 21.4 Performance matrix

4. Calibration (peer reviews)

Groups of managers meet to review the pattern of each other's ratings and challenge unusual decisions or distributions. This process of calibration or moderation is time consuming but is possibly the best way to achieve a reasonable degree of consistency, especially when the calibration group members share some knowledge of the performances of each other's staff. Manager workshops to review ratings were held by 16 per cent of the respondents to the CIPD 2003/4 survey.

5. Monitoring

The distribution of ratings is monitored by HR, which challenges any unusual patterns and identifies and questions what appear to be unwarrantable differences between departments' ratings. This is the approach favoured by many organizations, although there is much to be said for supporting it with training and peer reviews.

An alternative visual approach to rating

An alternative approach to rating was developed by Ann Cummins of Humanus Consultancy for a client in the financial services sector. This involves an agreement between the manager and the individual on where the latter should be placed on a matrix or grid as shown in Figure 21.4. This provides a 'snapshot' of their overall contribution which is presented visually and as such provides a better basis for analysis and discussion than a mechanistic rating. The assessment of contribution refers both to outputs and to behaviours, attitudes and overall approach.

The review guidelines accompanying the matrix are as follows:

> You and your manager need to agree an overall assessment. This will be recorded in the summary page at the beginning of the review document. The aim is to get a balanced assessment of your contribution through the year. The assessment will take account of how you have performed against the responsibilities of your role as described in the Role Profile; objectives achieved and competency development over the course of the year. The assessment will become relevant for pay increases in the future.
>
> The grid on the annual performance review summary is meant to provide a visual snapshot of your overall contribution. This replaces a more conventional rating scale approach. It reflects the fact that your contribution is determined not just by results, but also by your overall approach towards your work and how you behave towards colleagues and customers.
>
> The evidence recorded in the performance review will be used to support where your manager places a mark on the grid.
>
> Their assessment against the vertical axis will be based on an assessment of your performance against your objectives, performance standards described in your role profile, and any other work achievements recorded in the review. Together these represent 'outputs'.
>
> The assessment against the horizontal axis will be based on an overall assessment of your performance against the competency level definitions for the role.
>
> Note that someone who is new in the role may be placed in one of the lower quadrants but this should not be treated as an indication of development needs and not as a reflection on the individual's performance.

A similar scheme is used by HalifaxBOS.

EVALUATION

Englemann and Roesch (11) have suggested that the following areas should be examined when evaluating a 'performance system':

- How well it supports the organization's objectives.
- How it is linked to the organization's critical success factors.
- How well it defines and establishes individual objectives.
- How well it relates to job responsibilities and performance expectations.
- How effectively it encourages personal development.
- How easy (or difficult) it is to use.
- How objective or subjective, clear or ambiguous evaluation criteria are.

- Whether it addresses company policies and procedures.
- Whether it is fairly and consistently administered.
- How well supervisors and employees are trained to use and live under the system.
- How it is linked to pay.

The respondents to the 2003/2004 CIPD survey of performance management listed the criteria for evaluating performance management. The top ten in order of importance were:

1. Proper discussion/communication between managers and individuals in formal and informal reviews
2. Increased profitability or productivity
3. Achievement of goals
4. Increased motivation
5. Regular feedback
6. Support of personal development
7. Management buy-in
8. Alignment with business strategy
9. Low employee turnover
10. Development of skills.

Evaluation of the effectiveness of performance management can take place by conducting opinion surveys or asking individuals to complete a questionnaire immediately following a review meeting. The survey or questionnaire could ask them to give their reactions (for example, fully agree, partly agree, partly disagree, fully disagree) to the following statements:

1. I was given plenty of opportunity to contribute to formulating my objectives.
2. I am quite satisfied that the objectives I agreed to were fair.
3. I felt that the meeting to agree objectives helped me to focus on what I should be aiming to achieve.
4. I received good feedback from my manager during the year on how well I was doing.
5. My manager was always prepared to provide guidance when I ran into any problems with my work.
6. The performance review was conducted by my manager in a friendly and helpful way.
7. My manager fully recognized my achievements during the year.
8. If any criticisms were made during the review, they were based on fact, not on opinion.

9. I was given plenty of opportunity by my manager to discuss the reasons for any problems with my work.
10. I felt that generally the comments made by my manager at the review meeting were fair.
11. The review meeting ended with a clear plan of action for the future with which I agreed.
12. I felt well-motivated after the meeting.

PERFORMANCE MANAGEMENT ISSUES

The main issues in performance management are obtaining management buy-in and ensuring that proper reviews take place which generate fair judgements. Considerable efforts are needed to encourage managers and to develop their skills.

REFERENCES

1 Purcell, J, Kinnie, K, Hutchinson S, Rayton, B and Swart, J (2003) *Understanding the People and Performance Link: Unlocking the black box*, CIPD, London
2 Egan, G (1995) A clear path to peak performance, *People Management*, 18 May
3 IDS Study No 626 (1997) *Performance Management*, Incomes Data Services, London, May
4 Armstrong, M and Baron, A (1998) *Performance Management: The new realities*, CIPD, London
5 Armstrong, M and Baron, A (2004) *Managing Performance: Action and impact*, CIPD, London
6 Deming, W E (1986) *Out of the Crisis*, Massachusetts Institute of Technology Centre for Advanced Engineering Studies, Cambridge MA
7 Armstrong, M (1976) *A Handbook of Personnel Management Practice*, Kogan Page, London
8 Kessler, I and Purcell, J (1992) Performance-related pay: objectives and applications, *Human Resource Management Journal*, **2** (3)
9 Armstrong, M and Murlis, H (2004) *Reward Management*, 5th edn, Kogan Page, London
10 Leventhal, G S (1980) What should be done with equity theory? in *Social Exchange: Advances in theory and research*, ed G K Gergen, M S Greenberg and R H Willis, Plenum, New York
11 Engelmann, C H and Roesch, C H (1996) *Managing Individual Performance*, American Compensation Association, Scottsdale, AZ

Part VI

Reward management for special groups

22

Rewarding directors and senior executives

Probably no aspect of remuneration has attracted as much attention in recent years as that of the pay of directors and senior executives. An IDS survey (1) found that in 2003 chief executives of FTSE 100 companies earned a basic salary of £625,000. With incentives and bonuses their total pay jumped to £1.2 million. In 2003 managers and professionals earned £135 for every £100 they earned in 1998 and over the same period FTSE 350 directors earned £263 for every £100. Average earnings of all workers in April 2003 were £25,170. The outcry over top executives reward levels has recently focused on the huge sums paid out to failed chief executives, but questions are asked frequently on the level of pay and the basis upon which the pay decisions are made.

In this chapter the considerations affecting the rewards of directors (board room pay) and senior executives are covered under the following headings:

● corporate governance;
● the role of remuneration committees;
● the main elements of the remuneration packages of directors and senior executives: incentives, benefits and service contracts.

CORPORATE GOVERNANCE

A UK company is owned by its shareholders, but the power and authority for running the company is devolved to its board of directors. In the UK (as in the USA) the board of directors is a single or 'unitary' structure, responsible for corporate governance as well as business decision making, including most decisions about pay.

Concern about corporate governance and the belief that directors' pay might be out of control, leading to decisions contrary to shareholders' interests, led to a series of reviews. The sequence started with the Cadbury Report (1993), was furthered by Greenbury (1985) and tied together by Hampel (1998). In addition, the Stock Exchange produced its Listing Requirements Relating to Remuneration in 1997. The main outcomes of these reviews were statements of principle concerning corporate governance, proposals on the role of remuneration committees and requirements for boards to disclose further detail of remuneration to shareholders who were given the right to challenge pay decisions, which in a number of recent cases they have.

Principles of corporate governance relating to remuneration

The key principles of corporate governance as it affects the remuneration of directors which emerged from the various reviews and the Stock Exchange requirements are as follows:

- Remuneration committees should consist exclusively of non-executive directors and should determine remuneration policy and the reward packages of individual executive directors which should appear as a section in the annual report. This report should include statements on remuneration policy and the methods used to form that policy and disclose details of the remuneration of individual directors.
- Remuneration committees must provide a remuneration package sufficient to attract, retain and motivate directors but should avoid paying more than is necessary. They should be sensitive to wider issues, eg pay and employment conditions elsewhere in the company.
- Performance-related elements should be designed to align the interests of directors and shareholders.
- Any new longer-term incentive arrangement should, preferably, replace existing executive share option plans, or at least form part of an integrated approach which should be approved by shareholders.
- The pension consequences and associated costs to the company of increases in base salary should be considered.

- Notice or service contract periods should be set at, or reduced to, a year or less. However, in some cases, periods of up to two years may be acceptable.
- Remuneration committees should take a robust line on the payment of compensation where performance has been unsatisfactory.

REMUNERATION COMMITTEES

The reports and codes on directors' pay have all emphasized the importance of having a committee with the responsibility for making decisions on the remuneration of chief executives and directors.

Purpose

The purpose of remuneration committees is to provide an independent basis for setting the salary levels and the rules covering incentives, share options, benefit entitlements and contract provisions for executive directors. Such committees are accountable to shareholders for the decisions they take and the non-executive directors who sit on them should have no personal financial interests at stake. They should be constituted as sub-committees of company boards and boards should elect both the chairman and the members.

Role

The role of the remuneration committee is to:

- set broad policy for executive remuneration as a whole as well as the remuneration packages of executive directors and, sometimes, other senior executives;
- focus on encouraging corporate performance contribution and ensure that individuals are fairly but responsibly rewarded for their individual contribution;
- comply with the appropriate codes (the Stock Exchange and Halpern);
- report and account to shareholders directly for their decisions on behalf of the board;
- ensure that the relationship between boardroom remuneration and policy for employees below this level remains consistent and sensible; and that
- proper and professional advice is obtained to assist in their deliberations.

Remuneration committees should be supported by a senior executive of the company who has suitable expertise in remuneration issues and should seek external help from consultants as required. The committee should obtain information on remuneration levels and practices in comparable companies from an internal or external adviser.

DIRECTORS' AND SENIOR EXECUTIVES' REMUNERATION

The main elements of directors' and senior executives' remuneration are basic pay, short- and long-term bonus or incentive schemes, share option and share ownership schemes, benefits and service contracts.

Basic pay

Decisions on the base salary of directors and senior executives are usually founded on largely subjective views about the market worth of the individuals concerned. Remuneration on joining the company is commonly settled by negotiation, often subject to the approval of a remuneration committee. Reviews of base salaries are then undertaken by reference to market movements and success as measured by company performance. Decisions on base salary are important not only in themselves but also because the level may influence decisions on the pay of both senior and middle managers. Bonuses are expressed as a percentage of base salary, share options may be allocated as a declared multiple of basic pay and, commonly, pension will be a proportion of final salary.

Bonus schemes

Virtually all major employers in the UK (90 per cent according to recent surveys by organizations such as Monks and Hay) provide annual incentive (bonus) schemes for senior executives. Bonus schemes provide directors and executives with cash sums based on the measures of company and, frequently, individual performance. Recent surveys have shown that about 90 per cent of participating organizations have bonus schemes for main board directors.

Typically, bonus payments are linked to achievement of profit and/or other financial targets and they are sometimes 'capped', that is, a restriction is placed on the maximum amount payable. There may also be elements related to achieving specific goals and to individual performance. Amongst FT-SE 50 companies with a December 2002 year end, the median bonus for the top executive role was 64 per cent of salary (average 77 per cent) and only seven paid less than 50 per cent. The level of payments appears high given that this was generally considered to be a difficult year for most businesses.

Bonuses are ostensibly intended to motivate directors to achieve performance improvements for the business. There is no evidence that this takes place. A more common, although not always disclosed, reason for bonuses is to ensure that what is believed to be a competitive remuneration package is available: 'Everyone else is doing it so we must too.'

Long-term bonuses

Cash bonus schemes can be extended over periods of more than one year on the grounds that annual bonuses focus too much on short-term results. The most common approach to providing longer-term rewards is through share ownership schemes as described later.

Deferred bonus schemes

Some companies have adopted deferred bonus schemes under which part of the executive's annual bonus is deferred for, say, two years. The deferred element is converted into shares, each of which is matched with an extra, free share on condition the executive remains employed by the company at the end of the deferral period. Such a scheme is designed to reward performance and loyalty to the company.

Scheme effectiveness

In an effective bonus scheme:

- targets will be tough but achievable;
- the reward should be commensurate with the achievement;
- the targets will be quantified and agreed;
- the measures used will refer to the key factors which affect company performance, and these performance areas will be those that can be directly affected by the efforts of those eligible for bonus payments;
- the formula will be simple and clear.

On the evidence of recent bonus payouts to failing company directors, it does not seem that these criteria are being applied successfully.

Share option schemes

Many companies have share option schemes which give directors and executives the right to buy a block of shares on some future date at the share price ruling when the option was granted. They are a form of long-term incentive on the assumption that executives will be motivated to perform more effectively if they can anticipate a substantial capital gain when they sell their shares at a price above that prevailing when they took up the option.

Conditions may be laid down to the effect that the company's earnings per share (EPS) growth should exceed inflation by a set amount over a number of years (often three) and that the executive remains employed by the company at the exercise date.

The arguments advanced in favour of executive share options are that, first, it is right for executives to share in the success of their company, to which, it is assumed, they have contributed, and, second, they encourage executives to align their interests more closely in the longer term with those of the shareholders as a whole (the latter reason is based on agency theory, although it is quite possible that those who advance it are unaware that such a thing as agency theory exists). The first point is valid as long as the reward for exercising share options is commensurate with the contribution of the executive to the improved performance of the business. The second point is dubious. The vast majority of shares acquired in this way are sold almost immediately and the gain is pocketed as extra income.

Performance share schemes

Some companies adopt performance share schemes under which executives are provisionally awarded shares. The release of the shares is subject to the company's performance, typically determined on a sliding scale by reference to the company's total shareholder return (a combination of share price growth and dividend yield) ranking against its chosen peer companies over a three-year period. Release is also conditional on the executive remaining employed by the company at the vesting date. Such a scheme rewards loyalty to the company and the value delivered to shareholders in the form of share price performance and dividends but does not link directly to business performance.

Share options have been severely criticized recently because of the enormous gains made by some executives. There is a strong feeling among some of the major investment institutions that share options do not achieve community of interest between executives and shareholders and are in effect no more than a form of cash bonus in which the payout has little or nothing to do with the executive's performance. In spite of this feeling, however, share option schemes may continue because they are well understood and have become an accepted feature of executive remuneration, although interest in share ownership as an alternative is increasing.

Executive restricted share schemes

Under such schemes free shares are provisionally awarded to participants. These shares do not belong to the executive until they are released or vested; hence they are 'restricted'. The number of shares actually released to the executive at the end of a defined period (usually three or, less commonly, five years) will depend on performance over that period against specific targets. Thereafter there may be a further retention period when the shares must be held although no further performance conditions apply.

BENEFITS

Employee benefits for executives may amount to over 20 per cent of the total reward package. The most important element is the pension scheme, and directors may be provided with a much higher accrual rate in a final salary scheme. This means that, typically, the maximum two-thirds pension can be achieved after 20 years' service rather than the 40 years it takes in a typical one-sixtieth scheme.

SERVICE CONTRACTS

Long-term service contracts for directors have been fairly typical, but they are disliked in the City because of the high severance payments to departing chief executives and directors which are made if the contract is two or three years, even when it was suspected or actually the case that they had been voted off the board because of inadequate performance. Rolling contracts for directors are now more likely to be restricted to one year.

REFERENCE

1   Incomes Data Services (IDS) (2004) *Executive Compensation Review*, IDS, London

23

Expatriate remuneration

As businesses expand globally, they tend to send an increasing number of staff abroad as expatriates. The assignment may be a short-term attachment to provide guidance and expertise. Or it may be a secondment to an overseas location which lasts two or three years. Managing expatriates presents a number of problems, for example persuading people to work in possibly unpleasant or even dangerous countries, convincing them that an overseas assignment is a good career move, dealing with the issues raised by the partners of employees who do not want their career or life at home disrupted, and coping with the fact that on returning to their home country, expatriates often find that real earnings have fallen. A particularly difficult problem is that of remuneration (pay, benefits and allowances) and this chapter considers the approaches available to solving it.

EXPATRIATE REMUNERATION POLICIES

Expatriate remuneration policies may be based on the following propositions:

- Expatriates should be neither better nor worse off as a result of working abroad.
- Home country living standards should be maintained as far as possible.
- Higher responsibility should be reflected in the salary paid (this may be a notional home salary).
- The remuneration package should be competitive.

- In developing the remuneration package, particular care has to be taken to giving proper consideration to the conditions under which the employee will be working abroad.
- Account should be taken of the need to maintain equity as far as possible in remuneration between expatriates, some of whom will be from different countries.
- Account also has to be taken of the problems that may arise when expatriates are paid more than nationals in the country in which they are working who are in similar jobs.
- The package should be cost effective, ie the contribution made by expatriates should justify the total cost of maintaining them abroad – assignment costs can total three or four times the equivalent package in the home country.

EXPATRIATE PAY

There are four approaches to calculating expatriate pay: home country, host country, selected country and hybrid.

Home country basis

The home-based method (sometimes called the balance sheet approach) 'builds up' the salary to be paid to the expatriate in the following steps:

1. Determine the salary that would be paid for the expatriate's job in the home country net of income tax and National Insurance contributions.
2. Calculate the 'home country spendable' or 'net disposable' income. This is the portion of income used for day-to-day expenditure at home.
3. Apply a cost of living index to the 'host country spendable income' to give the equivalent buying power in the host country. This is used as a measure of expenditure levels in the host country and is an important yardstick which is used to ensure that the expatriate will be no worse off abroad than at home.
4. Add extra allowances for working abroad (see below).

This is the most popular approach because it demonstrates that individuals will not lose by going abroad (in fact they will probably gain) and because it is easier to operate when expatriates are working in several countries.

Host country basis

This involves paying the market rate for the job in the host country. Allowances may be paid for the expenditure incurred by expatriates because they are living abroad, for example second home costs, children's education.

Selected country basis

The salary structure in a selected country (often where the company's headquarters are sited) provides the base and this built up as in the home country method.

Hybrid basis

This approach divides the expatriate's salary into two components. One – the local component – is the same for all expatriates working in jobs at the same level irrespective of their country of origin. The other local component is based on a calculation of the expendable income in the host country required to maintain a UK standard of living.

ALLOWANCES

Companies add a number of allowances, as described below, to the expatriate's salary to calculate the total expatriate remuneration package. They are designed to compensate for disruption and to make the assignment attractive to the employee. Most are applied to the notional home salary but one of them, the cost-of-living allowance, is based on spendable income:

- *Cost-of-living-allowance* – the cost-of-living allowance is reached by applying an index to the home country spendable income. The index measures the relative cost, in the host country, of purchasing conventional 'shopping basket' items, such as food and clothing.
- *Incentive premium* – this offers the expatriate a financial inducement to accept the assignment. It may be intended to compensate for disruption to family life. But companies are tending to reduce this premium or do away with it altogether, particularly for intra-European assignments. They are questioning why an employee should receive 10–15 per cent of gross salary for simply moving from one culturally similar country to another when no such allowance would be payable in the case of a relocation within the UK.
- *Hardship allowance* – this compensates for discomfort and difficulty in the host country such as an unpleasant climate, health hazards, poor communications, isolation, language difficulties, risk, and poor amenities.
- *Separation allowance* – this may be paid if expatriates cannot take their family abroad.
- *Clothing allowance* – a payment for special clothing and accessories which expatriates need to buy.

- *Relocation allowance* – this covers the cost of expenses arising when moving from one country to another.
- *Housing/utilities* – any additional costs of accommodation or utilities.

BENEFITS

The benefits provided to expatriates include cars, the costs of educating children, special health home leave, and rest and recuperation leave if the expatriate is working in a high hardship territory.

24

Rewarding sales and customer service staff

Rewards for sales staff are often different from those provided for employees. Sales representatives are more likely to be eligible for commission payments or bonuses on the grounds that their sales performance will depend on, or at least be improved by, financial incentives. Many companies believe that the special nature of selling and the type of person they need to attract to their sales force require some form of additional bonus or commission to be paid. The nature of the work of sales representatives means that it is usually easy to specify targets and measure performance against them and sales incentive schemes are therefore more likely to meet the line-of-sight requirement (that is, that there should be a clear link between effort and performance) than schemes for other staff such as managers and administrators. Sales or customer service staff in retail establishments are often paid spot rates with a commission on sales. The approaches to rewarding sales staff described in this chapter are:

- salary only;
- basic salary plus commission;
- basic salary plus bonus;
- commission only;
- sales incentives.

Table 24.1 at the end of the chapter summarizes the different schemes, their advantages and disadvantages and when they may be appropriate.

SALARY ONLY

Companies may adopt a salary-only (no commission or bonus) approach when sales staff have little influence over sales volume, when representing the company and generally promoting its products or services is more important than direct selling, and when the company wants to encourage sales staff to build up good and long-term relationships with their customers, the emphasis being on customer service rather than on high-pressure selling.

Basic salary only may also be paid to sales staff who work in highly seasonal industries where sales fluctuate considerably and in businesses where regular orders for food and other consumer goods give little opportunity for creative selling.

However, companies that do not pay commission or bonus may have a pay-for-contribution scheme which provides for consolidated increases based on an assessment of performance and competence in such areas as teamwork, customer relations, interpersonal skills and communications. Where sales staff have to work together to achieve results or where it is difficult to apportion a successful sale to individuals, a team pay approach may be adopted. Additionally, salary-only sales representatives may be eligible for incentives in the form of prizes, as described later.

If no commission or bonus is offered, it is necessary for companies to ensure that the salaries paid to their sales staff are competitive. They have to take account of the total earnings of sales staff in markets from which they recruit people or where their own staff move. If they cannot or do not want at least to match these earnings they may have to offer other inducements to join or stay with the company. These can include opportunities for promotion, learning new skills, more stable pay and greater security.

BASIC SALARY PLUS COMMISSION

Salary plus commission plans provide for a proportion of total earnings to be paid in commission, the rest being paid in the form of a fixed salary. The commission is calculated as a percentage of the value of sales. The proportion of commission varies widely. As a general rule it is higher when results depend on the ability and effort of individuals or when there is less emphasis on non-selling activities. As a rule of thumb, most sales managers believe that the commission element will not motivate their staff unless they have a reasonable opportunity to earn at least 20 per cent.

The commission may be a fixed percentage of all sales, possibly with a 'cap' or upper limit on earnings. Alternatively the commission rate can increase at higher levels of sales on a rising scale to encourage sales representatives to make even greater efforts.

BASIC SALARY PLUS BONUS

Cash bonuses may be paid on top of basic salary. They are based on the achievement of targets or quotas for sales volume, profit or sales 'contribution' (sales revenue minus variable expenses). They differ from commission payments in that the latter are based simply on a percentage of whatever sales have been attained. In a bonus scheme, targets or objectives may be set just for sales volume but they can also focus on particular aspects of the results that can be achieved by sales staff which it is felt should be stimulated. These may include the sales of high-margin or more profitable products or services in order to encourage staff to concentrate on them rather than simply aiming to achieve sales volume with low-margin products that are easier to sell. They may also cover reviving moribund accounts, promoting new products and minimizing bad debt. Other criteria may include the level of customer service, the volume of repeat business, the number of productive calls made, product knowledge, teamwork and quality of administration.

There are many ways in which bonuses can be determined. The method used will take into account the following considerations:

- the formula for relating bonuses to sales – a bonus may be triggered when a sales threshold is reached and additions related to increased sales directly or on an accelerated basis;
- the size of bonus payments available at different levels of performance;
- the maximum bonus that will be paid out;
- the bonus criteria; sales revenue is often used, but some companies use profit or contribution to encourage sales representatives to focus on selling high-margin products rather than going for volume;
- any other factors to be included in the bonus plan, such as those mentioned above.

COMMISSION ONLY

Sales staff who are at the 'hard' end of selling (for example, double glazing) may receive only a straight commission based on a percentage of the value of their sales. No basic salary is paid.

ADDITIONAL NON-CASH REWARDS

While it is possible that the prime motivator for a typical sales representative is cash, there are a number of other effective non-cash ways of providing motivation, as described below.

Incentives

Gifts and vouchers provide a tangible means of recognizing achievements. They may be linked to the achievement of specified targets but should not be restricted too much to the 'super sales representatives'; the solid dependable sales person also needs motivating through the recognition that such incentives provide. Gifts are subject to income tax.

Competitions

Prizes can be awarded to individuals or teams for notable sales achievements, for example bringing in new business. However, competitions can de-motivate those who do not win prizes and they should be designed to ensure that all those who are doing well feel that they have a good chance of getting a prize.

Cars as perks

Sales representatives can be motivated by the opportunity to get a bigger and better car if they are particularly successful. The car may be retained for a defined period and made available again if the high performance is maintained.

Non-financial motivators

Sales people typically have high levels of achievement motivation but they still like to be recognized and given the opportunity to make even better use of their talents in more challenging (and remunerative) work. Public applause (for example, sales representative of the month) and private 'thank you's are both important.

SUMMARY OF METHODS

Table 24.1 Summary of payment and incentive arrangements for sales staff

Method	Features	Advantages	Disadvantages	When appropriate
Salary only	Straight salary, no commission or bonus	Encourages customer service rather than high-pressure selling; deals with the problem of staff who are working	No direct motivation through money; may attract under-achieving people who are	When: representing the company is more important than direct selling; staff have little

(Continued)

Table 24.1 *Continued*

Method	Features	Advantages	Disadvantages	When appropriate
		in a new or unproductive sales territory; protects income when sales fluctuate for reasons beyond the individual's control	subsidized by high achievers; increases fixed costs of sales because pay costs are not flexed with sales results	influence on sales volume (they may simply be 'order takers'); customer service is all-important
Salary plus commission	Basic salary plus cash commission calculated as a percentage of sales volume or value	Direct financial motivation is provided related to what sales staff are there to do, ie generate sales; but they are not entirely dependent on commission – they are cushioned by their base salary	Relating pay to the volume or value of sales is too crude an approach and may result in staff going for volume by concentrating on the easier-to-sell products, not those generating high margins; may encourage high-pressure selling as in some financial services firms in the 80s and 90s	When it is believed that the way to get more sales is to link extra money to results but a base salary is still needed to attract the many people who want to be assured of a reasonable basic salary which will not fluctuate but who still aspire to increase that salary by their own efforts
Salary plus bonus	Basic salary plus cash bonus based on achieving and exceeding sales targets or quotas and meeting other selling objectives	Provide financial motivation but targets or objectives can be flexed to ensure that particular sales goals are achieved, eg high-margin sales, customer service	Do not have a clear line of sight between effort and reward; may be complex to administer; sales representative may find them hard to	When: flexibility in providing rewards is important; it is felt that sales staff need to be motivated to focus on aspects of their work other

(Continued)

Table 24.1 *Continued*

Method	Features	Advantages	Disadvantages	When appropriate
			understand and resent the use of subjective judgements on performance other than sales	than simply maximizing sales volume
Commission only	Only commission based on a percentage of sales volume or value is paid; there is no basic salary	Provide a direct financial incentive; attract high-performing sales staff; ensure that selling costs vary directly with sales; little direct supervision required	Lead to high-pressure selling; may attract the wrong sort of people who are interested only in sales and not customer service; focus attention on high volume rather than profitability	When: sales performance depends mainly on selling ability and can be measured by immediate sales results; staff are not involved in non-selling activities; continuing relationships with customers are relatively unimportant
Additional non-cash rewards	Incentives, prizes, cars, recognition, opportunities to grow	Utilize powerful non-financial motivators	May be difficult to administer; do not provide a direct incentive	When it is believed that other methods of payment need to be enhanced by providing additional motivators

25

Shop floor pay

Shop floor payment systems and statutory for manual workers which have not been 'harmonized', that is, brought into line with the reward system for staff, frequently differ from the systems described elsewhere in this book, in three ways. First, the use of time rates, second, the use of spot rates rather than graded structures, and third, the use of payment-by-results schemes. This chapter reviews the factors affecting shop floor pay and describes the characteristics of manual workers' pay mentioned above. It ends with a discussion of harmonization and single status.

FACTORS AFFECTING SHOP FLOOR PAY

The three main factors affecting shop floor pay are, first, bargaining arrangements, second, local labour market rate pressures, and third, trends in the use of technology on the shop floor.

Bargaining arrangements

Shop floor pay is often influenced strongly by national and local agreements with trade unions which will determine rates for particular jobs or skill levels. This consitutes an aspect of the effort bargain. The objectives of workers and their trade union officials and representatives is to strike a bargain with management about what they consider to be a reasonable amount of pay which should be provided by their employer in return for their contribution. It is, in effect, an agreement between workers and management which lays down the amount of work to be done for an agreed wage, not just the hours to be worked. Explicitly or implicitly, all employers are in a bargaining situation with regard to payment systems. A system will not be effective until it is agreed as being fair and equitable by both sides.

Local labour market pressures

Shop floor workers are usually recruited from the local labour market where the laws of supply and demand can have a marked effect on the rates of pay for particular occupations when there is a skills shortage or reluctance on the part of workers to carry out certain jobs. The local labour market is a fairly perfect market in one of the senses used by economists, that is, there is widespread and easily available knowledge on rates of pay (the price of labour) and there may also exist, although not for every occupation, a fair degree of choice by both buyers and sellers of where they obtain labour or where they provide it.

Technology

The increased use of technology on the shop floor, for example in the form of computer-aided manufacture, has meant that the demand for a number of the traditional skills has diminished while the demand for new technical skills has increased. Computer controlled machines are more likely to be operated by technicians than by members of the old skilled trades. This is one of the factors that has led to pressures to harmonize shop floor and office or laboratory payment systems.

TIME RATES

Time rates, also known as day rates, day work, flat rates or hourly rates, provide workers with a predetermined rate for the actual hours they work. The rate is fixed by formal or informal negotiations, on the basis of local rates or, less often, by reference to a hierarchy produced by job evaluation. The rate varies only with time, never with performance or output. However, additional payments are made on top of base rates for overtime, shift working, night work, call outs, adverse working conditions and, sometimes, location.

The situation when time rates are most commonly used is when it is thought that it is impossible or undesirable to use a payment-by-results system, for example in maintenance work. From the viewpoint of employees the advantage of time rates is that their earnings are predictable and steady and they do not have to engage in endless arguments with rate fixers and supervisors about piece rate or time allowances. The argument against them is that they do not provide a direct incentive relating the reward to the effort or the results. Two ways of modifying the basic time rate approach are to adopt high day rates, as described below, or measured day work, as covered later in this chapter.

Time rates may take the form of what are often called high day rates. These are higher than the minimum time rate and may contain a consolidated bonus rate element. The underlying assumption is that higher base rates will encourage greater effort without the problems created when operating an incentive scheme. This is in line with the theory of the economy of high wages mentioned in Chapter 6. High day rates are usually above the local market rates to attract and retain workers.

PAYMENT-BY-RESULT SCHEMES

Payment-by–result (PBR) schemes provide incentives to workers by relating their pay or, more usually, part of their pay to the number of items they produce or the time taken to do a certain amount of work. The main types of PBR or incentive schemes for individuals are piecework, work measured schemes, measured day work and performance-related pay. Team bonus schemes are an alternative to individual PBR and plant-wide schemes can produce bonuses which are paid instead of individual or team bonuses or in addition to them. Each of these methods is described below and summarized, with an analysis of their advantages and disadvantages and the situations when they may be appropriate, in Table 25.1 (page 319). First, however, it is necessary to deal with the general considerations affecting the design and use of PBR schemes.

General considerations

The general considerations to be taken into account in developing and maintaining incentive schemes are the criteria of effectiveness and their advantages and disadvantages.

Criteria of effectiveness

Incentive schemes aim to motivate employees to exert greater effort. They will do so effectively only if:

- the link between effort and reward is clear and easily understood;
- the value of the reward is worth while in relation to the effort;
- individuals are able to influence their level of effort or behaviour in order to earn a reward;
- rewards closely follow the effort;

- the integrity of the scheme is preserved – it is not allowed to degenerate and cannot be manipulated so that individuals are over-rewarded.

The rationale for incentive schemes

The basic rationale of incentive schemes is the simple proposition that people are motivated by money. It is believed that they will work harder if rewards are tied directly to the results they achieve. Certainly the experience of most people who have installed a PBR scheme in a workplace where it did not previously exist is that productivity increases substantially when the scheme is new, although the level of increase is not always maintained. Studies in the United States by Lawler (1), Guzzo *et al* (2), Nalbantian (3) and Binder (4) have shown productivity increases of between 15 and 35 per cent when incentive schemes have been put into place.

PBR schemes are used in the belief that they yield increased output, lower the cost of production and provide higher earnings for the workers concerned. It is also commonly believed that less supervision is needed to keep output up. Indeed, when direct supervision is difficult, PBR is often advocated as the only practicable form of payment.

Disadvantages of incentive schemes

The argument that people work harder only when they are paid more is regarded by some people as overwhelming. They do not accept the proposition that intrinsic and non-financial motivators can have an equally, if not more, powerful and longer-lasting impact.

The disadvantages of shop floor PBR schemes are that they can:

- *Be unfair* – earnings may fluctuate through no fault of the individual because of lack of work, shortage of materials, design modifications or the need to learn new skills. It may also be felt that the method of altering rates is unfair.
- *Be ineffective* – workers may have their own ideas about how much they want to earn or how hard they want to work and regulate their output accordingly.
- *Penalize skill* – the more skilled workers may be given the more difficult and often less remunerative jobs.
- *Cause wage drift* – the difficulty of conforming to criteria such as clearly relating pay to effort and the lax approach of some organizations to the management of incentive schemes contribute to increases in earnings at a higher rate than productivity. Degeneration and wage drift are a particular problem with work-measured schemes, as discussed later in this chapter.
- *Lead to management escaping its responsibilities* – team leaders and supervisors may rely on the incentive scheme to control output. Instead of taking poor performers

to one side and informing them that their work is not up to standard, they are tempted to take the soft option and simply point to the figures.

- *Be costly to maintain* – extra work-study engineers, rate fixers and inspectors are often needed to maintain the scheme and exercise quality control.
- *Produce strife in the workplace* – arguments about rates and accusations of unjustified rate-cutting are common in workshops where incentive schemes are used.
- *Result in poor quality work* – concentration on output can lead to neglect of quality.
- *Lead to poor teamwork* – individual incentive schemes by definition encourage individual rather than team effort.
- *Result in accidents and health hazards* – workers may be tempted to cut corners and ignore safety precautions to achieve output targets; repetitive strain injury (RSI) may result if they work too hard on tasks requiring repeated small movements.

These are powerful arguments but shop floor incentive schemes persist. The number of workers paid on this basis may have diminished but this is because of structural (the reduction in manufacturing) and technological reasons rather than because managements have turned against it.

Payment-by-result schemes

The main types of PBR or incentive schemes are described below. Their characteristics and advantages and disadvantages are summarized in Table 25.1 on page 319.

Piecework

Piecework is the oldest and simplest form of shop floor incentive scheme. Operators are paid at a specific rate according to their output or the number of 'pieces' they produce. Pay is directly proportional to output, although most piecework schemes provide a fall-back rate as minimum earnings level. The proportion of the minimum rate to average earnings varies. It is typically set at 70 or 80 per cent, although it can be as low as 30 per cent.

Work-measured schemes

Work-measured schemes are the most popular form of incentive plan for shop floor workers. They use work measurement techniques to determine standard output levels over a period or standard times for tasks. The incentive pay is then linked with the output achieved relative to the standard, or to the time saved in performing each task.

The form of work measurement used is time study. Jobs are broken down into their constituent parts or tasks and the time taken by workers to complete each part is measured with a stopwatch by a work study or industrial engineer. A number of measurements will be made of the time taken by different workers on the same task or the same worker carrying out the task at different times of the day and night. Time study is based on objective measurements, but account has to be taken of the fact that there will probably be significant differences between the rate at which operators work – the effort they put into the job. Work study engineers have therefore to assess what that rate is, a process known as effort rating.

Individual effort is rated in terms of 'standard performance'. This is the performance that a qualified and motivated worker should be able to achieve without over-exertion. The effort needed to achieve standard performance is sometimes represented as equivalent to walking at four miles an hour (that is, quite briskly). All the operators studied are given an effort rating relative to this standard. The raw times observed by the work study are then adjusted by the work study engineer to produce a basic time which represents a rating of 100 to indicate the performance of an average operator working conscientiously without financial motivation. This involves a large element of subjectivity, although experienced and well-trained engineers should be capable of making reasonably accurate and consistent assessments.

The basic time will be further adjusted to incorporate allowances for relaxation, personal needs, fatigue and any time regularly taken up by other aspects of the work such as cleaning or resetting machines. The result is the standard time for the task, usually expressed as 'standard minutes'.

Work measured schemes can use performance ratings which are calculated by a formula as in the following example:

Number of units produced per day (132) = 528 × 100 = 110%
× standard minutes per unit (4)

Actual time taken in minutes per day (480)   480

In the most common proportionate system of payment, the performance rating is applied directly to the base rate so that in the above example the incentive payment would be an additional 10 per cent.

The problem with time study is that, although it is based on objective measurements, the standard time that is ultimately obtained is the product of a number of additional subjective judgements. Employees who are being timed may deliberately restrict their performance in order to achieve low standard times and therefore higher bonuses with less effort. It is up to the work study engineer's skill and judgement to detect such restrictions, and this can lead to arguments and even strife. In organizations with trade unions it is common practice to train some representatives in work measurement techniques to promote the achievement of acceptable judgements on standard times.

Alternatively, PBR payments can be based on the time saved principle. The amount of the bonus depends on the difference between the actual time taken to perform the task and the standard time allowed. If a task is done in less than the standard time, then the percentage of time saved is applied to the base rate to calculate the bonus. The standard times may be determined by work measurement, although traditionally 'rate fixers' were employed to make more subjective and therefore often more controversial judgements.

Measured day work

Measured day work schemes were originally developed for large batch or mass-production factories in the 1950s and 1960s, when it became evident that, despite all efforts, it was impossible to control wage drift. They are, however, much less common now. Manufacturing firms often prefer to pay a high day rate.

When they exist, measured day work schemes provide for the pay of employees to be fixed on the understanding that they will maintain a specified level of performance, but in the short term pay does not fluctuate with their performance. The arrangement depends on work measurement to define the required level of performance and to monitor the actual level. The fundamental principles of measured day work are that there is an incentive level of performance and that the incentive payment is guaranteed in advance, putting employees under the obligation to perform at the effort level required. In contrast, a conventional work-measured incentive scheme allows employees discretion as to their effort level but relates their pay directly to the results they achieve. Between these two extremes there are a variety of alternatives, including banded incentives, stepped schemes and various forms of high day rate.

Performance-related pay

Performance-related pay systems such as those described in Chapter 17 can be used for manual workers. Employees receive a high base rate and an additional performance-related payment which is either a lump sum bonus or consolidated into basic pay. The award is governed by assessments of skill and performance ratings under headings such as quality, flexibility, contribution to team working and ability to hit targets. The percentage award is usually small – up to 5 per cent.

Performance-related pay is sometimes introduced for manual workers as part of a programme for harmonizing their conditions of employment with those of salaried staff. It can be appropriate in circumstances where work measurement is difficult or impossible to use, in high-technology manufacturing where operations are computer controlled or automated and teamwork and multiskilling are important, in organizations where the emphasis is on quality, and in those where just-in-time systems are used.

Group or team incentive schemes

Group or team incentive schemes provide for the payment of a bonus to members of a group or team related to the output achieved by the group in relation to defined targets or to work-measured standards.

Factory or plant-wide schemes

Factory or plant-wide schemes pay a bonus to individuals which is related to the performance of the factory as a whole and may be measured in terms of added value as in a gain-sharing scheme (see Chapter 19) or some other index of productivity (for example, units produced, cost per unit of output).

Assessment of schemes

Table 25.1 contains an assessment of the advantages and disadvantages of each type of scheme from the viewpoint of employers and employees and a review of the circumstances when the scheme is more likely to be appropriate.

SINGLE STATUS AND HARMONIZATION

Single status means that all employees have the same status so that shop floor workers on wages are on salaried terms and conditions and are entitled to the same conditions of employment, such as sick pay, as other members of staff. Harmonization means the reduction of differences in the pay structure and other employment conditions between categories of employee, usually manual and staff employees. It involves the adoption of a common approach and criteria to pay and benefits for all employees.

The pressure for harmonization has occurred because of the belief that status differentials between people in the same employment cannot be justified. Harmonization facilitates the more flexible use of labour and the impact of technology has enhanced the skills of shop floor workers and made differential treatment harder to defend. Equal pay legislation has been a major challenge to differentiation between staff and manual workers.

ACAS (5) has suggested that organizations, before pursuing a programme of harmonization, should seek answers to the following questions:

- What differences in the treatment of groups of employees are a rational result of differences in the work or the job requirements?
- Is it possible to estimate the direct costs of removing these differences?

Table 25.1 Comparison of shop floor incentive and bonus schemes

Scheme	Main features	For employers		For employees		When appropriate
		Advantages	Disadvantages	Advantages	Disadvantages	
Piecework	Bonus directly related to output.	Direct motivation; simple, easy to operate.	Lose control over output; quality problems.	Predict and control earnings in the short term; regulate pace of work themselves.	More difficult to predict and control earnings in the longer term; work may be stressful and produce RSI.	Fairly limited application to work involving unit production controlled by the person, eg agriculture, garment manufacture.
Work-measured schemes	Work measurement used to determine standard output levels over a period or standard times for job/tasks; bonus based by reference to performance ratings compared with actual performance or time saved.	Provides what appears to be a 'scientific' method of relating reward to performance; can produce significant increases in productivity, at least in the short term.	Schemes are expensive, time consuming and difficult to run and can too easily degenerate and cause wage drift because of loose rates.	Appear to provide a more objective method of relating pay to performance; employees can be involved in the rating process to ensure fairness.	Ratings are still prone to subjective judgement and earnings can fluctuate because of changes in work requirements outside the control of employees.	For short-cycle repetitive work where changes in the work mix or design changes are infrequent, downtime is restricted, and management and supervision are capable of managing and maintaining the scheme.
Measured day work	Pay fixed at a high rate on the understanding that a high level of performance against work-	Employees are under an obligation to work at the specified level of performance.	Performance targets can become easily attained norms and	High predictable earnings are provided.	No opportunities for individuals to be rewarded in line with	Everyone must be totally committed to making it work; high standards of work measurement are essential;

(Continued)

Table 25.1 Continued

Scheme	Main features	For employers		For employees		When appropriate
		Advantages	Disadvantages	Advantages	Disadvantages	
	measured standards will be maintained.		may be difficult to change.		their own efforts.	good control systems to identify shortfalls on targets.
Performance-related pay	Payments on top of base rate are made related to individual assessments of performance.	Reward individual contribution without resource to work measurement; relevant in high-technology manufacturing.	Measuring performance can be difficult; no direct incentive provided.	Opportunity to be rewarded for own efforts without having to submit to a pressured PBR system.	Assessment informing performance pay decisions may be biased, inconsistent or unsupported by evidence.	As part of a reward harmonization (shop floor and staff) programme; as an alternative to work measured schemes or an enhancement of a high day rate system.
Group or team basis	Groups or teams are paid bonuses on the basis of their performance as indicated by work measurement ratings or the achievement of targets.	Encourage team cooperation and effort; not too individualized.	Direct incentive may be limited; depends on good work measurement or the availability of clear group output or productivity targets.	Bonuses can be related clearly to the joint efforts of the group; fluctuations in earnings minimized.	Depend on effective work measurement, which is not always available; individual effort and contribution not recognized.	When team working is important and team efforts can be accurately measured and assessed; as an alternative to individual PBR if this is not effective.
Factory-wide bonuses	Bonuses related to plant performance – added value or productivity.	Increase commitment by sharing success.	No direct motivation.	Earnings increased without individual pressure.	Bonuses often small and unpredictable.	As an addition to other forms of incentive when increasing commitment is important.

- What differences in status are explicitly recognized as part of the 'reward package' for different groups in the labour force?
- What would be the possible repercussive effects of harmonization?
- How do the existing differences affect industrial relations in the organization?

REFERENCES

1   Lawler, E E (1971) *Pay and Organizational Effectiveness*, McGraw-Hill, New York
2   Guzzo, R A, Jette, R D and Katsell, R A (1985) The effect of psychological-based intervention programmes on worker productivity: a meta analysis, *Personnel Psychology*, **38**, 275–91
3   Nalbantian, H (1987) *Incentives, Cooperation and Risk Sharing*, Rowman & Littlefield, Totowa, NJ
4   Binder, A S (1990) *Paying for Productivity*, Brookings Institution, Washington, DC
5   ACAS (1982) *Developments in Harmonization: Discussion Paper No 1*, ACAS, London

Part VII

Employee benefits and pension schemes

26

Employee benefits

Employee benefits consist of arrangements made by employers for their employees which enhance the latter's well-being. They are provided in addition to pay and form important parts of the total reward package. As part of total remuneration, they may be deferred or contingent, like a pension scheme, insurance cover or sick pay, or they may be immediate like a company car or a loan. Employee benefits also include holidays and leave arrangements, which are not strictly remuneration. They are sometimes referred to dismissively as 'perks' (perquisites) or 'fringe benefits', but benefits such as those mentioned above, with the exception of company cars, which fundamentally cater for personal security or personal needs, could hardly be described as 'fringe'.

Employee benefits are a costly part of the remuneration package. They can amount to one-third or more of basic pay costs and therefore have to be planned and managed with care.

This chapter covers:

- the rationale for employee benefits;
- employee benefit strategies and policies;
- types of benefit;
- choice of benefit;
- the administration of benefits;
- tax considerations affecting benefits.

Flexible benefit systems are dealt with in Chapter 27 and pensions in Chapter 28.

RATIONALE FOR EMPLOYEE BENEFITS

Employee benefits provide for the personal needs of employees and they are a means of increasing their commitment to the organization and demonstrating that their employers care for their well-being. Not all employers care, but they, like the ones that do, provide benefits to ensure that the total remuneration package is competitive. And some benefits, such as maternity leave, have to be provided by law.

EMPLOYEE BENEFIT STRATEGIES AND POLICIES

Employee benefit strategies will be concerned in general terms with the direction the organization wants to go with regard to the range and scale of benefits it wants to provide and the costs it is prepared to incur. The strategy forms the foundation for the formulation of employee benefit policies.

Employee benefit policies are concerned with:

- the types of benefits to be provided, taking into account their value to employees, their cost, and the need to make the benefit package competitive;
- the size of the benefits;
- the need to harmonize benefits (harmonization policies are considered in Chapter 25);
- the total costs of benefits provision in relation to the costs of basic pay;
- the use of flexible benefits, as described in Chapter 27.

TYPES OF BENEFIT

The main benefits other than personal pensions (see Chapter 28), as described below, are concerned with personal security, financial assistance, personal needs, holidays, company cars and voluntary benefits.

Personal security

Personal security benefits include:

- *Health care* – the provision through medical insurance of private health care to cover the cost of private hospital treatment (permanent health insurance), making periodic health screening available and, sometimes, dental insurance.
- *Insurance cover* – for death in service (if not already provided in a pension scheme), personal accident and business travel.

- *Sick pay* – providing full pay for a given period of sickness and a proportion of pay (typically half-pay for a further period). Sick pay entitlement is usually service related. Sick pay can be costly unless attendance management and control practices are introduced.
- *Redundancy pay* – additions can be made to the statutory redundancy pay, including extra notice compensation, extra service-related payments (eg one month per year of service) and ex gratia payments to directors and executives in compensation for loss of office (sometimes called golden handshakes).
- *Career counselling* (outplacement advice) – can be provided by specialist consultants to employees who have been made redundant.

Financial assistance

Financial assistance can take the following forms:

- *Company loans* – interest-free modest loans, or low interest on more substantial loans which are usually earmarked for specific purposes such as home improvements.
- *Season ticket loans* – interest-free loans for annual season tickets.
- *Mortgage assistance* – subsidized interest payments on mortgages up to a given price threshold. This benefit is most likely to be provided by financial services companies.
- *Relocation packages* – for staff who are being relocated by the organization or recruited from elsewhere, the costs of removal and legal/estate agent's fees may be refunded.
- *Fees to professional bodies* – eg the CIPD.

Personal needs

Employee benefits satisfying personal needs include:

- maternity and paternity leave and pay above the statutory minimum;
- leave for personal reasons;
- childcare through workplace nurseries or vouchers;
- pre-retirement counselling;
- personal counselling through employee assistance programmes;
- sports and social facilities;
- company discounts – employees can buy the products or services offered by the company at a reduced price;
- retail vouchers to buy goods at chain stores.

Holidays

Before the European Working Time Directive in 1998, there was no statutory obliga-tion to offer any paid holiday except for the standard 'bank' holidays. Employers are now obliged to offer a minimum of 20 days' paid holiday per year, including bank holidays.

In practice, most organizations have always offered annual leave well in excess of this minimum, with few UK companies giving less than four weeks to employees at any level. Basic holiday entitlements are typically five weeks plus bank holidays, with some organizations offering up to six weeks for senior executives (who in practice may rarely have time to take full advantage of the provision) or on a service-related basis to more junior staff. The entitlement to holiday begins to accrue on the first day at work.

Organizations are obliged by statute to provide paid maternal and paternal leave and unpaid family leave.

Company cars

Although the tax liability for individuals with company 'status' cars has increased steadily over the past decade, they still remain one of the most valued perks, perhaps because people do not have to make a capital outlay, do not lose money through depreciation and are spared the worry and expense of maintenance.

Voluntary ('affinity') benefits

Voluntary benefit schemes provide opportunities for employees to buy goods or ser-vices at discounted prices. The employer negotiates deals with the providers but the scheme does not cost them anything.

Popular voluntary benefits include:

- *health*: private medical insurance, dental insurance, health screening;
- *protection*: critical illness insurance, life insurance, income protection insurance, personal accident insurance;
- *leisure*: holidays, days out, travel insurance, computer leasing, bicycle leasing, pet insurance, gym membership;
- *home:* household goods, online shopping.

Voluntary benefits schemes may have more in common with an online shopping portal than traditional employee benefits.

CHOICE OF BENEFITS

Some benefits, such as holidays, maternity leave and redundancy pay, have to be provided by statute – there is no choice except on the extent to which statutory provisions may be enhanced. For a responsible employer there is no real choice over the provision of pensions, life insurance or sick pay. Company cars for executives are still popular in spite of the tax provisions because of the felt need to be competitive.

Some optional benefits such as health insurance, childcare and low interest loans may be selected because they will be appreciated and also because they are frequently offered by other employers. The CIPD 2004 Reward Management Survey (1) found that the percentage of employers providing the different types of benefit other than pensions were as follows:

'Wellness' (health care etc)	87%
Family-friendly	52%
Financial assistance	36%
Voluntary benefits	12%

The factors affecting the choice of or provision or scale will be:

- what employees want as established by opinion surveys;
- what other employers are providing as established by market surveys;
- what the organization can afford.

ADMINISTERING EMPLOYEE BENEFITS

Employee benefits can be expensive and it is necessary to monitor the costs of providing them and the extent to which cost/benefit comparison justifies continuing with them on the present scale or at all. There should be a budget for employee benefit costs and expenditure should be monitored against it. Regular surveys should be undertaken of the attitude of employees to the benefits package. They may suggest where benefit expenditure could be redirected to areas where it would be more appreciated. They may also suggest that there is a need to adopt a flexible benefit policy, as described in the next chapter.

TAX CONSIDERATIONS

The following summary of tax considerations represents the situation in 2004. It is liable to change.

General principles

Emoluments from employment are subject to income tax under Schedule E. Emoluments are defined by legislation as 'all salaries, fees, wages, perquisites, or profits whatsoever'. In the courts, emoluments have been defined as rewards for 'services rendered, past, present and future' or, more broadly, payments made 'in return for acting as, or being, an employee'.

In general, much of the taxation on benefits applies only to directors and employees earning over £8,500 a year – in most organizations this is likely to be just about all full-time workers. Such employees are sometimes known as P11D employees, P11D being the form on which employers have to report the benefits received by employees to the Inland Revenue. A non-cash benefit such as a gift is taxable on the price it would command if sold. A benefit which cannot be turned into cash by the recipient is taxable on the annual cost incurred by the employer. For employees earning less than £8,500 a year, such 'non-convertible' benefits are not taxed. Regulations on the taxation of benefits are summarized below as they applied in 2004. They are frequently changed and it is advisable to keep up to date through such publications as the IDS annual guide to taxation for personnel managers.

Taxable benefits

There are a number of employee benefits offered by companies which are taxable on the employee as a benefit in kind. These include:

- Company cars – if a car is made available to a director or employee who is paid more than £8,500 a year, the employee will be liable to tax based on the value of the benefit. This value is calculated by reference to the list price of the car and the level of CO_2 (carbon dioxide) emissions. Until 6 April 2002 the car benefit was calculated on the list price of the car, with deductions available for the amount of business mileage and the age of the car. There are now no discounts available for higher levels of business mileage or for older cars. Cars which are made available to employees or to their families are considered to be derived from employment and taxed as employment income accordingly. The cash equivalent for the car benefit is reduced for any periods when the car was unavailable. This also applies to the provision of fuel benefit. If the employee is required to contribute to the cost of private fuel and the car, provided it is solely done to cover the business rules, then the cash equivalent is reduced to nil.

  If employees use their own car for business purposes, they can claim a deduction for a business proportion of their running costs, eg insurance, road tax, petrol, etc. Mileage allowances paid are taxable if they exceed the tax-free allowance.

The current fixed profit car scheme for 2004/2005 is as follows: 40p up to 10,000 business miles and 25p for each additional mile over 10,000.

- Fuel benefit – from 6 April 2003, the new car fuel benefit regime is linked to the level of the car's CO_2 emissions. The CO_2 emissions' percentages that apply to determine the company car benefit are also used in the car fuel calculation. However, instead of applying the percentage to the list price of the car, the percentage is applied to a specified amount. For the 2003/04 tax year, the specified amount is £14,400; however, the Treasury does have the power to change the defined specified amount.

  The benefit of fuel has been eroded over the past few years due to the increase in the scale charges. It is necessary for an employee to cover significant private mileage in a year to realize the value of fuel benefit.

- Private medical insurance.
- Entertaining clients or those who are not employees.
- The cash equivalent of a loan subsidy (ie the difference between the interest paid by the employee and the official rate of interest).
- Payments for expenses which have not been wholly, exclusively and necessarily incurred in the performance of relevant duties of the employee.
- Awards offered as part of incentives or in recognition of excellent performance, eg store vouchers, catalogue-based incentives in kind (which need to be grossed up for tax to avoid de-motivating surprises).

The basic principles of benefit taxation are not clear cut and it is always advisable to get a ruling from the Inland Revenue on any specific new benefit under consideration. In addition, it is important to ensure that employees are fully aware of the tax liabilities on their benefits in kind.

Benefits not usually subject to tax include:

- Approved pension schemes.
- Accommodation – if this is used solely for the purpose of the job, ie it is wholly, exclusively and necessarily for the purposes of the job, this is a non-taxable benefit.
- Meals – provided they are served to employees in general.
- Car parking space – provided this is close to or at work.
- Subscriptions – to approved professional institutions/bodies.
- Christmas parties and other annual functions.
- Gifts from third parties are exempt where the cost does not exceed £250.
- Long-service awards – a tax-free award can be made to employees with a minimum of 20 years' service.
- Counselling services to redundant employees.

- Mobile phones are also exempt, even when available for personal use by employers in respect of an employee's household expenses where the employee regularly works from home.
- In the 2003 Finance Act, the Inland Revenue indicated that up to £2 a week may be paid without the need to provide supporting evidence of the actual costs.
- Costs relating to employee liability insurance, professional indemnity insurance and work-related uninsured liabilities are not a taxable benefit if paid by the employer. If it is paid by the employee, it is allowable as a deduction against earnings.
- If an employee is away from home overnight on business, he or she is not assessable for tax on the reimbursement of the cost of, or provision of, non-cash vouchers in connection with personal expenses, eg newspapers, telephone calls up to a maximum of £5 a night.
- The costs in connection with work-related training are also exempt. The exemption also covers learning materials, fees for registration and exams.
- If an employee is relocated, qualifying removal expenses and benefits from the time of the job change to the end of the tax year are exempt up to a maximum of £8,000 per move. If expenses exceed £8,000, they do attract a withholding obligation but the amount does need to be reported on the year-end return.
- Payments given as compensation for loss of office – these are taxable if they exceed £30,000, subject to current tax legislation.
- Loans – an interest-free loan up to the value £5,000 is not taxable on the employee.
- Workplace nurseries – these are not considered to be taxable benefits in kind provided they are places which are made available by the employer.

REFERENCE

1 Chartered Institute of Personal and Development (2004) *Reward Management Survey*, CIPD, London

27

Flexible benefits

Flexible benefit schemes give employees a choice, within limits, of the type or scale of benefits offered to them by their employers. A wide variety of approaches is available. Interest in such schemes has been generated because employee benefits are not all equally wanted or appreciated by the staff who receive them and, from the employer's point of view, some benefits will not therefore provide value for money. The number that have introduced formal schemes is relatively small – only 12 per cent of the respondents to the CIPD 2004 Reward Management Survey (1) had them – but interest is high. In this chapter the reasons for introducing flexible benefits are set out, the different types of flexible benefit schemes are defined and the steps required to introduce a scheme explained.

REASONS FOR INTRODUCING FLEXIBLE BENEFITS

Flexible benefit schemes may be introduced in order to:

- meet the diverse needs of employees and increase the perceived value of the package to them – to a degree, they can decide for themselves what benefits they want and the size of particular benefits to suit their own lifestyle rather than being forced to accept what their employers think is good for them;
- enable employers to get better value for money from their benefits expenditure because it meets the needs and wants of employees;

- control costs by providing employees with a fund to spend rather than promising a particular level of benefits;
- aid recruitment and retention – flexible benefits are generally preferred by employees to fixed benefits of equivalent value;
- help to harmonize terms and conditions in a merger.

TYPES OF FLEXIBLE BENEFITS SCHEMES

There are many ways in which benefits can be flexed and the main types of schemes are described below.

Flex individual benefits

Employees are given the opportunity to vary the size of individual benefits, paying extra if they want more or, in effect, being paid cash if they want less. A typical example is a flexible car scheme which enables people to pay more for a better model or, if they decide to downsize, receive the reduction in cost to the company in cash. Choices are made on recruitment or replacement.

Another common arrangement is to provide scope, within limits, to buy or sell holiday time over the holiday year; for example, so many extra days could be 'bought' at the daily rate of the employee, or so many could be 'sold' and the amount at the daily rate added to pay.

This is a simple approach which is easy to introduce and administer and is therefore the most common method of flexing benefits. The disadvantage is that the impact may be limited.

Flex existing entitlement

Employees may choose to increase, decrease or end their current benefits and select new benefits from the menu provided. The value of the benefits bought and sold is then aggregated and the net amount added to or deducted from pay.

An example of how this might look for an employee whose salary is £30,000 pa is shown in Table 27.1.

This arrangement can be simplified by making only two or three benefits flexible. The rules often stipulate that such essential core benefits as pensions and life insurance cannot be reduced and limits may be placed on the scope for flexing other benefits, for example holidays.

Table 27.1 Example of variation around existing entitlement

Benefit	Standard entitlement	Selected entitlement	Monthly cost saving or (extra cost)
Holidays	25 days	22 days	£35
Car	Lease cost £300 per month	£240 per month	£60
Company pension contribution	10% of salary	10% of salary	Nil
Private medical insurance	Cover for self	Cover for self, partner and child	(£45)
Dental insurance	Nil	Nil	Nil
Childcare vouchers	Nil	£200 per month	(£200)
Total monthly adjustment			(£150)

(Source: Michael Armstrong and Helen Murlis (2004) *Reward Management*, 5th edn, Kogan Page, London)

Flex fund

Employees are allocated a fund of money to 'spend' on benefits from a menu. This is therefore sometimes described as the 'cafeteria' approach. Certain 'core' compulsory benefits, such as pensions and life insurance, have to be maintained. The value of the flex fund is big enough to enable individual employees to 'buy' their existing benefits and thus retain them without additional cost.

A simplified example of a flex fund benefits choice menu for someone with a salary of £30,000 and a flex fund of £12,000 is shown in Table 27.2.

The impact of the choices made is shown in Table 27.3.

The overspend would be funded by salary sacrifice. Had less than £12,000 been spent, the unspent flex fund would be paid as a monthly, non-consolidated cash sum.

Most common flexible benefits

The most common flexible benefits as established in a survey by Hewitt Associates (2) are:

	% of plans
Private medical cover/insurance	80
Holidays	75
Dental insurance	74
Company car	70
Health screens	59
Critical illness insurance	59

Table 27.2 Example of flex fund benefits choice menu

Benefit	Minimum choice	Maximum choice	Price
Holidays	20 days	30 days	0.4% of salary per day
Lease car	£300 per month (£3,600 per annum)	£500 per month (£6,000 per annum)	Annual lease times 1.25 (to allow for insurance and maintenance)
Company pension contribution	5% of salary	15% of salary	Face value less 10%*
Private medical insurance	Cover for self only	Cover for self, partner and children	£500 each per adult. £200 for one or more children
Dental insurance	n/a	Level 3 cover for self, partner and children	£40, £100, £180 per individual for Level 1, 2 or 3 cover, respectively
Childcare vouchers	n/a	20% of salary	Face value less 5%*

(Source: Michael Armstrong and Helen Murlis (2004) *Reward Management*, 5th edn, Kogan Page, London)
* The adjustment reflects the fact that Employer NICs (12.8% for 2004/5) are not payable on these benefits. The adjustment for childcare vouchers is lower to allow for the charge payable to the provider.

INTRODUCING FLEXIBLE BENEFITS

The steps required to introduce flexible benefits are described below:

1. *Define business need* – the benefits in terms of meeting the diverse needs of employees, helping recruitment and retention and getting better value for money from expenditure on employee benefits.

Table 27.3 Example of impact of flex fund choices made (shown in Table 27.2)

Benefit	Choice	Cost
Holidays	25 days	£3,000
Lease car	£350 per month	£5,250
Company pension contribution	10% of salary	£3,000
Private medical insurance	Cover for self and partner	£1,000
Dental insurance	Level 2 cover for self and partner	£200
Childcare vouchers	Nil	Nil
Total		**£12,450**
Flex fund		£12,000
Over (under) spend		£450

(Source: Michael Armstrong and Helen Murlis (2004) *Reward Management*, 5th edn, Kogan Page, London)

2. *Seek views* – conduct an opinion survey of employees on what they think of present benefit arrangements, what they think about flexible benefits and what benefits they would like to be eligible for flex (this could be accompanied by information about how flexible benefits might work and would therefore be the first shot in a communications campaign – communicating about flexible benefits is important).

3. *Decide strategy* – management should draw up a flexible benefits strategy for approval by top management. This will include broadly the extent to which it is believed that the approach should be to go for a full scheme based either on flexing existing benefits or a flex fund, or whether the approach should be to flex individual benefits. There may be something to be said for starting with the latter simpler approach (which will be cheaper to install), with the possibility of extending it at a later stage when experience has shown that it is working well. The strategy should also explore the need for outside advice and, on the basis of initial discussions with potential advisers, how much would need to be spent on developing and maintaining the scheme. One of the common objections to flexible benefits is the costs involved, especially when the proposed scheme is a fairly complex one and outside professional advice and support are required. Preliminary decisions need to be made at this stage on the likelihood that such advice is required so that the costs involved can be estimated. It is also necessary to decide on the need for a project team with employee involvement.

4. *Set up project team* – this could be a joint management/employee team (involvement is very desirable) with the responsibility of planning and overseeing the development programme.

5. *Decide who is going to carry out the development work* – someone from within the organization should be in charge of the project, with help as required and available from flexible benefit, finance, tax and pensions specialists. The development of a scheme requires considerable expertise in these areas in developing and costing schemes, exploring tax considerations and setting up the administration.

6. *Decide finally on approach* – a choice will need to be made on the basic approach.

7. *Design scheme* – this involves deciding on core benefits which have to be maintained, identifying benefits that can be flexed, deciding on any limits to the extent to which these benefits can be flexed, costing the benefits as necessary to enable menus to be produced and flex funds set up, if appropriate, and considering how the scheme should be administered. Simple schemes can be administered on paper but there is software available to administer more elaborate ones. An intranet can be used to help with administration – employees can make their choice of benefits from the screen and calculate the financial implications.

8. *Communicate details of the scheme* – employees need to be given detailed but easily understood information about the proposed scheme – how it will work, how it will affect them, its advantages, and how and when it will be introduced.
9. *Pilot test* – there is much to be said for piloting the scheme in a part of the organization to test reactions and administrative arrangements.
10. *Introduce scheme* – the earlier communications need to be reinforced generally at this stage and arrangements need to be made to provide individual employees with advice through personal contact, a help line or a help screen on the intranet.

REFERENCES

1 Chartered Institute of Personnel and Development (2004) *Reward Management Survey*, CIPD, London
2 Hewitt Associates (2003) *Survey of Flexible Benefits*, unpublished

28

Pension schemes

Pensions provide an income to employees when they retire and to their surviving dependant on the death of the employee, and deferred benefits to employees who leave. Schemes offered by organizations (occupational pensions), as distinct from state pensions, are funded by contributions from the organization and usually, but not always, the employee. Pensions are the most significant benefit and are a valuable part of the total reward package. But they are perhaps the most complex part.

The aim of this chapter is to present an outline of why pensions are provided, what they provide and the main types of schemes, including the State Pension scheme. The reasons for the shift from defined benefits (final salary) schemes to defined contribution (money purchase schemes) are discussed and the chapter ends with a summary of the law relating to providing pensions advice.

WHY PENSIONS ARE PROVIDED

Pensions are provided because they demonstrate that the organization is a good employer concerned about the long-term interests of its employees who want the security provided to be a reasonable pension when they retire. Good pension schemes help to attract and retain high-quality people by maintaining competitive levels of total remuneration. According to the CIPD, they are 'a well-perceived and often expected benefit among employees' (1).

WHAT PENSION SCHEMES PROVIDE

The range and level of benefits from pension schemes depend on the type of scheme and the level of contributions. In general, schemes provide:

- *Benefits on retirement* – these are related to the final salary of individuals when they retire or the amount that has been paid into a defined contribution scheme while the individuals were members.
- *Benefits on death* – the pensions of widows or widowers and children are normally related to the member's anticipated pension; the most common fraction is half.
- *Benefits on leaving an employer* – individuals leaving an employer can elect to take one of the following options: a deferred pension from the occupational scheme they are leaving, the transfer of the pension entitlement from the present employer to the new employer (but this is not always possible), or refund of their contributions, but only if they have completed less than two years' membership of the pension scheme.

THE TWO MAIN TYPES OF SCHEME

The two main types of scheme are described below. Other types are covered in the next section.

Defined benefit (final salary) schemes

The main features of defined benefit schemes are as follows.

Pension entitlement on retirement

- On retiring, the employee is entitled to a pension which is calculated as a fraction of their final salary (on retirement or an average of the last two or three years) multiplied by the length of pensionable service.
- The maximum proportion of salary allowed by the Inland Revenue is two-thirds of final salary after 40 years' service.
- The amount of the pension depends on the final salary, the value of the annuity that provides the pension and the accrual rate. The accrual rate refers to the fraction of final salary that can be earned per year of service. When a pension is described as 1/60th it means that 40 years' service would produce a two-thirds of final salary pension, and 30 years would produce a pension of half the final salary. This is a fairly typical fraction in private sector firms.

Employer and employee contributions

- Employer contributions can be a fixed percentage of salary. Alternatively, the percentage increases with service or is a multiple of the employee's contribution (eg the employer contributes 15 per cent if the employee contributes 5 per cent). The 2003 Survey by the National Association of Pension Funds (2) found that the level of employer contribution averages 16 per cent.
- Employee contribution rates vary considerably. The Hay Group Survey of Employee Benefits in 2003 (3) found that for staff and middle managers these range from 3 per cent to 15 per cent with a median of around 8 per cent.

Pension fund

- Employee and employer contributions are paid into a combined fund and there is no direct link between fund size and the pensions paid.
- The money remaining in the fund after any lump sums have been taken out is invested in an annuity to provide a regular income, the amount of which may be revised upwards periodically to compensate for inflation.

Dependants

- Dependants are entitled to a percentage of the employee's pension entitlement if he or she dies during retirement or in service with the company.

Lump sum

- Part of the pension may be exchanged for a tax-free lump sum up to a maximum under Inland Revenue rules of 1/80th per year for up to 40 years' service.

Defined contribution (money purchase) schemes

The main features of defined contribution schemes are as follows.

Pension entitlement

- The employee receives a pension on retirement which is related to the size of the fund accumulated by the combined contributions of the employee and employer. The amount of the pension depends on the size of contributions, the rate of return on the investment of the accumulated fund and the rate of return on an annuity purchased by the employer. It is not related to the employee's final salary.

Contributions

- The employer contributes a defined percentage of earnings which may be fixed, age-related or linked to what the employee pays. The 2003 Survey by the National Association of Pension Funds (2) found that the level of employer contribution averages 6 per cent.
- The employee also contributes a fixed percentage of salary.

Pension fund

- The contributions are invested and the money used at retirement to purchase a regular income, usually via an annuity contract from an insurance company. The retirement pension is therefore whatever annual payment can be purchased with the money accumulated in the fund for a member.
- Members have individual shares of the fund, which represent their personal entitlements and which will directly determine the pensions they receive.

Dependants

- Dependants receive death in service and death in retirement pensions.

Lump sum

- One-quarter of the pension can be taken as a tax-free lump sum on retirement.

Comparison of defined benefits and defined contribution schemes

The main differences are that a defined benefits (final salary) scheme provides a guaranteed pension to the employee but the employer is unable to predict the costs, which can fluctuate unfavourably. Conversely, a defined contribution (money purchase) scheme provides an uncertain pension and the cost to the employer is predictable. The differences are summarized in Table 28.1.

Defined benefit or defined contribution?

Defined benefit scheme costs and risks

Defined benefit schemes are more costly to employers (16 per cent average contribution) than defined contribution schemes (6 per cent average contribution). They are also more risky for employers because the pension is based on a guaranteed formula and the cost of providing this guaranteed benefit may be higher than expected. Typically, employee contributions are fixed and those of the employer vary on the

Table 28.1 Comparison of defined benefit and defined contribution schemes

Defined benefit (final salary)	Defined contribution (money purchase)
Benefits defined as a fraction of final pensionable pay	Benefits purchased as an annuity by an accumulation of contributions invested
Benefits do not depend on investment returns or annuity rates	Benefits dependent on investment returns, contributions, and cost of annuities at retirement
Employer contributes necessary costs in excess of employee contributions	Employer contributions are fixed
Employer takes financial risk	Member takes financial risk
Not easily portable to other employers	Easily portable to other employers
Benefits appropriate for long-serving employees with progressive increases in pensionable pay	Benefits appropriate for short-serving employees or those whose pensionable pay fluctuates

basis of specialist advice from the scheme actuary. Hence, the risk of higher than expected costs falls on the employer. Costs might exceed expectations for a number of reasons, for example pensioners are living longer (an important factor in putting up costs), the fund investments perform less well than expected (another important factor recently) or salaries grow faster than expected. Costs have in fact increased significantly in many schemes and as a result some large pension funds are in deficit.

Defined contribution scheme costs and risks

In a defined contribution scheme the cost of employer contributions is predictable and generally lower than in defined benefit schemes. However, there is a risk that the resulting pension falls short of expectations because the fund investments perform poorly or because the annuity rate (that is, the conversion rate from lump sum to regular pension) is unfavourable. This risk falls on the employee.

The move toward defined contribution schemes

Many leading companies have questioned the financial wisdom of final salary provision. Defined benefit schemes provide much more value to older and longer-serving employees but greater labour mobility has led many employers to question this emphasis, particularly in newer industries with young, high-turnover workforces.

However, defined benefit schemes are still the most popular. The CIPD 2004 Reward Management Survey (4) established that, on average, 62 per cent of employers had such schemes, while 37 per cent had defined benefit schemes. There has, however, been a shift towards providing defined contribution schemes for new employees

– an average of 47 per cent compared with an average of 37 per cent for defined benefit schemes (employees also provide hybrid, stakeholder, or personal schemes as described below). The trend towards defined contribution schemes has been pronounced in labour-intensive sectors but the public sector has so far mostly retained its defined benefit schemes.

Defined benefit schemes are liked by employees and trade unions because they produce a guaranteed income. Trade unions are therefore always hostile to any move towards defined contribution schemes. Such a move will appear to threaten personal security and be detrimental. Even if the change is restricted to new staff, existing employees may well believe that it will be applied to them sometime. To avoid a major upset in employee relations, employers have to convince their staff that they will not be affected in the future, and they have to mean what they say. If they don't, any trust that exists between them and their employees will be destroyed.

Rather than change to a defined contribution scheme, some companies have taken steps to reduce final salary scheme costs. This means retaining final salary provision but with some benefits scaled back. For example, employers have reduced the accrual rate from 1/60th per year of service to 1/80th or, more commonly, have increased employee contributions. Employees and unions are likely to resist such changes but may eventually be persuaded that they are better than a move towards defined contribution provision.

OTHER TYPES OF PENSION SCHEME

Hybrid schemes

Hybrid schemes aim to split the risk between both parties, although only 3 per cent of the CIPD respondents had them. Examples of such schemes include:

- *Combined final salary/defined contribution scheme* – under this approach, both types of scheme are in operation. A final salary scheme might be provided for staff who meet an age and/or service qualification, with defined contribution provision applying to other staff.
- *Career average revalued earnings (CARE) scheme* – this is a type of defined benefit scheme. Instead of pension being based on final salary, the employee receives a pension proportional to service and career average salary, with salary from earlier years revalued by the Retail Price Index. These produce lower pensions than a final salary scheme.
- *Cash balance scheme* – employees are provided with a guaranteed individual retirement fund proportional to service and final or average salary. As in a defined contribution scheme, a proportion may be taken as cash, with the balance being used to buy an annuity.

- *Schemes with an element of discretion* – low-level guaranteed benefits are provided, perhaps on a final salary or career average basis. However, there is discretion to provide enhanced pensions as and when the scheme's funding position allows it. A variant of this approach is to operate a defined contribution scheme with a modest final salary (or career average salary) guarantee.
- *Capped final salary* – a self-imposed cap is applied to pensionable salary, with defined contribution provision on the excess salary. The logic here is that it is reasonable to transfer some risk to the employee once a basic level of guaranteed retirement income has been built up.

Personal pensions

Employers cannot compel their employees to join their scheme. As an alternative, employees can take out their own personal pension plan from an approved provider, either as an alternative to an occupational scheme provided by the employer or because there is no occupational scheme available. Personal pension schemes can be contracted out of the State pension scheme and may take contributions from an employer. They are defined contribution (that is, money purchase) schemes, which means that the pension is based on what has been paid into the scheme and not on final salary.

Group schemes

Group schemes are in effect a bundle of individual personal pensions for which the employer carries out a payroll function by remitting contributions to a pensions provider.

Stakeholder pension

A stakeholder pension is a government-sponsored scheme, primarily designed for individuals earning less than about £20,000. Employers who do not provide a suitable pension scheme for their employees are required by law to offer access to a stakeholder scheme. A suitable pension scheme will be either an occupational pension scheme or a group scheme.

A stakeholder pension is a defined contribution arrangement that satisfies certain conditions, designed to ensure that it provides good value for money and that members' interests are protected. These conditions are:

- *flexible contributions* – members must be free to pay whatever contributions they wish, when they wish;
- *charges* – the maximum charge is 1 per cent of the fund;
- *transfers* – the scheme will be required to accept transfer payments;

- *FSA regulation* – all stakeholder schemes will be regulated by the Financial Services Agency;
- *investments* – the scheme must offer a default investment scheme for members who are unwilling to choose between different funds.

Executive pensions

In the private sector, executive pensions are typically provided for by a defined benefit scheme with an accelerated accrual compared to that for other staff. Instead of providing a maximum two-thirds pension after 40 years of service (an accrual rate of 1/60th per year of service), a full pension may be earned after only 20 or 30 years' service (equivalent to an accrual rate of 1/30th or 1/45th). The two-thirds pension provided is normally inclusive of any pensions from previous employments.

THE STATE PENSION SCHEME

State pension arrangements are subject to change, and this section is based on the current (2004) arrangements. The State pension scheme has two parts, as described below.

The State Flat Rate Benefit (SFRB)

The SFRB is paid at a standard rate which may be increased each year as long as the required number of National Insurance contributions have been paid.

The State Earnings Related Pension Scheme (SERPS)

SERPS pays a pension on earnings for which Class 1 National Insurance contributions have been paid over the years which fall between the lower and the upper earnings limit. The lower earnings limit corresponds roughly with the flat rate pension (SFRB) for a single person, while the upper limit is currently about eight times the lower earning limit. Both limits are adjusted from time to time.

Contracting out

Employers and individuals with a personal pension plan can contract out of SERPS. Occupational pension schemes will be able to contract out if they meet an overall quality test. When a scheme is contracted out, both the employer and the employee pay National Insurance contributions at a lower rate.

ADVISING EMPLOYEES ON PENSIONS

The Financial Services Act 1986 and the Pensions Act 1995 place restrictions on the provision of financial advice to employees. Only those who are directly authorized by one of the regulatory organizations or professional bodies are permitted to give detailed financial advice on investments which include personal pensions. Information can, however, be given to employees:

- on the company's occupational pension scheme, since it is not classed as an investment;
- about the general principles to be borne in mind when comparing an occupational pension scheme with a personal pension; these could include spelling out the benefits of the company's scheme, thus leaving employees in a better position to compare the benefits with whatever an authorized adviser may indicate are the benefits from a personal plan – what should not be done is to tell people categorically that they will be better off with the company's scheme or to advise them to look elsewhere;
- on their rights for staff who are leaving to preserve their pension and the advisability of finding out from their prospective employer whether existing rights can be transferred to their scheme and, if so, what the outcome will be in terms of pension rights at the new company;
- the general advantages of making additional voluntary contributions.

HR specialists should restrict themselves to giving information. They should never suggest what people should do. If in any doubt as to how to respond to a request for information or advice it is best to refer the matter to the company's own pension specialist or adviser or, if none is available, suggest that the employee should talk to an authorized adviser, for example the individual's own insurance company or bank.

DEVELOPING AND COMMUNICATING PENSIONS POLICIES

The pension benefits provided by employers should be developed as an important part of a coherent total reward package. Good schemes demonstrate that employers care about the future security and well-being of their employees and pensions are a valuable means of gaining and keeping employee commitment to the organization. Younger and more mobile employees are often indifferent to pensions but the older they get the more they are concerned and these mature employees contribute largely to organizational success.

Careful consideration needs to be given to telling employees about the scheme. They need to know how it works and how it benefits them – it is too easy for employees to take pensions for granted. It is particularly important to communicate the reasons for any changes and staff should be involved in discussing the reason for the proposed arrangements and given the opportunity to comment on them. As stated by the CIPD (1), HR professionals have a key role to play 'in being honest about the real picture and its alternatives, and educating their staff'.

REFERENCES

1   Chartered Institute of Personnel and Development (2002) *Pensions and HR's Role*, CIPD, London
2   National Association of Pension Funds (2003) *2003 Survey of Pensions*, NAPF, London
3   The Hay Group (2003) *Survey of Employee Benefits in 2003*, Philadelphia, PA
4   Chartered Institute of Personnel and Development (2004) *Reward Management 2004: A survey of policy and practice*, CIPD, London

Part VIII

Reward management procedures and case studies

29

Managing reward

Managing reward systems is a complex and demanding business. This chapter deals with the subject in seven parts:

1. *Reward management roles*: HR or reward specialists (reward system development and administration, and advising line managers), devolving responsibility to line managers, and the use of reward management consultants.
2. *Reward procedures:* for grading jobs, determining levels of pay and hearing appeals.
3. *Controlling reward:* preparation and use of forecasts and budgets, costing, monitoring and evaluating reward policies and practices and obtaining value for money.
4. *Conducting general and individual pay reviews.*
5. *Communicating to employees*, collectively and individually.
6. *Managing the development of reward systems:* the process, involving employees, managing change.
7. *The use of computers in reward management.*

REWARD MANAGEMENT ROLES

HR and reward specialists

HR and reward specialists develop and implement reward strategies, policies and processes, administer and audit existing systems and provide advice and guidance to line managers. They deal with employee relations issues such as involvement, communications, negotiations, appeals and grievances.

Line managers

Increasingly, responsibilities for managing reward are being devolved to line managers to recognize the fact that people are their major resource and that they should play a full part in managing them. Full devolution, which means that managers are given the authority within budgets and in accordance with policy guidelines to decide on pay increases, gradings and salaries on appointment or promotion, is fairly rare. It is more usual to give them the responsibility for making recommendations which are subject to approval by a higher authority. Even if full devolution takes place, their decisions are likely to be monitored by senior managers and HR. In practice, the amount of authority devolved to individual line managers will depend on their experience and their proven ability to make fair, equitable and consistent decisions. HR will 'hold the hands' of inexperienced managers when they are first involved in pay decisions and will progressively let go as the managers demonstrate their capability. If line managers do not learn then this means that their competence as managers is questioned.

The risk of unfair, inequitable, biased and inconsistent decisions can be alleviated by close monitoring, but this defeats the purpose of devolution which is to encourage managers to act responsibly in managing their own affairs. Managers must be briefed thoroughly on pay policies and the application of pay review guidelines. They should be given training, guidance and help as required. The basic training should cover how pay reviews should be carried out, including the use of software or spreadsheets and how the data supplied by HR on market rates and the existing distribution of pay for their staff should be interpreted. It should also deal with performance management processes, including how to be fair and consistent when rating performance if rating is part of the system. The approaches used by AEGON and Lloyds TSB to devolving reward responsibilities to line managers are described in Chapter 30.

Using reward consultants

Reward consultants are used frequently to help with major development projects by providing expertise and additional resources (an extra pair of hands). They can conduct diagnostic reviews and employee attitude surveys, and provide disinterested advice. Effective consultants add credibility and value because they have the knowledge of good practice and project management which may not be available in the organization. To make good use of consultants it is necessary to:

- spell out terms of reference, deliverables and the timetable;
- take great care when selecting them to ensure that they have the expertise and experience required and will 'fit' into the organization, and that they produce realistic and acceptable indications of the cost of their fees and expenses;
- meet and vet the consultant who is going to carry out the work, not just the senior consultant who presents the proposal;
- agree up front how they will work alongside line management, HR and trade unions and the basis upon which the project will be monitored and controlled;
- ask for regular reports and hold 'milestone' meetings in order to review progress and costs.

REWARD PROCEDURES

Reward procedures deal with grading jobs, fixing rates of pay and handling appeals.

Grading jobs

The procedures for grading jobs set out how job evaluation should be used to grade a new job or re-grade an existing one. A point-factor evaluation scheme which has defined grades may be used for all new jobs and to deal with requests for re-grading. However, an analytical matching process (see Chapter 9) may be used to compare the role profiles of the jobs to be graded with grade or level profiles or profiles of benchmark jobs. This is likely to be the case in large organizations and for broad-banded structures.

Fixing rates of pay on appointment

The procedure should indicate how much freedom line managers and HR have to pay above the minimum rate for the job. The freedom may be limited to, say, 10 per cent above the minimum or two or three pay points on an incremental scale. More scope is sometimes allowed to respond to market rate pressures or to attract particularly well-qualified staff by paying up to the reference point or target salary in a pay range, subject to HR approval and bearing in mind the need to provide scope for contingent pay increases. If recruitment premia are used, the rules for offering them to candidates must be clearly defined.

Promotion increases

The procedure will indicate what is regarded as a meaningful increase on promotion, often 10 per cent or more. To avoid creating anomalies, the level of pay has to take account of what other people who are carrying out work at a similar level are paid and it is usual to lay down a maximum level which does not take the pay of the promoted employee above the reference point for the new range.

Equal pay reviews

The procedure for conducting equal pay reviews (see Chapter 12) should be defined.

Appeals

It is customary to include the right to appeal against gradings as part of a job evaluation procedure (see Chapter 10). Appeals against pay decisions are usually made through the organization's grievance procedure.

CONTROLLING REWARD

The implementation of reward policies and procedures should be monitored and controlled to ensure that value for money is obtained. Control is easier if the grade and pay structure is well defined and clear guidelines exist on how it and the benefits arrangements should be managed. Control should be based on forecasts, budgets and costings, and by monitoring and evaluating the implementation of reward policies as described below.

Reward forecasts

It is necessary to forecast future payroll costs taking into account the number of people employed and the impact of pay reviews and contingent pay awards. The cost implications of developments such as a revised job evaluation scheme, a new grade and pay structure or a flexible benefits scheme also have to be forecast.

Reward budgets

Pay review budgets set out the increase in payroll costs that will result for either general or individual pay reviews and are used for cost forecasts generally and as the basis for the guidelines issued to line managers on conducting individual reviews.

Total payroll budgets are based on the number of people employed in different jobs and their present and forecast rates of pay. In a budgetary control system they are aggregated from the budgets prepared by departmental managers but HR provides guidance on the allowances that should be made for pay increases. The aim is to maintain control over payroll costs and restrain managers from the temptation to overpay their staff.

Costing reward processes

Proposed changes to the reward system need to be costed for approval by senior management. The costs would include development costs such as consultants' fees, software, literature, additional staff and, possibly, the opportunity costs arising when staff are seconded to a development project.

Implementation costs also have to be projected. A new grade and pay structure, for example, can easily result in an increase to the payroll of three or four per cent. New contingent pay schemes may also cost more, although the aim should be to make them self-financing.

Auditing reward systems

The effectiveness of reward policies and practices should be monitored and evaluated against the requirements of the organization. Evaluation should compare outcomes with the objectives set for the new practice (this is why setting objectives for reward initiatives is so important). Twenty aspects of reward policy and practice which need to be monitored and evaluated are set out below:

1. The existence of realistic, innovative and integrated reward strategies.
2. Progress towards developing a total reward approach.
3. The practicality and comprehensiveness of reward policies and how well they are applied.
4. The effectiveness of the job evaluation scheme from the point of view of the extent to which it has decayed, how relevant it is to present working arrangements, the degree to which it provides the basis for fair and equitable grading decisions and for preventing grade drift and whether or not it is too bureaucratic or time consuming.
5. Progress towards achieving equal pay for work of equal value (using equal pay review procedures as explained in Chapter 12).
6. The availability of accurate and usable information on market rates.
7. The appropriateness of the grade and pay structure using the criteria set out in Chapter 16 as the basis for evaluation.

8. The distribution of actual salaries and the extent to which it conforms to policy guidelines by reference to compa-ratios as described in Chapter 15. These can be used to measure the relationship between actual and policy rates of pay.

9. The extent to which pay levels are competitive and contribute to the attraction and retention of high-quality staff.

10. Whether or not value for money is being obtained from the contingent pay arrangements, with reference to their costs and benefits (the latter assessed as far as possible in terms of their impact on motivation and the degree to which they contribute to developing a performance culture).

11. The incidence of attrition to pay costs which takes place when employees enter jobs at lower rates of pay than the previous job holders and the implications for pay policy (large attrition rates may reduce and therefore justify contingent pay costs).

12. The effectiveness of performance management processes with regard to how they function in terms of fairness, equity and consistency, the contribution they make to achieving total reward objectives, and the quality of the outcomes as means of informing contingent pay decisions.

13. The range of employee benefits provided and the extent to which they provide value for money in terms of increasing employee job satisfaction and commitment.

14. The benefits provided by the pension scheme and its cost.

15. The quality of the budgetary control arrangements.

16. The cost of the implementation of pay reviews against budget.

17. The degree to which the benefits of reward innovations justify the costs.

18. The opinions of employees about the reward system, which can be obtained by means of regular attitude surveys – an example of a survey is given in Appendix 4.

19. The capacity of line managers to carry out their managing reward duties.

20. The quality of the communications to employees about the reward system and the extent to which they understand how it operates.

Obtaining value for money

Assessing the value for money provided by existing practices, or by new practices when they are implemented, is a major consideration when monitoring and evaluating reward management processes. Evaluating the cost of innovations may lead to the reconsideration of proposals to ensure that they will provide value for money. Evaluating the value for money obtained from existing reward practices leads to the identification of areas for improvement.

Affordability is, or should be, a major issue when reviewing reward management developments and existing practices. Value for money is achieved when the benefits of a reward practice either exceed its cost or at least justify the cost. At the development stage it is therefore necessary to carry out cost/benefit assessments. The two fundamental questions to be answered are: (1) 'What business needs will this proposal meet?' and (2) 'How will the proposal meet the needs?' The costs and benefits of existing practices should also be assessed on the same basis.

CONDUCTING PAY REVIEWS

Pay reviews are *general or 'across-the-board'* reviews in response to movements in the cost of living or market rates or following pay negotiations with trade unions, or *individual reviews* which determine the pay progression of individuals in relation to their performance or contribution, or individual reviews. They are one of the most visible aspects of reward management (the other is job grading) and are an important means of implementing the organization's reward policies and demonstrating to employees how these policies operate.

Employees expect that general reviews will maintain the purchasing power of their pay by compensating for increases in the cost of living. They will want their levels of pay to be competitive with what they could earn outside. And they will want to be rewarded fairly and equitably for the contribution they make.

GENERAL REVIEWS

General reviews take place when employees are given an increase in response to general market rate movements, increases in the cost of living or union negotiations. General reviews are often combined with individual reviews but employees are usually informed of the general and individual components of any increase they receive. Alternatively, the general review may be conducted separately to enable better control to be achieved over costs and to focus employees' attention on the performance-related aspect of their remuneration.

Some organizations have completely abandoned the use of across-the-board reviews. They argue that the decision on what people should be paid should be an individual matter, taking into account the personal contribution people are making and their 'market worth' – how they as individuals are valued in the marketplace. This enables the organization to adopt a more flexible approach to allocating pay increases in accordance with the perceived value of individuals to the organization.

The steps required to conduct a general review are:

1. Decide on the budget.
2. Analyse data on pay settlements made by comparable organizations and rates of inflation.

3. Conduct negotiations with trade unions as required.
4. Calculate costs.
5. Adjust the pay structure – by either increasing the pay brackets of each grade by the percentage general increase or by increasing pay reference points by the overall percentage and applying different increases to the upper or lower limits of the bracket, thus altering the shape of the structure.
6. Inform employees.

INDIVIDUAL REVIEWS

Individual pay reviews determine contingent pay increases or bonuses. The e-research 2004 survey of contribution pay (1) found that the average size of the contingent pay awards made by respondents was 3.3 per cent. Individual awards may be based on ratings, an overall assessment which does not depend on ratings or ranking as discussed below.

Individual pay review steps

The steps required to conduct an individual pay review are:

1. Agree budget.
2. Prepare and issue guidelines on the size, range and distribution of awards and on methods of conducting the review.
3. Provide advice and support.
4. Review proposals against budget and guidelines and agree modifications to them if necessary.
5. Summarize and cost proposals and obtain approval.
6. Update payroll.
7. Inform employees.

It is essential to provide advice, guidance and training to line managers as required. Some managers will be confident and capable from the start. Others will have a lot to learn.

There are three basic approaches to conducting reviews as explained below.

Individual pay reviews based on ratings

Managers propose increases on the basis of their performance management ratings within a given pay review budget and in accordance with pay review guidelines. Forty-two per cent of the respondents to the CIPD 2003/4 performance management

	Percentage pay increase according to performance rating and position in pay range (compa-ratio)			
	Position in pay range			
Rating	80–90%	91–100%	101–110%	111–120%
Excellent	12%	10%	8%	6%
Very effective	10%	8%	6%	4%
Effective	6%	4%	3%	0
Developing	4%	3%	0	0
Ineligible	0	0	0	0

Figure 29.1 PRP pay matrix

survey (2) used ratings to inform contingent pay decisions. Approaches to rating were discussed in Chapter 17.

There is a choice of methods. A pay matrix may be used as illustrated in Figure 29.1.

Sixty-four per cent of the respondents to the e-research 2004 contingent pay survey with ratings (1) used a pay matrix.

Alternatively, there is a direct link between the rating and the pay increase for example:

Rating	% Increase
A	6
B	4
C	3
D	2
E	0

Thirty-one per cent of the respondents to the e-research 2004 contingent pay survey with ratings (1) used this approach.

Individual reviews without ratings

As mentioned in Chapter 17, many people argue that linking performance management too explicitly to pay prejudices the essential developmental nature of performance management. However, realistically it is accepted that decisions on performance-related or contribution-related increases have to be based on some form of assessment. One solution is to 'decouple' performance management and the pay review by holding them several months apart. Forty-five per cent of the respondents to the CIPD 2003/4 survey separated performance management reviews from pay reviews (43 per cent of the respondents to the e-research 2004 survey (1) separated the review). There is still a read-across but it is not so immediate.

Some try to do without formulaic approaches (ratings and pay matrices) altogether, although it is impossible to dissociate contingent pay completely from some form of assessment.

Twenty-seven per cent of the respondents to the 2004 e-research survey of contingent pay (1) did without ratings. The percentage of respondents to the 2003/4 CIPD performance management survey (2) who did not use ratings was 52 per cent (this figure is too high to be fully reliable and may have been inflated by those who treat service-related increments, which do not depend on ratings, as contingent pay).

Holistic approach

Some companies adopt what might be called an holistic approach. Managers propose where people should be placed in the pay range for their grade, taking into account their contribution and pay relative to others in similar jobs, their potential, and the relationship of their current pay to market rates. The decision may be expressed in the form of a statement that an individual is now worth £21,000 rather than £20,000. The increase is 5 per cent, but what counts is the overall view about the value of a person to the organization, not the percentage increase to that person's pay.

Example: HalifaxBOS

The criteria used by HalifaxBOS to guide individual pay reviews without ratings are:

1. The size of the role as determined by job evaluation.
2. Market data and location to determine the average salary that would be expected for the role.
3. How the individual has performed over the last 12 months: Have they contributed what was expected of them? Have they contributed above and beyond their peers? Have they under-performed in respect of what was required of them? NB: these are not ratings, they are simply guidelines given to managers as to whether the individual should be given an average, above average or below average award.
4. If a manager has, for example, six people carrying out the same role and are delivering at the same level and are all competent, they should be getting similar salaries.
5. Individuals paid below the market rate who are performing effectively may get a bigger pay rise to bring them nearer the market rate for their role.

Example: oil exploration company

Broadly the same method is used by an oil exploration company as follows:

- Managers reach an agreement with individual members of their teams on their level of contribution, whether, broadly, it meets (high) expectations, is above expectations or below expectations. There is no rating but the aim is to ensure that both parties are in complete agreement about the assessment.
- At the later pay review, managers are given information on the pay of each member of their staff and on market rates for the jobs they hold.
- Managers are then expected to make a judgement on the rate of pay of individuals by reference to the assessment of their overall contribution and by making comparisons with their peers and the individual's market worth based on market rate data and an assessment of the risk of their leaving for higher pay.
- Individuals whose pay is lagging behind what is earned by their peers who are making the same level of contribution, or below market rate, may receive a greater increase to bring them in line or at least progress their pay in the right direction.
- The review results in a decision on what the individual's pay should be; it is not expressed as a percentage increase.
- Managers are given a budget for the total amount available for the review and the authority to distribute the budget in accordance with the guidelines, subject to monitoring by HR.

Other examples

Companies such as Bass and Zurich, which adopt a similar approach, provide managers with spreadsheets containing information on salaries in their department to enable them to carry out the review in accordance with a budget and review guidelines. This is accompanied by data on market rates. Managers can then model alternative distributions of awards while keeping the total within budget. To help them with their decisions, the data can be given in a scattergram as illustrated in Figure 29.2, which shows a pay progression guideline which indicates where people might be paid in relation to an assessment of their contribution. The market rates (median and upper quartile) are also shown. The rate of pay for staff in the job concerned is entered to show relativities. Managers are then in a position visually to assess how the pay of an individual might be adjusted, taking into account an assessment of contribution (not rated), progression guidelines, market rates and relativities. More examples of approaches to pay reviews without the use of ratings or a pay matrix at AEGON, B&Q, GlaxoSmithKline and Lloyds TSB are given in Chapter 30.

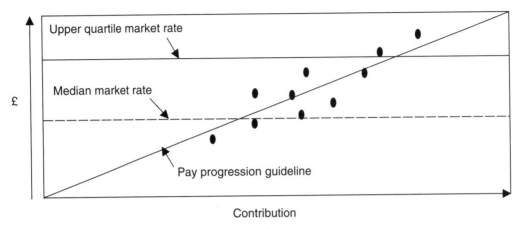

Figure 29.2 Pay review without ratings: data presentation

Approaches to review without ratings used by e-research survey respondents

Examples are given below of the criteria or approaches used by the respondents to the 2004 e-research survey of contingent pay (1) who did not use ratings:

- 'Individual market worth.'
- 'Most people will get the standard annual increase, but their increase may be withheld if they have documented performance problems. A few individuals may receive slightly more than the standard increase if they are judged to be high performers.'
- 'Basic salaries are determined in relation to position against the market and what stage of development is at, assuming competent performance.'
- 'Based on "informed subjectivity" – considering ongoing performance in the form of overall contribution.'
- 'Employee's performance (without formal numerical rating), level of skills, budget control, market salaries.'
- 'Senior managers' pay is reviewed by considering individual contribution, organizational performance, and the relevant external employment markets. The first component is not formally linked to the performance review process.'
- 'Consideration of performance, responsibility level, 360 degree feedback and market rates.'
- 'Broad reference to development, career progression and scarce resources.'
- 'Mostly subjective – based on market rates and internal relativities but performance based for key individual performers.'
- 'General assessment of competence and performance in line with benchmark rate for the role.'

Ranking

Ranking is carried out by managers who place staff in a rank order according to an overall assessment of relative contribution or merit and then distribute performance ratings through the rank order. The top 10 per cent could get an A rating, the next 15 per cent a B rating and so on. The ratings determine the size of the reward. But ranking depends on what could be invidious comparisons and only works when there are a number of people in similar jobs to be ranked.

Guidelines to managers on conducting individual pay reviews

Whichever approach is adopted, guidelines have to be issued to managers on how they should conduct reviews. These guidelines will stipulate that they must keep within their budgets and may indicate the maximum and minimum increases that can be awarded with a indication of how awards could be distributed; for example, when the budget is 4 per cent overall, it might be suggested that a 3 per cent increase should be given to the majority of their staff and the others given higher or lower increases as long as the total percentage increase does not exceed the budget. Managers in some companies are instructed that they must follow a forced pattern of distribution but, as noted in Chapter 21, only 8 per cent of the respondents to the 2003/4 CIPD survey used this method. To help them to explore alternatives, managers may be provided with a spreadsheet facility in which the spreadsheets contain details of the existing rates of staff and can be used to model alternative distributions on a 'what if' basis. Managers may also be encouraged to 'fine-tune' their pay recommendations to ensure that individuals are on the right track within their grade according to their level of performance, competence and time in the job compared with their peers. To do this, they need guidelines on typical rates of progression in relation to performance, skill or competence and specific guidance on what they can and should do. They also need information on the relative positions of their staff in the pay structure in relation to the policy guidelines.

COMMUNICATING TO EMPLOYEES

Transparency is important. Employees need to know how reward policies will affect them and how pay and grading decisions have been made. They need to be convinced that the system is fair.

Communicating to employees collectively

Employees and their representatives should be informed about the guiding principles and policies that underpin the reward system and the reward strategies that drive it.

They should understand the grade and pay structure, how grading decisions are made, including the job evaluation system, how their pay can progress within the structure, the basis upon which contingent pay increases are determined and policies on the provision of benefits, including details of a flexible benefits scheme if one is available.

Communicating to individual employees

Individual employees should understand how their grade, present rate of pay and pay increases have been determined and the pay opportunities available to them – the scope for pay progression and how their contribution will be assessed through performance management. They should be informed of the value of the benefits they receive so that they are aware of their total remuneration and, if appropriate, how they can exercise choice over the range or scale of their benefits through a flexible benefits scheme.

MANAGING THE DEVELOPMENT OF REWARD SYSTEMS

The development process is illustrated in Figure 29.3.

Involving employees

Employees should be treated as stakeholders and give every opportunity to contribute to the development of reward policies and practices. This is a matter of involvement in working parties, project teams and panels, not just consultation, although the normal consultative channels have to be used.

Trade unions and their representatives should be involved in the initial stages, to sound out their opinions and reach as much agreement as possible on what needs to be done, especially if this affects job evaluation, pay structures, contingent pay schemes and flexible benefits.

Change management

The introduction of new job evaluation schemes, pay structures and contingent pay arrangements all concern employees who may be alarmed at the possibility that they will be adversely affected. It is therefore necessary to pay particular attention to change management during the development and implementation of reward practices. The following approaches should be adopted:

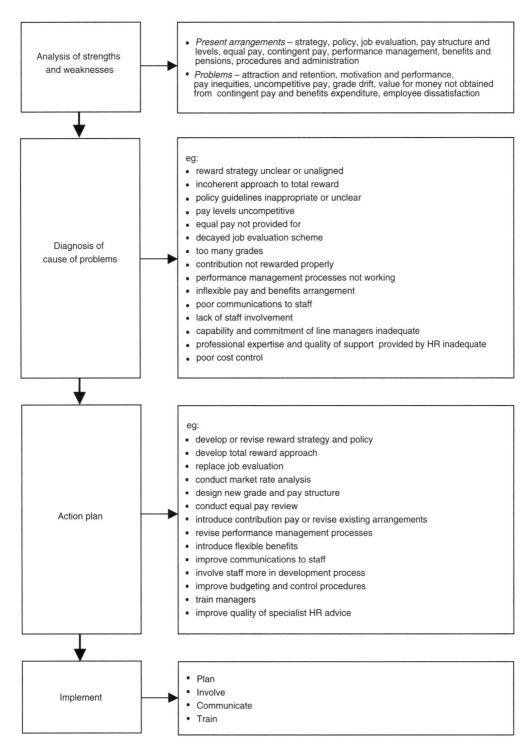

Figure 29.3 Development of reward processes

1. Mobilize commitment to change through the joint analysis of problems.
2. Develop a shared vision of how to organize and manage change to achieve agreed goals.
3. Foster consensus for the new vision, competence to enact it, and cohesion to move it along.
4. Institutionalize change through formal policies, processes and practices.
5. Monitor and adjust policies and practices in response to problems emerging during the change process.

The key points emerging from these suggestions are the need for involvement (giving managers and employees a voice), and communications and training as part of a planned approach to implementation.

HR practitioners have an important role in managing change. Lynda Gratton (3) stresses the need for them to: 'Understand the state of the company, the extent of the embedding of processes and structures throughout the organization, and the behaviour and attitudes of individual employees.' She believes that 'the challenge is to implement the ideas' and the solution is to 'build a guiding coalition by involving line managers, which means creating issue-based cross-functional action teams that will initially make recommendations and later move into action'. This approach 'builds the capacity to change'.

Peter Harris, Reward and Benefits Manager, Friends Provident, commented to the e-reward researcher in 2004 that:

> We often read that 'the only constant thing is change itself' and during periods of change 'communicate, communicate, communicate'. How right they are. Over the past four years we have continuously reviewed and evolved our reward and benefits package to ensure we can differentiate reward by performance, have a set and range of benefits that are valued and which are effectively communicated. The changes we have made have certainly helped to move the company forwards, given us the opportunity to reinforce the link between individual performance, company performance and reward, and personally given me the opportunity to make a positive difference. I'm confident that the latter is true for all reward specialists.

Excellent practical advice on the management of change when developing reward systems is also provided by the heads of reward in B&Q, Diageo, Lloyds TSB and Tesco, as set out in Chapter 30. Paul Craven, Compensation Director, R&D GlaxoSmithKline, summed it up when he said: 'Don't expect people to change overnight and don't try to force change. It is better to reinforce desirable behaviour than to attempt to enforce a particular way of doing things.'

THE USE OF COMPUTERS IN REWARD MANAGEMENT

The ever-evolving world of IT and electronic communications has changed how salary data is reviewed and managed quite radically in the past decade. Applications and data can now be accessed and assessed from almost anywhere in the world; organizations are making increasing use of the Internet, data on market rates and pay settlements is published on the Internet and users can communicate at speed through e-mail. Computers and the software are becoming more and more powerful and sophisticated. HR or reward specialists can analyse the implications of new grade structures, cost pay review matrices and plan salary reviews, and options can rapidly be costed through simple changes on a spreadsheet. Increasing use is being made of IT to speed up and support reward administration and generate information to assist in decision making in the areas of:

- providing an employee reward database;
- job evaluation;
- grade and pay structure modelling;
- pay review modelling;
- equal pay reviews.

The employee reward database

The employee reward database stores data on employees' pay, earnings and benefits so that it can be updated, processed and communicated as information to users. The database consists of systematically organized and interrelated sets of files (collections of records serving as the basic unit of data storage) and allows for combinations of data to be selected as required by different users. The database contains information imported from the payroll or personnel information system. This information may include personal and job details, job grade, basic pay, position in the pay range (compa-ratio), earnings through variable pay, pay history (progression, and general and individual pay increases), performance management ratings, details of employee benefits, pension contributions, contributions to Save-as-you-earn schemes and the choices made under a flexible benefits system, including pension contributions.

The database can be used to:

- produce listings of employees by job category, job grade, rate of pay, position in range and size in actual or percentage terms of the last increase and, if required, previous individual performance pay increases;
- generate reports analysing distributions of pay by grade, including compa-ratios for each grade and the organization as a whole – extracts from these reports can

be downloaded to the personal computers of managers responsible for pay decisions to assist them in conducting pay reviews;
- initiate and print notifications of pay increases and update the payroll database;
- use electronic mail facilities to transmit data.

In using the database it is necessary that the provisions of the Data Protection Act 1998 are met. This requires *inter alia* that personal data held for any purpose should not be used or disclosed in any manner incompatible with that purpose, and appropriate security measures must be taken against unauthorized access to, or disclosure of, those data. If data are going to be downloaded it will be essential to control who gets what. The importance of data protection will also have to be spelt out to managers.

Computer-assisted job evaluation

Computers can be used to help directly with job evaluation processes, as described in Chapter 9.

Software packages

Micro-based software packages have been developed to carry out the various processes referred to above. Proprietary software is usually designed as a standard software shell within which there are a number of functions that allow users to customize the system to meet their own needs.

Grade and pay structure modelling

Software packages available from firms such as Link Consultants and Pilat UK use the output from a computerized job evaluation exercise contained in the database to model alternative grade structures by reference to the distribution of points scores against the existing pay rates for the jobs covered by job evaluation. The computer produces a scattergram and a trend line showing the relationship between pay and the job evaluation scores. The program will then enable a proposed grade structure to be superimposed on the scattergram which identifies those jobs above or below the new grade boundaries. The cost of bringing the pay of those below the new boundaries to the minimum rate for their new grades is then calculated by the computer.

Alternative grade configurations can then be superimposed on the scattergram to find out if the number of jobs below the lower limits of their new grades will be reduced. The computer then calculates the lower costs of bringing the fewer jobs up to the minimum. This modelling process can continue until the optimum configuration of grades from the point of view of costs is achieved. A decision can then be made as to whether this grade structure or one of the others should be selected. The lowest cost option would not necessarily be chosen as it might produce an unmanageable grade structure, for example too few grades with too much scope for pay progression within them.

Pay review modelling

General reviews

The computer can use the database to provide information on the total cost of a proposed general pay review and the effect this will have on other costs, for example pensions. They can then model alternative levels. Computers can model the effect on costs of alternative increases.

Individual reviews

It is now increasingly typical to manage pay reviews for an organization on an Excel or Lotus 1-2-3 spreadsheet, through which a number of alternative options can be tested. They provide line managers with a worksheet, divided into cells, into which can be inserted text, numbers or formulae. This allows the user to carry out complex 'what if' analyses of the impact on the pay review budget of alternative distributions of awards to staff. Analyses can be saved as a separate file for future recall when the proposals are approved. Spreadsheets can be printed out in report or graphical form, for example a scattergram as illustrated in Figure 29.2. In some organizations line managers carry out the modelling themselves using a spreadsheet with data provided by HR and their conclusions can be reviewed, approved and aggregated into an overall cost of the review analysed by departments. In others, HR and reward specialists carry out salary reviews for each function or department with the relevant line managers on-site using a laptop.

The problem with spreadsheets is that they can be quite complex and do not always work well in larger applications. Software such as the Pay Modeller marketed by Link Consultants may be the answer to these problems.

Equal pay reviews

Software is available to support equal pay reviews and analyses. These range from database tools that enable data to be imported from a range of sources to generate pay gap analyses such as the e-review Equal Pay toolkit, to more sophisticated tools that allow for a broader range of analysis possibilities using different data cuts, including the tool developed by Link.

REFERENCES

1   e-research (2004) *Survey of Contingent Pay*, e-reward.co.uk Ltd, Stockport, Cheshire
2   Armstrong, M and Baron, A (2004) *Managing Performance: Action and impact*, CIPD, London
3   Gratton, L A (2000) Real step change, *People Management,* 16 March, pp 27–30

30

Reward case studies

The 11 case studies in this chapter provide information on reward strategies and practices and development programmes in 10 leading UK companies and the UK Audit Commission. They have been condensed from the research carried out by e-reward between 2002 and 2004 which resulted in a total of 17 cases, the full versions of which can be obtained from e-reward.co.uk:

- AEGON
- Audit Commission
- B&Q
- British Airways
- Diageo
- GlaxoSmithKline
- Lloyds TSB
- Nationwide
- Norwich Union Insurance
- PriceWaterhouseCoopers
- Tesco

SIGNIFICANT POINTS

The overall impression from these case studies is that the organizations concerned have generally adopted a strategic and integrated approach to the development of their reward systems. The total reward concept is mentioned specifically by three organizations but, by implication, it is very much on the agenda in others. There is a general belief that reward is strongly linked to talent management, the creation of 'compelling employment opportunities' and ensuring that the organization is 'a great place to work'. Several heads of reward emphasized that the differentiator between companies from the viewpoint of attraction and retention of staff was not so much levels of pay but the total reward package, especially those parts of it concerned with intrinsic and non-financial rewards which tend to be unique to the organization that provides them. Recognition and flexible benefit schemes are used in a number of organizations. There is a move away from narrow-graded pay structures to career families or broad bands in a number of organizations. Excellent advice was given by a number of heads of reward on how to develop new reward systems. Heads of reward in a number of organizations were very much aware of the need to plan reward developments and manage change with great care.

The general points emerging from the case studies are:

- advice on developing reward systems – B&Q, Diageo, Lloyds TSB;
- reduced use of analytical job evaluation – AEGON, Tesco;
- approaches to devolving reward responsibilities to line managers – AEGON, Lloyds TSB;
- details of reward philosophies and guiding principles – Audit Commission, B&Q, British Airways, Diageo, Lloyds TSB, Tesco;
- approaches to strategic reward – B&Q, Diageo, GlaxoSmithKline, Lloyds TSB, Norwich Union Insurance;
- approaches to total reward – GlaxoSmithKline, Lloyds TSB, Norwich Union Insurance, PriceWaterhouseCoopers;
- conducting pay reviews – AEGON, B&Q, GlaxoSmithKline, Lloyds TSB.

The case studies also provide information on the use of:

- the balanced scorecard – Lloyds TSB, Norwich Union Insurance;
- bonuses – GlaxoSmithKline;
- broad-banded structures – GlaxoSmithKline, Norwich Union Insurance, Tesco;
- career/job families – AEGON, Nationwide, Norwich Union Insurance;
- flexible benefits – Lloyds TSB, PriceWaterhouseCoopers;
- performance pay – GlaxoSmithKline, Lloyds TSB, Norwich Union Insurance;
- recognition schemes – GlaxoSmithKline;
- reference points and target rates – AEGON, Tesco;
- zones – AEGON, GlaxoSmithKline.

The information obtained from each organization is set out below.

AEGON

AEGON UK has 4,200 employees and is one of the UK's leading providers of individual and group pension, protection and investment products. It is part of the AEGON Group, one of the world's largest listed insurance companies.

Integrated approach to HR

Like many companies, AEGON UK's pay systems and supporting processes, such as job evaluation and performance appraisal, used to stand alone, apart from other HR processes. The company adopted a more holistic approach to the development of its new reward system – which it calls the *Human Resources Integrated Approach* – so that from whatever angle staff now look at the elements of pay management, performance, career development and reward, they are consistent and linked.

The reward system

AEGON UK has gradually overhauled its reward system since January 2000. In addition to a flexible benefits scheme, the main components are as follows.

Career family structure

At the heart of AEGON UK's new reward system is a career family structure which gives 'greater clarity in the link between jobs and pay rates'. It was developed to replace a traditional graded structure containing 27 grades, with pay progression related to individual performance. In what was once a typical multi-graded pay structure, the emphasis was very much on hierarchy: the only way ahead was upward, through promotion or re-grading. The focus is now on flexible roles, individual career development and competency growth, and more priority is now given to external competitiveness. Gone are the days when pay progression and career development at AEGON UK were simply a matter of getting promotion to a higher grade.

The company defines a career family as 'a group of jobs where the technical knowledge and behavioural skills are similar and recognizable by the external labour market'. The career family structure consists of what are in effect four job families:

1. Operations delivery
2. Team leader and technical
3. Junior management, professional and senior technical
4. Management and senior professional.

One of its main aims is to provide information on development opportunities and career paths that, as part of a performance management process, can contribute to performance development and training. Within each career family there are defined career paths for progressing to higher levels by clarifying what skills individuals have to demonstrate if they wish to move to a new career path. The career families can therefore provide the foundation for personal development planning by defining the knowledge and skills required at higher levels or in different functions and what needs to be learnt through experience, education or training.

Employees are able to understand not only how they can develop their skills and competence within their current role, but also how they can move through their career path to specialist roles. Routes are also shown into career paths in other parts of the organization.

Target rates

Target rates are defined as the 'rate that a competent and experienced individual should be paid when he or she has consistently demonstrated that he or she is performing at a competent level over time'. This is in relation to:

- the capsule role descriptions which accompany the career family pay chart;
- the individual's performance and achievement of objectives when compared with the competency framework applicable to the role and evidenced through the performance management review system.

Each target rate supports three *performance zones* which 'help managers and staff understand the relationship between individual performance and their pay level'. These zones provide some guidance on the pay range for different roles within the band. The lower level of pay is as much as 25 per cent below the reference point, while the higher level is more than 10 per cent above that point.

The three performance zones are:

- *Learning zone* (75–90 per cent of target rate): Individuals are still progressing and have yet to consistently demonstrate their use of the full range of behavioural and technical competencies required for the role.
- *Competent zone* (90–110 per cent of target rate): Individuals are consistently demonstrating full use of the behavioural and technical competencies.
- *Advanced zone* (over 110 per cent of target rate): Individuals are consistently delivering a superior performance based upon their use of behavioural competencies and advanced technical knowledge.

Flexible pay and incentives

Pensionable, lump-sum bonus payments are awarded on a non-consolidated basis. An incentive scheme enables line managers to recognize and reward outstanding contribution by individuals or teams outside of the annual pay cycle, ensure that rewards are valued by the recipient due to the wide choice available for the redemption of vouchers, and make awards quickly with the minimum bureaucracy in respect of form completion and management approval.

The AEGON UK bonus scheme is based on the following three measures:

1. annual premium income;
2. customer satisfaction and industry reputation;
3. operating expenses.

AEGON UK also offers a variety of financial and non-financial awards in recognition of personal development and the ongoing contribution that employees make towards the overall effectiveness and efficiency of the company.

Devolution to line managers

In some parts of the business, pay decisions have increasingly been devolved to line managers who have been given freedom to manage the pay of their staff in accordance with policy guidelines and within their budgets (by reference to information on market rates and relativities within their departments).

Factors affecting individual pay levels

The reward system at AEGON UK is designed to recognize three core factors which affect the level of pay that individuals should receive for their 'personal commitment and consistent contribution within their roles'. These are:

1. *internal job value* – the bigger the job, the higher the reward;
2. *external job value* – the level of reward will be influenced by external market rates and the degree to which market forces affect the salaries required to attract and retain quality staff;
3. *value of the person* – individual employees may be rewarded at a higher level because they are making a greater contribution, are performing better, meeting objectives and have achieved a higher level of skill or competence than their colleagues (measured through the performance management process).

As an internal policy statement explains: 'Whilst the first two factors are the primary responsibility of the compensation and benefits in group personnel, line managers are best placed to manage the third factor for all staff within their reporting teams.'

Job evaluation

Job evaluation now relies on whole-job comparisons consisting of internal benchmarking or matching along with external benchmarking against survey data, using generic role definitions. The relative emphasis on job evaluation and detailed, common standards of internal job measurement and grading has been reduced.

AUDIT COMMISSION

The reward policy is based on the principle that the systems must:

- encourage and give significant and appropriate recognition through pay progression and/or other one-off rewards to high-quality performance, in achieving business goals;
- differentiate between those who achieve and those who do not;
- align pay determination and budget responsibility;
- identify a clear relationship with 'market rates', recognizing these may differ on a geographic and functional basis;
- support the recruitment and retention of staff with competencies relevant to present and future business need;
- be affordable in the short and long term;
- support a culture and style of management which is open and which aims to secure staff credibility and support;
- encourage and reward the development of competencies appropriate to the role of the individual and the business needs of the organization;
- whilst providing reward mainly through base pay, offer a combination of pay and non-pay benefits which is flexible to enable staff to gain maximum value from their personal package;
- in applying pay systems, seek to ensure fairness and consistency in decision making;
- comply with legal requirements (eg on equal pay) and with other appropriate constraints such as government guidelines on public sector pay;
- be communicated in a timely, clear, concise and accurate way to existing and new staff;
- not discriminate on grounds of age, colour, creed, ethnic origin, gender reassignment, marital status, personal disability, race, sex or sexual orientation.

B&Q

B&Q is the UK's leading DIY and garden retailer with 25,000 full-time employees.

Pay structure for customer advisers

A new spot rate pay structure for the 20,000-strong customer advisers in the stores was launched in February 2001, but it has taken a further two years to design and develop the new learning and development framework which supports the structure and identifies how employees progress up the scale.

The 20,000 customer advisers are paid in the upper quartile of similar jobs on one of six different spot rates. These spot rates are 'market competitive and place us as one of the top paying retailers in the UK'. Spot rates are reviewed each February. All new recruits come in at the same *minimum rate*. After 13 weeks they move to the *established rate* for the job if they successfully complete their initial induction and training period and meet the requirement of the job. This is the rate that is paid to good performers who are fully competent in this role and the rate that most customer advisers receive. The established rate is the one B&Q uses when benchmarking how it pays in comparison to retail and other industries.

Pay progression is based on the acquisition – and application on the shop floor – of skills and knowledge. There are four additional spot rates beyond the established rate, designed to reward 'excellence in the role'. Each additional level represents an hourly increase up to a maximum rate. Pay is reviewed against the learning and development framework which, in the words of Will Astill, Reward Manager at B&Q, 'underpins the delivery of the service levels we aspire to'. As part of the establishment of a new learning and development framework, roles have been redefined and the skills required at each level have been profiled. Training plans have also been introduced to help employees progress through the framework.

The framework has been created around the key business areas B&Q wanted to see improved: stock control, shrinkage, customer service, level of product knowledge and increases in the number of multiskilled staff in store teams. Will Astill says: 'Better trained staff will lead to improved business performance.' The aim of the framework is to help support the expansion of the business by providing opportunities for those who want to progress their career but also seeks to recognize those employees who want to help colleagues learn and give great customer service.

All customer advisers are given a written job description, called 'What is my role?', which provides an overview of the key accountabilities. This helps managers and the employee identify those areas where the individual could improve his or her DIY knowledge. It also provides details of each pay level and the standard of job performance needed, as well as the type of behaviour B&Q is looking for at each level. Customer advisers will now be able to see how they are performing and whether they have fulfilled all the criteria for the role. If the employee has met the required performance standard and the budget exists, he or she will be put forward to progress to the next level.

There is also a store team bonus, based on sales, shrinkage (resulting from losses such as theft and stocktaking errors) and customer service measures set at store level, and a formal recognition scheme.

Advice on developing reward systems

On the basis of his experience of a major reward system development programme, Will Astill, recommends the following guiding principles:

1. *Without cooperation, change strategies are likely to fail.* A key challenge is getting the people in all of the different departments involved in the project – recruitment, employment policy, internal communications, human resources and reward – to work together. If change strategies do not carry everyone in the organization willingly forward, the process can be painful and even damaging. So it's vital that the reward manager builds relationships with the right people. 'You need to get key individuals to work together without them feeling that they are losing control of their initiatives,' says Will Astill.

2. *Secure directors' 'buy-in' right away.* You will need to build a compelling case for the recommended approach and it should be accepted and supported by directors at an early stage. As Will Astill puts it: 'Don't go to the board meeting without having talked the directors through it beforehand. There's simply not enough time at the board meeting. They have to have made the decision beforehand.'

   Additionally, time spent thinking about each and every individual decision-maker is time well spent. Says Will Astill: 'You must sell it to every individual. For example, with the new store team bonus we had to anticipate how it would impact on the finance director and the property director. You must build that into the project management process.'

   Will Astill is keen to extol the virtues of a more strategic use of reward: 'Reward is so strategic. If it is not being discussed in the boardroom, you are doing something wrong. It has so much impact on change management, performance, and business strategy. You cannot hope to design a reward strategy if you are not close to the board.'

3. *Never underestimate the value of in-depth employee consultation.* As Will Astill explains: 'It is necessary to spend money on professional research – market research, HR consultants to design and facilitate focus groups – as though you are conducting a market research exercise. Employees are consumers. You need to sell the initiative to them and help them understand why it is taking place.'

4. *Remember that strategy formulation is an evolutionary process.* 'Our business is changing rapidly and there are significant differences in our business needs compared with, say, the early 1990s, so we need policies, procedures and people to follow them,' says Will Astill. 'We work on the basis of an emerging strategy and there is always a three-year rolling plan. New challenges emerge through the business changing. There are whole new profit areas of B&Q that simply didn't exist a few years ago, for example the financial services and installation part of the business. Clearly, this has an impact on the type of people we recruit and the way we reward them. Customer advisers now need to be educated to sell financial services.'

5. *Look at how much you spend on communicating your reward package.* Does every employee have an effective induction? Do they know what the total package is worth? Do they know how their bonus has been tracking?

6. *No initiative should be implemented without examining the return on investment.* This means that processes and schemes will not be introduced or updated at B&Q without assessing the effect they are expected to have on the business. 'Make a business case for everything,' says Will Astill. 'The return on investment analysis also justifies what priority you assign to implementation.'

7. *Evaluate the effectiveness of programmes and take action as required.* B&Q carries out a post-implementation review one year after implementation to ensure that the scheme is meeting its key objectives and it examines what will need to change next year.

8. *Budget well in advance.* Will Astill begins his budgetary process in May for the financial year starting the next February. By the end of May everything which is planned to take place in the next financial year is fully costed. B&Q operates a three-year rolling plan for its reward activities.

9. *Never take your eye off future European Union and UK legislation.* 'It's imperative that you budget well in advance for statutory changes. You need to make sure that you are not in a position where you haven't got the money for, say, new maternity and paternity provisions,' says Will Astill.

A final word

An overriding theme running through our review was on the desirability of adopting a strategic approach. It wasn't a case of 'let's follow best practice' nor were we lured into adopting the latest 'fads' and 'fashions'. Applying a bespoke system – taking what someone has done before and adapting to your organization – will not push you ahead of rivals. Our emphasis throughout the two-year process was on what's right for the business. – Will Astill, Reward Manager

BRITISH AIRWAYS

Reward vision

The vision for the reward system at British Airways is that it should:

- support the attraction and retention of employees through effective use of total reward;
- help motivate employees by rewarding their contribution and recognizing their value to the company;
- ensure that reward will be aligned to both individual and company performance;
- support the delivery of BA's business strategy and plans.

Reward principles

- Total reward is aligned to the business strategy. It engages and involves people in the achievement of business goals.
- Reward is aligned to company performance and supports a performance culture.
- Reward helps employees understand how their efforts contribute to company success.
- Rewards will be cost effective.
- Total reward is actively supported in the business.
- Individual value is recognized through base pay; delivery of results is linked to variable pay.
- Reward will take into account market forces and drivers.

Reward strategy

The airline recognizes that reward strategy is an important means of reinforcing cultural change. 'Reward strategy and plans should support major change programmes,' says Neil Buswell, International Reward Manager. 'Thus our overall approach at macro level flows from business and people strategies and individual reward work areas will take the same approach on a micro level.'

DIAGEO

Diageo is one of the world's leading beverage alcohol businesses, with a string of international brands and 24,000 employees worldwide. It is known as one the best places to work, having won awards as one of the top 10 'most admired' companies in the UK and for being a 'great employer' not only in the UK, but also in Australia,

Hungary, Ireland, Italy, Jamaica, Kenya, Portugal and Spain. From an HR perspective, the aim is to 'release the potential of every employee to deliver Diageo's performance goals'.

Recognition and reward principles

Diageo's approach to recognition and reward is based around four key principles:

1. *Performance:* rewards are developed that reflect team and individual achievements.
2. *Market:* rewards reflect the market in which an employee is based, whether that be geographical or functional, and compare favourably with those of competitors.
3. *Communication:* Diageo aims to explain to 'everyone the components and value of their reward package, the criteria that affect it, and how they can influence it'.
4. *Effectiveness:* the company seeks out 'best practice' and ensures its benefits programmes 'remain effective for the business and our employees'.

Role of reward

The role of reward in Diageo comprises five key elements:

1. *Support and enable the talent agenda.* 'Our role in reward is to help to provide the talent the business needs, at the right time, in the right place and for the right price,' says Nicki Demby, Diageo's Performance and Reward Director. 'This means developing reward processes and plans that will hire the best talent, keep it and develop it. We simply can't buy all the talent that we need to take the organization into its future. We need to grow our own.'
2. *Provide clear principles to enable decision- making in the business.* By developing clear principles, Diageo hopes that when line managers are faced with choices, the right decisions will be more obvious. 'Less demand will be placed on reward "experts" in the business, who can spend more of their time on value creating enhancements to our processes, plans and communications,' comments Nicki Demby.
3. *Align the reward approach with Diageo business strategy.* The success of the reward strategy depends heavily on developing appropriate performance measures in incentives, the cost-effective delivery of reward and consistent processes.
4. *Enable every employee to understand why they get paid what they get paid.* 'We need to have a big push on communication,' admits Nicki Demby. 'People do not necessarily understand what they are paid and how we perform. The connection between performance and reward needs to become visceral. As a formal part of each business review, we are telling people the impact the performance of their business is likely to have on their pay. It helps people to

make the connections between the business decisions that they make and the likely personal impact.'

5. *Have a customer service ethic that results in great execution.* The reward team's ethic is now based on a much greater orientation towards the needs of employees – its internal customers. 'This demands great planning, great communication and great execution,' says Nicki Demby.

Diageo recognizes, of course, that rewards are not just about pay and bonuses. That's why it aims to provide a range of benefits to meet the differing needs of individual employees, according to lifestyle, family and domestic circumstances through flexible benefits programmes. The company also believes in providing an environment where people can grow, learn and have fun. Above all, Diageo considers it just as important to provide ongoing development and a stimulating work culture as to offer competitive financial rewards.

Strategy

Diageo has well-articulated and integrated business, HR and reward strategies.

Business strategy

Diageo's business goal is straightforward: to create the world's leading premium drinks business. As the CEO, Paul S Walsh, stated in the 2003 Annual Report: 'We are more committed than ever to our ambition for Diageo to become one of the most revered names in consumer products. This is a bold and ambitious goal. To reach it we must continually deliver outstanding performance, judged by the most exacting global standards.'

Human resource strategy

Diageo prefaced the development of its new HR strategy with a major consultation exercise. It canvassed the opinions of middle managers, team leaders, line managers and employees generally through a series of 70 focus groups. Three broad strands emerged:

1. *Reward and recognition*: use recognition and reward programmes to stimulate outstanding team and individual performance contributions.
2. *Talent management*: drive the attraction, retention and professional growth of a deep pool of diverse, talented employees.
3. *Organizational effectiveness*: ensure that Diageo adapts its organization to maximize employee contribution and deliver performance goals.

The outcome was what Diageo calls its *Organization and People Strategy*. 'Our *Organization and People Strategy* has provided direction to our talent, operational effectiveness and performance and reward agendas,' says Nicki Demby. The company's underlying thinking is that the people strategy is not for the human resource function to own but is the responsibility of the whole organization, hence the title 'Organization and People Strategy'.

Reward strategy

Nicki Demby pointed out the significance of changes in the business strategy:

> This is a key issue. This changes reward strategy. Put simply, your organization's fundamental purpose may be revised. Major long-term goals in terms of outcomes and achievement of performance objectives may change. As a result, what your organization has to be good at doing to fulfil its mission and achieve its strategic goals may need refining.... Whenever you change your business strategy and/or your HR strategy, your reward strategy may need to respond, We are just getting to grips with the profound and detailed implications of a shift in our business strategy in the last two or three years.

Implications for reward

The organization needed to develop a coherent set of reward principles that would apply to all levels in the organization. However, as Nicki Demby explained, putting this idea into action is fraught with difficulties. 'We considered consistency to be vitally important but we had to recognize the fundamental tensions. You want a common framework and principles but in many ways reward is fundamentally a local intervention in terms of practice, labour markets and legislation. So, there is no way you can apply one-size-fits-all approaches to reward and hope that they will work. You just can't be dogmatic.'

When it came to reviewing its approach to reward, Diageo's ambitious goal can be distilled down to two words: 'massive simplification'. As Nicki Demby recalls: 'Historically, the centre had set policy but local managers found a way to work around it, adapting it to "my market" because everyone felt that their needs were different. This has led to an inordinate amount of complexity. But is this value-creating complexity?'

It was essential at Diageo to assess the extent to which changes will add value rather than create work. Nicki Demby explains: 'Reward processes and schemes will not be introduced or updated without assessing whether there is a good reason for doing so. Does it give energy or take it away? For example, is the reward plan so complicated that by the time you have waded through it you wish you hadn't? If so, you are taking away a rather effective management tool.'

So how will Diageo take complexity out of the reward system? 'Our mantra is now "keep it simple, but simple isn't easy!" It's just as hard as making something complicated, but in terms of effectiveness, well-thought-through simplicity can pay huge dividends,' says Nicki Demby.

Lessons learnt from the development programme

Nicki Demby describes what she sees as the more successful elements of the Diageo change management process.

First and foremost, one particularly noteworthy learning point was the desirability of ensuring that the human resource department is not developing policies and practices on its own, which are then tagged as just another HR initiative rather than as something which is owned by the organization as a whole. At Diageo, senior HR leaders drawn from across the company's global operations teamed up with senior finance people to discuss a number of broad reward themes. 'Together they came up with some really powerful ideas,' says Nicki Demby. 'Everyone worked together, sparking ideas off one another, on forging links between performance and reward. The meeting was very powerful and energetic. We achieved cut-through on a number of issues. According to the coach who facilitated this meeting, it was hard to distinguish between the HR and finance people who took part. Issues were characterized as business rather than HR problems.'

Broad-based representation in the project proved beneficial in other ways. When developing changes to the annual incentive plan, at the outset Diageo formed a steering committee responsible for agreeing and signing off the approach, with an oversight role throughout the project. The majority of the steering group was formed of executives representing the business, for example managing directors across major, key and venture markets. 'HR was leading the process but the business was used as a sounding board,' says Nicki Demby. 'We had to create that connectivity with the business across the world and it was worth its weight in gold.'

The third lesson learnt by Nicki Demby concerns the communications exercise. Quite clearly, an essential feature of any implementation programme is the very clear, effective and regular communication of aims, methods of operation and the impact. Transparency is essential. But for Nicki Demby it is imperative not only to explain the planned changes, the rationale behind them, and how it affects the workforce, but also to communicate details of who was involved in the development process so that unnecessary fears are allayed. 'Cross-functional teams develop better solutions,' says Nicki Demby.

A final word

Great incentives should be used to drive great business performance. Great performers will always perform. Great reward programmes can help the whole organization to perform. – Nicki Demby, Performance and Reward Director

GLAXOSMITHKLINE (GSK)

GSK is the UK's largest pharmaceutical company, with 22,000 employees. Its mission is stated as follows: 'Our global quest is to improve the quality of human life by enabling people to do more, feel better and live longer.' The key business drivers are:

- portfolio – building the best pipeline (that is, the time it takes to bring a drug to market);
- product commercialization – developing products from a 'molecule' into a block-buster drug;
- global competitor – having a global mindset where appropriate;
- operational excellence – to be the best-managed organization; processes should be slick, smooth and efficient;
- people – 'We want GSK to be a place where the best people do their best work.'

Total reward strategy

Paying for performance is the ultimate goal at GSK, and this is championed at the highest level, by the chief executive. *TotalReward*, the name by which GSK refers to its approach to reward, consists of three elements:

1. *Total Cash* (base salary and bonus), plus long-term incentives for managers and executives;
2. *Lifestyle Benefits* (health care, employee assistance, family support, dental care);
3. *Savings Choices* (pension plan, *ShareSave*, *ShareReward*).

The complete package, the concept of which is based on employees understanding the total value of all the rewards they receive, not just the individual elements, is designed to attract, retain, motivate and develop the best talent. The proposition for employees is that *TotalReward* gives them the opportunity to share in the company's success, makes it easier to balance home and working life, and helps them to take care of themselves and their families.

Total Cash

The first element of *TotalReward* is *Total Cash*. This consists of base salary and bonus. The philosophy behind this is that superior performance deserves superior reward. This, says the company, is 'performance with a sense of urgency and integrity, performance that enables our patients and consumers to do more, feel better and live longer, and performance that will enable GSK to achieve its strategic goals'.

Total Cash has been designed to reinforce the achievement of business objectives – when GSK and the business unit do well, the individual employee will do well too. The key features of *Total Cash* are:

- Pay for performance is a basic principle.
- GSK and business unit performance drive bonus plans.
- It is aligned with the achievement of business objective.
- It reflects competitive leading market practices.
- It rewards team and individual contributions.
- It is aligned with roles and responsibilities.

Base salary

GSK has five bands: A and B for are for top executives, band C is for directors and managers, band D covers professional and technical staff and band E comprises administrative staff. These bands determine benefit entitlements. Pay for manufacturing staff is negotiated with the trade unions; these job grades are subject to local agreement and are not included in the grading structure.

For pay purposes, each band is divided into a number of zones. For example, band D is divided into six zones, and band E has five zones. The combination of band and zone produces the grade, and there are 29 grades in total. These grades are also important for determining bonus entitlement. The pay for each grade ranges approximately 25 per cent either side of the range mid-point.

This kind of job-evaluated multi-graded structure can sometimes cause problems with grade drift, as there may not be the flexibility to reward lateral development within pay bands. Where this happens, individuals who take on extra responsibilities expect to be promoted. This is not a problem at GSK. First, there is a fair degree of flexibility as to how managers can use the ranges. Staff can be recruited high or low within a grade, if this is necessary to keep pace with the market. Managers can be paid one grade above or below the grade at which their job has been evaluated, again to keep their pay relative to their capabilities and hence in line with the market. Secondly, there are a number of career ladders (such as the HR and R&D scientific career ladders), which provide an established means of moving up the structure. Finally, while staff are not automatically promoted or given a salary increase when they move laterally as part of their development plan, this is likely to lead to promotion in the long run.

With the introduction of the new grading process, individuals were, and continue to be, allocated to their grades using a home-grown factor-based scheme which is based around a combination of a number of different job evaluation schemes found in the market. This was a demanding exercise, keeping many of the company's compensation team busy for around nine months.

Pay ranges are benchmarked against the market. The company's policy is to base pay rates on the median, but for total cash to range from median to the 65th percentile for good performers.

Paying for performance

The main method of paying for performance each year is through the bonus scheme, but individuals are also able to progress through their grade range. There is no formal system of advancing people to their mid-points. Salaries are reviewed annually, usually in April. For individuals on grades A to E, their pay rise is determined by:

- their achievement of objectives;
- their 'behaviours';
- their position in the range;
- their position with regard to their peers;
- their salary in relation to the market;
- the position of the pay ranges with regard to the market;
- the available budget.

The annual pay rise is intended to reward continuing performance, whereas the bonus is more focused on the current year's performance. Unionized manufacturing staff receive a negotiated across-the-board increase which does not depend on their individual performance.

There is a two-way performance and development planning process whereby individuals agree their objectives with their manager and identify development needs for the forthcoming year. Managers are 'strongly guided' to have at least two other appraisal meetings with their staff throughout the year, making a total of three, so that there are 'no surprises'.

Bonuses are the main vehicles for pay for performance. The payments are substantial – worth as much as 22.5 per cent for a senior professional or technical specialist. The design of the bonus plan is common across all GSK's businesses in the UK.

An individual's bonus is driven by the performance of their bonus unit, their job grade and, for the majority of grades, their individual performance over the year.

Recognition

The recognition scheme is seen as another and more immediate way to motivate staff and reward good performance rather than having to wait for the annual bonus.

GSK feels the scheme is 'well used', for example within the R&D business, where, in any one year, around a third of staff will receive an award. The scheme gives financial recognition to effort over and above the normal job requirements and there are four different levels of award – bronze, silver, gold and platinum – with taxable payouts ranging from £50 to £5,000.

The pot for recognition awards is part of the manager's overall staff budget. The company is planning to track awards on the intranet, in order to learn from demonstrations of outstanding staff effort or achievement.

A final word

> Don't expect people to change overnight and don't try to force change. It is better to reinforce desirable behaviour than to attempt to enforce a particular way of doing things. – Paul Craven, Compensation Director, R&D

LLOYDS TSB

Lloyds TSB has 70,000 full- and part-time employees in the UK and 80,000 worldwide. Lloyds TSB is among the 10 largest organizations in the UK and now ranks as the second biggest bank in Europe based on market capitalization. Over 50 per cent of staff are in direct service roles, offering a range of financial products available to customers on a 24-hour, 7-day-week basis.

Approach to reward

Lloyds TSB is not simply offering more enticing pay packages to give it the edge in luring and keeping these valued employees who are so critical to high-quality work and customer service. Instead, Lloyds TSB is thinking about reward in a much broader sense, which means embracing more intangible rewards like work environment, performance and development, career management and resourcing as the cornerstones of an effective recruitment and retention policy.

Since the mid-1990s, the compensation and benefits team has been busy rewriting the rules of reward management in the organization in a bid to hold on to their most valued staff. Pivotal to the emergence of a new, more integrated total reward approach was the formulation in 1994 of a far-reaching vision statement. In essence, its message was that the bank could not afford to remain trapped in the ways of doing things as in the past – the reward management landscape in the organization had to be transformed. The merger between Lloyds Bank and TSB in autumn 1995 was also to have a lasting impression on terms and conditions in the two companies.

The era in which reward at Lloyds TSB was just about cash is long gone; increasingly the emphasis is on creating a 'compelling employment offer' – one that is more individually focused, tailored to employees' needs and interests, and more in tune with the expectations of a diverse workforce. By focusing on monetary rewards it is all too easy to overlook ways of succeeding that rivals cannot readily copy. But with competitive pressures so strong, the need for Lloyds TSB to differentiate its reward package from other financial services employers has never been more intense. The bank decided that what really gives an employer the edge as they struggle to woo and retain scarce talent is appealing to the beliefs, personal values and lifestyle choices of today's employees. Its total reward package, called *Flavours*, replete with one of the biggest flexible benefits schemes in the UK and a new share incentive plan, seeks to integrate all aspects of the work experience so that prominence is given not only to remuneration but also to less tangible rewards.

Business and reward strategies

Lloyds TSB's corporate goal is straightforward: put simply, it is to maximize shareholder value. Basically, it does that in three main ways. The company:

- aims to be the leader in its chosen markets;
- wants to be the first choice for customers;
- wants to facilitate investment in its people by driving down day-to-day operating costs.

The principal challenge from a reward perspective is for Lloyds TSB to 'tie back' all of its reward practices and processes to satisfy these three corporate needs so that developing a distinctive reward strategy contributes effectively to achieving longer-term business goals. The strategy of the organization provides a sense of purpose and the general direction in which reward management must go to provide help in dealing with these issues. What's more, for the compensation and benefits team it establishes priorities for developing and acting on reward plans if they are to secure the investment they want from the group's executive board.

Guiding principles of reward at Lloyds TSB

The guiding principles governing the design of the reward system are as follows:

- Basic pay is linked to the market.
- Benefits are market driven and individually focused.
- Pay decisions are devolved to line managers.

- Pay reflects individual contribution in a high-performance organization.
- Complying with equal pay principles.
- Variable pay is linked to performance.
- Wealth creation and share ownership are encouraged.
- Reward and HR practices are managed in an integrated way.

The pay structure

Lloyds TSB opted in 1997 to replace its fairly typical multi-graded pay structure with eight broader bands where each job type/family is linked to a wide salary range comprising a minimum and maximum salary related to market comparisons. Subsequently, in 2001, the maximum pay point was abandoned to provide more flexibility in the reward system.

Devolution of pay decisions to line managers

The final stage in the development of the new system was to scrap the variable pay matrix. Line managers were given freedom to manage the pay of their staff within pay budgets held locally, in accordance with policy guidelines and by reference to information on market rates and relativities within their departments. The system is designed to provide greater scope for progressing individual pay according to a line manager's judgement about an employee's performance, competence and contribution in relation to market trends.

Lloyds TSB's starting point was to make absolutely clear to all concerned from the outset that no one should expect to move to the upper reaches or top of a band unless they had earned it through increased competence, career development, the assumption of greater responsibilities and the consistent delivery of higher levels of contribution and added value.

Local pay management requires immense care when being introduced to ensure that it will work. It is not an easy option, or a quick fix. It constitutes a major culture change. It is important not only to get the basic design right but also to ensure that the various processes required to manage it are developed systematically. The processes have to be strong enough to cope with the increased demands that will be placed on HR and line managers. And they have to be developed and described in ways that clarify for employees how the system will work, how it is different, and how they will be affected by it.

Guidelines

The basic control mechanism is the pay review budget – line managers are required to keep strictly within their budgets. But detailed guidelines are issued to all line managers on the size of pay increases to help them manage pay within the new devolved framework. They are also trained on the principles governing the system.

To ensure that salary awards are fair and consistent, when making pay decisions for individuals, Lloyds TSB's broad guidelines suggest that managers should consider:

- what their current role and pay position is in the salary range
- what people in the same or similar roles are being paid;
- how they value the individual's skills, competencies and performance in this role, relative to the nearest pay reference point;
- what the function and geographical market rate is for this role;
- what recent pay awards have they received;
- expectations – they should conduct a dialogue with their people about where they are and where they could be;
- any other relevant factors, such as the degree of challenge of the job, the amount of learning required, and their recent performance history.

Line managers are now provided with a pay pot, which could be worth, say, 3.5 per cent of the pay budget, and are free to distribute their pay pot to reflect each individual's contribution. As Tim Fevyer, Senior Manager, Compensation and Benefits at Lloyds TSB, explains: 'The focus is really on where the employee is in the salary scale and where you want them to be in relation to their development of competencies and skills, given consistent annual performance over a sustained period of time. Pay is also governed by whether the employee is experienced and fully effective as well as market rate information.'

Controlling costs

Line managers are supplied with details of the salaries they would be expected to pay a typical employee who is fully experienced and consistently delivers a fully effective level of performance over a sustained period of time in a given role. This illustrates where Lloyds TSB expect them to be paid according to their skills, competencies and performance.

Additionally, managers are supplied with details of actual salaries in their department or area to enable them to make comparisons against the relevant internal market. They are also given the pay reference points for the appropriate benchmark roles. An individual may be paid at, below or above this pay reference point, depending on the contribution of their role relative to the nearest benchmark role, and on their experience, skills and contribution in their particular role.

Pay decisions are made on the basis of the manager's overall budget, pay pot, the market and internal equity, and they are scrutinized by the manager's manager and the HR manager for fairness and consistency. There is a perceived need to exercise control to achieve what is regarded as a proper degree of equity and consistency. Besides adherence to the pay budget, additional control is provided by careful monitoring of the distribution of pay in bands to ensure that anomalies do not occur. But the structure provides line managers with much greater flexibility to manage the career development and pay of their staff. 'HR now has a support or consultative role rather than a decision-making role,' says Tim Fevyer.

Performance-related pay

One of the forces that led to the overhaul of the existing performance management system was that performance-related pay increases were being added cumulatively to basic pay on an annual basis (that is, consolidated). This annuity approach has been described as the 'gift that goes on giving', and it raises questions such as 'why should this person still be rewarded now for an isolated achievement which took place many years ago?' The consolidation of merit increases means that pay costs will escalate without any guarantee that such extra costs are financed by increases in performance and productivity.

'People were being rewarded every year for perhaps something they had done only in one year,' say Tim Fevyer. 'That didn't seem right and didn't seem flexible enough for us. The focus has now moved away from annual performance to performance in much broader sense, performance over time and, of course, consideration of competencies and skills.'

Pay reflects contribution

Lloyds TSB's new approach to pay is based on three 'pay zones'. Pay is linked, in an open and transparent way, to distinct differences in individual contribution – comprising ongoing performance, knowledge, behaviours, competences and skills. Employees will receive a pay increase if their individual performance justifies it – they won't if it doesn't. If an employee consistently delivers a superior performance, that will be reflected in pay which will be managed in or towards the top of the three pay ranges.

Introduction of pay zones

Every role in Lloyds TSB is currently aligned to a pay market – put simply, each role has a market reference point, which indicates the normal rate of pay for a fully effective performer. In April 2004, the company will be introducing new pay zones within each band from 2 to 8 to help indicate normal progression and to give 'more structure and openness to the way we manage pay'. An internal briefing paper sent to all staff explains: 'The zones mean that you'll be able to see more clearly how your pay is managed in line with your contribution, and how your salary should increase as you develop in your role.'

There is a published salary range for each band (in other words, a minimum and maximum salary) based on pay rates within the market and these are reviewed every April to keep them in line with market movements.

Each band has three zones – primary, market and high performance – which will indicate the normal range of pay for someone who is developing in a particular role, fully effective over a sustained period of time (and which will be aligned to the market indicators), or displaying superior performance in the role:

- *Primary zone* – for people new to the role and still developing in that role. Typically – but not normally in every case – Lloyds TSB expects an employee to be performing to a 'fully effective' level after two or three years in the role and to move to the next zone. If an employee's salary is currently below the bottom zone and his or her work is judged satisfactory, pay will automatically be adjusted upwards.
- *Market zone* – if an employee is fully effective in a role, his or her pay should be managed towards or in the 'market' zone (if an employee moves to a new role, pay will start in the market zone as long as he or she has the necessary knowledge, competencies and skills to be fully effective from the outset).

  Broadly speaking, the market zone reflects the rate that other employers would pay for a particular job. These rates are set with data provided by independent pay consultants.
- *High-performance zone* – if an employee 'consistently makes a superior contribution to the business', his or her pay should be managed towards or in the high-performance zone. If an employee's salary is above the top zone, they will not receive an increase in basic pay in because they are already paid 'very high' in relation to the market.

Total reward strategy

The total reward strategy at Lloyds TSB comprises four elements:

1. Performance and development
2. Employee involvement
3. Career management and resourcing
4. Reward.

A basic tenet underpinning the concept of total reward at Lloyds TSB is that sacred managerial pursuits, such as improving commitment, encouraging better performance and generating a culture of innovation, can rarely be achieved through cash alone. As Tim Fevyer sees it, what comes across loud and clear from much of the research on what really motivates and engages people within organizations is that traditional pay elements tend to come somewhere down towards the bottom of the list.

'It is the non-financial rewards like work/life balance, meaningful work, the way people are managed which come right at the top of the list.'

Embracing a wider range of initiatives than just pay and benefits helps Lloyds TSB focus on the needs of employees for recognition, achievement, responsibility and personal growth. The company sees these as having a deeper and longer-lasting impact on retention, motivation and commitment.

For Tim Fevyer, traditional rewards – such as base pay and benefits – remain important fundamentals that companies must get right in order to compete for and retain key talent – otherwise much damage can be done. If individuals are not treated fairly, pay becomes a symbol of the unfairness and a source of dissatisfaction. 'Therefore I think we need to focus on getting pay right, particularly in light of equal pay. If you get it wrong, it has a negative effect. Then we need to concentrate on those things that are really going to make a difference to people,' says Tim Fevyer.

Tailoring rewards to employee needs

By thoroughly assessing and then addressing what it is that employees need in the reward package to feel well rewarded and motivated, you can start to create a working environment that will help you to hold on to and inspire your best people. According to Tim Fevyer, that is one of the principal reasons why Lloyds TSB introduced its flexible benefits scheme. As he explains: 'Giving people the opportunity to buy and sell up to five days' holiday really has a significant impact for them as individuals. As a consequence, that has a potentially significant impact for the organization, because if we are providing people with something that really meets their agenda, the chances are that they are more likely to think positively about the organization, and be more likely to stay in the organization. So, it enhances our ability to recruit people.'

Tailoring the total reward package to meet individual needs and offering flexibility may be the most effective way of responding to recruitment and retention difficulties. But Lloyds TSB views it as only part of the solution. Says Tim Fevyer: 'Flexible benefits are absolutely necessary but they are not in themselves sufficient. They are not going to solve all of our turnover issues, nor are they the perfect panacea for all of the organization's issues. But we actually have to do it.' In this context, the provision of a tax-free computer or five days' extra holiday might not mean that an employee will definitely stay at Lloyds TSB. 'But when it comes to thinking about whether you are going to leave or not it's another consideration,' says Tim Fevyer, 'and what we need to do is develop other considerations.'

The total reward programme

The Lloyds TSB total reward programme consists of four elements designed to create a 'compelling offer'.

Performance and development	Employee involvement
Career management and resourcing	Reward

Performance and development

Performance and development is the first part of Lloyds TSB's total reward programme. These are viewed as critical issues for the business. Quite clearly, with an increasingly competitive world market, it has never been more vital for employers to know that they are maximizing the capabilities of their employees.

Competency-based frameworks

Lloyds TSB also relies heavily on competencies. Every single job in the organization, regardless of level, has competencies linked to it. Competency is defined in terms of what people have to know and to be able to do to perform well. Great care has been taken to develop competency frameworks and performance management processes which ensure that competency is assessed against agreed criteria and by reference to evidence of how well competencies have been developed and used.

Balanced scorecard

The size and complexity of the organization means that some sense of accountability can get lost along the way. Lloyds TSB 'rolled out' a balanced scorecard from January 2003 so that staff can see how they are performing and be recognized and rewarded for their success.

A host of tangible rewards and incentives are linked to an individual's job. Clearly, in such a situation there is a danger of encouraging employees to focus on short-term quantifiable financial results to the exclusion of all else in order to achieve the reward. All too often the emphasis can be on quantity at the expense of quality. Lloyds TSB recognized that *how* results are achieved is as important as the results themselves.

The Lloyds TSB balanced scorecard blends a mix of financial metrics and non-financial indicators to provide a single integrated measure of performance that focuses on key indicators, from which a true reflection of organization performance can be accomplished. The scorecard thus enables the organization to focus on a small number of critical measures that create value for the organization, thereby rewarding employees not only for what they do but also how they do it.

All employees have a balanced scorecard or personal set of performance objectives, setting out clearly what is expected of each person. The bank feels that at an individual level, a balanced scorecard can help everyone understand how his or her performance contributes to the overall success of the business. It captures what every individual is seeking to achieve, how progress will be measured and what specific targets need to be attained.

The balanced scorecard sets out five key areas – finance/contribution; franchise growth and operational development; customer and service quality; risk; and people development – which align individual objectives with wider objectives as a business unit and as a group.

Lessons learnt

The management of reward at Lloyds TSB has undergone a profound transformation over the past decade as the company has strived to strengthen its competitiveness, enhance attractiveness to employees and increase shareholder returns. By daring to be different, by creating a unique employment offer that is more in tune with employees' needs and interests and more consistent with the expectations of a diverse workforce, Lloyds TSB is confident that it will be more able to attract and retain talented people.

Tim Fevyer believes the bank's employees are now unlikely to jump ship simply because of the basic pay they receive – they are much more likely to look at the overall employment package when deciding whether to stay or go. By adopting a total rewards strategy, the company maintains that it has a competitive advantage because it is able raise employee awareness and remind staff about the total value of their employment package. 'A quick glance at the total reward statements lets employees see all of the things that make up working at Lloyds TSB. *Flavours* draws it all together.'

Just one year old in 2003, the flexible benefits scheme has already generated extensive take-up among staff – 50 per cent of employees have opted to change one or more benefits. More importantly, according to Lloyds TSB, there has been a 10 per cent increase in satisfaction with benefits. Says Tim Fevyer: 'We are delighted with the take-up because it means there must be things of interest to people. But actually having a choice is the thing that is really important. Employees may not want to exercise that right today but they know that next year they might choose to flex holidays. They want that option.'

What's more, almost a third of Lloyds TSB staff now work flexibly – everything from four-day working to compressed hours, days that employees choose to job sharing. The number of employees choosing to work flexibly is increasing by 10 per cent a year.

So, it seems that companies that consciously take a holistic approach to total reward may then be able to push themselves ahead of rivals in the recruitment and retention race. Lloyds TSB's argument is that there is a demonstrable link between HR and reward practices that promote high levels of employee satisfaction and employees' willingness to 'go the extra mile'. As Tim Fevyer explains: 'The ability to buy and sell holidays, change your work patterns to suit your own needs and "flex" a raft of benefits means that employees are more likely to work harder, delivering an excellent return on the organization's investment.'

Developing new reward systems

When developing new reward systems, Tim Fevyer recommends these guiding principles:

1. 'The success of new reward systems depends heavily on talking to people, and asking what they would like to see,' argues Tim Fevyer. There is much to be said for involving line managers and listening to what employees and their representatives regard as important. Indeed, involvement is seen as a cornerstone of the bank's total reward programme. A range of approaches are used to involve employees, to capture meaningful data and to gain an understanding of employee needs and the rewards that motivate them to deliver results. But Lloyds TSB finds that the best ways are through carefully crafted attitude surveys, focus groups and the like.

    'When creating our compelling employment offer, we talked to people and found out what the key trends were. We undertook research about what is really compelling for employees. It is an essential preliminary to any reward strategy,' says Tim Fevyer.

2. Lloyds TSB feels it is imperative to communicate to staff at every stage of the process – even in advance of launch, explaining the planned changes, the rationale behind them, and how it affects the workforce. You then need to continue to give progress reports to employees and obtain their input on an ongoing basis thereafter. It requires consistent communication to employees, who must have a clear understanding of why total reward is being introduced and how it will affect them.

    But, as Tim Fevyer admits, communicating a wide-ranging change programme is onerous: 'Getting a consistent message across and getting people to understand what the business is trying to achieve is very difficult when rolling out a reward strategy over six, seven and eight years.'

3. The success of any total reward programme will hinge on the degree to which employees feel a sense of ownership. The aim is to get 'ownership' – a feeling among people that the change is something that they are happy to live with

because they have been involved in its planning and introduction – it has become *their* change.

4. Remember to ensure that employees are aware of what is available in terms of benefits provision. Employee research demonstrated that staff not only significantly underestimated the company's investment in employee benefits, but were completely unaware of some benefits that were available.

5. It's vital that you get pay right – otherwise much damage can be done. 'But once it is,' says Tim Fevyer, 'don't treat it like a sophisticated lever to influence motivation and empowerment.' He reckons that employees place a great deal more emphasis on intangible rewards when deciding where to work and the level of commitment to give their work. 'Pay is no longer the great differentiator. The only way we are going to keep people is by engaging them,' says Tim Fevyer.

6. A central message of some of the new pay advocates in the USA is the role of reward as a change agent: their central thesis is that pay can be a positive force for organizational change. But this is still a decidedly minority view. Much evidence seems stacked against it. For the Lloyds TSB compensation and benefits team, reward processes can indeed underpin structural and cultural change and support the achievement of business goals. But not on their own, and they do not lead change. As Tim Fevyer puts it: 'Pay can support business change and consolidate key messages, but it can't drive it.' In his view, pay should be regarded as one of the instruments available to achieve transformation, working in conjunction with other instruments as part of top management's overall strategy. Importantly, it must be integrated with the other key areas of business strategy to reinforce the achievement of corporate goals.

    At the heart of the bank's approach is the idea that the quality of leadership and management style are critical factors engaging employees for business success. Tim Fevyer explains: 'A significant element of changing employee behaviour is about the local situation with manager, individual and team – how it feels to work in a particular environment, the atmosphere of the workplace. Key elements of this are the way people are managed and coached, the way people are supported by their manager. Like the other elements of the total reward package, pay should aim to support business in what it is trying to achieve rather than driving business.'

7. Creating a compelling offer requires excellent support and information systems. You need to develop the capability of the organization in terms of information access – pay clubs, market survey and so on – and analysing the data.

8. Tim Fevyer is certain that applying off-the-shelf compensation strategies will not push your company ahead of rivals. Good reward strategies are about customization and tailoring. As he puts it: 'You simply can't copy.' Fevyer also has another important message for other reward professionals: 'We need to get away from

adapting new initiative after new initiative. We need to move away from a culture of "flavour of the month".'

9. Although a fundamentally simple concept, nobody should pretend that total reward is not a difficult and time-consuming process to put into practice. If you are looking for a quick-fix solution, forget it. There are no 'three easy steps' to engaging employees' hearts and minds. Companies discover that engaging people in the drive for improved business performance is a long-term change process. It is incredibly complex out there. As Tim Fevyer explains: 'Total reward require serious commitment to a long-term programme in terms of cost. This commitment is really about investment.'

10. The best thing you can do when creating a more compelling employment offer tailored to employee needs is to look more closely at whether people think the new flexible arrangements are better, rather than whether they have actually exercised that right to change their benefits mix. 'It might be that what they want is to have the ability to buy and sell holidays,' argues Tim Fevyer.

11. All reward initiatives should be prioritized – only those processes and schemes that are expected to generate the greatest value will be introduced.

A final word

You cannot succeed without focusing on business goals and understanding what these mean for your core people goals. Shareholder value was our ultimate objective. But we unbundled this objective and examined how we would generate shareholder value through our reward strategy. We wanted to recruit, retain and engage good people. You might do that in the short term by throwing more money at people but we wanted a long-term solution that really focused on the individual and their contribution within the business. Meeting individual needs by providing flexibility within a framework has enabled us to generate significant value for both employees and the company. – Tim Fevyer, Senior Manager, Compensation and Benefits, Lloyds TSB

NATIONWIDE

Nationwide's job family pay structure has five levels and eleven job families (see Table 30.1). The five levels are:

1. Service and support
2. Advice and team leading
3. Senior management
4. Executive management
5. Director.

Table 30.1 Nationwide's five job-family levels

Job family level	Level title	Nature of jobs	Job families at this level
Level 1	Service and support	This level contains those roles in which decision making extends over a few days or weeks and the work is fairly well patterned, involving people working individually.	Customer services Support services Specialist services General services
Level 2	Advice and team leading	For technical and professional employees where work cannot always be specified in advance. Decision making tends to involve tasks with a time span of between three months and one year.	Customer relationships Leading people Specialist advice
Level 3	Senior management	Decision making tends to involve tasks with a time span of between one and two years. These managers are often responsible for other managers and may include senior specialists who refine professional practices.	Leading implementation Professional development
Level 4	Executive management	This level contains general managers whose work involves designing and developing new systems, services and products with strategic direction and turning corporate strategies into action. The decision making would tend to involve tasks with a time span of between two and five years.	Strategy development
Level 5	Director	Decision making tends to involve tasks with a time span of between one and five years.	Strategic direction

Design details

- Every level consists of a number of job families, each of which contains a group of similar jobs.
- The levels reflect the extent of employees' decision-making responsibilities, which range from level 1, where decision making extends over a few days or weeks, to level 5, director level, where strategic decision making involves tasks with a time span of between one and five years.
- Job families do not cross levels; if an individual moves to a job at a higher level then their new job will be in another job family.

- Most jobs are in levels 1 and 2, which are currently divided into a number of sub-levels (three for level 1 and two for level 2), so there are a total of eight levels – just half the sixteen grades on which the previous structure was based.
- There are, however, more salary ranges than levels: level 1 has three sub-levels but five ranges, while level 2 has seven ranges despite having only two sub-levels.
- All the ranges in a level overlap, and have a span of 80 to 120 per cent. The maximum of each range is the target (100 per cent) for the next range up, while the target for each range is the minimum for the next one up.
- The two ranges for level 3 are exactly the same as the top two ranges for level 2. This means that there will not necessarily be any salary advantage in moving from one level to the other, so seeking promotion in order to get an increase in pay has largely become a thing of the past.
- The large number of ranges is designed to ensure that the jobs positioned within them on the basis of knowledge, skills or decision making can be rewarded in line with the market.

NORWICH UNION INSURANCE

Norwich Union Insurance (NUI) has 15,000 employees. It is the general insurance arm of Aviva, the largest insurer in the UK and the world's seventh largest insurance group. When Norwich Union Insurance merged with CGU (which later became Aviva) in 2000, it was faced with a stark choice: whether to harmonize or to opt for a completely new reward approach. Not wanting to keep employees in suspense while it went through a protracted harmonization process, it initially confirmed staff on existing terms and conditions. The company then embarked on a radical redesign of its pay structure.

Arrangements before the merger

Both Norwich Union and CGU had operated pay matrix systems underpinned by Watson Wyatt job evaluation and pay benchmarking, which was to prove useful when attempting to bring the two systems together. Each year, staff received a percentage increase on their salary which varied according to their position in the pay range and their performance. Individuals whose existing salaries were below the mid-point secured higher salary rises than those above, even where those above the mid-point were much better performers.

Norwich Union Insurance managers had some discretion when determining the pay awards of their staff, but they invariably used it to bring staff up to the mid-point. CGU managers had less discretion.

Another important difference in the pay and performance systems of the two organizations was the handling of employee development. Norwich Union's twice-yearly formal appraisal meetings focused on development, whereas CGU's newly designed system – Objective Setting and Performance (OSAP)– focused more on reward. This had only been in place for just over a year, but managers claimed that it was rigid, time consuming, had a short-term perspective and needed more clarity in objective setting. More measurable objectives were required.

As Martin Todd, Head of Reward, points out: 'Under the existing reward structure managers were unable to give sufficient levels of reward to high performers. But the financial services sector is beginning to realize that matrix systems are no longer as effective. They are designed to reward competent performers, whereas companies now want more flexibility to reward high performers.'

Reward goals

NUI wanted a reward strategy that was flexible, transparent, fair, consistent, and would reward high performers. The strategy that has been devised in response to this challenge encompasses four elements: salary, variable pay, an all-employee share option plan, and local incentive awards, together with much greater emphasis on, and support for, employee development.

New total reward strategy

Progression, Performance and Pay is the name given to Norwich Union Insurance's new total reward strategy. It comprises four main elements:

1. *Reward* – salary and benefits, variable pay, all-employee share option plan and incentive awards.
2. *Career framework* – meaningful job content and career opportunities.
3. *Performance* – challenging work; recognition and brand supporting behaviours.
4. *Development* – learning opportunities and personal development.

The wider context

As stated in the NUI documentation and illustrated in Figure 30.1:

> These initiatives... support our commitment to the one team culture reflected in our balanced scorecard. The Progression, Performance and Pay framework is underpinned by the brand values: Progressive, Shared benefit and Integrity. These should be reflected in the way we agree objectives and use the skills, knowledge and behaviours model.

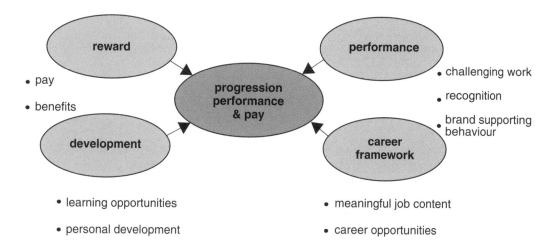

Figure 30.1 The Norwich Union Insurance Progression, Performance & Pay framework

Progression, Performance and Pay moves us towards 'total reward' where financial reward is just one element of the reward package. Other elements are benefits, recognition of performance, career opportunities and personal development. In our model these are expressed through reward, performance, career framework and development. This gives us the tools to help build NUI as a great place to work which attracts and retains quality staff.

The framework was accompanied by a commitment from senior management:

- 'to recognize our best people through career opportunities and reward packages;
- to develop all staff to their full potential;
- to widen career opportunities for all;
- to provide managers with the means to recognize and reward performance locally'.

New structure

The new reward structure was devised by a managerial focus group. The organization sees itself as a market leader in terms of its products, so the focus group discussed what that meant for reward. It took the view that reward is not just about money, since pay packages throughout the financial services sector are broadly similar. Recruitment, retention and performance issues suggested that enabling improved career development for all should be an important part of the new arrangements. When HR asked the managerial focus group what it wanted to reward, two key priorities emerged. The first was to be able to establish clear links between the organization's balanced scorecard and individual objectives, and the second was the flexibility to reward high performers.

The resulting structure was based on two broad bands, seven generic occupational groups and nineteen career families, as described below. The new structure provides the underpinning for:

- *progression arrangements* which pay out substantially more to high performers;
- *variable pay*, which links individual objectives to the company's balanced scorecard (see below), and rewards those who exceed objectives with non-pensionable payments of up to 7 per cent of salary for those in broad band 1 and 15 per cent for those in broad band 2;
- *skills and behaviours models* (competencies) for each generic group to support career development, performance improvement and progression.

The balanced scorecard

Norwich Union Insurance describes its balanced scorecard as a 'mechanism for implementing our strategy and measuring performance against our objectives and critical success factors to achieve the strategy'. The scorecard is cascaded throughout the organization to measure the operational activities that are contributing to the overall company strategy.

The balanced scorecard changes from year to year. In 2002 it set out to achieve three goals: positive benefit, staff impacts, financial performance – in short, service, morale and profits.

In 2001 the emphasis was predominantly on profit, in order to deliver the promises made to the City and shareholders, but the company feels that more focus is now needed on service and morale.

Moving to total reward

Norwich Union Insurance believes that reward is about more than money. Career development is a far more significant element of its performance management than under the previous arrangements, and this has gone down well with staff, according to a recent staff opinion survey. The first survey was carried out in 2001, fairly soon after the merger, and the second took place this year.

The organization is also planning to introduce personal reward statements in the first half of 2003. It does not, as yet, 'flex' many of its benefits, although holidays can be bought and sold and Norwich Union products are offered at discount to staff.

Career framework

The career framework describes the new structure created to help staff to understand how their jobs fit within their business unit and the organization as a whole, and to help them develop their careers by moving up or sideways.

The first building block of the framework was to divide all jobs into two broad bands. This was done mainly for benefits and variable pay purposes: staff in broad band 1 receive different benefits and potentially higher variable pay than those in broad band 2.

Then, all the jobs in the organization were classified into seven generic roles, each of which involves similar levels of responsibility (see Table 30.2). This means that within each of the 19 business units there can be no more than seven roles.

After this, 19 different career families were identified (see Table 30.3). For Norwich Union Insurance, a career family is a cluster of jobs with similar skill requirements and activities. Levels of responsibility vary within the family.

These career families are intended to support movement across the organization, since individuals can identify jobs at a similar level in other families which they might like to join. An HR manager, for example, might wish to become a manager in another career family, and the skills, knowledge and behaviours profile published for each role in each family would enable the HR manager to identify whether he or she had the necessary competencies for another managerial role. Career families also aim to facilitate the payment of market rates, since jobs can be benchmarked more directly with comparable jobs elsewhere.

Once the career families had been devised, the business units sent representatives from each career family to workshops set up to identify the roles in each family. While a family could have no more than seven roles, it could have less; several have just four.

Following the rollout of career families, focus groups were established for each career family and a cross-section of staff from NUI business units worked together to agree and place roles into the appropriate family at the appropriate level.

The whole career framework rests on individual job profiles, which set out the individual skills and behaviours required.

New pay structure

Once the career framework structure, with its nineteen job families and a maximum of seven roles within each family, had emerged, the time had come to attach a salary structure to it.

HR recommended that each career family should have its own pay structure, so that rates could be tracked and implemented more easily than if several career families were combined. In the event, only 11 pay structures were identified, so that some

Table 30.2 Career framework at Norwich Union Insurance

Broad bands	Generic groups	
1	**Technical**	**Managerial**
	Managing consultant	Business manager
	Consultant	Team manager
2	**Lead adviser**	
	Adviser	
	Support	

structures apply to more than one family. As time goes by, however, it may be necessary to move towards the idea of 'one family, one structure'.

The new market salary guide structures were designed to give managers maximum flexibility in rewarding their employees, dependent on level of performance.

The salary ranges were devised by benchmarking roles against the external market, using the Watson Wyatt database of salaries in the financial services and/or insurance sector. Each structure contains between four and seven ranges, one for each generic group (see Table 30.2). The salary ranges have an 80 per cent minimum, a market salary guide for competent performance and no maximum.

For example, for an individual in broad band 1, in a consultant role within the claims career family:

- the 'market salary guide' is currently £20,000 to £27,000 (representing median pay in the insurance industry for someone whose role is evaluated at consultant level);
- the minimum is £16,000 – that is, 80 per cent of £20,000;
- there is no maximum.

Paying for performance

Individual performance is rewarded through annual pay increases and through variable pay – non-pensionable bonuses. Both elements are designed to reward excellent

Table 30.3 Norwich Union Insurance career families

Accountants	Actuaries	Business solutions practitioners	Claims
Customer services	Direct sales	Finance	HR
Risk management	Marketing	Planning and MI	Pricing
Project management	Purchasing	Relationship management	Legal
Secretarial and administration	Underwriting	Operational support	

performers – the new pay structure enables rapid salary progression and variable pay delivers significant payments (up to 15 per cent) for such individuals.

Annual pay increases

Salary progression is based on a review of the achievement of agreed objectives, based on accountabilities and the skills, knowledge and behaviour model, which Norwich Union Insurance describes as 'what people do to add value and bring about a result'. In contrast, variable pay rewards 'actual results', related to the balanced scorecard.

Four ratings are used for the purposes of annual pay increases:

- *Outperforming* – overall contribution exceeds all aspects of the relevant skills, knowledge and behaviours model and is demonstrated through superior delivery of individual accountabilities of the role.
- *Performing* – overall contribution fulfils all aspects of the relevant skills, knowledge and behaviours model and is demonstrated through the competent delivery of individual accountabilities of the role.
- *Developing* – overall contribution does not currently fulfil all relevant aspects of the skills, knowledge and behaviours model and is demonstrated through progress towards delivery of individual accountabilities of the role.
- *Underperforming* – overall contribution failing to demonstrate the skills, knowledge and behaviours model relevant to the role.

The previous pay structure provided an annual progression increase for satisfactory and better performers, based on a percentage of salary. It took between five and six years to reach the mid-point. The new structure is designed to move good performers through the range much faster. It gives increases based on a percentage of the market salary guide, which means that all those in a generic group rated as delivering a particular level of performance get the same monetary pay increase.

For example, using 2001 performance year percentage increases, for a consultant with a market salary guide of £20,000 to £27,000:

- underperformers receive 0 per cent;
- developing performers secure a pay increase of 1.5 per cent of £20,000 (£300), the lower point in the market salary range;
- performers receive 4 per cent of £27,000 (£1,080), the higher point in the market salary range;
- outperformers gain 7 per cent of £27,000 plus a percentage – 10 per cent last year – of £29,700. This yielded a salary increase of £2,074. The intention here is to give those ranked as 'outperforming' 7 per cent of an upper quartile salary, rather than the percentage of the median given to developing and performing staff.

Variable pay

Variable pay at Norwich Union Insurance rewards performance against the balanced scorecard objectives for the year. Payments, in the form of a percentage of salary, are made in March for performance in the previous calendar year.

Since performance objectives can be either individual or team, variable pay may be based on the achievement of *individual or team objectives* or a mixture of both. Where variable pay is based on team performance, it is intended to help staff understand how objectives can be achieved through working as a team.

PRICEWATERHOUSECOOPERS (PWC)

PwC is the world's largest multi-professional services firm, with 16,000 employees in the UK and 125,000 worldwide. Price Waterhouse and Coopers & Lybrand merged in 1998 to form PwC. The merger gave rise to the need for harmonization of terms and conditions, including benefits. IBM has recently acquired the PwC Consulting arm of the organization, but this has had no immediate repercussions on its approach to reward.

PwC considers itself engaged in the 'war for talent'. It recruits hundreds of graduates each year, and seeks to attract the best. The average age of the firm's employees is only 27, so its attitude to reward is pitched towards the aspirations and needs of this age group in the sense that younger workers are likely to demand fulfilling careers, excellent development and competitive pay as well as work/life balance.

To meet its employees' requirements, PwC has therefore adopted a total reward policy – replete with a competitive reward package, flexible benefits, genuine work/life choices, flexible working and a strong emphasis on personal development, advancement and recognition.

PwC, explains Sasha Hardman, Head of Reward and Recognition, is seeking to 'bring together and maximize the effectiveness of teams of people with different and complementary skills, ideas and experience, which will produce better solutions for our clients'.

Pay

PwC sees itself as a meritocracy and aims to pay for performance. PwC's reward strategy is market driven and output focused, with a strong emphasis on the total package. Individuals are paid on the basis of a combination of performance and market rates.

Pay for non-managerial staff is more structured than that for other grades. Most new recruits are students on three-year training contracts while they qualify as accountants, tax specialists or actuaries. New trainees are paid set starting rates which vary by region. As staff progress through the organization, there is greater opportunity for differentiation dependent on performance.

Pay is determined by line managers, subject to their budgets, broad bands and market rates. Market intelligence is gathered centrally from surveys and pay networks.

As staff become more senior, there is a greater element of variable pay – bonuses are paid on the basis of both individual and organizational performance.

Approach to total reward

PwC's UK board is committed to total reward, and in the summer of 2001 refocused its people agenda, designed to deliver the goal of making PwC 'a great place to work'. The agenda groups actions to achieve this into four areas, called 'beacons', because they 'point the way to a vision of success'.

The four beacons are:

1. Diversity
2. Advancement and recognition
3. Pride
4. Resourcing/recruitment.

Flexible benefits plan

When Price Waterhouse merged with Coopers & Lybrand in 1998, only the former had a flexible benefits plan. Flex had been successful in Price Waterhouse, the two approaches needed to be harmonized and Coopers' staff made it clear that they also wanted flexibility, so *Choices*, its new flexible benefits plan, was introduced for all 20,000 UK employees in April 1999.

Apart from harmonization, the company had other pressing reasons why it wanted staff to have the flexibility to tailor their benefits packages to suit their own personal needs. It wanted, primarily, to raise staff awareness of the value of their total remuneration package and the value of their benefits in particular. What's more, it was seeking to introduce a leading-edge approach to reward. Giving staff flexibility was part of the organization's overall approach to working at PwC, and it believed that this would prove to be a valuable recruitment tool.

Easing the administration

When *Choices* was first introduced, it was a 'tick-box paper-based system'. As Sasha Hardman admits, administration was problematic in the beginning, with many pieces of paper travelling about. PwC has a commitment to be 'process light' and has introduced an electronic benefit processing system for the administration of *Choices*, with queries handled by the Employee Service Help desk.

Employees have a six-week period in which to request their *Choices* for each benefit year, which begins on 1 October. News articles, posters, e-mails and voice messages publicize this, but, inevitably, in the first couple of years all too many left their requests until the last minute, and the help desk handled around 1,000 calls a day in the last week or so before the deadline. But as staff have got used to the process there is no longer quite such a mad rush as the deadline approaches.

In 2002, 80 per cent of staff requested changes to their benefits, suggesting that the flexibility to do so is of real value, since so many take advantage of it.

What's on the flex menu?

PwC provides all staff with certain minimum benefits – known as the core benefits. These are benefits which are provided to staff, the value of which cannot be used for other benefits or taken as cash (for example: death in service cover, personal accident insurance and private medical insurance). The standard holiday entitlement is 20 days a year, but up to 10 further days can be requested, in units of one day. Staff can request to extend insurance cover and include dependants too.

There is a wide range of benefits that can be requested under *Choices*, as shown in Table 30.4.

Many benefits offer advantages because PwC's superior buying power means that a benefit is cheaper than it would be if the employee bought it in the open market. As Sasha Hardman points out, the travel insurance offered through *Choices*, for example, is such good value that half the workforce takes it. Retail vouchers, which can be used at high street retailers, including Tesco, Marks & Spencer and John Lewis, offer discounts of between 5 and 7 per cent.

Anyone, including a newly recruited trainee, can request a company car, as long as they maintain the minimum amount of salary they are required to take.

Calculating entitlement

The total reward for an employee is made up of base pay plus a benefit premium. It is the total reward figure that is important for the *Choices* plan – it is this amount from which staff are able to request benefits and the *Choices* price is applied to this figure.

Staff are placed in one of four '*Choices* categories' – A to D. PwC uses a formula for each benefit category to calculate the size of the benefit premium for an employee. There is a fixed element as well as an element that is based on a percentage of base pay. The formula means that the size of the benefit premia increases as staff move through categories A to D:

Table 30.4 Choice of benefits at PwC

Pensions	Pet insurance
A company car	Travel insurance
Retail vouchers	Dental insurance
Health screening	Private medical insurance
Permanent health and life assurance	Critical illness cover
Childcare vouchers	Personal accident insurance

A	Non-managerial staff, including graduate trainees and administration staff
B	Junior managers
C	Senior managers
D	Directors

Staff are allowed to use up to 20 per cent of their base pay plus their benefit premium to request benefits. Retail vouchers are ignored for the purposes of the calculation. Benefits requesting was limited to 20 per cent of the total package when the plan was set up in order to stop staff using a disproportionate amount of their salary for, say, a very expensive car. But the company is now reconsidering this limit. Staff should be trusted to make these decisions for themselves, Sasha Hardman says.

Concierge services at PwC

PwC began to offer a concierge service on a year-long trial to its staff in 2001. Concierge services originated in the USA in response to the long-hours culture which limited personal time away from the workplace. Businesses benefit from providing these services because they enable staff to concentrate on their jobs by freeing them from mundane personal tasks such as waiting at home for deliveries or getting their car serviced.

Services provided generally include dealing with home and car repair and maintenance, financial services, buying presents, restaurant reservations, theatre tickets and travel arrangements.

At PwC, staff can pay £10 a month for a limited number of requests, and £15 a month for unlimited requests. Requests can be for anything from shopping or arranging a plumber to event planning – 'so long as it's legal'.

TESCO

Tesco has over 200,000 employees and 1,000 stores, three-quarters of which are in the UK. Tesco is expanding rapidly; it is opening more stores, using different store formats, and operating overseas. The retailer found that its 22-grade pay structure and job evaluation processes were inflexible and did not provide a sufficient link between pay and performance. They also inhibited the career development and horizontal movement the organization needs to manage in a period of expansion and change. The company's response has been to introduce a six-level broad-banded structure which gives line managers more discretion over how they develop and pay their staff. Tesco is also moving towards total reward, introducing some flexibility in its benefit provision and underpinning its 'values' with a company-wide recognition scheme.

Desire for more flexibility

Tesco wanted much greater flexibility in how it approached pay. The company was expanding rapidly, especially overseas, and required a system that would foster management movement and development internationally. What's more, it was moving into new product markets, such as personal finance.

Grade structure

There was a strong belief that the company was over-managed; with 22 grades, everyone had someone breathing down their neck, which suggested that a reduction in the number of grades or bands was highly desirable.

The benefits and challenges of Tesco's previous narrow grading system were analysed as shown in Table 30.5.

Job evaluation

The use of a proprietary analytical job evaluation scheme encouraged individuals to try to inflate their jobs to achieve higher scores and thus higher salaries, while the job evaluation panel had to work slowly and bureaucratically so the process was very drawn out. It was concluded that job evaluation added no value to the business and was contrary to the company's preferred way of doing things. Instead, job slotting – a non-analytical method of matching jobs – was introduced, and in January 2000 work began on designing the broad-banded pay system which was finally installed in 2003.

Reward goals

Tesco sets out its reward principles as:

- 'We will provide an innovative reward package that is valued by our staff and communicated brilliantly to reinforce the benefits of working for Tesco.

Table 30.5 Tesco: benefits and challenges of previous narrow-graded structure

Benefits	Challenges
Consistent message	Grade drift
Easy to understand	Inflexible
Career path mapped out	Too rigid
Grade reflected contribution	Encouraged empire building
Control of cost	Discouraged movement
	Created hierarchies
	People over-managed
	Inconsistently applied
	Caused discontent

- Reward investment will be linked to company performance so that staff share in the success they create and, by going the extra mile, receive above average reward compared to local competitors.
- All parts of the total reward investment will add value to the business and reinforce our core purpose, goals and values.'

The retailer's overall reward strategy supports these principles by:

- 'Being on the right side of the competition on total reward, with the reward package being above the median.
- Focusing on making reward investment deliver more rather than reducing the size of the pot.
- Reinvesting to ensure that every element of reward adds value to the business and is valued by staff.
- Building a simplified, global pay and grading system that enables mobility and flexibility and supports the values which are critical to future business growth.
- Ensuring the affordability of the reward package is sustainable, and using Tesco's buying power to deliver as much unbeatable value to staff as to customers.
- Focusing on rewarding staff for their contribution in a way that enables them to benefit directly from the success they help to create.
- Ensuring more transparency so that the reward package offered by the company is fully understood and valued.'

The new broad-banded structure

The new structure at Tesco 'converts' the previous 22 grades, which covered all staff from the shop floor to the main board, into six 'work levels' – this is the essential idea that the retailer is trying to get across to employees:

- *Work level 1* covers all clerical and some administrative (non-executive) jobs.
- *Work levels 5 and 6* are for main board and senior directors, whose pay is determined on an individual basis.
- All other jobs are covered by *work levels 2, 3 and 4*, and it is the occupants of these posts who are covered by the new broad-banded pay structure.

As can be seen from Table 30.6, there is a considerably wider spread between the minimum and maximum pay limits of bands (the pay range or span). Indeed, the maximum of each of the bands is at least 100 per cent above the minimum. The company also considered having no maxima for its six bands, but when managers were consulted they said that they wanted some boundaries.

Reference points

The new Tesco system has what the company calls *pay reference points*, which have been developed for around 100 benchmark roles across the whole new structure. These are *not* market rates, to be aimed for by all competent performers, and they do not replace existing market rates – 'Market rates are for average performers and we want something better,' says Richard Sullivan, Group Reward Manager. Pay reference points are, instead, 'aspirational', being based on pay practice in around 20 blue-chip service companies, including the major retailers, according to a salary survey conducted by Tesco each year. These organizations are already paying well in the market, and Tesco's pay reference points are set between the median and upper quartile of pay in them. They are thus designed to reward staff who perform at the level of the very best individuals in the most successful organizations.

Actual pay rates at Tesco are expected to cluster around 10 per cent below pay reference points. There are as many as 10 benchmark roles per function, and these are benchmarked annually against this external market.

In the new Tesco structure, there are no mid-points or zones, simply very substantial pay bands, which line managers can use to reward individuals for their contribution, although the process is moderated both by senior departmental managers and by human resource managers.

Allocating roles to bands

Roles are allocated to work levels at Tesco by reference to the complexity of decisions in seven aspects of accountability:

1. *resource complexity* – accountability for the resources that are needed to deliver business plans;

Table 30.6 Tesco broad-banded pay structure July 2002

| Job | Pay band | Previous structure 2000/2001 | | | Pay band | New broad-band structure 2002 | |
		Min, £pa	Mid-point, £pa	Max, £pa		Min, £pa	Max, £pa
Director	D2	69,930	87,412	104,895	WL4	75,000	150,000
	D1	58,661	73,326	87,991			
Manager	M7	45,131	56,414	67,697	WL3	35,000	82,500
	M6	38,658	48,322	57,987			
	M5	33,327	41,658	49,990			
Manager	M4	28,419	35,523	42,628	WL2	20,000	48,000
	M3	25,118	31,398	37,678			
	M2	21,987	27,484	32,981			
	M1	19,279	24,099	28,919			
Executive	E3	17,079	21,349	25,619			

2. *problem solving* – the type of problems that need to be solved, from largely operational to problems that are more strategic, and require conceptual thinking;
3. *change* – accountability for driving innovation;
4. *natural work team* – the team with which the role holder must work to achieve his or her accountabilities;
5. *external interaction* – the people outside Tesco with whom the role holder must work to achieve his or her accountabilities;
6. *timeframe* – the typical amount of time needed to see the impact of the decisions for which the role is accountable;
7. *nature of work* – summary of the key accountabilities.

Movement within bands

Broad-banding relaxes or even removes clearly defined and absolute pay limits for pay progression. The tendency in traditional pay structures has been for most staff to progress inexorably to the top of their grade. What is to stop this happening, at great expense, in a much broader band?

The starting point for Tesco is to make absolutely clear to all concerned that no one should expect to move to the upper reaches or top of a band unless they have earned it through increased competence, career development, the assumption of greater responsibilities and the delivery of higher levels of contribution and added value. After all, it should not be too difficult to convince people that their pay spans have not magically increased from say, 30 to 100 per cent.

It is 'important to create the right level of expectation', say the Tesco guidelines. 'Relatively few individuals will achieve the highest possible pay for their band. The upper limit represents the highest amount that Tesco might pay for a role in that work level and is likely to be achieved by those in the most challenging roles within that work level, whose performance and contribution in their work level is self-evidently outstanding. The pay level for each work level is broad enough to accommodate the different types of roles and different levels of contribution in that level, as well as the different external markets for different roles.'

Pay progression

The old system of semi-automatic progression has gone. Instead, part of the pay budget is now being spent on increases when people move roles, continuity payments to recognize those who deliver sustained high performance in the same role, year on year, and stretch payments (linked to and reinforcing a talent-spotting process) for rapidly developing performers who are capable of a move to the next work level within the next 12 months:

- *Continuity payments* – recognize sustained good performance over several years. These are for individuals who are happy in their existing role and do not wish to move out of it but who nonetheless perform very well in the same role, year on year. Managers can make this award to anyone whose performance has been consistently good over at least three years. The award is worth around 5 per cent of base pay, usually delivered as a one-off lump sum. This assumes the individual is already well rewarded against their peer group, having been rewarded for their high performance in successive annual pay reviews. If this is not the case, the award may be made as an increase to base pay. Another continuity payment can be made after a further three years of green performance ratings. Payments are typically made in May, after the annual performance review discussions.
- *Stretch payments* – recognize that individuals have been identified by the talent-spotting process as having the potential to move to the next work level within 12 months, based on the criteria for each successive work level set out in the work level handbook. Awards are made after the annual talent-planning meeting in October. They are typically a 5 per cent increase to base pay.
- *Rewarding moves within a work level* – managers are able to move individuals through their work-level pay band by appointing them to a different role, either one that significantly broadens their skill and experience elsewhere in the business or one that makes a significantly bigger contribution.

Avoiding broad-banding problems

To avoid broad-banding problems, Richard Sullivan recommends that the following guiding principles should be borne in mind:

1. Don't underestimate the old culture – it will take time to change it.
2. Deal with the move to broad bands as a conversion rather than a new initiative, to minimize change issues.
3. Be prepared to challenge any return to the old ways.
4. Management capability is key to communicating issues.
5. Deal with cost issues before changing to broad bands.
6. If broad bands are not used for all staff, explain why carefully.
7. Consider equal pay issues.
8. Use market data, but ensure that it is credible before making it public.
9. Allow at least nine months to move to broad-banding.
10. Employee communication is key to having the new system understood.
11. Don't have fewer than five layers across the business in a broad-band system.
12. Obtain managers' input when designing the new process; this will help them explain it to others and will increase their commitment to it.

Verdict

Tesco does not use pay to motivate staff. It wants pay to reward performance and contribution and to be seen as fair. But the objective of its new broad-banded structure was to have the flexibility to reward rather than to penalize staff when they developed their careers horizontally, and also to reward good performers who do not want to move jobs.

A final word

Our old structure did not link pay and performance in the way we thought it should. It was bureaucratic and encouraged empire building rather than the sort of development we wanted. Now our line managers have the freedom to reward performance, contribution and potential, and we are going to see that they use this to produce the top class staff we need to enable Tesco to continue to succeed. It took a long time – 18 months – to design and implement broad-banding and we haven't finished yet. It has still to be rolled out to store staff and communicated fully to others. But we know that all the hard work has been worthwhile, and the 5,000 employees who have already been placed in work levels seem to agree. – Richard Sullivan, Group Reward Manager, Tesco

Appendix 1

Reward bibliography

Reward management general

Books

ACAS (1994) *Introduction to Payment Systems*, London

Armstrong, M (1999) *Rewards and Benefits Audit*, Cambridge Strategy Publications, Cambridge

Armstrong M (2002) *Employee Reward*, 3rd edn, Chartered Institute of Personnel and Development, London

Armstrong, M and Brown, D (2001) *New Dimensions in Pay Management*, Chartered Institute of Personnel and Development, London

Armstrong, M and Murlis, H (2004) *Reward Management*, 5th edn, Kogan Page, London

Beer, M (1984) Reward systems, in *Managing Human Assets*, ed M Beer, B Spector, P R Lawrence and D Quinn Mill, The Free Press, New York

Berger, L A and Berger, D R (eds) (1999) *The Compensation Handbook*, 4th edn, McGraw-Hill, New York

Chartered Institute of Personnel and Development (2001) *Reward Determination in the UK*, CIPD, London

Chartered Institute of Personnel and Development (2001) *The Future of Reward*, CIPD, London

Chartered Institute of Personnel and Development (2003) *Reward Management 2003: A survey of policy and practice*, CIPD, London

Chartered Institute of Personnel and Development (2004) *Reward Management 2004: A survey of policy and practice*, CIPD, London

Cox, A and Purcell, J (1998) Searching for leverage in pay systems, in *Motivation and Commitment: A reader*, ed S Perkins, SRRC, Faringdon

Druker, J and White, G (2000) *Reward Management: A critical text*, Routledge, London

Flannery, T P, Hofrichter, D A and Platten, P E (1996) *People, Performance, and Pay*, The Free Press, New York

Gomez-Mejia, L R and Balkin, D B (1992) *Compensation, Organisational Strategy, and Firm Performance*, Southwestern Publishing, Cincinnati

Haymarket Business Publications (1997) *Reward Strategy*, London

Heneman, R L (ed) (2002) *Strategic Reward Management: Design, implementation, and evaluation*, Information Age Publishing, Greenwich, CT

Homans, G and Thorpe, R (2000) *Strategic Reward Systems*, FT Prentice Hall, London

Incomes Data Services (1990) *Putting Pay Philosophies into Practice*, IDS, London

Kanter, R M and Wilson, T B (2002) *Innovative Reward Systems for the Changing Workplace*, 2nd edn, McGraw-Hill, New York

Lawler, E E (1971) *Pay and Organisational Effectiveness*, McGraw-Hill, New York

Lawler, E E (1990) *Strategic Pay*, Jossey-Bass, San Francisco

Lawler, E E (1994) Effective reward systems, in *Diagnosis for Organizational Change: Methods and models*, ed A Howard, Guilford Press, New York

Lawler, E E (2000) *Rewarding Excellence: Pay strategies for the new economy*, Jossey-Bass, San Francisco

Leventhal, G S (1980) What should be done with equity theory? in *Social Exchange: Advances in theory and research*, ed G K Gergen, M S Greenberg and R H Willis, Plenum, New York

Martocchio, J (2003) *Strategic Compensation: A human resource*, 3rd edn, Prentice Hall, New York

Murlis, H (1996) *Pay at the Crossroads*, Institute of Personnel and Development, London

Pfeffer, J (1998) *The Human Equation: Building profits by putting people first*, Harvard Business School Press, Boston

Purcell, J, Kinnie, K, Hutchinson S, Rayton, B and Swart, J (2003) *Understanding the People and Performance Link: Unlocking the black box*, CIPD, London

Stredwick, J (1997) *Case Studies in Reward Management*, Kogan Page, London

Suff, P (2001) *The New Reward Agenda IRS Management Review* 22, Industrial Relations Service – Eclipse Group, London

Thompson, M (1998) Trust and reward, in *Trust, Motivation and Commitment: A reader*, ed S Perkins, SRRC, Faringdon

Tyler, T R and Bies, R J (1990) Beyond formal procedures: the interpersonal context of procedural justice, in *Applied Social Psychology and Organizational Settings*, ed J S Carrol, Lawrence Erlbaum, Hillsdale, NJ

Wright, A (2003) *Reward Management in Context*, CIPD, London

Journal articles

Case, J (2001) When salaries aren't secret, *Harvard Business Review*, **79** (5), May, pp 37–49

Gherson, D J (2000) Getting the pay thing right, *Workspan*, **43** (6), June, pp 47–51

Giles, P (2001) Building a foundation for effective pay programs, *Workspan*, **44** (9), September, pp 28–32

Pfeffer, J (1998) Six dangerous myths about pay, *Harvard Business Review*, May/June

Watson, S (2002) Heart stoppers: creating change with harming performance, *Workspan*, **45** (5), May, pp 58–62

Strategy

Books

Ashton, C (1999) *Strategic Compensation*, Business Intelligence Ltd, London

Boxall, P and Purcell, J (2003) *Strategic Human Resource Management*, Routledge, London

Brown, D (2001) *Reward Strategies: From intent to impact*, CIPD, London

Lawler, E E (2000) Pay strategy: new thinking for the new millennium, *Compensation & Benefits Review*, **32** (1), January–February, pp 7–12

Manas, T M and Graham, M D (2002) *Creating a Total Reward Strategy: A toolkit for designing business based plans*, AMACOM, New York

Mintzberg, H, Quinn, J B and James, R M (1988) *The Strategy Process: Concepts, contexts and cases*, Prentice-Hall, Englewood Cliffs, NJ

Schuster, J R and Zingheim, P K (2000) *Pay People Right!: Breakthrough reward strategies to create great companies*, Jossey-Bass, San Francisco

Total reward

Books and reports

Bowen, R B (2000) *Recognizing and Rewarding Employees*, McGraw-Hill, New York

Chartered Institute of Personnel and Development (2002) *Total Reward*, CIPD, London

Manas, T M and Graham, M D (2002) *Creating a Total Rewards Strategy: A toolkit for designing business-based plans*, AMACOM, New York

Herriot, P (2000) *The Employment Relationship: A psychological perspective*, Routledge, London

Lawler, E E (2003) *Treat People Right!: How organizations and individuals can propel each other into a virtuous spiral of success*, Jossey-Bass, San Francisco

Manus, T M and Graham, M D (2002) *Creating a Total Rewards Strategy: A toolkit for designing business-based plans*, AMACOM, New York

O'Neal, S (1998) The phenomenon of total rewards, *ACA Journal*, **7** (3)

Thomas, K W (2003) *Intrinsic Motivation at Work: Building energy and commitment*, Berrett-Koehler, San Francisco

WorldatWork (2000) *Total Rewards: From strategy to implementation*, Scottsdale, AZ

Journal articles

Ben-Ora, D and Lyons, F H (2002) Total rewards strategy: the best foundation of pay for performance, *Compensation & Benefits Review*, **34** (2), April, pp 34–40

Motivation, engagement and commitment

Books

Alderfer, C (1972) *Existence, Relatedness and Growth*, The Free Press, New York

Goleman D, Boyatzis, R and McKee, A (2002) *Primal Leadership, the Hidden Driver of Great Performance*, Harvard Business School Press, Boston

Gratton L (2004) *The Democratic Enterprise – Liberating Your Business with Freedom, Flexibility and Commitment*, FT Prentice Hall, London

Hay Group (2002) *Engage Employees and Boost Performance*, Hay Group, London

Herzberg, F, Mausner, B and Snyderman, B (1957) *The Motivation to Work*, New York, Wiley

Katzenbach, J R (2000) *Peak Performance: Aligning the hearts and minds of your employees*, Harvard Business School Press, Cambridge, MA

Maslow, A (1954) *Motivation and Personality*, Harper & Row, New York

Porter, L and Lawler, E E (1968) *Management Attitudes and Behaviour*, Irwin-Dorsey, Homewood, IL

Thomas, K W (2003) *Intrinsic Motivation at Work: Building energy and commitment*, Berrett-Koehler, San Francisco

Vroom, V (1964) *Work and Motivation*, New York, Wiley

Articles

Adams, J (1965) Injustice in social exchange, in *Advances in Experimental Psychology*, ed L Berkowitz, Academic Press, New York

Gupta, N and Shaw, J D (1998) Financial incentives *are* effective!, *Compensation & Benefits Review*, March/April, pp 26, 28–32

Herzberg, F (2003) One more time: how do you motivate employees? (Classic reprint), *Harvard Business Review*, **81** (1), January, pp 87–96

Hollyforde, S and Whiddett, S (2002) How to nurture motivation, *People Management*, **8** (14), 11 July, pp 52–3

Kessler, I and Purcell, J (1992) Performance-related pay: objectives and applications, *Human Resource Management Journal*, **2** (3), pp 16–33

Kohn, A (1993) Why incentive plans cannot work, *Harvard Business Review*, September–October, pp 54–63

Latham, G and Locke, E A (1979) Goal setting – a motivational technique that works, *Organisational Dynamics*, Autumn, pp 68–80

Lawler, E E (1969) Job design and employee motivation, *Personnel Psychology*, **22**, pp 426–34

Murlis, H and Watson, S (2001) Creating employee engagement – transforming the employment deal, *Benefits and Compensation International*, **30** (8), April, pp 25–29

Watson, S (2003) Total rewards: building a better employment deal, *Workspan*, **46** (12), December, pp 48–51

Job evaluation

Books and reports

Advisory Conciliation and Arbitration Service (2003) *Job Evaluation: an Introduction*, ACAS, London

Armstrong, M, Cummins, A, Hastings, S and Wood, W (2003) *Job Evaluation: A guide to achieving equal pay*, Kogan Page, London

Grayson, D (1987) *Job Evaluation in Transition*, ACAS, London

Incomes Data Services (2003) *IDS Studies Plus: Job evaluation*, IDS, London

International Labour Office (1986) *Job Evaluation*, Geneva

Jaques, E (1961) *Equitable Payment*, Heinemann, Oxford

Pritchard, D and Murlis H (1992) *Jobs, Roles and People*, Nicholas Brealey, London

Quaid, M (1993) *Job Evaluation: The myth of equitable settlement*, University of Toronto Press, Toronto

Journal articles

Emerson, S M (1991) Job evaluation: a barrier to excellence, *Compensation & Benefits Review*, January–February, pp 4–17

Heneman, R L (2001) Work evaluation: current state of the art and future prospects, *WorldatWork Journal*, **10** (3), third quarter, pp 65–70

Lawler, E E (1986) What's wrong with point-factor job evaluation?, *Compensation & Benefits Review*, March–April, pp 20–28

Equal pay
Books

Chartered Institute of Personnel and Development (2001) *Equal pay guide*, CIPD, London
EOC (2003) *EOC Good Practice Guide – Job Evaluation Free of Sex Bias*, EOC, Manchester
Equal Pay Task Force (2001) *Just Pay*, Equal Opportunities Commission, Manchester
Falconer, H (2003) *One Stop Guide: Equal pay reviews*, Personnel Today Management Resources – Reed Business Information, London
Hastings, S (1989) *Identifying Discrimination in Job Evaluation Schemes*, Trade Union Research Unit, Oxford
Hastings, S (1991) *Developing a Less Discriminatory Job Evaluation Scheme*, Trade Union Research Unit, Oxford
Kingsmill, B (2001) *Review of Women's Employment and Pay*, HMSO, Norwich
National Institute for Economic and Social Research (2001) *The Gender Pay Gap*, Women and Equality Unit, Department of Trade and Industry, London

Journal articles

Arvey, R D (1986) Sex bias in job evaluation procedures, *Personnel Psychology*, **39**, pp 315–35
IRS Employment Review (2003) Chasing progress on equal pay, *IRS Employment Review*, No 774, 18 April, pp 19–22
Paddison, L (2001) How to conduct an equal pay review, *People Management*, **7** (12), 14 June, pp 58–59

Grade and pay structures
Books and reports

Armstrong, M and Brown, D (2001) *New Dimensions in Pay Management*, CIPD, London
Braddick, C A, Jones, M B and Shafer, P M (1992) A look at broad-banding in practice, *Journal of Compensation and Benefits*, July/August, pp 24–38
Gilbert, D and Abosch, K S (1996) *Improving Organisational Effectiveness Through Broadbanding*, ACA, Scottsdale, AZ

Journal articles

Armstrong, M (2000) Feel the width, *People Management*, 3 February, pp 34–38

Armstrong, M (2004) What's happening to broad-banding?, *IDS Executive Compensation Review*, June

Fay, C H, Schulz, E, Gross, S E and Van De Voort, D (2004) Broadbanding, pay ranges and labour costs: an empirical test, *WorldatWork Journal*, **13** (2), second quarter

LeBlanc, P V and Ellkis, M E (1995) The many faces of broad-banding, *ACA Journal*, Winter, pp 52–56

Richter A S (1998) Paying the people in black at the big blue, *Compensation & Benefits Review*, May–June, pp 51–59

Performance management

Books and reports

Armstrong, M and Baron, A (1998) *Performance Management: The new realities*, CIPD, London

Armstrong, M and Baron, A (2004) *Performance Management: Action and impact*, CIPD, London

Baguley, P (2002) *Performance Management in a Week*, 2nd edn, Hodder Arnold, London

Egan, G (1995) A clear path to peak performance, *People Management*, 18 May

Grint, K (1993) What's wrong with performance appraisal? A critique and a suggestion, *Human Resource Management Journal*, Spring, pp 61–77

Incomes Data Services (2003) *IDS Studies: Performance management*, IDS, London

Personnel Today and PeopleSoft (2004) *Performance Management Survey*, Personnel Today Management Resources – Reed Business Information, London

Suff, P (2001) *Performance Management – Revisited (IRS Management Review 21)*, Industrial Relations Service – Eclipse Group, London

Journal articles

Lawler, E E and McDermott, M (2003) Current performance management practices: examining the varying impacts, *WorldatWork Journal*, **12** (2), second quarter, pp 49–60

McGregor, D (1957) An uneasy look at performance appraisal, *Harvard Business Review*, May–June, pp 89–94

Morris, E and Sparrow, T (2001) Transforming appraisals with emotional intelligence, *Competency & Emotional Intelligence Quarterly*, **9** (1), Autumn, pp 28–32

Peiperl, M A (2001) Getting 360 degree feedback right, *Harvard Business Review*, **79** (1), January, pp 142–47

Stiles, P, Gratton, L, and Truss, C (2001) Performance management and the psychological contract, *Human Resource Management Journal*, **7** (1), pp 57–66

Williams, V (2001) Making performance management relevant, *Compensation & Benefits Review*, **33** (4), July–August, pp 47–51

Winstanley, D and Stuart-Smith, K (1996) Policing performance: the ethics of performance management, *Personnel Review*, **25** (6), pp 66–84

Contingent pay

Books and reports

Armstrong, M (2000) *Rewarding Teams*, CIPD, London

Armstrong, M and Brown, D (1999) *Paying for Contribution: Real performance-related pay strategies*, Kogan Page, London

Cannell, M and Wood, S (1992) *Incentive Pay*, IPM, London

Chartered Institute of Personnel and Development (2002) *Guide to Bonus and Incentive Plans*, CIPD, London

Cross, M (1992) *Skill-based Pay*, IPM, London

Geldman, A, Holroyd, K and Suff, P (eds) (2003) *Managing Best Practice No. 105 – Restructuring performance-related pay*, The Work Foundation, London

Incomes Data Services (2003) *IDS Studies Plus: Employee recognition schemes*, IDS, London

Marsden, D and French, S (1998) *What a Performance: Performance-related pay in the public services*, Centre for Economic Performance, London

Parker, G, McAdams, J and Zielinski, D (2000) *Rewarding Teams: Lessons from the trenches*, Jossey-Bass, San Francisco

Reilly, P (ed) (2003) *New Reward: Team, skill and competency based pay*, Institute for Employment Studies, Brighton

Rose, M (2001) *Recognising Performance: Non-cash rewards*, CIPD, London

Thompson, M (1992) *Pay and Performance: The employer experience*, Institute of Manpower Studies, Brighton

WorldatWork (2001) *The Best of Variable Pay: Incentives, recognition and rewards*, WorldatWork, Scottsdale, AZ

Journal articles

Fisher, J (2001) How to design incentive schemes, *People Management*, **7** (1), 11 January, pp 38–39

Freeman, R (2001) Upping the stakes (employee share ownership feature), *People Management*, **7** (3), 8 February, pp 25–29

IRS (2003) Sharing the spoils: profit-share and bonus schemes, IRS Employment Review 784, *Pay and Benefits Bulletin*, 19 September, pp 28–33

Keegan, B P (2002) Incentive programs boost employee morale and productivity, *Workspan*, **45** (3), March, pp 30–33

Luo, S (2003) Does your sales incentive plan pay for performance?, *Compensation & Benefits Review*, **35** (1), January–February, pp 18–24

Employee benefits

Books and reports

Chartered Institute of Personnel and Development (2002) *Pension and HR's Role: A guide*, CIPD, London

Chartered Institute of Personnel and Development (2004) *Flexible benefits*, CIPD, London

House of Commons Work and Pensions Committee (2003) *The Future of UK Pensions, Third Report of Session 2002–03*, The Stationery Office, London

Hutchinson, P (2002) *Flexible Benefits: A practical guide*, Butterworths Tolley, London

Journal articles

Daugherty, C (2002) How to introduce flexible benefits, *People Management*, **8** (1), 10 January, pp 42–43

IRS Employment Review (2003) Benefits and allowances (Annual survey), *IRS Employment Review*; Part 1, No 776, 23 May, pp 29–34; Part 2, No 777, 6 June, pp 30–5; Part 3, No 778, 20 June, pp 28–34

Lewin, C (2003) Pension developments in the UK, *Benefits & Compensation International*, **32** (9), May, pp 19–21

Appendix 2

Reward management guiding principles

Overall reward management principles

- Align reward strategies with the business and HR strategy.
- Align reward policies with the culture of the organization and use them to underpin that culture and, as required, help to change it.
- Value employees according to their competence and contribution.
- Aim to achieve equity, fairness and consistency in the operation of reward policies and practices.
- Ensure that reward processes are transparent and that staff are treated as stakeholders.
- Adopt an integrative approach which ensures that no innovations take place and no practices are changed without considering how they relate to other aspects of human resource management so that they can become mutually supportive.
- Provide managers with the authority and skills needed to use rewards to help achieve their goals, but ensure that they are given the training, guidance and continuing support required to develop and use these skills well.
- Remember that reward policies and practices express what the organization values and is prepared to pay for – they are driven by the need to reward the right things to convey the right message about what is important.

● Concentrate overall on developing reward management as a strategic, innovative and integrative process designed to meet the evolving needs of the organization and the people who contribute to its success.

Developing pay structures

The guiding principles on the processes involved in the development of pay and grade structures are that:

● the design should take place within the context of articulated reward strategies which should be integrated with the corporate and HR strategies of the organization;
● the design should be based on a thorough analysis of the needs of the organization and of its employees;
● stakeholders should be involved in the design of the structure;
● the structure should be based on an analytical form of job evaluation;
● the structure should provide for pay progression in accordance with agreed principles and policies;
● performance management processes should be developed which, if required, will inform decisions on pay progression as well as, importantly, providing guidance on continuous development;
● equal value considerations should be at the forefront of the design process;
● it should be remembered that grade structures can and should provide valuable information on career ladders as the basis for career planning;
● the cost implications of a new structure should be evaluated;
● the introduction of new pay structures will probably involve considerable changes which may create major concerns amongst those affected by them – close attention will therefore have to be given to how such change should be managed when designing and implementing the structure.

Pay structure principles

Pay structures should:

● be appropriate to the objectives, culture and structure of the organization;
● meet the needs of the organization and its members;
● take into account the nature of the roles covered by the structure;
● cater for all staff;
● enable the management of relativities between jobs;
● help to achieve fairness, equity and consistency in grading posts;
● facilitate the achievement of equal pay for work of equal value;

- provide scope if required for rewarding contribution (performance and competence);
- clarify reward and career opportunities;
- be constructed logically and clearly on the basis of an analysis of relative job values or size;
- be defined so as to achieve transparency and understanding;
- operate with an appropriate degree of flexibility;
- be manageable with the resources available;
- facilitate control to maintain equity and contain costs within budgets.

Pay progression principles

Pay progression policy and practices should:

- ensure that people are valued and rewarded fairly according to their contribution;
- provide rewards for those skills and behaviours that support the future success of the individual and the organization, not just immediate past results;
- deliver a clear message to staff on what the organization believes to be important in terms of performance (results) and behaviour;
- adopt a fair, consistent and transparent approach to measuring and assessing performance and competence which is based on agreed expectations and success criteria;
- ensure that as far as possible judgements on performance and contribution are based on evidence, not opinion;
- recognize that performance may be a function of effective teamwork as well as individual effort;
- be developed in consultation with those concerned – managers, employees and union representatives;
- be communicated to staff so that they understand the operation of the process, the part they and their managers play and its impact on them;
- devolve the maximum amount of responsibility to managers in operating the system but provide safeguards to ensure that fair and consistent decisions are made within the framework of policies and guidelines, including budgets;
- provide training and guidance for managers on the system and their role in operating it.

Job evaluation principles

The pay and grade structure should be designed and managed with the aid of a system of job evaluation which should:

- enable fair, equitable consistent and transparent judgements to be made about the relative value or size of jobs;
- help in the management of job relativities and in making decisions on the grading of posts;
- provide guidance on the design and maintenance of rational and orderly grade and pay structures;
- be analytical in the sense that judgements on the size of jobs are based on an analysis of the key factors in terms of job demands and working arrangements which affect relative values – the scheme should be thorough in analysis and capable of impartial implementation;
- have been equality-proofed;
- ensure that the factors used in the scheme cover the whole range of jobs to be evaluated without favouring any particular type of job or occupation and without discriminating on the grounds of gender or for any other reason;
- ensure that any weighting contained in the scheme is justified and non-discriminatory;
- provide the basis for ensuring that equal pay for work of equal value is achieved, including the data required to conduct equal pay audits;
- ensure that the processes used for evaluating jobs are conducted fairly and openly and involve those affected;
- be communicated to staff so that they understand how it operates;
- only be introduced if those involved receive thorough training in its operation;
- contain provision for appeals against job gradings resulting from job evaluation;
- be reviewed regularly to ensure that it is operating effectively.

Appendix 3

Examples of role and level profiles

1. Role profile: higher education lecturer

Elements	Role analysis
1 Teaching and learning support	• Plan, design and deliver a number of modules within subject area. • Deliver at undergraduate and/or postgraduate levels across a range of modules. • Use appropriate teaching, learning support and assessment methods. • Supervise projects, field trips and, where appropriate, placements. • Supervise postgraduate students. • Identify areas where current course provision is in need of revision or improvement.

(Continued)

Elements	Role analysis
	• Contribute to the planning, design and development of course objectives and material.
	• Ensure in conjunction with colleagues that modules complement other courses taken by students.
	• Set, mark and assess course work and examinations and provide feedback to students.
2 Research and scholarship	• Develop research objectives and proposals, obtain funding and design research projects.
	• Conduct individual and collaborative research projects, lead small research teams or play a major part in research teams.
	• Identify sources of funding and contribute to the process of securing funds.
	• Extend, transform and apply knowledge acquired through scholarly activities.
	• Write and referee journal articles, or write or contribute to text books and make presentations at national and international conferences.
3 Communication	• Communicate straightforward through to complex information to a variety of audiences, including students, peers and external contacts.
	• Use high level presentation skills and a range of media.
4 Liaison and networking	• Liaise with colleagues in other departments and/or institutions on professional matters.
	• Participate in departmental and other committee meetings.
	• Join external networks to foster collaboration and share information and ideas.
	• May represent the department at external meetings.
5 Managing people	• Lead the delivery of teaching in a module or programme: plan the timetable, allocate teaching responsibilities, and monitor the delivery of programmes to ensure that they achieve learning objectives and are meeting quality standards.
	• Lead small research teams.
	• Act as mentor to more junior lecturers.
	• Appraise staff and advise them on their personal development.
6 Teamwork	• Attend and actively participate in regular team meetings at which course development and delivery issues are discussed.
	• Collaborate with colleagues to identify and respond to students' needs.
7 Pastoral care	• Use listening, interpersonal and pastoral care skills to deal with sensitive issues concerning students and provide support.

(Continued)

Elements	Role analysis
	• Refer students as appropriate to services providing further help.
	• Act as personal tutor.
8 Initiative, problem solving and decision making	• Identify the need for developing the content or structure of a course and put proposals together in conjunction with colleagues on how this should be achieved.
	• Develop creative ideas as a result of research and scholarship.
	• Deal with admission queries and problems concerning student performance.
	• Sole responsibility to decide how to deliver own modules and assess students.
9 Planning and managing resources	• As module leader or tutor, liaise with colleagues on content and method of delivery.
	• May plan and implement consultancy projects to generate income for the institution.
10 Emotional demands	• Work under pressure to deliver results.
11 Work environment	• Work in a stable environment or a laboratory or workshop.
12 Expertise	• Possess in-depth knowledge of the subject.
	• Possess the required levels of expertise in teaching and research.
	• Update skills and knowledge continuously.
	• Understand equal opportunity issues as they impact upon the delivery of teaching and collegiate working.

2. Generic role profile: team leader

Overall purpose of role

To lead teams in order to attain team goals and further the achievement of the organization's objectives.

Key result areas

1. Agree targets and standards with team members which support the attainment of the organization's objectives.
2. Plan with team members work schedules and resource requirements which will ensure that team targets will be reached, indeed exceeded.
3. Agree performance measures and quality assurance processes with team members which will clarify output and quality expectations.

4. Agree with team members the allocation of tasks, rotating responsibilities as appropriate to achieve flexibility and the best use of the skills and capabilities of team members.
5. Coordinate the work of the team to ensure that team goals are achieved.
6. Ensure that the team members collectively monitor the team's performance in terms of achieving output, speed of response and quality targets and standards and agree with team members any corrective action required to ensure that team goals are achieved.
7. Conduct team reviews of performance to agree improvement.

Competencies

- Builds effective team relationships, ensuring that team members are committed to the common purpose.
- Encourages self-direction among team members but provides guidance and clear direction as required.
- Shares information with team members.
- Trusts team members to get on with things – not continually checking.
- Treats team members fairly and consistently.
- Supports and guides team members to make the best use of their capabilities.
- Encourages self-development by example.
- Actively offers constructive feedback to team members and positively seeks and is open to constructive feedback from them.
- Contributes to the development of team members, encouraging the acquisition of additional skills and providing opportunities for them to be used effectively.

3. Career family level profile: local authority

	Level 5 Overall: deal with all aspects of directing a department	
Role characteristic	*Key activities and competence requirements*	*JE level*
Knowledge and expertise	First degree or full professional qualification.	5
Operational knowledge and experience	Able to direct a range of internal and external policies and procedures requiring a high level of theoretical and practical knowledge.	6
Problem solving	Able to lead on a wide range of problems involving sensitive or high-profile situations or people management issues.	5
Fact finding and analysis	Take final judgements involving a range of facts or situations which require analysis or comparison and are often complex or highly technical.	5

(Continued)

Role characteristic	Key activities and competence requirements	JE level
Initiative, innovation and creativity	Review large-scale departmental and organizational operations and make recommendations on major changes. Reach creative conclusions on a range of departmental issues.	6
Planning and organizing	Plan and organize a large portfolio of short- and long-term projects. Think strategically in leading the achievement of the department business plan. Integrate planning with over-arching Authority strategies and plans. Contribute to Authority strategic planning process.	5
Developing policies	Direct the development of departmental policies and contribute to policy developments for the Authority.	5
Freedom to act and decision making	Make strategic operational decisions on own initiative within framework of Authority policies, procedures, regulations and plans and the department's budget. Decisions are often complex and concerned with unique situations:	5
Impact of decisions	Decisions impact on whole department and across the organization.	6
Communications	Influence people and persuade them to agree to or take a course of action at a senior level within the Authority and with elected members on relevant committees. Provide and receive complex, sensitive and contentious information. Produce written reports presenting facts and making recommendations upon which high-profile decisions affecting the whole Authority will be made.	6
Range of contacts	Daily contacts with elected members, VIPs and senior officers.	5
Impact of relationships with others	Considerable influence on major policy initiatives in Authority concerning departmental affairs. Resolve conflicts on policy and operational issues. Represent the Authority on departmental affairs in ways that will enhance its reputation.	6
Working environment and demands	Work in an office environment with minimal exposure to disagreeable working conditions.	2

4. Career band profiles: Friends Provident

Career band A

Job example: clerical and administrative staff

Technical knowledge/ business experience and qualifications	Developing a knowledge of one or more key areas within the function or business unit, together with an understanding of the systems utilized. Ensures that technical information is appropriately presented and correct.
Problem solving	Solves problems by following well-defined procedures and precedents. Will consult with more experienced colleagues on more difficult or novel situations.

(Continued)

| Leadership | Takes responsibility for management of own workload, delivering against performance standards and individual/ team objectives. |
| Communication/influence | Communicates information clearly and concisely, applying standards of common courtesy to all contacts. |

Career band B

Job example: customer services consultant

Technical knowledge/ business experience and qualifications	Demonstrates a good understanding of a range of non-standard processes, procedures and systems to be utilized in carrying out responsibilities. Is likely to have two or more years' relevant experience working within the function or business unit or have gained relevant experience elsewhere. May be starting to study for specific technical exams, eg FPC or ACII.
Problem solving	Works within procedures and precedents determining solutions from a number of appropriate alternatives.
Leadership	Offers guidance and technical support to less experienced members of the team.
Communication/influence	Applies developed communication skills in effectively handling more challenging contacts.

Career band C

Job example: customer services team leader

Technical knowledge/ business experience and qualifications	Fully conversant with the procedures, policies and systems applied within the function or business unit, having gained relevant experience over a period of five or more years. Demonstrates a comprehensive understanding of one or more well-defined areas for which they will provide technical leadership. Is developing an understanding of the relationship between different subject areas/business units. Is likely to have gained a qualification in a technical subject in a relevant discipline.
Problem solving	Applies specialist knowledge of own area in making judgements based on the analysis of factual information in straightforward situations.
Leadership	Plans and coordinates the work of the team and/or provides technical leadership, eg through delivery of on-the-job training, quality audits or application of developed specialist skills and knowledge.
Communication/influence	Explains technical information clearly and effectively, adopting a style of communication to fit differing levels of audience understanding. Is able to persuade colleagues and gain commitment to new ideas or approaches by expressing own views confidently and logically.

(Continued)

Career band D

Job examples: customer services team manager, analyst, programmer

Technical knowledge/ business experience and qualifications	Is able to apply and consolidate specialist skills and knowledge gained over a period of eight or more years' relevant experience to ensure essential procedures are followed and standards maintained. Demonstrates an understanding of the relationship between different subject areas and applies this knowledge in delivering cross-functional support, projects or advice.
	As a professional entrant to the business, will be developing professional skills through exam success and be increasing their contribution to the business.
Problem solving	Uses analytical skills and evaluative judgement, based on the analysis of factual and qualitative information to solve problems of a non-routine or more complex nature. Will be guided by precedents.
Leadership	In a team management role will be handling staff management issues including recruitment, resource management, training, coaching and performance management, and playing a leading role in determining salary recommendations for team members. Alternatively, will be a technical specialist with well-developed technical skills and specialist knowledge.
Communication/influence	Demonstrates strong verbal and written communication skills in influencing the outcome of decisions. Involves appropriate contacts in developing the final solution.

5. COLT Telecom: job level descriptions

Senior managing director: level 1a

- Leads and directs a major complex pan-European business function.
- Develops organization-wide strategy for business function.
- Influences business strategy throughout the organization.
- Makes a significant contribution to company revenues.
- Capacity to have a significant impact on business results.
- Thought leader, initiating and driving change across the whole function.
- Makes a significant contribution to the creation of shareholder value.

Senior managing director: level 1b

- Leads and directs a major complex pan-European business function.
- Develops organization-wide strategy for business function.
- Influences business strategy throughout the organization.

- Capacity to have a significant impact on business results.
- Thought leader, initiating and driving change across the whole function.
- Likely to make a significant contribution to the creation of shareholder value.

Senior director: level 2

- Makes a significant contribution to the formulation of strategy across the whole function, including discrete sub-specialisms.
- Plans current and future resourcing requirements for a major business activity(ies).
- Leads a major organization-wide multi-disciplinary operating activity or the strategic framework for an entire function.
- Thought leader for a complex, multi-specialist area – probably developing new business concepts.
- May require a high level of analytical and long-term planning skills.
- Accountable for the delivery of major programmes/projects which have a potentially significant impact on the company's overall commercial performance.
- Will have seasoned professionals as direct reports.

Director: level 3

- Leads a significant area of excellence, company-wide, and is responsible for resourcing, budgets and delivery.
- May have significant accountabilities for product or multi-product/regional margins.
- Alternatively, delivers primary functional support to a major business stream.
- Refines, packages and executes delivery of company products for local customers.
- Implements the framework (eg standards and processes) within which others operate, with potentially far-reaching consequences/high impact.
- Leads major change processes throughout the organization – occasionally influencing business strategy.
- A recognized thought leader in their area of expertise – an accomplished professional.
- Influences, and to some extent drives, strategy in a major specialist area, product category or functional area.

Associate director: level 4

- Partners others in the identification and development of specialist/technical functions.
- Implements (and occasionally contributes to the development of) functional strategy for a major geography or specialist area.

- Accountable for the provision of operational support to a significant customer group.
- Often dependent on cross-functional collaboration to achieve goals.
- Sets technical or service standards for others to follow – implying job holder has a high level of technical/professional knowledge themselves.
- Likely to head up a team of technical specialists or senior project managers within a much larger service area.
- Alternatively, leads a team which includes a small number of technical specialists in a small centre of excellence, company-wide.
- Might manage a discrete portfolio of products within a specialist channel.
- May be lead functional representative for a large country or small cluster.

Senior manager: level 5

- Anticipates internal and external business and legislative/regulatory issues impacting all areas of the business.
- Understands business strategy and contributes to the achievement of goals through the setting of short- and long-term objectives.
- Develops long-term partnerships with internal and external customers.
- Likely to be a key technical contributor offering specialist advice and guidance throughout the organization.
- Leadership of professional and technical teams within a specialist function which may be geographically diverse.
- Actions will have functional or company-wide impact/influence.
- Defines and takes accountability for team deliverables and team priorities.
- Identifies emerging needs of the business.
- Manages costs and profitability of projects. Will have a key role in budget setting.
- Source of complex and strategic problem solving and resolution.

Manager: level 6

- Manages own time and develops plans for work activities in own area, may support strategic planning activities.
- Supervises daily activities of operational/technical team members within a functional area. Defines and takes accountability for team deliverables.
- Generates innovative solutions to problems within functional area through creative actions while identifying short- and longer-term priorities.
- Recognized as having expertise in own professional/specialist area. May be a key technical, individual contributor offering guidance to a specific function or geographical area.
- May have a role in budget setting or contribution to budgetary discussions.

Professional: level 7

- Works within a more complex/critical environment.
- Completes own role independently or with minimal guidance.
- Improves, modifies procedures and develops new problem solving in own area.
- Experienced and fully competent in own area.
- Shares own experience/knowledge with others and provides guidance and support to others.
- May coordinate activities of others.

Senior administrative: level 8

- Works within well-established procedures and may improve or modify procedures in own area.
- Completes own role with moderate or minimal guidance.
- Demonstrates competence in own area and shares own expertise with others.
- May still acquire higher-level skill.

Administrative: level 9

- Works within well-established, clearly defined procedures.
- Limited autonomy, with a need for guidance and supervision.
- Demonstrates competence in own area and in general business principles.
- Acquires higher-level skill.

Appendix 4

Example of reward attitude survey

Please state the extent to which you agree or disagree with the following statements by placing a circle around the number which most closely matches your opinion.

		Strongly agree	Agree	Disagree	Strongly disagree
1	My contribution is adequately rewarded	1	2	3	4
2	Pay increases are handled fairly	1	2	3	4
3	I feel that my pay does not reflect my performance	1	2	3	4
4	My pay compares favourably with what I could get elsewhere	1	2	3	4
5	I am not paid fairly in comparison with other people doing similar work in the organization	1	2	3	4
6	I think the organization's pay policy is overdue for a review	1	2	3	4
7	Grading decisions are made fairly	1	2	3	4
8	I am not clear how decisions about my pay are made	1	2	3	4
9	I understand how my job has been graded	1	2	3	4
10	I get good feedback on my performance	1	2	3	4

(Continued)

		Strongly agree	Agree	Disagree	Strongly disagree
11	I am clear about what I am expected to achieve	1	2	3	4
12	I like my job	1	2	3	4
13	The performance pay scheme encourages better performance	1	2	3	4
14	I am proud to work for the organization	1	2	3	4
15	I understand how my pay can progress	1	2	3	4
16	The job evaluation scheme works fairly	1	2	3	4
17	The benefits package compares well with those in other organizations	1	2	3	4
18	I would like more choice about the benefits I receive	1	2	3	4
19	I feel motivated after my performance review meeting	1	2	3	4
20	I do not understand the pay policies of the organization	1	2	3	4

Appendix 5

Guidelines for employee reward students

The following guidelines are for use by students taking the CIPD Employee Reward examination. They are set out under the following headings:

- General guidance
- Guidance on tackling the examination case study
- Guidance on tackling the questions

GENERAL GUIDANCE

1. Study the Indicative Content of the Employee Reward Professional Standards as summarized below.

Section	Standard	Handbook page reference
1 The employee reward contribution	Employee reward systems: processes and elements	6–9
	Role and aims of employee reward	3–4

(Continued)

Section	Standard	Handbook page reference
2 The conceptual framework	Corporate, national and international context	49–53
	Influence of organizational culture	47–48
	Factors affecting reward levels – economic theories	57–62
	The psychological contract	85–87
	Motivation theory	72–76
	Role of financial and non-financial rewards in a total reward system	6, 7, 9, 12–15
	Equity, fairness, consistency and transparency	4–6
3 Employee reward processes	Reward philosophies (and guiding principles)	31–32, 34, 35, 429–32
	Reward strategy	25–28, 34–35
	Reward policies	41–46
	Auditing and analysing the reward system	28–30, 355–56
	Developing the reward system	364–66
	Approaches to employee reward in a range of organizations	371–417
4 Job evaluation	Purpose, methodology, key features and limitations	92–94, 104
	Types of job evaluation and their advantages and disadvantages	94–98, 101–02
	Computer-assisted job evaluation	98–99, 122
	Job and role analysis	173–78
5 Pay and benefit surveys	Concept of a market rate	158–59
	Sources of data	163–70
	Criteria for data	162–63, 168
	Presenting, interpreting and using data	170–72
6 Pay structures	Purpose	181
	Criteria for effectiveness	201–02
	Types of structure and their advantages and disadvantages	183–99, 203–04
	Pay structures for manual workers	311–13
	Designing and operating pay structures	202–21
7 Pay discrimination and equal pay	Reasons for pay discrimination	131–32
	The legal framework	134–38
	The EOC Code of Practice on Equal Pay	138–45
	Designing and implementing a non-discriminatory pay structure	221–22
	Developing a job evaluation scheme free of sex or other bias	141–42
8 Contingent pay	Arguments for and against contingent pay	233–35
	Criteria for contingent pay	236–37
	Development and management of contingent pay schemes	253–54
	Change management in development programmes	364, 366
	Types of contingent pay: nature, advantages and disadvantages	237–50, 252–53

(Continued)

2. Ensure that where appropriate you can at least define any key concept or practice succinctly (up to 50 words) so that when it comes to the exam you can start impressively when dealing with a particular question. For example:

- *Job evaluation* – a systematic process for defining the relative worth or size of jobs within an organization in order to establish internal relativities.
- *Grade structure* – a grade structure consists of a sequence or hierarchy of grades, bands or levels into which groups of jobs which are broadly comparable in size are placed.
- *Performance-related pay* – provides pay increases related to individual performance as indicated by the achievement of agreed results defined as targets or outcomes.

3. Make sure that you know at least 50 per cent (preferably 75 per cent) of the key headings or features of any of the main areas of employee reward covered by the standards. For example:

- *Economic factors affecting levels of pay:*
  - the labour theory of value
  - the nature of the external and internal labour market
  - the economic 'laws' of supply and demand
  - efficiency wage theory
  - human capital theory
  - agency theory.

- *Approaches to rewarding sales staff:*
  - salary only
  - basic salary plus commission
  - basic salary plus bonus
  - commission only
  - sales incentives.

- *Uses of computers:*
  - providing an employee reward database
  - job evaluation
  - grade and pay structure modelling
  - pay review modelling
  - equal pay reviews.

4. Know the main advantages and disadvantages of specified reward practices. For example: Performance-related pay:

- *Advantages*
  - May motivate (but this is uncertain)
  - Links rewards to objectives
  - Meets the need to be rewarded for achievement
  - Delivers message that good performance is important and will be rewarded.

- *Disadvantages*
  - May *not* motivate
  - Prejudicial to teamwork
  - Focuses on outputs, not quality
  - Relies on judgements of performance which may be subjective
  - Relies on good performance management processes.

5. To help with the above, read and absorb the various summary tables in this handbook dealing with:

    - motivation theories – pages 82–83;
    - job evaluation schemes – pages 101–02;
    - sources of market rate data – pages 169–70;
    - grade and pay structures – pages 203–04;
    - contingent pay schemes – pages 252–53;
    - sales staff pay – pages 308–10;
    - shop floor incentive schemes – pages 319–20.

6. Know about the key writers or researchers on the subject such as Adams, Brown, Guest, Lawler, Latham and Locke, Pfeffer, Purcell, Thompson and Vroom, so that their names and ideas can be referred to briefly (not quoted in detail) to support your answer and demonstrate that you are effective in the 'thinking' dimension of the personnel and development professional as a 'thinker performer'.

7. Keep up to date with the latest ideas and examples by reading *People Management* (which, however, neglects the subject shamefully), the IRS Pay and Benefit Bulletin, the various IDS publications, and by contacting the e-reward website, e-reward.co.uk (the latter, which is free, provides an immediate and constantly updated source of reward data). If you can convince the examiner by pertinent references to reward material that you know what's going on, you will be given extra credit.

    Support your answers wherever possible with brief examples drawn from your own experience or your reading.

THE CASE STUDY

Purpose and features of the case study

The case study is designed to test your ability to use your knowledge to tackle a practical situation. You will be expected to demonstrate that you can carry out a critical analysis and diagnosis and come up with convincing solutions. You should adopt the perspective of someone who is acting as a 'business partner' and 'thinking performer'.

Cases are mostly about organizations where the development or improvement of reward management policies and practices is necessary to enhance organizational performance, or where there are specific issues and problems concerning current reward management practices which need to be dealt with. The cases are therefore often about problem solving and the introduction and management of change.

Tackling the case study

As in real life, the cases require you to adopt an analytical and diagnostic approach to answer the questions – 'What is happening in this context? Why is it happening? What should be done about it?' This leads to the problem-solving activities of assessing and evaluating the options which in turn lead to a choice of the preferred option (often a balanced judgement). Finally, the costs and benefits of the proposed action have to be assessed and the resources and programme required to implement it set down in the form of an action plan. The case study often puts you in the position of an HR professional who is asked to assess a situation and make recommendations. This means persuading people to take a course of action and you will be expected to be persuasive on a realistic (cost/benefit) basis in your answer.

Overall, you should ensure that you take account of the context when carrying out your analysis. There is nothing more likely to lose marks than when candidates dive into their reservoir of theoretical knowledge and reel out a string of recommendations which have little or nothing to do with the organization to which the case study refers or to the issues facing it as described. Put another way, your answer must fit – be contingent to – the situation. This is even truer in real life than in a case study.

However, while your answer must be contextualized, you should not spend too much time feeding back details of the case word for word to the examiner who will (a) be bored and (b) think you are padding, which could be the case. You simply need to sum up the context in a smallish paragraph and then proceed to your analysis and diagnosis.

Bear in mind also that the examiner will almost certainly ask you to assume a role and do something for someone which is related to the case study situation; for example, as an HR Officer, prepare a recommendation for the HR Director. Remember therefore to bear in mind two questions: 'Who am I?' and 'What am I doing for whom?' and angle your answer accordingly.

Check list

The following is a 10-point check list to assist in dealing with the case study:

1. What's the context? (organizational, cultural etc analysis)
2. What's going on here – issues and problems? (critical analysis)
3. What are the reasons for the problems? (diagnosis)
4. What's the business need? (assessment drawn from analysis and diagnosis)
5. What alternative ways are available to address the issues and meet the business need? (a list of the main options – not more than two or three – and an evaluation of their merits in cost/benefit terms)

6. Which is the most appropriate alternative and why? (the business case, its benefits and its costs)
7. Who is going to be affected? (top management, line managers, employees and their representatives generally)
8. What are their reactions likely to be? (anticipation of objections)
9. How do we convince them that this approach is desirable? (listing benefits, dealing with possible concerns of management about affordability)
10. How do we implement? (programme, timing, resources/help required, involvement, consultation, negotiation, training)

Example of case study

The Exford Building Society is a medium-sized building society based in Exeter and covering the South-Western region. It is a mutual society (that is, it is owned by its members) and intends to remain one. The Society is well established in the South-West. It has been run on very traditional lines with a high degree of centralization, a lot of bureaucracy, a generally inflexible approach to operations *and* people, and a strong culture of command and control. Little attention has been given to team working in the branch network or at headquarters.

The situation over the last decade has, however, changed. Many of the big building societies have demutualized and competition is much fiercer. They are offering higher pay and better prospects and Exford is losing some experienced staff.

The staff consists of 450 managers and assistants in the branch network (50 branches) and 350 managers, professional, IT, finance and clerical staff in head office. The staff are represented by a recognized union: membership is strongest in the branches. Relationships with the union are not too good.

There is a conventional graded structure supported by an analytical job evaluation scheme. Progression within grades is by increments related to service. There is no performance-related pay but all staff are eligible for an annual bonus based on the Society's performance.

In response to the competitive challenges faced by the Society, the recently promoted chief executive decided that 'Project 2005' should be instituted. The aim of this project was to develop a corporate strategy for introduction in 2005, covering all aspects of the Society's operations and processes. A new head of HR has been appointed, also promoted from within, and she is a member of the senior management team. The Chief Executive has set up a special Project 2005 team consisting of himself, the head of branch operations, the head of customer servicing, the head of finance and the head of HR. The remit of the team is to produce the strategic plan. The first act of the project team was to develop a statement of strategic objectives which can be summarized as follows:

- Maintain market share (in a growth market).
- Operate more efficiently (it was felt that both headquarters and the branch network were overstaffed).
- Provide better and higher quality services to customers.
- Develop a culture which is more adaptive and flexible in the face of new demands.
- Improve the quality of staff.
- Improve staff morale generally.
- Value staff according to their contribution.
- Develop better relationships with the union.
- Improve teamwork.
- Develop a more attractive employment proposition to attract and retain high-quality staff.

You are the HR manager and you have been asked by the Head of HR to produce a brief paper setting out your thoughts on how reward strategies could be developed which would support the achievement of the Society's strategic objectives and could be incorporated in the final Project 2005 plan. She has suggested to you that the report should:

(a) indicate the issues that will need to be addressed;
(b) suggest the lines along which reward strategy should be developed and describe why and how any specific proposals or new system/processes would support the achievement of the corporate strategy;
(c) indicate how reward strategy proposals should be integrated with other aspects of HR strategy, particularly recruitment, retention and employee development;
(d) outline an action plan for implementing any proposals, with costings where appropriate.

It is suggested that in dealing with this case study candidates should allocate their time broadly as follows:

(a) issues – 10%
(b) proposals – 40%
(c) integration – 30%
(d) action plan – 20%

Answer

The objective of this case study is to test the ability of candidates to think strategically and to act as a business partner. They are expected to:

- show they understand the context in which the case study is set and the business issues arising from that context – ie this is a mutual building society facing fierce competition which must develop and implement a business strategy to meet that competition by improving the effectiveness of all aspects of the organization, transforming itself in the process of doing so;
- identify the people/issues including the need for better teamwork, high staff turnover, inflexibility, a command and control culture, over-staffing, poor industrial relations, the likelihood of downsizing;
- note that the reward system is a highly traditional one;
- develop a reward strategy which fully recognizes these issues and specifically focuses on supporting the achievement of strategic objectives, generally or specifically;
- justify any proposals they make in terms of how they will contribute to the strategic development of the Society – candidates should not simply produce a string of recommendations (eg broad-banding, performance management, contribution-related pay or team pay); they must explain the purpose of their proposals in the context of the organization and in relation to its business needs;
- pay particular attention, as briefed, to developing an integrated approach, not only one that fits the business strategy, but also one that links to other aspects of HR strategy, eg resourcing, employee development; for example, a career family structure might be proposed associated with the development of a competency framework and career planning (talent management) processes;
- develop a realistic and contextualized action plan; this must take account of the industrial relations climate in a situation where downsizing may take place and where proposals such as, possibly, abandoning the fixed incremental system and introducing contribution-related pay would almost certainly meet with union opposition; it must also suggest a realistic timetable for implementation;
- spell out not only the costs but also, in summary form, how the proposed reward strategy will contribute to increasing organizational effectiveness, improving the employment proposition and achieving business objectives, and will also be affordable (provide value for money).

THE QUESTIONS

Points to bear in mind

To do well in answering the seven out of ten questions you must:

- Answer the question – this may sound like boringly familiar advice but it is astonishing how often candidates fail to do so. You must look at questions and ask yourself: 'What is the examiner getting at?' 'What is wanted in the reply?' 'If this is a question asking me to respond to a request for information or advice, how do I express my reply in a way that meets this requirement?'

- Ensure that you adopt a realistic approach and show that you understand the business considerations relevant to the question.
- Emphasize the practicalities in terms of what impact this particular aspect of employee reward makes on the motivation, commitment, morale and performance of employees and on organizational effectiveness.
- Define briefly any terms or concepts to which you refer.
- Show that you understand the key features of any of the reward policies or practices you are asked to comment on and how they can be applied by setting out your knowledge of the major theories, concepts and research findings. This should be based on information gained by studying the literature.
- Refer briefly wherever possible to effective and relevant reward practices in your own and other organizations. If appropriate, you should take pains to understand thoroughly the reward policies of your own organization by studying them and talking to HR people and line managers who are involved. You can build up some useful examples of good and, sometimes, not so good practice in this way. Read any case studies you can get hold of from journals, magazines and books, including this one. They will provide you with a view of reward management in action which is an essential part of this highly practical subject.
- Present your arguments for a particular approach or practice in a clear and persuasive way.
- As in the case study, when answering a typical contextualized question involving action (eg question 6 below), remember to ask, and answer, the questions: 'Who am I?' and 'What am I doing for whom?'

Example of a question paper (Section B)

(seven to be answered out of ten)

1. Outline and justify the main points you would include when you give a brief talk to the local CIPD branch entitled: 'Total reward systems: how employers benefit'.
2. What are the key areas in which reward policies may need to be formulated? Illustrate your answer with examples from your own organization.
3. In the light of published research findings, justify the criteria you would use to review a pilot scheme for performance management that is completing its first cycle.
4. You have been invited for interview as principal reward adviser with an HR consultancy. As part of the interview you are to make a brief presentation on the

nature and benefits of conventional graded pay structures. What main points will you include and why?

5. Justify the steps that should be taken by an organization to ensure that its analytical job evaluation scheme is free of bias (gender, disability or race).

6. Your HR director is convinced that your company's performance-related pay scheme is ineffective as a motivator and should be replaced. He asks you to evaluate in summary form the alternative approaches that are available. How will you answer?

7. You have been asked by your chief executive to explain briefly how a flexible benefits system works and what benefits the organization would obtain by introducing one. Draft your response.

8. What are the considerations that should be taken into account when developing pay and benefits policies for expatriates, and why?

9. At a careers evening a bright young school leaver points to a claim in company literature that your pay package is in the upper quartile range. She asks what that means and why it matters. How will you answer in explanation of both the term and the organization's philosophy?

10. Outline an argument explaining how computers can be used to aid reward management that will convince your senior management team to authorize investment.

Points for inclusion in answers

1. Define the concept of a total reward system and explain that each aspect of reward, namely base pay, contingent pay, employee benefits and non-financial rewards, which include intrinsic rewards from the work itself, are linked together and treated as an integrated and coherent whole. Illustrate this with actual examples. Explain that the benefit to employers of a total reward approach is that it will maximize the combined impact of a wide range of reward initiatives on motivation, commitment and job engagement. Ideally, quote a well-known American commentator, Sandra O'Neal, who stated that: 'Total reward embraces everything that employees value in the employment relationship.'

2. Define the concept of reward policy and describe the significance of each of the following policy areas:

    ● achieving external competitiveness and internal equity;
    ● use of contingent pay schemes;
    ● use of job evaluation;
    ● design of pay structures;
    ● range of employee benefits, including the use of flexible benefits.

3. Refer to CIPD research (2003/4) and list at least five of the top ten methods of evaluating performance management used by respondents to the survey, namely:
   - proper discussion/communication between managers and individuals in formal and informal reviews;
   - increased profitability or productivity;
   - achievement of goals;
   - increased motivation;
   - regular feedback;
   - support of personal development;
   - management buy-in;
   - alignment with business strategy;
   - low employee turnover;
   - development of skills.

4. The main features that should be mentioned are:
   - jobs allocated into a number (often 10 or more) of grades by the use of job evaluation;
   - pay ranges related to market rates are attached to each grade, typically 30–40 per cent above the minimum, to provide scope for progression the pay ranges may overlap.

The main benefits are that such structures clearly indicate pay relativities and pay progression steps, facilitate control and are easy to understand.

5. Ensure that:
   - the scheme fits the jobs it covers;
   - the factors are non-discriminatory, cover all aspects of the jobs, do not involve double-counting and do not discriminate by commission or omission;
   - weightings do not discriminate and there is a rationale for them;
   - the scheme does not perpetuate existing hierarchies.

6. The alternatives to be evaluated are:
   - competence-related pay;
   - contribution-related pay;
   - team pay;
   - bonus related to organizational performance (eg profit-sharing).

At least three of these should be evaluated in terms of their main advantages and disadvantages.

7. Define flexible benefit schemes as ones that give employees a choice within or between benefits. The main advantage includes the fact that they give freedom of choice in accordance with individual needs and help to focus benefit expenditure more on those needs. The disadvantages include the problems of costing benefits and the administrative problems such schemes create.

8. State that the basic choice is between using either the home-based pay or host-based pay approach. These should be defined and the main advantages and disadvantages of both summarized. Mention that policies have also to be formulated for allowances and benefits.

9. Define upper quartile as, strictly, the value above which one-quarter of the individual values in a distribution fall. Mention that the term is used more loosely in assessing pay policy or market stance (pay levels in the organization in relation to market rates) as the top quarter of any distribution. Indicate that this means that the organization pays well compared with other organizations because it wants to attract and retain high-quality people and demonstrate that they are valued highly.

10. Describe the following uses:

   - create and maintain a pay database;
   - model alternative proposals for pay reviews;
   - assist job evaluation;
   - model pay structures;
   - aid equal pay reviews.

Explain how in each case IT will significantly reduce costs by speeding up reward administration processes and will also generate information quickly to assist in decision making.

Index

Also by **Michael Armstrong**

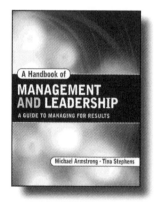
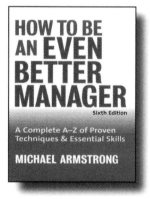

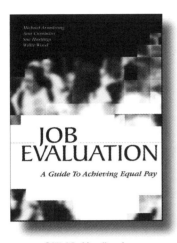

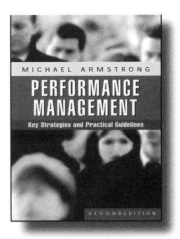
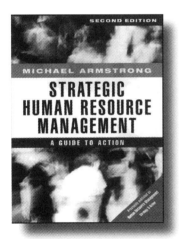

ALSO AVAILABLE FROM KOGAN PAGE

Keeping Well at Work
A TUC Guide
2nd Edition
Philip Pearson

"Extremely helpful and practical. A copy of this should be in every office." – Executive PA

£9.99 Paperback ISBN 0 7494 4152 6 304 pages 2004

Leading the Professionals
How to Inspire and Motivate Professional Service Teams
Geoff Smith

"A fascinating insight into leadership in practice and in context – that of the professional service firm... offers perceptive analysis, thoughtful guidance and practical illustration."
– Professor Michael Osbaldeston, Director of the Cranfield School of Management

£18.99 Paperback ISBN 0 7494 3996 3 256 pages 2004

The Employer's Handbook
An Essential Guide to Employment Law, Personnel Policies and Procedures
2nd Edition
Barry Cushway

"Easy to read and clearly presented... a source of practical information for any small- to medium sized employer." – Training Journal

£37.50 Hardback ISBN 0 7494 4133 X 320 pages 2004

The Handbook of Model Job Descriptions
With FREE CD ROM containing over 200 job descriptions
Barry Cushway
Endorsed by Institute of Directors

- Unique and unrivalled source of job descriptions based on actual jobs
- Accompanying CD ROM can be used to create reliable and accurate job descriptions

£49.95 Hardback ISBN 0 7494 3824 X 448 pages 2004